W9-AQG-869

Complete
American
Presidents
Sourcebook

Complete American Presidents Sourcebook

Volume 1
George Washington through Martin Van Buren
1789–1841

Roger Matuz
Lawrence W. Baker, Editor

AN IMPRINT OF THE GALE GROUP

DETROIT · NEW YORK · SAN FRANCISCO
LONDON · BOSTON · WOODBRIDGE, CT

Complete American Presidents Sourcebook

Roger Matuz

Staff

Lawrence W. Baker, *U•X•L Senior Editor*
Gerda-Ann Raffaelle, *U•X•L Contributing Editor*
Carol DeKane Nagel, *U•X•L Managing Editor*
Thomas L. Romig, *U•X•L Publisher*

Rita Wimberley, *Senior Buyer*
Dorothy Maki, *Manufacturing Manager*
Evi Seoud, *Assistant Manager, Composition Purchasing and Electronic Prepress*
Mary Beth Trimper, *Manager, Composition Purchasing and Electronic Prepress*

Cynthia Baldwin, *Senior Art Director*
Michelle DiMercurio, *Senior Art Director*
Kenn Zorn, *Product Design Manager*

Shalice Shah-Caldwell, *Permissions Associate (text and pictures)*
Maria L. Franklin, *Permissions Manager*
Kelly A. Quin, *Editor, Imaging and Multimedia Content*
Pamela A. Reed, *Imaging Coordinator*
Leitha Etheridge-Sims, *Image Cataloger*
Mary Grimes, *Image Cataloger*
Robert Duncan, *Imaging Specialist*
Dan Newell, *Imaging Specialist*
Randy A. Bassett, *Image Supervisor*
Barbara J. Yarrow, *Imaging and Multimedia Content Manager*

Marco Di Vita, Graphix Group, *Typesetting*

Library of Congress Cataloging-in-Publication Data

Matuz, Roger.
   Complete American presidents sourcebook / Roger Matuz ; Lawrence W. Baker, editor.
     p. cm.
   Includes bibliographical references and indexes.
   ISBN 0-7876-4837-X (set) — ISBN 0-7876-4838-8 (v. 1) — ISBN 0-7876-4839-6 (v. 2) — ISBN 0-7876-4840-X (v. 3) — ISBN 0-7876-4841-8 (v. 4) — ISBN 0-7876-4842-6 (v. 5)
     1. Presidents—United States—Biography—Juvenile literature. 2. Presidents' spouses—United States—Biography—Juvenile literature. 3. United States—Politics and government—Sources—Juvenile literature. I. Baker, Lawrence W. II. Title.

E176.1 .M387 2001
973'.09'9—dc21
[B]
                                              00-056794

Cover illustration of Abraham Lincoln is reproduced courtesy of the Library of Congress; Franklin and Eleanor Roosevelt, reproduced by permission of the Corbis Corporation; George W. Bush, reproduced by permission of Archive Photos; Thomas Jefferson, reproduced by permission of the National Portrait Gallery, Smithsonian Institution; Washington Monument, reproduced by permission of PhotoDisc, Inc.; Clintons, Bushes, Reagans, Carters, and Fords, reproduced by permission of Archive Photos; Theodore Roosevelt, reproduced by permission of Archive Photos.

Printed in the United States of America

10 9 8 7 6 5 4 3 2 1

Contents

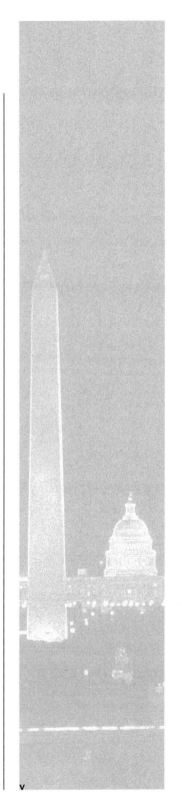

Volume 2

Volume 4

Volume 5

Reader's Guide

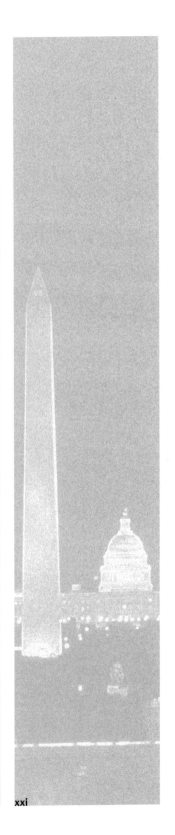

An "embarrassed pause" fell on the gathering of delegates at the Constitutional Convention of 1787 when James Wilson of Pennsylvania suggested the idea of a chief executive. Wanting "no semblance of a monarch," as Edmund Randolph of Virginia put it, delegates moved on to other matters.

So went the first real "discussion" about the office of president, according to Virginia delegate James Madison. Madison, later nicknamed "the Father of the Constitution," took lengthy notes on the proceedings. They were published in 1840 in a book, *Journal of the Federal Convention*.

The Convention was called to address the weakness of the American government formed under the Articles of Confederation that was approved in 1781. By the end of the Convention of 1787, delegates had cautiously agreed on a new system. They had debated ideas of government ranging in history from ancient Greece and Rome to the "Age of Enlightenment" (eighteenth century) in Europe; they considered the workings of the Iroquois confederacy of Native American tribes as well as the state governments in America; and they held to their ideals of liberty and their dislike of monarchy, a system in which one person rules a country for life. The delegates eventually returned to Wilson's suggestion and debated it. The new system of government they cautiously agreed to in the end did indeed include an elected chief executive—the president.

"President" was a title used for the position of governor in three states—Delaware, Pennsylvania, and New Hampshire. They were among the first nine states to ratify the Constitution, helping provide the majority (nine of thirteen states) needed for the Constitution to become legally binding.

The process of ratification was not easy. In Virginia, for example, which finally approved the Constitution in 1788 by a slim majority (89-79), there were significant concerns about the powers of the president. Former Continental congressman and former Virginia governor Patrick Henry called it "a squint toward monarchy."

The delegates of Virginia, however, had an example of the kind of leader envisioned when the office of president was created. George Washington had presided over the Constitutional Convention. He introduced no ideas and seldom participated in debates, but he kept delegates focused on the cause of improving the system of government. Washington was known for his honesty and for not being overly ambitious. Americans had turned to him to lead their military struggle in the Revolutionary War (1775–81). After the Constitution was ratified (approved), delegates turned to him to lead the new nation as its first president.

Washington's example as president reveals the realities of political leadership. He was voted unanimously into office, and left office in the same high regard, but he had faced resistance in between. Some viewed his version of the federal government as being too powerful: he had called on state militias to put down a rebellion in Pennsylvania against taxes; and for economic reasons, he sided in foreign relations with Great Britain—still a hated enemy to some Americans— over France, the nation that had assisted Americans in winning independence.

Washington was among those presidents who made firm decisions, then awaited the consequences. Some had viewed the presidency as being more impartial. Such are the perils of the presidency. John Adams, the second president, followed the more forceful actions of members of his party and became so unpopular that he had no real hope for reelection. Thomas Jefferson, whose ideals shaped the Declaration of Independence, lost much popularity by the time he left office as the third president. Jefferson had ordered foreign trade restrictions to assert America's strength and to demand respect from Great Britain and France, but the action ended up hurting the American economy.

Like the Constitution, the office of the president was never intended to be perfect. The Constitution is flexible, meant to be used and adapted to form "a more perfect union." The presidency has ranged at times from being a near monarchy to having little real strength. President Andrew Jackson was dubbed "King Andrew" by his opponents, who felt he overstepped his power in several instances. Franklin D. Roosevelt was given tremendous powers and support, first in 1933 to combat the effects of the Great Depression (1929–41), and later to direct the nation's economy during World War II (1939–45). But when Roosevelt tried to change the Supreme Court, he was met with swift criticism. Roosevelt was the only president elected to office four times, the last time being 1944. (In 1945, he died only three months into his fourth term.) By 1951, a constitutional amendment was passed to limit presidents to two terms in office.

Other presidents were far less powerful or effective. Prior to the Civil War, two presidents from the North (Franklin Pierce and James Buchanan) supported the rights for states to decide whether to permit slavery. Abraham Lincoln was elected to challenge that notion, and the Civil War (1861–65) followed. Lincoln took a more aggressive approach than his two predecessors, and he emerged in history as among the greatest presidents.

After Lincoln's assassination in 1865, the presidency was dominated by Congress. In 1885, future president Woodrow Wilson criticized that situation in a book he wrote, *Congressional Government,* while he was a graduate student at Johns Hopkins University. By the time Wilson was elected president in 1912, a series of strong presidents—Grover Cleveland, William McKinley, and Theodore Roosevelt—had reasserted the president's power to lead.

The presidency, then, has passed through various stages of effectiveness. The dynamics of change, growth, and frustration make it fascinating to study. Different ideas of leadership, power, and the role of government have been pursued by presidents. Chief executives have come from various backgrounds: some were born in poverty, like Andrew Johnson and Abraham Lincoln, and others had the advantages of wealth, like the Roosevelts and Bushes; some were war heroes, like Ulysses S. Grant and Dwight D. Eisenhower, others were more studious, like Thomas Jefferson and Woodrow Wilson. Some came to the presidency by accident, like John Tyler and Gerald R. Ford, others campaigned long and hard for the position, like Martin Van Buren and Richard Nixon.

There are various ways to present information on the presidency. In 2000, a Public Broadcasting System (PBS) television series called *The American President* divided presidents into ten categories (such as presidents related to each other, those who were prominent military men, and chief executives who became compromise choices of their parties). The same year, a group of presidential scholars also used ten categories (such as crisis leadership, administrative skills, and relations with Congress) to rank presidents in order of effectiveness

Complete American Presidents Sourcebook uses a chronological approach, beginning with George Washington in 1789, and ending with George W. Bush in 2001. Each president's section contains three types of entries.

Biography of the president

Each of the forty-two men who have served in the nation's top political office is featured in *Complete American Presidents Sourcebook*.

- Each entry begins with a general overview of the president's term(s) in office, then follows his life from birth, through his service as president, to his post-presidency (if applicable).

- Outstanding events and issues during each presidential administration are described, as are the president's responses in his role as the nation's highest elected official.

- Sidebar boxes provide instant facts on the president's personal life; a timeline of key events in his life; a "Words to

Know" box that defines key terms related to the president; results of the president's winning election(s); a list of Cabinet members for each administration; and a selection of homes, museums, and other presidential landmarks.

- A final summary describes the president's legacy—how his actions and the events during his administration influenced the historical period and the future.

Biography of the first lady

Forty-four first ladies are featured in *Complete American Presidents Sourcebook*. Though some of the women died before their husbands became president, all had an important influence on the men who would serve as president. The profiles provide biographical information and insight into the ways in which the women lived their lives and defined their public roles. Like the presidents, first ladies have responded in different ways to their highly public position.

Primary source entry

Another important feature of interest to students is a selection of forty-eight primary source documents—speeches, writings, executive orders, and proclamations of the presidents. At least one primary source is featured with each president.

In the presidents' own words, the documents outline the visions and plans of newly elected presidents, the reasons for certain actions, and the responses to major world events. Students can learn more about key documents (such as the Declaration of Independence and the Monroe Doctrine); famous speeches (such as George Washington's Farewell Address and Abraham Lincoln's Gettysburg Address); presidential orders (the Emancipation Proclamation issued by Abraham Lincoln in 1863 and Harry S. Truman's executive order on military desegregation in 1946); responses to ongoing issues, from tariffs (William McKinley) to relations between the government and Native Americans (Chester A. Arthur); different views on the role of the federal government (from extensive programs advocated by Franklin D. Roosevelt and Lyndon B. Johnson, to reducing the influence of government by Warren G. Harding and Ronald Reagan); and many inaugural addresses, including the memorable speeches of Abraham Lincoln and John F. Kennedy.

Each document (or excerpt) presented in *Complete American Presidents Sourcebook* includes the following additional material:

- **Introduction** places the document and its author in a historical context.

- **Things to remember** offers readers important background information and directs them to central ideas in the text.

- **What happened next** provides an account of subsequent events, both during the presidential administration and in future years.

- **Did you know** provides significant and interesting facts about the excerpted document, the president, or the subjects discussed in the excerpt.

- **For further reading** lists sources for more information on the president, the document, or the subject of the excerpt.

Complete American Presidents Sourcebook also features sidebars containing interesting facts and short biographies of people who were in some way connected with the president or his era. Within each entry, boldfaced cross-references direct readers to other presidents, first ladies, primary sources, and sidebar boxes in the five-volume set. Finally, each volume includes approximately 70 photographs and illustrations (for a total of 350), a "Timeline of the American Presidents" that lists significant dates and events related to presidential administrations, a general "Words to Know" section, research and activity ideas, sources for further reading, and a cumulative index.

This wealth of material presents the student with a variety of well-researched information. It is intended to reflect the dynamic situation of serving as the leader of a nation founded on high ideals, ever struggling to realize those ideals.

Acknowledgments from the author

Many individuals, many institutions, and many sources were consulted in preparing *Complete American Presidents Sourcebook*. A good portion of them are represented in bibliographies and illustration and textual credits sprinkled throughout the five volumes. The many excellent sources and the ability to access them ensured a dynamic process that made the project lively and thought-provoking, qualities reflected in the presentation.

Compilation efforts were organized through Manitou Wordworks, Inc., headed by Roger Matuz with contributions from Carol Brennan, Anne-Jeanette Johnson, Allison Jones, Mel Koler, and Gary Peters. On the Gale/U•X•L side, special recognition goes to U•X•L publisher Tom Romig for his conceptualization of the project. Thanks, too, to Gerda-Ann Raffaelle for filling in some editorial holes; Pam Reed, Kelly A. Quin, and the rest of the folks on the Imaging team for their efficient work; and Cindy Baldwin for another dynamite cover.

The author benefited greatly through his association and friendship with editor Larry Baker and his personal library, tremendous patience, and great enthusiasm for and knowledge of the subject matter.

Finally, with love to Mary Claire for her support, interest (I'll miss having you ask me the question, "So what new thing did you learn about a president today?"), and understanding from the beginning of the project around the time we were married through my frequent checking of the latest news before and after the election of 2000.

Acknowledgments from the editor

The editor wishes to thank Roger Matuz for a year and a half of presidential puns, for putting up with endless Calvin Coolidge tidbits, and—above all—for producing a tremendously solid body of work. You've got my vote when Josiah Bartlet's time in office is up. Thank you, Mr. Author.

Thanks also to typesetter Marco Di Vita of The Graphix Group who always turns in top-quality work and is just a lot of fun to work with; Terry Murray, who, in spite of her excellent-as-usual copyediting and indexing, still couldn't resist suggesting a sidebar for Zachary Taylor's horse, Old Whitey (um, no . . . maybe if we do *Complete American Presidents' Pets Sourcebook);* and proofer Amy Marcaccio Keyzer, whose sharp eye kept the manuscript clean and whose election e-mails kept me laughing.

In addition, the editor would be remiss if he didn't acknowledge his first family. Decades of thanks go to Mom & Dad, for starting it all by first taking me to the McKinley Memorial in Canton, Ohio, all those years ago. Love and appreciation go to editorial first lady Beth Baker, for putting up with all of the presidential homes and museums and grave markers and books, but who admits that touring FDR's Campobello during a nor'easter storm is pretty cool. And to Charlie & Dane—please don't fight over who gets to be president first!

Finally, a nod to Al Gore and George W. Bush for adding some real-life drama to the never-ending completion of this book . . . and who *did* fight over who got to be president first!

Comments and suggestions

We welcome your comments on the *Complete American Presidents Sourcebook* and suggestions for other topics in history to consider. Please write: Editors, *Complete American Presidents Sourcebook,* U•X•L, 27500 Drake Rd., Farmington Hills, Michigan 48331-3535; call toll-free: 800-877-4253; fax to 248-414-5043; or send e-mail via http://www.galegroup.com.

Timeline of the American Presidents

1776   The Declaration of Independence is written, approved, and officially issued.

1781   The Articles of Confederation are approved, basing American government on cooperation between the states. Congress is empowered to negotiate treaties, but has few other responsibilities.

1787   A national convention called to strengthen the Articles of Confederation develops the U.S. Constitution instead, defining a new system of American government. The powers of Congress are broadened. Congress forms the legislative branch of the new government, and the Supreme Court forms the judicial

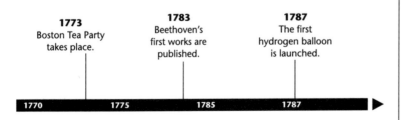

1773
Boston Tea Party
takes place.

1783
Beethoven's
first works are
published.

1787
The first
hydrogen balloon
is launched.

1770   1775   1785   1787

branch. An executive branch is introduced and will be led by an elected official, the president. The president and vice president are to be inaugurated on March 4 of the year following their election (a date that remains in practice until 1933, when the Twentieth Amendment is ratified, changing inauguration day to January 20).

1787   Three of the original thirteen colonies—Delaware, Pennsylvania, and New Jersey—ratify the Constitution, thereby becoming the first three states of the Union.

1788   Eight of the original thirteen colonies—Georgia, Connecticut, Massachusetts, Maryland, South Carolina, New Hampshire, Virginia, and New York—ratify the Constitution, thereby becoming the fourth through eleventh states of the Union. The Constitution becomes law when New Hampshire is the ninth state to ratify it (two-thirds majority of the thirteen states had to approve the Constitution for it to become legally binding).

1789   One of the original thirteen colonies—North Carolina—ratifies the Constitution, thereby becoming the twelfth state of the Union.

1789   The first presidential election is held. Voting is done by electors appointed by each state, and the number of electors are based on the state's population. Each elector votes for two candidates. Whomever finishes with the most votes becomes president, and whomever finishes second becomes vice president.

1789   Revolutionary War hero George Washington is elected president, receiving votes from each elector.

1789   The French Revolution begins.

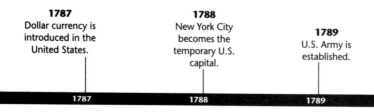

1787
Dollar currency is introduced in the United States.

1788
New York City becomes the temporary U.S. capital.

1789
U.S. Army is established.

1787   1788   1789

1789   George Washington is inaugurated in New York City. A site for the national capital is selected along the Potomac River in Washington, D.C., and the federal government will be situated in Philadelphia, Pennsylvania, until the new capital is completed.

1789   One of the original thirteen colonies—Rhode Island— ratifies the Constitution, thereby becoming the thirteenth state of the Union.

1789   Political factions solidify. Federalists, who support a strong federal government, are led by Secretary of the Treasury Alexander Hamilton, and Anti-Federalists, who support limited federal power and strong states' rights, are led by Secretary of State Thomas Jefferson.

1791   Vermont becomes the fourteenth state of the Union.

1792   President George Washington is reelected unanimously.

1792   Kentucky becomes the fifteenth state of the Union.

1794   American forces defeat a confederacy of Native American tribes at the Battle of Fallen Timbers in Ohio, opening up the midwest for settlement.

1796   When Vice President John Adams finishes first and former Secretary of State Thomas Jefferson finishes second in the presidential election, two men with conflicting political views and affiliations serve as president and vice president. Political parties—the Federalists and the Democratic-Republicans—become established.

1796   Tennessee becomes the sixteenth state of the Union.

1798   The United States engages in an undeclared naval war with France.

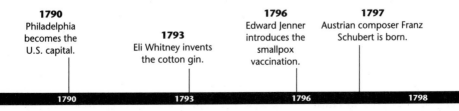

1790
Philadelphia becomes the U.S. capital.

1793
Eli Whitney invents the cotton gin.

1796
Edward Jenner introduces the smallpox vaccination.

1797
Austrian composer Franz Schubert is born.

1790   1793   1796   1798

1798   Federalists in Congress pass and President John Adams signs into law the Alien and Sedition Acts. The laws, which expand the powers of the federal government, prove unpopular and bolster the prospects of anti-Federalists.

1800   The seat of government moves from Philadelphia, Pennsylvania, to Washington, D.C.; President John Adams and first lady Abigail Adams move into the White House (officially called The Executive Mansion until 1900).

1800   In the presidential election, Vice President Thomas Jefferson and former New York senator Aaron Burr (both of the Democratic-Republican Party) finish tied with the most electoral votes. The election is decided in the House of Representatives, where Jefferson prevails after thirty-six rounds of voting.

1803   The historic *Marbury v. Madison* decision strengthens the role of the U.S. Supreme Court to decide constitutional issues.

1803   The Louisiana Purchase more than doubles the size of the United States.

1803   Ohio becomes the seventeenth state of the Union.

1804   The Twelfth Amendment to the Constitution mandates that electors must distinguish between whom they vote for president and vice president (to avoid repeating the problem of the 1800 election, where most voters selected both Jefferson and Burr with their two votes).

1804   President Thomas Jefferson wins reelection. He selects a new running mate, New York governor George Clinton, to replace Vice President Aaron Burr.

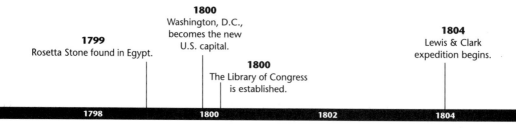

1800
Washington, D.C., becomes the new U.S. capital.

1799
Rosetta Stone found in Egypt.

1804
Lewis & Clark expedition begins.

1800
The Library of Congress is established.

1798   1800   1802   1804

1804 After losing an election for governor of New York, outgoing vice president Aaron Burr kills former U.S. secretary of the treasury Alexander Hamilton in a duel. Hamilton had influenced voters against Burr in the presidential campaign of 1800 and during Burr's campaign to be governor of New York in 1804.

1806 The Lewis and Clark expedition, commissioned by President Thomas Jefferson, is completed when explorers Meriwether Lewis and William Clark return to St. Louis, Missouri, after having traveled northwest to the Pacific Ocean.

1807 President Thomas Jefferson institutes an embargo on shipping to England and France, attempting to pressure the nations to respect American rights at sea. The embargo is unsuccessful and unpopular.

1807 Former vice president Aaron Burr is tried and acquitted on charges of treason.

1808 Secretary of State James Madison, the "Father of the Constitution," is elected president. Vice President George Clinton campaigns and places third as a member of the Independent Republican Party after having accepted Madison's offer to continue in his role as vice president.

1811 At the Battle of Tippecanoe, American forces (led by future president William Henry Harrison) overwhelm a Native American confederacy led by Shawnee chief Tecumseh.

1811 Vice President George Clinton casts the tie-breaking vote in the U.S. Senate (a responsibility of the vice president under the U.S. Constitution) against rechartering the National Bank, and against President James Madison's wishes.

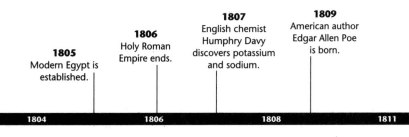

1805 Modern Egypt is established.

1806 Holy Roman Empire ends.

1807 English chemist Humphry Davy discovers potassium and sodium.

1809 American author Edgar Allen Poe is born.

1804   1806   1808   1811

1812	War of 1812 (1812–15) begins.
1812	President James Madison is reelected.
1812	Louisiana becomes the eighteenth state of the Union.
1813	After having suffered military defeats in Canada, U.S. naval forces win control of the Great Lakes.
1814	British military forces burn the White House and the Capitol during the War of 1812.
1815	The Battle of New Orleans, where American forces (led by future president Andrew Jackson) rout a superior British force, occurs after an armistice was agreed on, but news had not yet reached Louisiana. The War of 1812 officially ends a month later.
1816	Secretary of State James Monroe is elected president. The "Era of Good Feelings" begins: the war is over, America is expanding, and Monroe is a popular president.
1816	Indiana becomes the nineteenth state of the Union.
1817	President James Monroe moves into an incompletely reconstructed White House.
1816	Mississippi becomes the twentieth state of the Union.
1818	Illinois becomes the twenty-first state of the Union.
1819	Alabama becomes the twenty-second state of the Union.
1819	Bank Panic slows economic growth.
1820	President James Monroe is reelected by winning every state. One elector casts a vote for John Quincy Adams as a symbolic gesture to ensure that George Washington remains the only president to win all electoral votes in an election.

1812
The Brothers Grimm publish their book of fairy tales.

1814
Francis Scott Key writes the "Star Spangled Banner."

1818
Mary Shelley writes *Frankenstein.*

1818
Congress adopts a U.S. flag.

1812   1815   1818   1820

1820 The Missouri Compromise sets a boundary (the southern border of present-day Missouri): slavery is not permitted north of that boundary for any prospective territory hoping to enter the Union.

1820 Maine, formerly part of Massachusetts, becomes the twenty-third state of the Union.

1821 Missouri becomes the twenty-fourth state of the Union.

1823 In his annual message to Congress, President James Monroe introduces what will become known as the Monroe Doctrine. Although not very significant at the time, the Doctrine, which warns European nations against expansionist activities in the Americas, sets a foreign policy precedent several later presidents will invoke.

1824 Electoral votes are based on the popular vote for the first time. Tennessee senator Andrew Jackson bests Secretary of State John Quincy Adams with over 45,000 more popular votes and a 99-84 Electoral College lead, but does not win a majority of electoral votes, split among four candidates. The election is decided in Adams's favor by the House of Representatives. The support of powerful Speaker of the House Henry Clay, who finished fourth in the election, helps sway the House in favor of Adams. When Adams names Clay his secretary of state, Jackson supporters claim a "corrupt bargain" had been forged between Adams and Clay.

1824 John Quincy Adams is the fourth straight and last president from the Democratic-Republican Party, which held the White House from 1800 to 1829. The party splits into factions around Adams and his elec-

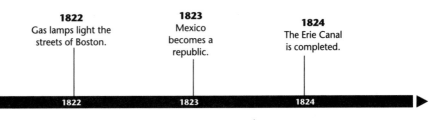

1822
Gas lamps light the streets of Boston.

1823
Mexico becomes a republic.

1824
The Erie Canal is completed.

1820   1822   1823   1824

tion opponent, Andrew Jackson (called Jacksonian Democrats), respectively.

1826   Former presidents John Adams and Thomas Jefferson die on the same day, July 4—fifty years to the day after the Declaration of Independence was officially issued.

1828   Former Tennessee senator Andrew Jackson defeats President John Quincy Adams. Modern-day political parties are established: Jackson leads the Democratic Party, and Adams leads the National Republican Party. The National Republicans are also represented in the 1832 presidential election, but most party members are joined by anti-Jackson Democrats to form the Whig Party in 1834.

1832   President Andrew Jackson is reelected. Candidates from the Nullifier Party (based on the proposition that states have the right to nullify federal laws) and the Anti-Masonic Party receive electoral votes. Future president Millard Fillmore was elected to the U.S. House of Representatives in 1831 as a member of the Anti-Masonic Party (a pro-labor group against social clubs and secret societies).

1832   The Black Hawk War leads to the taking of Native American land west to the Mississippi River. Future president Abraham Lincoln is among those fighting.

1832   President Andrew Jackson vetoes the charter for the Second National Bank (the federal banking system), creating great controversy between Democrats (favoring states' rights) and proponents for a strong federal government, who gradually unite to form the Whig Party in 1834.

1833   Running water is installed in the White House.

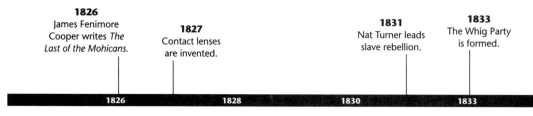

1826
James Fenimore Cooper writes *The Last of the Mohicans.*

1827
Contact lenses are invented.

1831
Nat Turner leads slave rebellion.

1833
The Whig Party is formed.

1826   1828   1830   1833

1834   Congress censures (publicly rebukes) President Andrew Jackson for having taken funds from the federal bank and depositing them in various state banks.

1836   Vice President Martin Van Buren is elected president after defeating three Whig candidates. Whigs hoped that their three regional candidates would win enough electoral votes to deny Van Buren a majority and throw the election to the House of Representatives, where Whigs held the majority.

1836   The last surviving founding father, James Madison, dies the same year the first president born after the American Revolution (Martin Van Buren) is elected.

1836   Arkansas becomes the twenty-fifth state of the Union.

1837   The Panic of 1837 initiates a period of economic hard times that lasts throughout President Martin Van Buren's administration.

1837   Michigan becomes the twenty-sixth state of the Union.

1840   Military hero and Ohio politician William Henry Harrision (known as "Old Tippecanoe") defeats President Martin Van Buren.

1841   President William Henry Harrison dies thirty-one days after being inaugurated president. A constitutional issue arises because the document is unclear as to whether Vice President John Tyler should complete Harrison's term or serve as an interim president until Congress selects a new president. Tyler has himself sworn in as president. Controversy follows, but Tyler sets a precedent on presidential succession.

1841   The President's Cabinet, except for Secretary of State Daniel Webster, resigns, and some congressmen con-

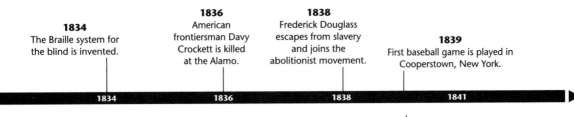

1834
The Braille system for the blind is invented.

1836
American frontiersman Davy Crockett is killed at the Alamo.

1838
Frederick Douglass escapes from slavery and joins the abolitionist movement.

1839
First baseball game is played in Cooperstown, New York.

1834   1836   1838   1841

sider impeachment proceedings against President John Tyler (but the impeachment fails to materialize). Though a member of the Whig Party, Tyler opposes the Whig program for expanding federal powers. He is kicked out of the Whig Party.

1842 The Webster-Ashburton Treaty settles a border dispute between Maine and Quebec, Canada, and averts war between the United States and Great Britain.

1844 Congress approves a resolution annexing Texas.

1844 Tennessee politician James K. Polk, strongly associated with former president Andrew Jackson, is elected president. The years beginning with Jackson's presidency in 1829 and ending with Polk's in March 1849 are often referred to historically as The Age of Jackson.

1845 Congress passes and President James K. Polk signs legislation to have presidential elections held simultaneously throughout the country on the Tuesday following the first Monday in November.

1845 Florida becomes the twenty-seventh and Texas the twenty-eighth states of the Union.

1845 The U.S. Naval Academy opens.

1846 The Mexican War begins.

1846 Iowa and Wisconsin expand the Union to thirty states.

1848 Gas lamps are installed in the White House to replace candles and oil lamps.

1848 The Mexican War ends. The United States takes possession of the southwest area from Texas to California.

1848 General Zachary Taylor, a Mexican War hero, is elected president in a close race. He had joined the Whig

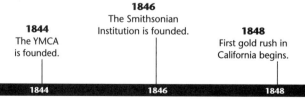

1844
The YMCA is founded.

1846
The Smithsonian Institution is founded.

1848
First gold rush in California begins.

| 1842 | 1844 | 1846 | 1848 |

Party but promised to remain above partisan causes and announced that he was against the expansion of slavery into new territories. Ex-president Martin Van Buren finishes a distant third as a candidate for the Free-Soil Party that also opposes the expansion of slavery into new territories. Van Buren likely drew enough votes from the Democratic candidate, former Michigan senator Lewis Cass, to tip the election to Taylor.

1849   The California Gold Rush brings thousands of people into the new American territory.

1850   President Zachary Taylor dies in office, and Vice President Millard Fillmore becomes president.

1850   President Millard Fillmore supports and signs into law the series of bills called the Compromise of 1850 that the late president Zachary Taylor had opposed. The Fugitive Slave Act, which forces northern states to return runaway slaves, becomes law.

1850   California becomes the thirty-first state of the Union.

1850   The Pony Express begins operation, providing mail service to the far west.

1852   Former New Hampshire senator Franklin Pierce is elected president.

1852   *Uncle Tom's Cabin,* by Harriet Beecher Stowe, is published and further fuels growing support in the North for complete abolition of slavery.

1853   The Gadsden Purchase adds southern areas of present-day New Mexico and Arizona as American territory.

1854   The Republican Party is formed by those against the expansion of slavery and by abolitionists wanting to outlaw the institution, drawing from the Whig Party

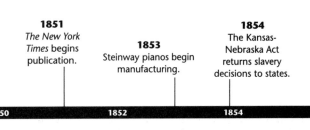

1851
The New York Times begins publication.

1853
Steinway pianos begin manufacturing.

1854
The Kansas-Nebraska Act returns slavery decisions to states.

1849   1850   1852   1854

(which becomes defunct) and Democrats opposed to slavery.

1854 Diplomatic and trade relations begin between the United States and Japan.

1856 Civil war breaks out in Kansas Territory between pro- and anti-slavery proponents.

1856 Former secretary of state James Buchanan, a states' rights advocate, is elected president. Former California senator John Frémont finishes second as the Republican Party's first presidential candidate. Former president Millard Fillmore finishes third with about twenty percent of the popular vote and eight electoral votes, as the nominee of the American Party (also nicknamed the Know-Nothing Party).

1857 The *Dred Scott* decision by the U.S. Supreme Court limits the power of Congress to decide on slavery issues in American territories petitioning to become states.

1858 The Lincoln-Douglas debates in Illinois, between U.S. Senate candidates Abraham Lincoln and incumbent Stephen Douglas, receive national press coverage.

1858 Minnesota becomes the thirty-second state of the Union.

1859 Abolitionist John Brown leads a raid on a federal arsenal in Harper's Ferry, Virginia (now West Virginia), hoping to spark and arm a slave rebellion.

1859 Oregon becomes the thirty-third state of the Union.

1860 Former Illinois congressman Abraham Lincoln is elected president despite winning less than forty percent of the popular vote. Democratic votes are split among three candidates. One of the party's candidates, Illi-

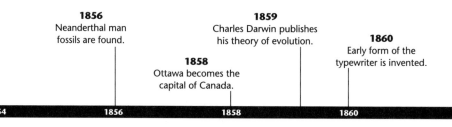

1856
Neanderthal man
fossils are found.

1859
Charles Darwin publishes
his theory of evolution.

1860
Early form of the
typewriter is invented.

1858
Ottawa becomes the
capital of Canada.

1854   1856   1858   1860

nois senator Stephen Douglas, finishes second in the popular vote but places fourth in electoral votes.

1860   South Carolina secedes from the Union.

1861   Confederate States of America formed; Civil War begins.

1861   Kansas becomes the thirty-fourth state of the Union.

1863   President Abraham Lincoln, sitting in what is now called the Lincoln Bedroom in the White House, signs the Emancipation Proclamation, freeing slaves in the states in rebellion.

1863   West Virginia becomes the thirty-fifth state of the Union.

1863   President Abraham Lincoln proposes a policy for admitting seceded states back into the Union on moderate terms.

1864   Pro-Union Republicans and Democrats unite as the National Union Party under President Abraham Lincoln (Republican) and Tennessee senator Andrew Johnson, who had remained in Congress after his southern colleagues walked out. The Lincoln-Johnson ticket wins 212 of 233 electoral votes.

1864   Nevada becomes the thirty-sixth state of the Union.

1865   The Civil War ends.

1865   President Abraham Lincoln is assassinated, and Vice President Andrew Johnson succeeds him as president.

1865   The Thirteenth Amendment to the Constitution, outlawing slavery, is ratified.

1867   Over objections and vetoes by President Andrew Johnson, Congress passes harsher Reconstruction

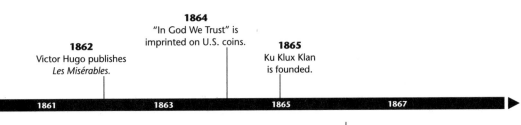

1862
Victor Hugo publishes
Les Misérables.

1864
"In God We Trust" is
imprinted on U.S. coins.

1865
Ku Klux Klan
is founded.

1861   1863   1865   1867

policies (terms under which former Confederate states can operate) than the Johnson (and Lincoln) plans.

1867 Nebraska becomes the thirty-seventh state of the Union.

1867 The United States purchases Alaska (a deal called "Seward's Folly" after Secretary of State William H. Seward, who negotiated the acquisition) from Russia.

1868 President Andrew Johnson becomes the first president to be impeached by the House of Representatives. He is acquitted by one vote in a trial in the U.S. Senate.

1868 Civil War hero Ulysses S. Grant is elected president.

1869 The Transcontinental railroad is completed.

1869 President Ulysses S. Grant fails in attempts to annex the Dominican Republic.

1872 President Ulysses S. Grant is reelected. His opponent, newspaper publisher Horace Greeley, dies shortly after the election, and his electoral votes are dispersed among several other Democrats.

1873 The Crédit Mobilier scandal reflects widespread corruption among some officials in the Ulysses S. Grant administration and some congressmen.

1876 Colorado becomes the thirty-eighth state of the Union.

1876 In the hotly contested presidential election, the Democratic candidate, New York governor Samuel J. Tilden, outpolls the Republican nominee, Ohio governor Rutherford B. Hayes, by over two hundred thousand votes, but falls one electoral vote short of a majority when twenty electoral votes (from the states of Florida, South Carolina, Louisiana, and Oregon) are contested with claims of fraud. The House of Representatives fails to resolve the issue.

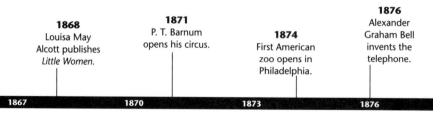

1868
Louisa May Alcott publishes *Little Women.*

1871
P. T. Barnum opens his circus.

1874
First American zoo opens in Philadelphia.

1876
Alexander Graham Bell invents the telephone.

1867   1870   1873   1876

1877   A special Electoral Commission is established to resolve the 1876 presidential election controversy. Days before the scheduled inauguration of the new president in March, the Commission awards the 20 disputed votes to Republican Rutherford B. Hayes, who edges Democrat Samuel J. Tilden, 185-184, in the Electoral College. Some historians refer to the decision as the Compromise of 1877, believing that Republicans and southern Democrats struck a deal: Hayes would be president, and Reconstruction (federal supervision of former Confederate states) would end.

1877   Federal troops are withdrawn from South Carolina and Louisiana, where troops had been stationed since the end of the Civil War to enforce national laws. Reconstruction ends, and southern states regain the same rights as all other states.

1878   Attempting to reform the civil service (where jobs were often provided by the party in power to party members), President Rutherford B. Hayes suspends fellow Republican Chester A. Arthur (a future U.S. president) as the powerful head of the New York Custom's House (which collects import taxes).

1879   The first telephone is installed in the White House. The phone number: 1.

1879   Thomas Edison invents the incandescent light bulb.

1880   Ohio congressman James A. Garfield is elected president.

1881   President James A. Garfield is assassinated by an extremist who lost his job under civil service reform. Chester A. Arthur becomes the fourth vice president to assume the presidency upon the death of the chief executive. Like the previous three (John Tyler, Millard

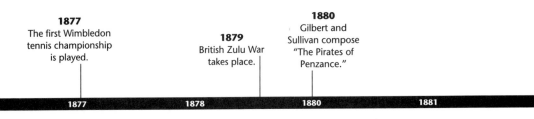

1877
The first Wimbledon
tennis championship
is played.

1879
British Zulu War
takes place.

1880
Gilbert and
Sullivan compose
"The Pirates of
Penzance."

1877   1878   1880   1881

Fillmore, and Andrew Johnson), Arthur is not selected by his party to run for the presidency after completing the elected president's term.

1883 The Pendleton Act, mandating major civil service reform, is signed into law by President Chester A. Arthur.

1884 New York governor Grover Cleveland is elected as the first Democrat to win the presidency since 1856. Tariffs (taxes on imported goods) and tariff reform become major issues during his presidency and the following three elections.

1885 The Statue of Liberty is dedicated.

1886 President Grover Cleveland marries Frances Folsom, becoming the only president to marry at the White House.

1888 Former Indiana senator Benjamin Harrison is elected president despite receiving 90,000 fewer popular votes than President Grover Cleveland. Harrison wins most of the more populated states for a 233-168 Electoral College advantage.

1889 North Dakota, South Dakota, Montana, and Washington enter the Union, expanding the United States to forty-two states.

1890 Idaho and Wyoming become the forty-third and forty-fourth states of the Union.

1891 Electric wiring is installed in the White House.

1892 Former president Grover Cleveland becomes the first person to win non-consecutive presidential terms by defeating incumbent president Benjamin Harrison (in the popular vote *and* the Electoral College). Iowa politician James B. Weaver of the People's Party (also

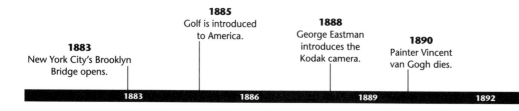

1883
New York City's Brooklyn Bridge opens.

1885
Golf is introduced to America.

1888
George Eastman introduces the Kodak camera.

1890
Painter Vincent van Gogh dies.

1883   1886   1889   1892

known as the Populists) finishes a distant third in the popular vote but garners twenty-two electoral votes.

1893 Lame duck (an official completing an elected term after having failed to be reelected) President Benjamin Harrison presents a treaty to annex Hawaii to the U.S. Congress.

1893 President Grover Cleveland rescinds former president Benjamin Harrison's treaty for the annexation of Hawaii and calls for an investigation of the American-led rebellion that overthrew the Hawaiian native monarchy.

1894 An economic downturn and numerous strikes paralyze the American economy.

1895 With gold reserves (used to back the value of currency) running low, President Grover Cleveland arranges a gold purchase through financier J. P. Morgan.

1896 Ohio governor William McKinley, the Republican Party nominee, is elected president over the Democratic candidate, former Nebraska congressman William Jennings Bryan.

1896 Utah becomes the forty-fifth state of the Union.

1898 The Spanish-American War takes place. The United States wins quickly and takes possession of overseas territories (the former Spanish colonies of Cuba, Puerto Rico, and the Philippines).

1898 President William McKinley reintroduces the Hawaii annexation issue and Congress approves it.

1899 President William McKinley expands U.S. trade with China and other nations through his Open Door Policy.

1900 President William McKinley is reelected by defeating William Jennings Bryan a second time.

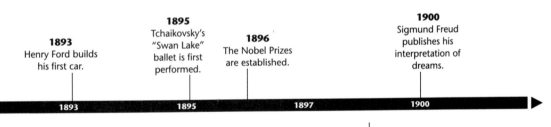

1893
Henry Ford builds his first car.

1895
Tchaikovsky's "Swan Lake" ballet is first performed.

1896
The Nobel Prizes are established.

1900
Sigmund Freud publishes his interpretation of dreams.

1893 1895 1897 1900

1900 Chinese nationalists take arms against growing foreign influences in their country, an uprising called the Boxer Rebellion. American military forces join those of other foreign nations to put down the uprising. American military forces are also stationed in the Philippines to combat revolts.

1901 President William McKinley is assassinated; Vice President Theodore Roosevelt assumes the presidency and, at age 42, becomes the youngest man to become president.

1902 To combat the growing influence of trusts (business combinations intended to stifle competition), President Theodore Roosevelt orders vigorous enforcement of antitrust laws, and an era of business and social reform gains momentum.

1903 The United States quickly recognizes and supports a rebellion in the nation of Colombia through which Panama becomes an independent nation. Through the Panama Canal treaty, which provides a strip of land to be developed by the United States, President Theodore Roosevelt spearheads plans to build a canal across Panama, linking the Atlantic and Pacific oceans.

1904 Theodore Roosevelt becomes the first president who assumed office upon the death of the elected president to win election for a full term.

1905 President Theodore Roosevelt serves as mediator during the Russo-Japanese War. His success at helping end the conflict earns him a Nobel Peace Prize.

1907 Oklahoma becomes the forty-sixth state.

1908 William Howard Taft, who served in the William McKinley and Theodore Roosevelt administrations, is

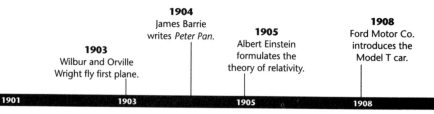

1904
James Barrie
writes *Peter Pan.*

1905
Albert Einstein
formulates the
theory of relativity.

1908
Ford Motor Co.
introduces the
Model T car.

1903
Wilbur and Orville
Wright fly first plane.

1901   1903   1905   1908

elected president. William Jennings Bryan loses in his third presidential bid.

1909 In a sign of the times, President William Howard Taft purchases official automobiles and has the White House stable converted into a garage.

1909 The North Pole is reached.

1912 New Jersey governor Woodrow Wilson is elected president. Former president Theodore Roosevelt, running as the Progressive Party candidate (nicknamed "the Bull Moose Party"), finishes second. Roosevelt outpolls his successor, President William Howard Taft, by about seven hundred thousand popular votes and wins eighty more electoral votes.

1912 New Mexico and Arizona enter the Union, expanding the United States to forty-eight states.

1912 The Sixteenth Amendment, authorizing the collection of income taxes, is ratified.

1912 The Federal Reserve, which regulates the nation's money supply and financial institutions, is established.

1913 The Seventeenth Amendment changes the system for electing U.S. senators. The popular vote replaces the system where most senators were elected by state legislatures.

1914 World War I begins.

1914 U.S. military forces begin having skirmishes with Mexican rebels in a series of incidents that last until 1916.

1914 The Panama Canal is opened.

1916 President Woodrow Wilson is reelected by a slim Electoral College margin, 277-254. He defeats the Repub-

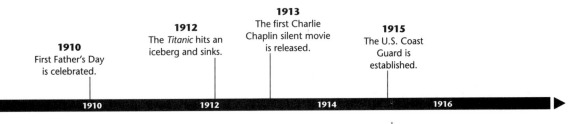

1910
First Father's Day
is celebrated.

1912
The *Titanic* hits an
iceberg and sinks.

1913
The first Charlie
Chaplin silent movie
is released.

1915
The U.S. Coast
Guard is
established.

1910   1912   1914   1916

lican candidate, former U.S. Supreme Court justice Charles Evans Hughes.

1916 President Woodrow Wilson acts as mediator for the nations in conflict in World War I.

1917 Citing acts of German aggression, President Woodrow Wilson asks Congress to declare war. The United States enters World War I. The Selective Service (a system through which young men are called on for military duty) is established.

1918 World War I ends.

1919 Congress rejects the Treaty of Versailles negotiated by President Woodrow Wilson and other leaders representing the nations involved in World War I. Congress also rejects American participation in the League of Nations that Wilson had envisioned.

1919 Attempting to rally support of the Treaty of Versailles and the League of Nations during a long speaking tour, President Woodrow Wilson collapses with a debilitating stroke. The public is not made aware of the severity of the affliction that leaves Wilson bedridden.

1919 The Eighteenth Amendment, outlawing the manufacture and sale of alcohol, is ratified.

1920 Women are able to participate in national elections for the first time.

1920 Ohio senator Warren G. Harding is elected president.

1922 Illegal deals are made by some officials of the Warren G. Harding administration. Two years later, they are implicated in the Teapot Dome scandal.

1923 President Warren G. Harding dies in San Francisco, California; Vice President Calvin Coolidge assumes the presidency.

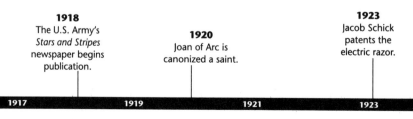

1918
The U.S. Army's
Stars and Stripes
newspaper begins
publication.

1920
Joan of Arc is
canonized a saint.

1923
Jacob Schick
patents the
electric razor.

1917　　　　1919　　　　1921　　　　1923

1924 Calvin Coolidge is elected president in a landslide, defeating West Virginia politician John W. Davis, the Democratic candidate. Progressive Party candidate Robert M. LaFollette, a future Wisconsin senator, garners over thirteen percent of the popular vote and wins thirteen electoral votes.

1925 The Scopes Trial is held in Dayton, Tennessee, after a public school teacher instructs his class on the theory of evolution in defiance of a state law.

1927 Charles Lindbergh becomes the first pilot to fly solo across the Atlantic Ocean.

1928 Former secretary of commerce Herbert Hoover, who also supervised international relief efforts during World War I, wins his first election attempt in a landslide (by over six million popular votes and a 444-87 Electoral College triumph).

1929 The stock market crashes.

1930 President Herbert Hoover assures the nation that "the economy is on the mend," but continued crises become the Great Depression that lasts the entire decade.

1932 The Bonus March, in which World War I veterans gather in Washington, D.C., to demand benefits promised to them, ends in disaster and death when military officials forcibly remove them and destroy their campsites.

1932 New York governor Franklin D. Roosevelt defeats President Herbert Hoover by over seven million popular votes and a 472-59 margin in the Electoral College.

1933 President Franklin D. Roosevelt calls a special session of Congress to enact major pieces of legislation to combat the Great Depression. Over a span called The

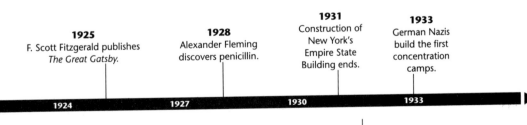

1925
F. Scott Fitzgerald publishes *The Great Gatsby.*

1928
Alexander Fleming discovers penicillin.

1931
Construction of New York's Empire State Building ends.

1933
German Nazis build the first concentration camps.

1924   1927   1930   1933

Hundred Days, much of Roosevelt's New Deal program of social and economic relief, recovery, and reform is approved.

1933 As part of the Twentieth Amendment to the Constitution, the inauguration date of the president is changed to January 20 of the year following the election.

1933 The Twenty-first Amendment repeals prohibition.

1936 President Franklin D. Roosevelt is reelected by a popular vote margin of eleven million and wins the Electoral College vote, 523-8.

1937 Frustrated when the U.S. Supreme Court declares several New Deal programs unconstitutional, President Franklin D. Roosevelt initiates legislation to add more justices to the court and to set term limits. His attempt to "stack the court" receives little support.

1939 World War II begins.

1939 Physicist Albert Einstein informs President Franklin D. Roosevelt about the possibility for creating nuclear weapons and warns him that Nazi scientists are already pursuing experiments to unleash atomic power.

1940 President Franklin D. Roosevelt wins an unprecedented third term by slightly less than five million popular votes and a 449-82 win in the Electoral College.

1941 Pearl Harbor, Hawaii, is attacked; the United States enters World War II.

1942 The success of the first nuclear chain reaction is communicated to President Franklin D. Roosevelt through the code words, "The eagle has landed." A secret program for manufacturing and testing atomic bombs begins.

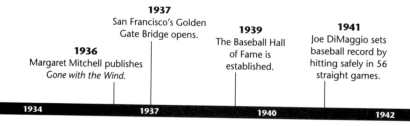

1937
San Francisco's Golden
Gate Bridge opens.

1936
Margaret Mitchell publishes
Gone with the Wind.

1939
The Baseball Hall
of Fame is
established.

1941
Joe DiMaggio sets
baseball record by
hitting safely in 56
straight games.

1934   1937   1940   1942

1944 President Franklin D. Roosevelt is elected to a fourth term by over five million popular votes and a 432-99 Electoral College triumph.

1945 President Franklin D. Roosevelt attends the Yalta Conference and meets with British prime minister Winston Churchill and Soviet leader Joseph Stalin to discuss war issues and the postwar world.

1945 President Franklin D. Roosevelt dies; Vice President Harry S. Truman becomes president. It is only then that Truman learns about development and successful testing of the atomic bomb.

1945 World War II ends in Europe.

1945 The United States drops atomic bombs on Japan. Japan surrenders, and World War II ends.

1946 The U.S. government seizes coal mines and railroads to avoid labor strikes and business practices that might contribute to inflation.

1947 An economic aid package called the Marshall Plan, named after its architect, Secretary of State George C. Marshall, helps revive war-torn Europe.

1947 The Cold War, a period of strained relations and the threat of nuclear war between the United States and the Soviet Union, and their respective allies, settles in and continues for more than forty years.

1948 Renovation of the White House begins. Four years later, the project has completely reconstructed the interior and added two underground levels.

1948 Despite the *Chicago Daily Tribune* headline "DEWEY DEFEATS TRUMAN" on the morning after election day, President Harry S. Truman wins the presidency,

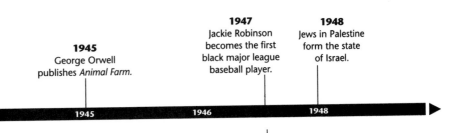

1945
George Orwell
publishes *Animal Farm.*

1947
Jackie Robinson
becomes the first
black major league
baseball player.

1948
Jews in Palestine
form the state
of Israel.

1944   1945   1946   1948

taking over two million more popular votes and winning 303-189 in the Electoral College. The State's Rights Party candidate, South Carolina governor J. Strom Thurmond, places third, slightly outpolling the Progressive Party candidate, former vice president Henry Wallace, and winning thirty-nine electoral votes. Thurmond led a contingent of Southern politicians away from the Democratic Party in protest of Truman's support for civil rights legislation.

1949   The North Atlantic Treaty Organization (NATO) is formed by the United States and its European allies to monitor and check acts of aggression in Europe.

1950   The United States becomes involved in a police action to protect South Korea from invasion by communist North Korea. The police action intensifies into the Korean War.

1951   The Twenty-second Amendment to the Constitution is ratified, limiting presidents to two elected terms and no more than two years of a term to which someone else was elected.

1952   Dwight D. "Ike" Eisenhower, famous as the Supreme Commander of Allied Forces during World War II, is elected president.

1953   An armistice is signed in Korea.

1954   The Army-McCarthy hearings are held. Wisconsin senator Joseph McCarthy presents accusations that the U.S. military and Department of State are deeply infiltrated by communists. McCarthy is eventually disgraced when most of his accusations prove groundless.

1954   In *Brown v. Board of Education,* the U.S. Supreme Court rules that racially segregated public schools are un-

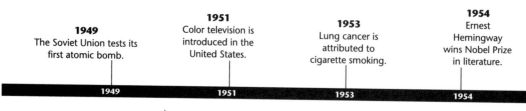

1949
The Soviet Union tests its first atomic bomb.

1951
Color television is introduced in the United States.

1953
Lung cancer is attributed to cigarette smoking.

1954
Ernest Hemingway wins Nobel Prize in literature.

1949   1951   1953   1954

constitutional. In 1957, President Dwight D. Eisenhower sends troops to Little Rock, Arkansas, to enforce desegregation of schools.

1956 An uprising in Hungary against Soviet domination is quickly crushed.

1956 President Dwight D. Eisenhower wins reelection, his second straight triumph over his Democratic challenger, former Illinois governor Adlai Stevenson.

1957 The Soviet Union launches the first space satellite, *Sputnik I.*

1958 The United States launches its first space satellite, *Explorer I,* and the National Aeronautics and Space Agency (NASA) is created.

1959 Alaska and Hawaii enter the Union as the forty-ninth and fiftieth states.

1960 The Cold War deepens over the *U2* incident, where a U.S. spy plane is shot down inside the Soviet Union.

1960 Massachusetts senator John F. Kennedy outpolls Vice President Richard Nixon by slightly more than 100,000 votes while winning 303-219 in the Electoral College. Kennedy, at age 43, is the youngest elected president. A dispute over nine thousand votes in Illinois, that might have resulted in Nixon winning that state instead of Kennedy, is stopped by Nixon. A change of electoral votes in Illinois would not have affected the overall electoral majority won by Kennedy.

1961 The District of Columbia is allowed three electoral votes.

1961 An invasion of Cuba by American-supported rebels at the Bay of Pigs fails when an internal rebellion does

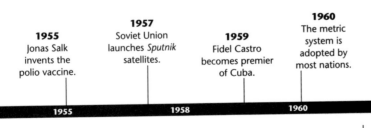

1955
Jonas Salk invents the polio vaccine.

1957
Soviet Union launches *Sputnik* satellites.

1959
Fidel Castro becomes premier of Cuba.

1960
The metric system is adopted by most nations.

1955   1958   1960   1961

not materialize and President John F. Kennedy refuses to provide military backing.

1962   The Cuban Missile Crisis puts the United States and the Soviet Union on the brink of nuclear war after the Soviets are discovered building missile launch sites in Cuba. After a tense, ten-day standoff, the missiles are removed.

1963   A military coup overthrows the political leader of South Vietnam, where American military advisors are assisting South Vietnamese to repel a communist takeover.

1963   A large civil rights march on Washington, D.C., culminates with the famous "I Have a Dream" speech by Rev. Martin Luther King Jr.

1963   President John F. Kennedy is assassinated; Vice President Lyndon B. Johnson assumes the presidency.

1964   President Lyndon B. Johnson steers major civil rights legislation through Congress in memory of the late president John F. Kennedy. The Twenty-fourth Amendment to the Constitution is ratified and ensures the right of citizens of the United States to vote shall not be denied "by reason of failure to pay any poll tax or other tax."

1964   President Lyndon B. Johnson is elected in a landslide, winning almost sixteen million more popular votes than Arizona senator Barry Goldwater.

1965   The Vietnam conflict escalates. President Lyndon B. Johnson is given emergency powers by Congress. Massive bombing missions begin, and U.S. military troops begin engaging in combat, although the U.S. Congress never officially declares war.

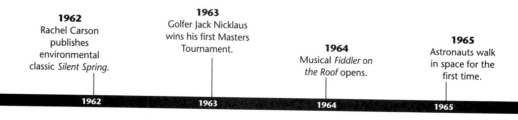

1962
Rachel Carson publishes environmental classic *Silent Spring.*

1963
Golfer Jack Nicklaus wins his first Masters Tournament.

1964
Musical *Fiddler on the Roof* opens.

1965
Astronauts walk in space for the first time.

1962   1963   1964   1965

1966   An unmanned American spacecraft lands on the moon.

1967   Protests, including a march on Washington, D.C., escalate against American involvement in the Vietnam War.

1967   Thurgood Marshall becomes the first African American Supreme Court justice.

1967   The Twenty-fifth Amendment to the Constitution is ratified and provides clear lines of succession to the presidency: "Section 1. In case of the removal of the President from office or of his death or resignation, the Vice President shall become President. Section 2. Whenever there is a vacancy in the office of the Vice President, the President shall nominate a Vice President who shall take office upon confirmation by a majority vote of both Houses of Congress."

1968   Civil rights leader Rev. Martin Luther King Jr. is assassinated in April, and leading Democratic presidential candidate Robert F. Kennedy is assassinated in June.

1968   Former vice president Richard Nixon is elected president, winning with 500,000 more popular votes than incumbent vice president Hubert H. Humphrey and a 301-191 Electoral College edge. Former Alabama governor George C. Wallace of the American Independent Party (for state's rights and against racial desegregation) nets over nine million popular votes and wins forty-six electoral votes.

1969   American troop withdrawals from South Vietnam begin.

1969   U.S. astronaut Neil Armstrong becomes the first man to walk on the moon.

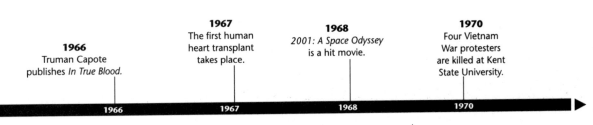

1966
Truman Capote publishes *In True Blood.*

1967
The first human heart transplant takes place.

1968
2001: A Space Odyssey is a hit movie.

1970
Four Vietnam War protesters are killed at Kent State University.

1966   1967   1968   1970

1972 President Richard Nixon reestablishes U.S. relations with the People's Republic of China that were ended after a communist takeover in China in 1949. He visits China and the Soviet Union, where he initiates a policy of détente (a relaxing of tensions between rival nations).

1972 An investigation of a burglary of Democratic National Headquarters at the Watergate Hotel and Office Complex in Washington, D.C., begins and leads to connections with officials in the Richard Nixon administration.

1972 President Richard Nixon is reelected in a landslide.

1973 The Paris Peace Agreement, between the United States and North Vietnam, ends American military involvement in the Vietnam War.

1973 Vice President Spiro T. Agnew resigns over income tax evasion; he is replaced by Michigan congressman Gerald R. Ford.

1974 Nationally televised U.S. Senate hearings on the Watergate scandal confirm connections between the 1972 burglary and officials of the Richard Nixon administration as well as abuses of power.

1974 The House Judiciary Committee begins impeachment hearings and plans to recommend to the House the impeachment of President Richard Nixon.

1974 President Richard Nixon resigns from office over the Watergate scandal. Vice President Gerald R. Ford assumes office.

1974 President Gerald R. Ford issues a pardon, protecting former president Richard Nixon from prosecution in an attempt to end "our national nightmare."

1972
Longtime FBI director J. Edgar Hoover dies.

1973
Skylab space missions take place.

1974
Hank Aaron passes Babe Ruth as baseball's all-time home run hitter.

1972   1973   1974   1975

1976 In a close election, former Georgia governor Jimmy Carter defeats President Gerald R. Ford.

1977 Beset by rising fuel costs and a continued sluggish economy, President Jimmy Carter calls an energy shortage "the moral equivalent of war" and attempts to rally conservation efforts.

1979 The Camp David Accords, the result of negotiations spearheaded by President Jimmy Carter, is signed by the leaders of Egyptian president Anwar Sadat and Israeli prime minister Menachem Begin in Washington, D.C.

1979 Fifty-two Americans are taken hostage in Iran following a religious revolution in that nation in which the American-supported leader was overthrown. The hostage crisis lasts 444 days, with the hostages released on the day President Jimmy Carter leaves office.

1980 Former California governor Ronald Reagan wins a landslide (489-49 in the Electoral College) over President Jimmy Carter. Independent candidate John Anderson, a longtime Republican congressman from Illinois, polls over five million votes. Reagan becomes the oldest president.

1981 Sandra Day O'Connor becomes the first female U.S. Supreme Court justice.

1982 Economic growth begins after a decade of sluggish performance.

1984 President Ronald Reagan is reelected in another landslide, drawing the most popular votes ever (54,455,075) and romping in the Electoral College, 525-13.

1987 A sudden stock market crash and growing federal deficits threaten economic growth.

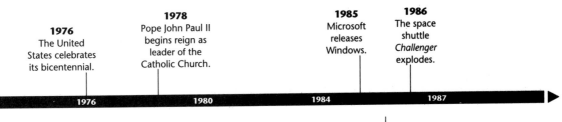

1976
The United States celebrates its bicentennial.

1978
Pope John Paul II begins reign as leader of the Catholic Church.

1985
Microsoft releases Windows.

1986
The space shuttle *Challenger* explodes.

1976 1980 1984 1987

1988 George Bush becomes the first sitting vice president since Martin Van Buren in 1836 to be elected president.

1989 Several East European nations become independent from domination by the U.S.S.R. Reforms in the U.S.S.R. eventually lead to the breakup of the Soviet Union; the former Soviet states become independent nations in 1991, and the Cold War ends.

1991 After the Iraqi government fails to comply with a United Nations resolution to abandon Kuwait, which its military invaded in August of 1990, the Gulf War begins. Within a month, Kuwait is liberated by an international military force. President George Bush's popularity soars over his leadership in rallying U.N. members to stop Iraqi aggression.

1992 An economic downturn and a huge budget deficit erode President George Bush's popularity. Arkansas governor Bill Clinton defeats Bush for the presidency. The Reform Party candidate, Texas businessman H. Ross Perot, draws 19,221,433 votes, the most ever for a third-party candidate, but wins no electoral votes. Clinton and running mate Al Gore are the youngest president–vice president tandem in history.

1994 An upturn in the economy begins the longest sustained growth period in American history.

1996 President Bill Clinton is reelected.

1998 President Bill Clinton is implicated in perjury (false testimony under oath in a court case) and an extramarital affair. The House Judiciary Committee votes, strictly on party lines, to recommend impeachment of the president, and the House impeaches the president for perjury and abuse of power.

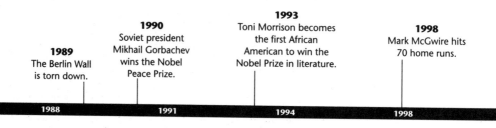

1989
The Berlin Wall is torn down.

1990
Soviet president Mikhail Gorbachev wins the Nobel Peace Prize.

1993
Toni Morrison becomes the first African American to win the Nobel Prize in literature.

1998
Mark McGwire hits 70 home runs.

1988   1991   1994   1998

1999   President Bill Clinton remains in office after being acquitted in a Senate trial.

2000   In the closest and most hotly contested election since 1876, Texas governor George W. Bush narrowly defeats Vice President Al Gore in the Electoral College, 271-266. Gore wins the popular vote by some three hundred thousand votes. The final victor cannot be declared until after a recount in Florida (with its twenty-five electoral votes at stake) takes place. Five weeks of legal battles ensue and Gore officially contests the results before Bush is able to claim victory in the state and, therefore, in the national election.

2000   Hillary Rodham Clinton becomes the first first lady to be elected to public office when she is elected U.S. senator from New York.

2000   In one of his last functions as president, Bill Clinton attends an international economic summit in Asia and visits Vietnam, twenty-five years after the end of the conflict that deeply divided Americans.

2001   George W. Bush is inaugurated the nation's forty-third president and becomes the second son of a president to become president himself.

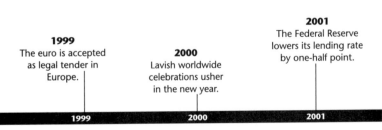

1999
The euro is accepted as legal tender in Europe.

2000
Lavish worldwide celebrations usher in the new year.

2001
The Federal Reserve lowers its lending rate by one-half point.

1999   2000   2001

Words to Know

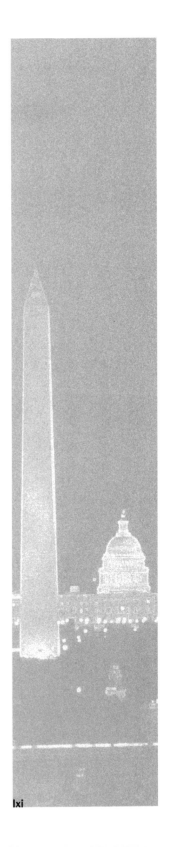

A

Abolitionists: People who worked to end slavery.

Agrarian: One who believes in and supports issues beneficial to agriculture.

Alien and Sedition Acts: Four bills—the Naturalization Act, Alien Act, Alien Enemies Act, and Sedition Act—passed by Congress in 1798 and signed into law by President John Adams. The Naturalization Act extended from five to fourteen years the waiting period before citizenship—and with it, the right to vote—could be obtained by new immigrants. The two Alien acts gave the president the right to deport or jail foreign citizens he deemed a threat to the nation's stability, especially during wartime. The Sedition Act criminalized criticism of the government. To write or publish views that disparaged the administration was punishable by harsh fines and jail terms.

Allied forces (allies): Alliances of countries in military opposition to another group of nations. Twenty-eight nations made up the Allied and Associated powers in World War I. In World War II, the Allied powers included Great Britain, the United States, and the Soviet Union.

Anarchist: One against any form of government.

Annexing: Adding a new state or possession to the existing United States of America.

Annual Message to Congress: A speech the president delivers before Congress each year. Originally called the Annual Message to Congress and delivered each November, the speech became known as the State of the Union Address and is delivered each January.

Anti-Federalists: A group who wanted a limited federal government and more power for individual states.

Antitrust: Government action against businesses that dominate a certain industry or market and that are alleged to have stifled competing businesses.

Appropriations: Funds authorized for a particular project.

Armistice: An agreement to cease fire while warring parties negotiate a peace settlement.

Articles of Confederation: From March 1, 1781, to June 21, 1788, the Articles served as the equivalent of the Constitution (1787). The Constitution replaced the Articles, which had failed to produce a strong central government, and the present-day United States was formed.

Axis: The countries that fought together against the Allies in World War II. Germany, Italy, and Japan formed the first coalition; eventually, they were joined by Hungary, Romania, Slovakia, Finland, and Bulgaria.

B

Bar: A term that encompasses all certified lawyers—those who have passed all official requirements (the bar exam) to be certified as lawyers.

Bar exam: A test that lawyers must pass in order to become legally certified to practice law.

Battle of the Bulge: Battles surrounding the last German offensive (1944–45) during World War II. Allied forces moving toward Germany from France following the D-Day invasion were stalled by bad weather along the German border. Germans launched a counteroffensive to divide American and British forces. Germans created a "bulge" in the Allied lines, but they were halted and then withdrew.

Bay of Pigs invasion: Failed U.S.-backed invasion of Cuba at the Bay of Pigs by fifteen hundred Cuban exiles opposed to Fidel Castro, on April 17, 1961.

"Big stick" foreign policy: Theodore Roosevelt's theory that in diplomatic efforts, it was wise to "speak softly and carry a big stick," meaning that one should attempt peaceful solutions while at the same time being prepared to back up the talk with action when necessary.

Bill of Rights: The first ten amendments to the American Constitution of rights and privileges guaranteed to the people of the United States.

Black Codes: Laws and provisions that limited civil rights and placed economic restrictions on African Americans.

"Bleeding Kansas": The conflict in Kansas in 1854 between slavery advocates and abolitionists—in the form of both residents and transients, and two different governments—that led to bloodshed. It was the first indication that the issue of slavery would not be settled diplomatically.

Bloc: A unified group able to wield power through its size and numbers.

Boston Tea Party: An event in 1773 in which colonists spilled shipments of tea into Boston harbor to protest taxes imposed on various products.

Bull market: A stock market term that describes a period of aggressive buying and selling of stock that proves profitable for most investors; in contrast, "bear market" is used to describe a more sluggish trading period.

Bureaucracy: A government or big business set up to be run by bureaus, or departments, that strictly follow rules and regulations and a chain of authority.

C

Camp David Accords: An agreement of peace following negotiations led by President Jimmy Carter and signed by Israeli prime minister Menachem Begin and Egyptian president Anwar Sadat on March 26, 1979.

Capitol Hill: A nickname for Congress, since the Capitol building where Congress holds sessions is located on a small hill.

Carpetbaggers: A term of contempt used by Southerners about agents, humanitarians, politicians, and businessmen who came to the South to assist or to exploit Reconstruction policies. The term suggests that Northerners could stuff everything they owned into a bag made from carpet.

Caucus: An organized vote by registered and designated members of a political party to determine the amount of support within a state for the party's presidential candidates.

Censure: To publicly condemn an individual; in Congress, the act of censure expresses Congress's condemnation of an individual's actions and is entered into the *Congressional Record.*

Central Intelligence Agency (CIA): A U.S. government agency charged with accumulating information on foreign countries.

Checks and balances: The system in which the three branches of the U.S. government can review and dismiss acts passed by one of the other branches.

Civil service: Positions under the authority of the federal government.

Civil War: Conflict that took place from 1861 to 1865 between the Northern states (Union) and the Southern seceded states (Confederacy); also known in the South as the War between the States and in the North as the War of the Rebellion.

Coalitions: Groups of people supporting a political issue or cause.

Cold War: A term that describes a period from 1945 to the late 1980s characterized by tense conflicts and failed diplomacy between the Soviet Union and the United States and their respective allies.

Communism: A system in which the government controls the distribution of goods and services and limits individual freedom.

Compromise of 1850: Legislation passed by Congress and signed into law by President Millard Fillmore consisting of five bills: (1) California was admitted as a free state; (2) Texas was compensated for the loss of territory in a boundary dispute with New Mexico; (3) New Mexico was granted territorial status; (4) the slave trade—but not slavery itself—was abolished in Washington, D.C; (5) and most controversially, the Fugitive Slave Law was enacted, allowing slaveowners to pursue fleeing slaves and recapture them in free states.

Confederate States of America (Confederacy): The eleven Southern states that seceded (separated) from the United States during the 1860s and fought the Union during the American Civil War.

Congressional Record: A document that records all speeches and votes made in Congress.

Conservative: A political philosophy of limited government influence and support for conventional social values.

Constitutional Convention: The 1787 convention attended by delegates to strengthen the Articles of Confederation. Instead, delegates adopted the American Constitution that formed the United States.

Constructionist: One who bases decisions on literal readings of the Constitution.

Consul: A diplomat stationed in a foreign country who advises people from his or her own country on legal matters.

Continental Army: The American army during the Revolutionary War against Great Britain.

Continental Congress: The group of representatives who met to establish the United States.

Coup: A sudden overthrow of a government, often by the country's military.

Covert operations: Secret, undercover acts used to help influence the outcome of events.

Cuban missile crisis: A showdown in October 1962 that brought the Soviet Union and the United States close to war over the existence of Soviet nuclear missiles in Cuba.

D

D-Day: A military term that describes the day when an event can be scheduled. D-Day in World War II was June 6, 1944, when Allied forces landed in Normandy, France.

Dark horse: A little-known candidate with modest chances for success who might emerge surprisingly strong.

Delegate: A member of a party or organization who has a vote that represents a larger group and helps determine the leader of that party or organization.

Democratic Party: One of the oldest political parties in the United States, developed out of the Democratic-Republican Party of the late eighteenth century. Andrew Jackson was one of its first leaders. In the years before the Civil War (1861–65), Democrats became increasingly associated with the South and slavery. Following the war, the party gradually transformed and became associated with urban voters and liberal policies. In the twentieth and twenty-first centuries, Democrats have generally favored freer trade, more international commitments, greater government regulations, and social programs.

Democratic-Republican Party: One of the first political parties in the United States, led by Thomas Jefferson and James Madison in the 1790s to oppose the Federalist Party and close ties with Great Britain. It was also called the Republican Party and the Jeffersonian Republican Party at the time, but the term Democratic-Republican helps distinguish that early political group from the Democratic and Republican parties that were formed later. The Democratic-Republican Party dissolved in the 1820s. Many former members began supporting the formation of the Democratic Party led by Andrew Jackson, who was elected president in 1828 and 1832. The modern-day Republican Party was formed in 1854.

Depression: *See* **Great Depression.**

Deregulation: Removal of guidelines and laws governing a business or financial institution.

Détente: A relaxing of tensions between rival nations, marked by increased diplomatic, commercial, and cultural contact.

Draft cards: From the mid-1960s through the mid-1970s, all males had to register for the draft upon turning eighteen. After registering, an individual received a draft card that contained a draft number. A lottery system was used to determine which available males would be "drafted"—required to serve in the military.

E

Election board: A group authorized to operate elections and count votes.

Electoral College: A body officially responsible for electing the president of the United States. In presidential elections, the candidate who receives the most popular votes in a particular state wins all of that state's electoral votes. Votes are distributed among states in ratios based on population. A candidate must win a majority of electoral votes (over fifty percent) in order to win the presidency.

Electoral votes: The votes a presidential candidate receives for having won a majority of the popular vote in a state. In presidential elections, the candidate who receives the most popular votes in a particular state wins all of that states' electoral votes. Votes are distributed among states in ratios based on population. A candidate must win a majority of electoral votes (over fifty percent) in order to win the presidency.

Emancipation: The act of freeing people from slavery.

Enfranchisement: Voting rights.

Expansionism: The policy of a nation that plans to enlarge its size or gain possession of other lands.

Exploratory committee: A group established by a potential political candidate to examine whether enough party, public, and financial support exists for the potential candidate to officially announce that he or she is running for an elected position.

F

Federal budget: The list of all planned expenditures the federal government expects to make over a year.

Federal budget deficit: When government spending exceeds income (from taxes and other revenue).

Federal Reserve System: The central banking system of the United States, which serves as the banker to the financial sector and the government, issues the national currency, and supervises banking practices.

Federalist: A proponent for a strong national (federal) government.

Federalist Party: An American political party of the late eighteenth century that began losing influence around 1820. Federalists supported a strong national government. Growing sentiments for states' rights and rural regions led to the demise of the party. Many Federalists became Democratic-Republicans until that party was split into factions in the mid-1820s. Those favoring states' rights became Jackson Democrats and formed the Democratic Party in 1832.

First Continental Congress: A group of representatives from the thirteen colonies who met in Philadelphia in 1774 to list grievances (complaints) against England.

Fiscal: Relating to financial matters.

Fourteen Points: Famous speech given by Woodrow Wilson that includes reasons for American involvement in war, terms for peace, and his vision of a League of Nations.

Freedmen's Bureau: An agency that provided federal help for freed slaves.

Fugitive Slave Law: The provision in the Compromise of 1850 that allowed Southern slaveowners to pursue and capture runaway slaves into Northern states.

G

General assembly: A state congressional system made up only of representatives from districts within that particular state.

Gerrymandering: A practice whereby the political party in power changes boundaries in a voting area to include more people likely to support the party in power. This can occur when Congressional districts are rezoned (marked off into different sections) following the national census that occurs every ten years.

Gold standard: The economic practice whereby all of the money printed and minted in a nation is based on the amount of gold the nation has stored. (Paper money is printed; coins are minted, or stamped.)

GOP: Short for "Grand Old Party," a nickname of the Republican Party.

Grand jury: A group empowered to decide whether a government investigation can provide enough evidence to make criminal charges against a citizen.

Grass roots: A term that describes political activity that begins with small groups of people acting without the influence of large and powerful groups.

Great Depression: The worst financial crisis in American history. Usually dated from 1929, when many investors lost money during a stock market crash, to 1941, when the last Depression-related relief effort to help impoverished and unemployed people was passed by the government. When America entered World War II (1939–45) in 1941, many more employment opportunities became available in war-related industries.

Great Society: A set of social programs proposed by President Lyndon B. Johnson designed to end segregation and reduce poverty in the United States.

Gross national product (GNP): An economic measurement of a nation's total value of goods and services produced over a certain period (usually a year); the GNP became an official economic statistic in 1947.

H

House of Burgesses: A representative body made up of Virginia colonists but under the authority of British rule.

Human rights: Principles based on the belief that human beings are born free and equal; governments must respect those rights or they can be accused of human rights violations.

I

Immunity: Protection from prosecution; usually extended to someone who can help the prosecution win its case.

Impeachment: A legislative proceeding charging a public official with misconduct. Impeachment consists of the formal accusation of such an official and the trial that follows. It does not refer to removal from office of the accused.

Imperialism: The process of expanding the authority of one government over other nations and groups of people.

Incumbent: The person currently holding an elected office during an election period.

Independent counsel: A federal position established during the 1970s to investigate federal officials accused of crimes. The Independent Counsel Act, intended to perform in a nonpartisan manner in rare occasions, was not renewed in 1999.

Indictment: An official charge of having committed a crime.

Industrialization: The use of machinery for manufacturing goods.

Inflation: An economic term that describes a situation in which money loses some of its value, usually because the cost of goods is more expensive.

Infrastructure: The system of public works—the physical resources constructed for public use, such as bridges and roads—of a state or country.

Injunction: A legal maneuver that suspends a certain practice until a legal decision can be reached.

Insurrections: Armed rebellions against a recognized authority.

Integration: The bringing together of people of all races and ethnic backgrounds without restrictions; desegregation.

Interest rates: The percentage of a loan that a person agrees to pay for borrowing money.

Internationalism: Interest and participation in events involving other countries.

Iran-Contra scandal: A scandal during the Ronald Reagan administration during which government officials made illegal sales of weapons to Iran. Money made from those sales were diverted to secret funds provided to the Contras in the civil war in El Salvador. This was illegal, since Congress must authorize foreign aid.

Iran hostage crisis: A 444-day period from November 4, 1979, to Inauguration Day 1981 when Iran held 52 American embassy officials hostage following the toppling of the American-backed Shah of Iran.

Iron Curtain: A term describing Eastern European nations dominated by the Soviet Union.

Isolationism: A national policy of avoiding pacts, treaties, and other official agreements with other nations in order to remain neutral.

K

Kansas-Nebraska Act: A U.S. law authorizing the creation of the states of Kansas and Nebraska and specifying that the inhabitants of the territories should decide whether or not to allow slaveholding.

Keynote address: The most important speech during opening ceremonies of an organized meeting.

Korean War: A war from 1950 to 1953 fought between communist North Korea and non-communist South Korea; China backed North Korea and the United Nations backed South Korea.

L

Laissez faire: A French term (roughly translated as "allow to do") commonly used to describe noninterference by government in the affairs of business and the economy.

Lame duck: An official who has lost an election and is filling out the remainder of his or her term.

League of Nations: An organization of nations, as proposed by President Woodrow Wilson, that would exert moral leadership and help nations avoid future wars.

Legal tender: Bills or coin that have designated value.

Lobbyist: A person hired to represent the interests of a particular group to elected officials.

Louisiana Purchase: A vast region in North America purchased by the United States from France in 1803 for $15 million.

Loyalists: Americans who remained loyal to Great Britain during the Revolutionary War (1775–83).

M

Manifest Destiny: The belief that American expansionism is inevitable and divinely ordained.

Marshall Plan: A post–World War II program led by Secretary of State George C. Marshall that helped rebuild European economies (also benefiting U.S. trade) and strengthened democratic governments.

Martial law: A state of emergency during which a military group becomes the sole authority in an area and civil laws are set aside.

Medicare: A government program that provides financial assistance to poor people to help cover medical costs.

Mercenaries: Soldiers hired to serve a foreign country.

Merchant marine: Professional sailors and boat workers involved with commercial marine trade and maintenance (as opposed to branches of the military such as the navy and the coast guard).

Midterm elections: Congressional elections that occur halfway through a presidential term. These elections can affect the president's dealings with Congress. A president is elected every four years; representatives (members of the House of Representatives), every two years; and senators, every six years.

Military dictatorships: States in which military leaders have absolute power.

Military draft: A mandatory program that requires that all males register for possible military service. Those who pass a medical test receive a draft number. A lottery system is used to determine which available males must serve in the military. Those whose numbers are drawn are "drafted" into military service.

Military governments: Governments supervised or run by a military force.

Military tribunal: A court presided over by military officials to try cases in an area under a state of war.

Militia: A small military group, not affiliated with the federal government, organized for emergency service.

Missing in action: A term that describes military personnel unaccounted for. They might have been captured by the enemy, in which case they become prisoners of war; they might be hiding out and attempting to return to safety; or they might have been killed.

Missouri Compromise: Legislation passed in 1820 that designated which areas could enter the Union as free states and which could enter as slave states. It was repealed in 1854.

Monarchy: A form of government in which a single person (usually a king or queen) has absolute power.

Monroe Doctrine: A policy statement issued during the presidency of James Monroe (1817–25) that explained the position of the United States on the activities of European powers in the western hemisphere; of major significance was the stand of the United States against European intervention in the affairs of the Americas.

Muckrakers: A circle of investigative reporters during Theodore Roosevelt's term in office who exposed the seamier (unwholesome) side of American life. These reporters thoroughly researched their stories and based their reports on provable facts.

N

National Security Council: A group of military advisors assisting the president.

Nationalism: Loyalty to a nation that exalts that quality above all other nations.

Nazi: The abbreviated name for the National Socialist German Workers' Party, the political party led by Adolf Hitler, who became dictator of Germany. Hitler's Nazi Party controlled Germany from 1933 to 1945. The Nazis promoted racist and anti-Semitic (anti-Jewish) ideas and enforced complete obedience to Hitler and the party.

Neutrality: A position in which a nation is not engaged with others and does not take sides in disputes.

New Deal: A series of programs initiated by the administration of President Franklin D. Roosevelt to create jobs and stimulate the economy during the Great Depression (1929–41).

North Atlantic Treaty Organization (NATO): An alliance for collective security created by the North Atlantic Treaty in 1949 and originally involving Belgium, Canada, Denmark, France, Great Britain, Iceland, Italy, Luxembourg, the Netherlands, Norway, Portugal, and the United States.

Nuclear test ban treaty: An agreement to stop testing nuclear weapons.

Nullification: Negatation; the Theory of Nullification was proposed by John C. Calhoun, a South Carolina congressman who later served as vice president to Andrew Jackson. In Calhoun's theory, a state has the right to nullify federal laws that it deems harmful to the state's interests.

O

Open Door Policy: A program introduced by President William McKinley to extend trade and relations with China, opening up a vast new market.

Oppression: Abuse of power by one party against another.

P

Pacifist: A person opposed to conflict.

Panic of 1837: An economic slump that hit the United States in 1837.

Pardon: A power that allows the president to free an individual or a group from prosecution for a crime.

Parliamentary government: A system of government in which executive power resides with Cabinet-level officials responsible to the nation's legislature. The highest-ranking member of the political party with a majority in such a system of government is usually made the nation's chief executive.

Partisan: Placing the concerns of one's group or political party above all other considerations.

Patronage system: Also called spoils system; a system in which elected officials appoint their supporters to civil service (government) jobs.

Peace Corps: A government-sponsored program that trains volunteers for social and humanitarian service in underdeveloped areas of the world.

Peacekeeping force: A military force sponsored by the United Nations that polices areas that have been attacked by another group clearly defined as aggressors.

Pearl Harbor: An American naval station in Hawaii attacked without warning by Japanese forces in December 1941.

Pendleton Civil Service Reform Act: A congressional act signed into law by President Chester A. Arthur that established the Civil Service Commission, an organization that oversees federal appointments and ensures that appointees do not actively participate in party politics while holding a federal job.

Perjury: The voluntary violation of an oath or a vow; answering falsely while under oath (having previously sworn to tell the truth).

Platform: A declaration of policies that a candidate or political party intends to follow if the party's candidate is elected.

Political boss: A politically powerful person who can direct a group of voters to support a particular candidate.

Political dynasty: A succession of government leaders from the same political party.

Political machine: An organized political group whose members are generally under the control of the leader of the group.

Populism: An agricultural movement of rural areas between the Mississippi River and the Rocky Mountains of the late nineteenth century that united the interests of farmers and laborers. In 1891, the movement formed a national political party, the People's Party, whose members were called Populists. Populist ideals remained popular even when the party faded early in the twentieth century.

Presidential primaries: Elections held in states to help determine the nominees of political parties for the general election. Each party disperses a certain number of delegates to each state. A candidate must win support of a majority of those delegates to win the party's presidential nomination. In states that hold primary elections, delegates are generally awarded to candidates based on the percentage of votes they accumulate; in some states, the leading vote-getter wins all of those state's delegates.

Presidential veto: When a president declines to sign into law a bill passed by Congress.

Primaries: *See* **Presidential primaries.**

Progressive "Bull Moose" Party: Party in which Theodore Roosevelt ran as a third-party candidate in 1912. He came in second to incumbent president William Howard Taft, but lost to New Jersey governor Woodrow Wilson.

Progressivism: A movement that began late in the nineteenth century whose followers pursued social, economic, and government reform. Generally located in urban areas, Progressivists ranged from individuals seeking to improve local living conditions to radicals who pursued sweeping changes in the American political and economic system.

Prohibition: The constitutional ban on the manufacture and sale of alcohol and alcoholic beverages from 1920 to 1933.

Prosecuting attorney: The attorney who represents the government in a law case.

Protectorate: A relationship in which an independent nation comes under the protection and power of another nation.

Proviso: A clause in a document making a qualification, condition, or restriction.

R

Racial desegregation: A policy meant to ensure that people of all racial origins are treated equal.

Rapprochement: Reestablishment of relations with a country after it has undergone a dramatic change in government.

Ratification: A vote of acceptance. A majority of the representatives from each of the thirteen colonies had to vote for the U.S. Constitution (1787) in order for the document to become legally binding.

Recession: A situation of increasing unemployment and decreasing value of money.

Recharter: To renew a law or an act.

Reciprocal trade agreements: When participating nations promise to trade in a way that will benefit each nation equally.

Reconstruction: A federal policy from 1865 to 1877 through which the national government took an active part in assisting and policing the former Confederate states.

Reconstruction Act of 1867: An act that placed military governments (governments supervised by a military force) in command of states of the South until the Fourteenth Amendment was ratified in 1868.

Regulation: Monitoring business with an established set of guidelines.

Reparations: Payments for damage caused by acts of hostility.

Republican government: A form of government in which supreme power resides with citizens who elect their leaders and have the power to change their leaders.

Republican Party: Founded in 1854 by a coalition (an alliance) of former members of the Whig, Free-Soil, and Know-Nothing parties and of northern Democrats dissatisfied with their party's proslavery stands. The party quickly rose to become one of the most important parties in the United States, and the major opposition to the Democratic Party. Republicans are generally associated with conservative fiscal and social policies. The Republican Party is not related to the older Democratic-Republican Party, although that party was often called the Republicans before the 1830s.

Riders: Measures added on to legislation. Riders are usually items that might not pass through Congress or will be vetoed by the president if presented alone. Congressmen attempt to attach such items to popular bills, hoping they will "ride" along with the more popular legislation.

S

Sanctions: Punishment against a nation involved in activities considered illegal under international law; such punishment usually denies trade, supplies, or access to other forms of international assistance to the nation.

Satellite nations: Countries politically and economically dominated by a larger, more powerful nation.

Secession: Formal withdrawal from an existing organization. In 1860–61, eleven Southern states seceded from the Union to form the Confederate States of America.

Second Continental Congress: A group of representatives from the thirteen colonies who began meeting in Philadelphia in 1775 and effectively served as the American government until the Constitution was adopted in 1787.

Sectionalism: The emphasis that people place on policies that would directly benefit their area of the country.

Segregation: The policy of keeping groups of people from different races, religions, or ethnic backgrounds separated.

Social Security: A government program that provides pensions (a regular sum of money) to American workers after they reach age sixty-five.

Social welfare: A term that encompasses government programs that provide assistance, training, and jobs to people.

Solicitor: An attorney who represents a government agency.

Solicitor general: An attorney appointed by the president to argue legal matters on behalf of the government.

South East Asia Treaty Organization: An alliance of nations founded in 1954 to prevent the spread of communism in Asian and Pacific island nations. Original members included Australia, France, Great Britain, New Zealand, Pakistan, the Philippines, Thailand, and the United States. The alliance disbanded in 1977.

Speaker of the House: The person in charge of supervising activity in the House of Representatives. The Speaker is elected by colleagues of the party with a majority in Congress.

Spin doctoring: A late twentieth-century term that describes the practice of having political aides offer the best possible interpretation of a political statement or the effects of an event on their political boss.

State militia: An organized military unit maintained by states in case of emergency; often called the National Guard.

Stock market crash: A sudden decline in the value of stocks that severely affects investors.

Strategic Arms Limitation Treaty (SALT): Missile reduction program between the United States and the Soviet Union.

Strategic Defense Initiative (SDI): A proposed—but never approved—technological system (nicknamed "Star Wars," after the popular movie) that combined several advanced technology systems that could, in theory, detect and intercept missiles fired by enemies of the United States.

Subpoena: A formal legal document that commands a certain action or requires a person to appear in court.

T

Taft-Hartley Act: Act that outlawed union-only workplaces, prohibited certain union activities, forbade unions to contribute to political campaigns, established loyalty oaths for union leaders, and allowed court orders to halt strikes that could affect national health or safety.

Tariff: A protective tax placed on imported goods to raise their price and make them less attractive than goods produced by the nation importing them.

Teapot Dome scandal: Incident that became public following the death of President Warren G. Harding that revealed that Navy secretary Edwin Denby transfered control of oil reserves in Teapot Dome, Wyoming, and Elk Hill, California, to the Department of the Interior, whose secretary, Albert Fall, secretly leased the reserve to two private oil operators, who paid Fall $400,000.

Tenure of Office Act: A law passed by Congress to limit the powers of the presidency.

Terrorist: A person who uses acts of violence in an attempt to coerce by terror.

Theater: A large area where military operations are occurring.

Thirteenth Amendment: An amendment to the U.S. Constitution that outlawed slavery.

Tonkin Gulf Resolution: Passed by Congress after U.S. Navy ships supposedly came under attack in the Gulf of Tonkin, this resolution gave President Lyndon B. Johnson the authority to wage war against North Vietnam.

Tribunal: A court of law.

Truman Doctrine: A Cold War–era program designed by President Harry S. Truman that sent aid to anticommunist forces in Turkey and Greece. The Union of Soviet Socialist Republics (U.S.S.R.) had naval stations in Turkey, and nearby Greece was fighting a civil war with communist-dominated rebels.

U

Underground railroad: A term that describes a series of routes through which escaped slaves could pass through free Northern states and into Canada. The escaped slaves were assisted by abolitionists and free African Americans in the North.

Union: Northern states that remained loyal to the United States during the Civil War.

V

Veto: The power of one branch of government—for example, the executive—to reject a bill passed by a legislative body and thus prevent it from becoming law.

Vietcong: Vietnamese communists engaged in warfare against the government and people of South Vietnam.

W

War of 1812: A war fought from 1812 to 1815 between the United States and Great Britain. The United States wanted to protect its maritime rights as a neutral nation during a conflict between Great Britain and France.

Warren Commission: A commission chaired by Earl Warren, chief justice of the Supreme Court, that investigated President John F. Kennedy's assassination. The commission concluded that the assassination was the act of one gunman, not part of a larger conspiracy. That conclusion remains debated.

Watergate scandal: A scandal that began on June 17, 1972, when five men were caught burglarizing the offices of the Democratic National Committee in the Watergate complex in Washington, D.C. This led to a cover-up, political convictions, and, eventually, the resignation of President Richard Nixon.

Welfare: Government assistance to impoverished people.

Whig Party: A political party that existed roughly from 1836 to 1852, composed of different factions of the former Democratic-Republican Party. These factions refused to join the group that formed the Democratic Party led by President Andrew Jackson.

Y

Yalta Conference: A 1944 meeting between Allied leaders Joseph Stalin, Winston Churchill, and Franklin D. Roosevelt in anticipation of an Allied victory in Europe over the Nazis. The leaders discussed how to manage lands conquered by Germany, and Roosevelt and Churchill urged Stalin to enter the Soviet Union in the war against Japan.

Research and Activity Ideas

The following research and activity ideas are intended to offer suggestions for complementing social studies and history curricula, to trigger additional ideas for enhancing learning, and to suggest cross-disciplinary projects for library and classroom use.

- The aftermath of the 2000 race between George W. Bush and Al Gore renewed debate over whether the Electoral College system should be abandoned in favor of the popular vote. Research the reasons why the Founding Fathers instituted the Electoral College. Write a paper on arguments for and against the Electoral College, or take one side and have a partner take the other side.

- Several Web sites on presidents are listed in the "Where to Learn More" section. Additional Web sites, linked to presidential libraries and historical sites, are listed at the end of many individual president entries. Using a president of particular interest to you, compare the descriptions of his life and his presidency on the various Web sites. The comparison will show how presidents are appraised by different sources. Pretend you are a media critic. Write a review of the various sites, comparing their different features, the ways they treat the president, and what you find interesting and not useful in each site.

- Plan a debate or a series of debates on important issues in American history. One issue could be the powers of the federal government in relation to the states. That issue can be explored and debated by contrasting the views of a president who took a different view of federal power from the president who preceded him. Such contrasting pairs include John Adams and Thomas Jefferson; James Buchanan and Abraham Lincoln; Herbert Hoover and Franklin D. Roosevelt; and George Bush and Bill Clinton.

- In contemporary times, when a president makes his State of the Union address each year, television networks provide equal time for a member of the opposing party to present his or her party's views. After reading and making notes on one of the speeches in the primary documents section, prepare a response—a speech that takes an opposite view on issues presented by the president.

- Create a timeline of a fifty-year period to parallel the "Timeline of the American Presidents," found on pages xxix–lix. Your timeline might list important inventions, world events, or developments in science and technology. Placing the timelines side by side, consider ways in which the events on your timeline might be connected with events in the presidential timeline.

- Using the resources of your local library, find magazines and newspapers that were published near the time you were born, or pick a date earlier in time. What were some of the big national news stories back then? How did the press view the performance of the president concerning those issues?

- Pretend you are a reporter preparing to interview one of the presidents. Just before your interview is to begin, the president is informed about a major event (select one from the president's entry). You are allowed to follow the president as he plans a course of action. Write an article providing an "insider's view" of the president in action.

- The Congressional cable network C-Span commissioned presidential scholars to rate presidents in ten categories (see http://www.americanpresidents.org/survey/histori-ans/overall.asp). Compare that ranking with other sources that rank presidents in terms of effectiveness. How are the rankings similar and different? What criteria do they use for judging presidents? Consider whether or not you feel the rankings are fair, and write an essay supporting your view.

- Visit a historical site or Web sites devoted to a particular president. Listings for both can often be found in each president's entry. Using biographical information about the president's childhood, his schooling, and his career as president, write a short play in which the president is surrounded by loved ones and aides at a crucial moment during his presidency.

- There were many different kinds of first ladies. Some were politically active (such as Sarah Polk and Eleanor Roosevelt), others believed they should not participate in politics because they were not the one elected to office (such as Bess Truman and Pat Nixon). Compare and contrast those different approaches by profiling several first ladies.

- Research more about a leading opponent of a particular president, perhaps someone he faced in an election. Imagine that the opponent was able to convince voters that he or she should be elected. Write about how history would have been different if the opponent had become president. The focus could be on an election that was very close (such as Rutherford B. Hayes over Samuel Tilden in 1876 or George W. Bush over Al Gore in 2000) or one in which the victor won by a large margin (such as Franklin D. Roosevelt over Alfred Landon in 1936 or Ronald Reagan over Walter Mondale in 1984).

Complete American Presidents Sourcebook

George Washington

First president (1789–1797)

George Washington

Born February 22, 1732
Westmoreland County, Virginia
Died December 14, 1799
Mount Vernon, Virginia

First president of the United States (1789–1797)

Used his popularity and political skills—and the blueprint of the U.S. Constitution—to build a new federal government

George Washington is called "the father of his country" for several reasons. Washington was an outspoken proponent for American independence from Great Britain. He commanded the American Continental Army in its long and ultimately successful struggle in the Revolutionary War (1775–83). After the war, Washington presided over the Constitutional Convention (1787), the assembly of representatives at which the United States was formed. Elected the nation's first president, Washington proved by example that the American system could work. He established a model of how the nation's chief executive should act.

Political differences among Americans threatened the unity of the young nation. Washington served a second term as president to keep the increasingly divided nation together. He avoided a war with Great Britain in the early 1790s that would have slowed the nation's progress. When Washington left office, the peaceful transition from one elected president to another proved that the American system of government was sound.

Washington was glorified by many myths following his death. In reality, he had a quick temper. Some historians

"Labour to keep alive in your breast that little spark of . . . fire—conscience."

George Washington

George Washington.
Courtesy of the Library of Congress.

3

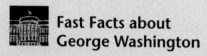

Fast Facts about George Washington

Full name: George Washington

Born: February 22, 1732

Died: December 14, 1799

Burial site: Washington Family Vault, Mount Vernon, Virginia

Parents: Augustine and Mary Ball Washington

Spouse: Martha Dandridge Custis (1732–1802; m. 1759)

Children: John Custis (1754–1781), Martha Custis (1755–1773) (stepchildren)

Religion: Episcopalian

Education: No formal education

Occupations: Surveyor; planter; general

Government positions: Virginia House of Burgesses member; Continental congressman; Constitutional Convention chairman

Political party: Federalist

Dates as president: April 30, 1789–March 4, 1793 (first term); March 4, 1793–March 4, 1797 (second term)

Age upon taking office: 57

feel he made several questionable strategic decisions as a military officer. He was also criticized for several actions during his presidency. Many felt, for example, that he was too lenient (not strict enough) as president in dealings with Great Britain.

These realities are balanced by his positive qualities and decision-making. He learned from his experiences about the landscape of America and the concerns of its people. Holding firm to his beliefs made him a victorious war leader and strong president. He displayed sound judgment, knowing when to act with authority or with diplomacy. That decisiveness for the American cause made him, as Henry Lee (1756–1818) stated, "First in war, first in peace, and first in the hearts of his countrymen." Lee, a Revolutionary War hero who was a representative from Virginia at the time of Washington's death in 1799, made that famous statement in Congress in his funeral oration for Washington.

Land surveyor

George Washington was born on February 22, 1732, in Westmoreland County, Virginia, on his father Augustine's farm, Wakefield. Augustine had two sons and a daughter before becoming a widower; his second wife, Mary Ball Washington, gave birth to six children, including George. The family moved to nearby Ferry farm in 1738. Augustine Washington died five years later, when George was eleven.

Schooled primarily at home, Washington was especially interested in mathematics. His enjoyment of mathematics

George Washington Timeline

helped him learn the art of land surveying. A surveyor measures land distances and maps the terrain, noting even the slightest rises and depressions (low points) in the landscape. Washington was close to his half-brother, Lawrence, who was fourteen years older. Lawrence married Anne Fairfax, who came from a wealthy and distinguished Virginia family. At age sixteen, Washington accompanied George Fairfax, Anne's brother, to survey the Fairfax family lands in western Virginia. They crossed the Blue Ridge Mountains into the Shenandoah Valley. Washington's surveying of the Fairfax property was so well done that at age seventeen he was named surveyor of Culpepper County, Virginia. Washington was growing into a large man. As an adult he stood six-foot two and wore size thirteen shoes.

In 1751, Washington accompanied Lawrence to Barbados, an island in the Caribbean Sea. Lawrence was suffering from tuberculosis and hoped that the warmer climate would help improve his health. (However, he died the following year.) In the meantime, Washington fell ill with smallpox. The disease left him with scars on his face, but the exposure helped build up his immune system (a system in the human body that fights off germs and disease). This moderate illness likely saved him later during the Revolutionary War, when many soldiers were badly afflicted with the disease under rough conditions.

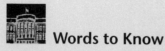

Words to Know

Anti-Federalists: A group who wanted a limited federal government and more power for individual states.

Appropriations: Funds authorized for a particular project.

Articles of Confederation: From March 1, 1781, to June 21, 1788, the Articles served as the equivalent of the Constitution (1787). They failed to produce a strong central government. The Constitution replaced the Articles to form the present-day United States.

Bill of Rights: The first ten amendments to the American Constitution of rights and privileges guaranteed to the people of the United States.

Boston Tea Party: An event in 1773 where colonists spilled shipments of tea into Boston harbor to protest taxes imposed on various products.

Constitutional Convention: The 1787 convention attended by delegates to strengthen the Articles of Confederation. Instead, delegates adopted the American Constitution that formed the United States.

Continental Army: The American army during the Revolutionary War against Great Britain.

Federalist: A proponent for a strong national (federal) government.

House of Burgesses: A representative body made up of Virginia colonists but under the authority of British rule.

Mercenaries: Soldiers hired to serve a foreign country.

Tariff: A tax a nation places on imported goods to increase their price, making imported goods as expensive or more expensive than similar products produced in the home nation.

Upon returning to Virginia, Washington inherited from Lawrence the family estate of Mount Vernon, which would be his home for the rest of his life. Appointed to his brother's vacated post as an officer in the Virginia militia, he was responsible for enlisting, inspecting, and commanding troops. Many militia groups formed during the American Revolution. A militia is not part of a regular army. Instead, citizens organize themselves for military service and are on call for emergency duty. In 1753, Virginia governor Robert Dinwiddie (1693–1770) dispatched Washington on a 300-mile journey to the Ohio River Valley. Washington was to present demands from King George II (1683–1760) of England to the French authorities. The king demanded that

French soldiers stop building a fort (Fort La Boeuf) in English territory. After French officers rejected the demand, Washington returned east through miserable winter conditions. Along the way, he memorized details of the landscape. When he returned to Virginia, he produced a map and pointed to a strategic location. There, he suggested, the British might build a fort.

Military ambitions thwarted

In 1754, Washington was commissioned as a lieutenant colonel and his idea for the fort was approved. Builders were sent ahead. When Washington arrived at the site (present-day Pittsburgh, Pennsylvania), French troops had scattered the builders and were constructing their own stronghold, which they called Fort Duquesne. Washington led an attack in which ten French soldiers were killed, including the commanding officer, Joseph Coulon (1718–1754).

Washington then built a stockade (an enclosed area protected by a large, strong fence) nearby, which he called Fort Necessity, and waited for reinforcements. Before the new troops arrived, Washington's own troops were overcome by a French outfit and were forced to surrender. The terms of surrender were lenient, but the actual paper that Washington signed was in French. He was unaware of a statement that claimed he had assassinated Coulon.

The skirmish (minor conflict) between Washington's forces and the French, as well as the surrender document that suggested the British force under Washington was the aggressor, contributed to the start of the French and Indian War (1754–63). The war was fought in frontier territory outside the thirteen colonies. The war was between British and French forces and their respective Native American allies.

When Washington returned to Williamsburg, then the capital of Virginia, he was viewed as a hero. He expected to receive a command position, but the British military allowed only men born in Great Britain to lead their troops. That decision and what Washington felt was arrogance toward colonists on the part of the British inspired his desire for American independence.

George Washington's early military experience took place during the French and Indian War (1754–63). By the war's end, he was a brigadier general.
Courtesy of the Library of Congress.

In 1755, Washington was appointed aide to British general Edward Braddock (1695–1755), who was to lead thirteen hundred men in an attack on Fort Duquesne. The attack was a failure: British soldiers fought in their conventional manner—in the open and in succeeding lines—while French and Indian fighters were scattered about and used the woods to their advantage. Washington and a group of colonial soldiers held their ground, but they soon joined the British retreat. The French and Indian tactics (military ideas) for using the natural environment would later be employed by Washington in the Revolutionary War.

Washington was appointed colonel of the colonial troops by Governor Dinwiddie. For the next few years, his assignment was to guard Virginia's three-hundred-mile-long frontier border from attack by the French. There were no attacks. After he accompanied a British regiment that recaptured Fort Duquesne in 1758, Washington resigned his commission.

Planter

On January 6, 1759, Washington married Martha Dandridge Custis (1732–1802; see entry on **Martha Washington** in volume 1), a wealthy widow with two children. He called her "Patsy." She had a home in Williamsburg and seventeen thousand acres of farmland to add to his holdings of five thousand acres and Mount Vernon. Washington, or "Old Man" (as Patsy called him, though she was a year older), settled into life as a gentleman farmer. He experimented with new agricultural methods, including crop rotation (the technique of planting different crops on a piece of land over a period of time; this is done because some plants use up soil nutrients, while others add nutrients to the soil). Washington also purchased the latest in farm implements. He failed to make money by growing tobacco, which he blamed on British agents who sold his goods in Great Britain at reduced prices. He turned to other crops, particularly wheat, and built a mill, fisheries, and ironworks. Washington served in Virginia's legislature, the House of Burgesses, as well.

From 1759 to 1774, Washington's anti-British sentiments deepened. He was annoyed by agents who sold his products at below market rates, by the poor workmanship of British-made products sold in the colonies, and by taxes that supported Great Britain. Other colonists felt the same way. Anti-British sentiments grew after several unpopular taxes—the Stamp Act (1765) and levies (taxes) on such goods as paper and tea—were imposed. The tea tax was opposed by angry colonists in Massachusetts in the Boston Tea Party in 1773. The colonists spilled shipments of tea into Boston harbor to protest the tax.

When Virginia's House of Burgesses grew increasingly rebellious, it was dissolved by British authorities. Washington made his growing anti-British activism clear in a secret meeting of former burgesses in the Raleigh Tavern in Williamsburg on May 27, 1774. The legislators—including Washington and **Thomas Jefferson** (1743–1826; see entry in volume 1)—voted to express sympathy for Massachusetts for refusing to recognize commercial (business) limitations imposed by the British. Washington was later chosen as a representative of Virginia to attend the first Continental Congress—a meeting of representatives from the thirteen colonies—in Philadelphia in 1774.

Long fight for independence

Washington was appointed to command five Virginia militia outfits in 1774. In 1775 he was chosen to be a delegate to the Second Continental Congress in Philadelphia. He arrived there in full military dress in the colors of the Fairfax Virginia militia: those colors—blue and buff (beige)—were adopted for the Continental Army. In June of 1775 the Congress elected Washington commander in chief of the army. The army was made up of all the local and state militias representing colonists against Great Britain as well as of new recruits for the American cause.

When Washington became head of the army, the Revolutionary War had already begun. On April 18, 1775, the Massachusetts militia (a civilian force called the Minutemen, because they could be ready at a moment's notice) had repelled a British force of around seven hundred men who planned to seize a stockpile of munitions (ammunition) at Concord. Concord was less than twenty miles from Boston. Minutemen fought surprisingly well at Concord against a superior force. The British returned to Boston, where militia companies kept them under siege (the act of surrounding and blockading a town).

Washington formally assumed command of American forces at Cambridge, Massachusetts, on July 2. While continuing to lay siege to Boston, he began training and organizing an army of about thirteen thousand men. Artillery (large guns mounted on wheels) captured from a British fort at Ticonderoga on Lake Champlain arrived in the Boston area. With these guns, Washington's forces occupied a hill outside of Boston and threatened to attack British troops. In March 1776, eleven thousand British troops under General William Howe (1729–1814) evacuated Boston by ship and sailed to Halifax, Nova Scotia, Canada.

Washington continued to organize the Continental Army while waiting for the return of British troops. Howe and his troops landed in New York at the end of June to begin reclaiming the colonies. Howe returned with thirty-two thousand soldiers, including eight thousand German mercenaries, and superior equipment. (Mercenaries are professional soldiers who fight for pay, not out of loyalty to a particular country. The German mercenaries were called Hessians, because most of the men were from the Hesse-Kassel and Hesse-Hanau regions of Germany.) The British troops quickly forced the Continental Army into a series of retreats—from Long Island to Manhattan, then into New Jersey, and then across New Jersey. On December 8, Washington led his retreating forces across the Delaware River from New Jersey into Pennsylvania. The British set up outposts in New Jersey, manned mostly by Hessians (about twelve hundred men). The British troops then withdrew back to New York for the winter.

Plagued by desertions, the Continental Army was fortunate to have escaped several battles during which supplies and soldiers were nearly completely overtaken. Washington himself said, "I think the game is pretty much up." But he made a bold move that won back some ground and cheered his weary troops. On a snowy Christmas night in 1776, he led his troops back across the Delaware River to New Jersey, where they overcame a Hessian force in the Battle of Trenton. The Continental Army took nine hundred prisoners in that battle. On January 3, 1777, Washington's army routed (forced out) three British units in the Battle of Princeton (New Jersey). Washington set up camp in Morristown, New Jersey, and began rebuilding his forces.

During the war, Washington remained careful to avoid a full-scale battle with the British. He preferred smaller skirmishes while patiently looking for an edge that could give American troops the advantage. It would take awhile (see accompanying American Revolution timeline).

General Washington and his American Revolutionary soldiers camped at Valley Forge, Pennsylvania, during the bitter winter of 1777–78. Many of Washington's men did not survive the frigid conditions.
Courtesy of the National Archives and Records Administration.

Washington and the American Revolution Timeline

September 1774: Continental Congress representing the thirteen colonies meets in Philadelphia, Pennsylvania, to define America's rights and to limit the British Parliament's power over the colonies. The Congress schedules a second meeting for May 1775.

April 18, 1775: Aware that Massachusetts militia members are being trained for immediate military service and that ammunition is being stockpiled, a British force of around seven hundred men sets out from Boston to seize munitions gathered at Concord (less than twenty miles from Boston). The American Committee of Safety (including Paul Revere) warns militia members that the British are coming. On April 19, the British force kills eight Americans in a battle at Lexington, Massachusetts, then proceeds toward Concord. Americans fight surprisingly well at Concord against a superior force; the British return to Boston with 273 casualties, while Americans suffer less than 100. Militia companies and then the Continental Army keep the British army under siege in Boston from April 20, 1775, to March 17, 1776.

May 10, 1775: The Second Continental Congress begins meeting in Philadelphia. Delegates establish the Congress as the central government for "The United Colonies of America" and unanimously vote to appoint George Washington as commander in chief of the Continental Army, which includes the Massachusetts militia. In New York, Colonel Ethan Allen and Vermont's Green Mountain Boys along with Colonel Benedict Arnold of Connecticut capture the British fort at Ticonderoga on Lake Champlain.

June 16, 1775: Americans under Colonel William Prescott occupy Breed's Hill, overlooking Boston, and withstand two British assaults. A third assault pushes Americans back to Bunker Hill. British forces gain ground but suffer twice as many casualties (about one thousand) than the Americans.

July 2, 1775: Washington formally assumes command of American forces. He begins training and organizing the Continental Army of about thirteen thousand men.

August 1775: American forces under General Richard Montgomery invade Canada. They take Montreal in November, but are defeated at Quebec in December.

March 4, 1776: American forces under Washington occupy Dorchester Heights, overlooking Boston, and place newly arrived artillery there. Eleven thousand British troops under General William Howe and more than one thousand Loyalists (those loyal to Great Britain) evacuate Boston in ships and sail to Halifax, Nova Scotia, Canada.

June 29, 1776: British forces led by Howe arrive in New York harbor with thirty-two thousand troops, including eight thousand German mercenaries (called Hessians because most are from the Hesse-Kassel and Hesse-Hanau regions of Germany).

July 4, 1776: The Continental Congress adopts the Declaration of Independence.

August 22, 1776: American forces are defeated in the Battle of Long Island and retreat across the East River to Manhattan on August 29 and 30. British forces continue to advance through skirmishes on Manhattan Island and the Battle of White Plains (October 28), taking all of New York City. Americans evade several close calls in which their supplies are nearly taken.

December 8, 1776: Having retreated across New Jersey, Washington's forces cross the Delaware River into Pennsylvania. Howe establishes several outposts in New Jersey, mostly manned by Hessians, and returns to New York for the winter. Washington tries to maintain morale among his poorly equipped and hungry army of less than three thousand men.

December 25, 1776: On a snowy Christmas night, Washington leads his troops across the Delaware River and overwhelms some twelve hundred Hessian soldiers in Trenton, New Jersey, taking more than nine hundred prisoners.

January 3, 1777: Washington's forces rout three British units in the Battle of Princeton (New Jersey) and establish camp in Morristown, New Jersey.

Summer 1777: A force of British and Native Americans under Colonel Barry St. Leger moves east from Lake Ontario through the Mohawk Valley of New York. St. Leger's forces are repelled by those of American major general Benedict Arnold.

July 1777: A British army under Major General John Burgoyne moving south from Montreal toward Albany, New York, retakes Fort Ticonderoga. A Hessian unit he sends into Vermont is routed in the Battle of Bennington by Vermont and New Hampshire militias.

August 25, 1777: Howe's forces march toward Philadelphia. Americans under Washington fail to stop his advance in the Battle of Brandywine Creek (Pennsylvania), and on September 26 Howe enters Philadelphia. Before his advance, the Continental Congress flees, first to York, Pennsylvania, and then to Baltimore, Maryland.

September 1777: Burgoyne's forces meet stiff resistance in two battles near Saratoga, New York, and on October 17 Burgoyne surrenders his army. The Battle of Saratoga is a major victory for the Continental Army.

→

October 4, 1777: Washington attacks Howe's forces at Germantown, just north of Philadelphia, then withdraws.

Winter 1777: Washington, with about eleven thousand men, spends the winter at Valley Forge in Pennsylvania.

February 1778: Impressed with American performances, France recognizes the independence of the colonies and signs a treaty of commerce and alliance with the new nation. France supplies arms, clothing, and money, and a French fleet commanded by Jean-Baptiste-Charles Henri-Hector d'Estaing, sails for America in April. Benjamin Franklin is a key diplomat in France and maintains contact with Washington through secret messages.

Spring 1778: Lieutenant General Sir Henry Clinton, who succeeds Howe, evacuates British troops from Philadelphia and returns to New York pursued by Washington. They battle at Monmouth Courthouse on June 28, but Americans retreat.

July 8, 1778: D'Estaing's French fleet with twelve battleships arrives off the mouth of the Delaware River, but after no opportunities for engagement arise d'Estaing sails for the West Indies on November 4.

1779: British forces move by sea from New York and capture Savannah, Georgia. Meanwhile, an American expedition under George Rogers Clark captures the British fort at Vincennes (in present-day Indiana). General John Sullivan, under orders from Washington, destroys the lands and villages of the Iroquois Confederacy in western New York for having aided the British.

July 1779: General "Mad Anthony" Wayne captures the British post at Stony Point on the Hudson River in New York.

August 1779: Major Henry Lee captures a small British garrison at Paulus Hook on the Jersey shore.

August 16, 1779: Lieutenant General Charles Cornwallis, second in command of the king's forces in British North America, routs an American force at Camden, South Carolina.

September 1779: Fleets and armies of France and Spain attack the British

In August of 1777, Howe's forces marched toward Philadelphia. Americans failed to stop his advance in the Battle of Brandywine Creek (Pennsylvania). In October, Washington attacked Howe's forces at Germantown, just north of Philadelphia, but was soon forced to withdraw. During the winter of 1777–78, Washington and about eleven thousand

fortress of Gibraltar in the Mediterranean Sea, drawing the British fleet to defend the valuable port.

October 7, 1779: British forces are overwhelmed in the Carolinas in the Battle of Kings Mountain.

July 1780: Six thousand French troops under General Jean Baptiste-Donatien de Vimeur arrive in Newport, Rhode Island.

September 1780: Major General Benedict Arnold is accused of treason for proposing to surrender West Point, New York, to the British. Warned that his plot has been discovered, Arnold escapes to a British warship.

January 17, 1781: After another defeat in the Carolinas, Cornwallis retreats north into Virginia and establishes camp at Yorktown.

March 22, 1781: With the British fleet engaged at Gibralter, twenty-nine French ships under Admiral François Joseph Paul sail to America.

August 14, 1781: After receiving word that Paul is steering his French fleet to Chesapeake Bay, Washington decides to attack Cornwallis at nearby Yorktown, Virginia. Washington's forces and those of French general Rochambeau (sixteen thousand total) will attack by land while the French fleet drives off a British fleet under Admiral Thomas Graves.

October 19, 1781: After several attempts to break through Washington's siege on Yorktown, Cornwallis surrenders.

March 1782: The British House of Commons declares its unwillingness to continue supporting the war in America. Minor skirmishes continue.

April 1783: Peace is declared.

September 3, 1783: The Treaty of Paris is signed, ending the war.

November 25, 1783: The last of the British military presence in the thirteen colonies is withdrawn.

December 4, 1783: Washington takes leave of his officers at Fraunces Tavern in New York City.

December 23, 1783: Washington resigns from his commission to Congress at Annapolis, Maryland.

men barely survived a frigid winter at Valley Forge in Pennsylvania.

Meanwhile, the performance of the Continental Army had impressed other enemies of Great Britain. Early in 1778, Washington received secret messages from Benjamin

Franklin (1706–1790; see accompanying sidebar), the American diplomat in France. Franklin informed Washington that France was prepared to recognize the independence of the colonies; to sign a treaty of commerce and alliance; and to supply arms, clothing, money, and a French fleet.

Washington also learned from sources in Great Britain that the nation was growing tired of the war. Washington wanted to have one more triumph in hopes of breaking British resolve. Still, the battles dragged on into 1781 before Washington found his opportunity. Twenty-nine French ships under Admiral François Joseph Paul (1722–1788) were sailing for Chesapeake Bay. With their help, Washington decided to attack the forces of British general Charles Cornwallis (1738–1805) camped at Yorktown, Virginia, in the summer of 1781. Washington's forces and those of French general Jean-Baptiste Rochambeau (1725–1807)—about sixteen thousand combined—attacked by land while the French fleet drove off a British fleet and cut British access to the sea from Yorktown. After several attempts to break through Washington's siege on Yorktown, Cornwallis surrendered on October 19, 1781.

Although several minor skirmishes continued to erupt, Yorktown proved to be the decisive battle of the war. In March 1782, the British House of Commons declared its unwillingness to continue supporting the war in America. Peace was declared in April of 1783. The Treaty of Paris, officially ending the war, was signed in September. On December 4, 1783, Washington took leave of his officers at Fraunces Tavern in New York City. Nineteen days later, Washington resigned from his commission to Congress at Annapolis, Maryland.

The Constitution

After the war, Washington returned to Mount Vernon with little money. He had used some of his own resources during the war and had refused pay for his services. He began to repair his farm. In 1784, he crossed the Blue Ridge Mountains to survey thirty thousand acres of land he owned in the Ohio Valley. Parts of the land had been claimed by settlers. Other areas were guarded by Native Americans.

Benjamin Franklin

Boston-born statesman Benjamin Franklin was a man of achievement as an author, diplomat, inventor, philosopher, and scientist. Born in 1706, by age fifteen he was writing anonymous (unsigned) observations about New England that were popular and rankled (continually annoyed) colonial authorities. After moving to Philadelphia, he bought the *Pennsylvania Gazette,* a weekly newspaper he made successful. He also began a series of other projects. He founded what was probably the first public library in America. He published *Poor Richard's Almanack* (which contained humorous, but useful, advice), became clerk of the Pennsylvania General Assembly, and organized the first fire company in Philadelphia. He invented the Franklin stove, which furnished greater heat with less fuel.

During the American Revolution, Franklin helped edit the Declaration of Independence and was one of the signers. At one point during the convention, he said to the delegates, "We must all hang together, or assuredly we shall all hang separately." Representing America in France, Franklin negotiated a 1778 treaty of commerce and alliance

Benjamin Franklin.
Courtesy of the Library of Congress.

with France that greatly helped the American cause. He later helped negotiate the peace treaty with Great Britain that ended the war. In 1787, he was elected a delegate to the convention that drew up the U.S. Constitution. One of his last public acts was to sign a petition to the U.S. Congress (as president of the Pennsylvania Abolition Society) urging the abolition of slavery and the suppression of the slave trade. He died in 1790.

The difficulty of passing over the mountains to reach the frontier led Washington to consider an alternate route. He planned a system of canals that could be extended from the Potomac River that borders Virginia and Maryland. He formed the Potomac Company and presented his idea to members of the Virginia and Maryland legislatures in March of 1785. The meeting of state representatives was so successful that Virginian **James Madison** (1751–1836; see entry in volume 1) sug-

Washington had one remaining tooth at the time of his inauguration and had worn dentures for years, but he knew the importance of dental hygiene. His six white horses had their teeth brushed each morning!

gested a convention that representatives from all states could attend to discuss issues of mutual interest. The following year, a convention was held in Annapolis, Maryland, but only five states sent delegates. Still, those present decided to hold another convention in May of 1787 in Philadelphia. Washington's canal idea never materialized, but once again he displayed his ability to bring Americans together.

Meanwhile, with little power to raise taxes or make binding decisions, the post-revolutionary colonial government was failing. The British government enacted commercial sanctions—official trade measures meant to intimidate the new country. Individual states responded differently to the sanctions. The growing presence of British forces on the frontier and the Great Lakes was a looming (close at hand) threat. Shays's Rebellion in 1786, an uprising by debt-ridden farmers in Massachusetts, further exposed the weakness of the central government. The convention in Philadelphia in 1787 was intended to firm up the Articles of Confederation that united the thirteen former colonies and to strengthen the government. Washington was elected to preside over the convention. These proceedings would become known in history as the Constitutional Convention.

The convention lasted throughout the summer. Representatives argued over many issues, including whether or not to form a strong federal government. Finally, in September of 1787, the Constitution of the United States was adopted by the convention. The Constitution became binding when nine of the thirteen former colonies approved it. In June of 1788, New Hampshire became the ninth state to ratify the Constitution. Among its provisions, the Constitution called for the election of a president.

For the first presidential election of the United States, each of the thirteen states was represented by electors. The number of electors in each state was based on its population. The electors each voted for two men. The man who received the most votes would become president. The man with the second highest number of votes became vice president. Washington was elected unanimously to serve as the nation's first president. **John Adams** (1735–1826; see entry in volume 1) became the first vice president.

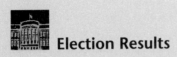

Election Results

1789

Presidential / Vice presidential candidates	Popular votes	Presidential electoral votes
George Washington	—	69
John Adams	—	34
John Jay	—	9
Others	—	15

1792

Presidential / Vice presidential candidates	Popular votes	Presidential electoral votes
George Washington	—	132
John Adams	—	77
George Clinton	—	50
Others	—	5

Popular votes were not yet part of the presidential elections of 1789 and 1792. (The public at large did not vote.) Washington received all 69 electoral votes for president in 1789 and all 132 electoral votes in 1792. Under the system then in place, votes for vice president were considered electoral votes; the person with the second highest number of electoral votes became the vice president.

At the time of the election, Washington was at Mount Vernon, concerned mostly about his debts. He had to borrow $600 to make the trip from Mount Vernon to New York City, where the seat of government was established. He took the oath of office on April 30, 1789, in a ceremony on Wall Street attended by Adams, congressmen elected to serve in the first Congress, and a lively crowd.

The president of precedents

Washington was extremely careful to set precedents for the behavior of future presidents. In many instances, he projected a model of what a president should be. For example, he acted with authority as the highest elected official of the land, but he did not attempt to influence Congress. Having presided over the Constitutional Convention, he was well aware of various opinions about the presidency. He was also

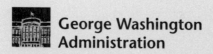

George Washington Administration

Administration Dates
April 30, 1789–March 4, 1793
March 4, 1793–March 4, 1797

Vice President
John Adams (1789–97)

Cabinet
Secretary of State
Thomas Jefferson (1790–93)
Edmund J. Randolph (1794–95)
Timothy Pickering (1795–97)

Secretary of the Treasury
Alexander Hamilton (1789–95)
Oliver Wolcott Jr. (1795–97)

Secretary of War
Henry Knox (1789–94)
Timothy Pickering (1795)
James McHenry (1796–97)

Attorney General
Edmund J. Randolph (1789–94)
William Bradford (1794–95)
Charles Lee (1795–97)

Postmaster General
Samuel Osgood (1789–91)
Timothy Pickering (1791–95)
Joseph Habersham (1795–97)

conscious of different views about the roles of states and the federal government. In a gesture of goodwill, he undertook two journeys—touring New England in 1789 and the South in 1791—to meet citizens.

Congress began discussing the Bill of Rights (see sidebar in **James Madison** entry in volume 1), which became the first ten amendments to the Constitution in 1789. Meanwhile, Washington wanted to form a cabinet of advisors who would assist him in his duties as president. Congress agreed on five cabinet posts: an attorney general to serve as the federal prosecutor; a secretary of war to run day-to-day operations of the military; a secretary of state to pursue the president's foreign diplomacy; a secretary of the treasury to oversee the nation's finances; and a postmaster general to run the nation's mail system. For these positions, Washington chose men who had varying views of government: Treasury Secretary Alexander Hamilton (1755–1804; see box) and War Secretary Henry Knox (1750–1806) had a Federalist viewpoint; they favored a strong central authority. Secretary of State Thomas Jefferson (1743–1826) and Attorney General Edmund Randolph (1753–1813) favored a federal government with more limited powers. Postmaster general Samuel Osgood (1748–1813) was less involved than the others in policy discussions.

Congress established the nation's court system with the Judiciary Act (1789). The Supreme Court was instituted with a chief justice—John Jay (1745–1829; see box)— and five associate justices. The First Congress also passed the first tax—a tariff that would make imported goods more costly. The tariff protected American manufacturers and would bring in much needed revenue (income) to the federal government.

Washington looked to Hamilton to establish a financial system for the United States. Hamilton introduced part of his plan to Congress in January 1790. It was immediately contested (challenged). Those who believed in limiting the powers of the federal government—led by Thomas Jefferson in the administration and James Madison in Congress—denounced Hamilton's Federalist plans. Nevertheless, after heated debate, most elements of Hamilton's financial plan passed through Congress and became law.

 Washington Slept Here

The nation's capital was located in New York when Washington first took office in 1789. The following year it was moved to Philadelphia. The District of Columbia was then agreed on as the site of the nation's capital. Construction began on the Capitol building beginning in 1793. Washington was the only president who did not live in Washington, D.C., during his presidency.

Jefferson and Hamilton were at odds over taxes. Jefferson cooled his opposition to taxes when Hamilton agreed to his plan to establish the nation's capital on land donated by the states of Virginia and Maryland. Jefferson's plan passed in July of 1790. (The District of Columbia was destined to be the nation's seat of government in 1800. Construction was soon underway. Washington laid the cornerstone of the White House in 1793.)

In December of 1790, Hamilton introduced the rest of his financial plan. He wanted to create a national bank. Jefferson called the measure unconstitutional, arguing that Congress was not authorized to charter a national bank. In his counterargument, Hamilton noted that Congress was granted by the Constitution the right to levy taxes, coin money, and pay the nation's debts—all of which would be functions of a national bank. After much debate, Congress chartered the First Bank of the United States. President Washington signed it into law in February 1791.

The controversy over taxes continued. The Excise Tax (1791) proved most unpopular among the several levies introduced by Hamilton. (An excise tax is a tax on the production or sale of a particular item.) This tax on whiskey, meant to pay off interest on the national debt, was especially hard on

President George
Washington (left) and four
Cabinet members: Secretary
of War Henry Knox;
Secretary of the Treasury
Alexander Hamilton;
Secretary of State Thomas
Jefferson; and Attorney
General Edmund Randolph.
Lithograph by Currier and Ives.
Reproduced by permission of
the Corbis Corporation.

small farmers. Because of high costs of shipping corn to market, many small farmers distilled some of their corn crop into whiskey, which they could store easily and sell locally.

Disagreements among different factions (groups) concerning the Constitution, taxes, federal authority, and the bank became so heated that the unity of the young nation was threatened. Washington had planned to retire to his Virginia estate following his term, but for the sake of the nation he was persuaded to run again for president in 1792. He again won unanimous approval from the electors—he was named on all 132 ballots. Adams remained his vice president.

Staying the course

Soon after Washington began his second term in March 1793, King Louis XVI (1754–1793) was executed in France during the French Revolution (1789–97). The new

French government declared war on England. Recognizing that the United States could not afford to become involved in war or lose revenue from trade with Great Britain, President Washington proclaimed America's neutrality (allegiance toward neither side). France and its American supporters, including Jefferson, were outraged. The French government felt betrayed, because the alliance treaty signed by America and France during the American Revolution was still in effect.

Washington asserted his authority as president. The Constitution decreed that Congress had the power to declare war, but it did not address the issue of declaring neutrality. To help ease tensions with France, Washington released an official statement that did not use the word *neutral*. He considered the alliance between France and the United States. Washington agreed to a cautious interpretation of the exact terms of the treaty and accepted the new French government's American diplomat.

Washington's stand was unpopular. Many Americans resented the British. Their cause was further inflamed when Britain began stopping American ships at sea. Britain claimed to be searching for British citizens who had deserted the army, but they began seizing all cargoes not bound for Great Britain on suspicion that they were intended for Britain's enemies. The situation grew worse in early 1794 when Britain closed off trade between the United States and the West Indies, a colony of Britain. With calls for war spreading throughout the land, Washington sent John Jay to England in May of 1794 to negotiate a settlement.

Meanwhile, unrest spread on the home front. Rioting occurred in western Pennsylvania, primarily over the Excise Tax. The Whiskey Rebellion (1794), as it was called, ended when Washington directed fifteen thousand troops—the militias of New Jersey, Virginia, and Maryland—to restore order. Further west, on the frontier of the Ohio Valley and the Great

 Constitutional Flexibility

The Federal Bank issue brought to the forefront one of the most fundamental questions of the American political system—the flexibility of the Constitution. Some argue that if the Constitution is to remain meaningful it must be followed literally. They are called "constructionists." Others contend that the document serves as a framework and guide. Its basic principles must be followed, but the Constitution is open to interpretation and flexible to change.

Alexander Hamilton

Alexander Hamilton was born on the small West Indies island of Nevis in 1755. He was the son of James Hamilton, a merchant, and Rachel Faucett. The couple was not married, because Danish law forbade the once-divorced Rachel from marrying again.

As a teen, Hamilton worked as a bookkeeper on the island of St. Croix. In 1773, he sailed to Boston, Massachusetts, and within a year entered King's College (now Columbia University) in New York. At eighteen, he published two articles that concluded that the colonies had every right to protect themselves from the tyranny of British Parliament.

Hamilton joined the New York infantry as a captain in the Revolutionary War (1775-83). In 1777, he was named the highest assistant for General George Washington, writing letters and handling appointments. Hamilton, however, desired a position in command of troops. In 1781, Washington gave Hamilton command of a battalion of light infantry. Hamilton distinguished himself in the famous battle at Yorktown.

Hamilton served in the Continental Congress from November 1782 through July 1783. From 1783 to 1789, Hamilton practiced law while advocating a stronger federal government. Hamilton favored reform of the Articles of Confederation and called for and attended the Constitutional Convention. His idea of the ideal government was one in which only property own-

ers should be allowed to vote; a president should be chosen by landholders to hold the office for life; and the president would have power over a popularly elected assembly that would have little voice in government. A second legislature would consist of propertied men elected for life by electors chosen by the people. The federal government would appoint a governor for each state, also for life, who would preside over a legislature and have absolute veto power. Hamilton viewed the Constitution, drawn up in 1787, as being frail, but he supported its experiment with a republican form of government. He contributed to a series of articles called the *Federalist Papers* that supported the new Constitution.

In 1789, with the Constitution in place, Washington was elected the nation's first president. The new government faced heavy debt from the Revolutionary War. As the first secretary of the treasury, Hamilton established a credit rating for the federal government by pledging to pay off all foreign debts incurred during the war. He also agreed to pay all debts incurred by individual states, as a way to unite the states.

Hamilton urged the formation of a national bank. Such a bank would develop a system of notes to serve as money and make the payment of taxes easier. It could also loan money to help build American businesses. As a control, the Treasury Department would supervise the bank's bookkeeping. Even before the bank proposal was made, however, some politicians—such as

Alexander Hamilton.
Portrait by John Trumbull. Courtesy of the National Archives and Records Administration.

Secretary of State Thomas Jefferson—were against it. Some states already had their own banks and currency. Hamilton contended the Constitution demanded that the government regulate trade, collect taxes, provide for a common defense, and promote the general welfare. He believed that some powers must be implied (suggested) by these sweeping demands, and one of these powers must be the ability to raise funds to meet such lofty goals. Establishing a national bank would allow the government to meet those financial demands.

The Bank of the United States was chartered in February 1791. But more important, Hamilton had succeeded in permitting the Constitution to be open for interpretation. The idea that the federal government has implied powers—not specifically stated in the Constitution—has long been a lively source of debate.

Hamilton left his Treasury post in 1795 and retired to law and politics in New York. Under President John Adams, Hamilton became inspector general of the army from 1798 to 1800. The relationship between the two soured, however. When it became clear that the incumbent Federalist president Adams would not win the 1800 election, fellow Federalist Hamilton tried to influence the election in favor of Democratic-Republican Jefferson, Adams's enemy at the time. Jefferson and Aaron Burr tied in electoral votes; in those days, the person with the most votes became president, and the second highest became vice president. Under the Constitution, Congress was authorized to settle the matter. Hamilton pushed his friends in Congress to elect Jefferson over Burr, helping Jefferson win by a single vote.

In 1804, Hamilton spoke out against Burr in his candidacy for governor of New York, calling him "a man of irregular and unsatiable ambition who ought not to be trusted with the reins of government." Burr took offense and a duel followed on July 12, 1804. Hamilton fired in the air, obviously intending to miss his mark, but Burr shot and wounded Hamilton. He died the next day at age forty-nine.

Washington bowed to visitors, believing that shaking hands was beneath a president.

Lakes, a series of Native American uprisings were threatening settlers. The situation was eased when a coalition of tribes was defeated on August 20, 1794, near present-day Toledo, Ohio, by the forces of General Anthony Wayne (1745–1796). The coalition (alliance) of tribes likely received aid from the British, who continued to operate several forts on the Great Lakes. Wayne concluded a treaty with the coalition of tribes that effectively ceased their claims on the Ohio River Valley and reopened the frontier.

Jay's Treaty, the treaty negotiated by Jay with Great Britain, did not address British aggression at sea. Although it was vastly unpopular, because the treaty did not allow the United States to restrict British imports and it did not open up the British-controlled West Indies to American trade, Washington agreed to the treaty and called a special session of Congress on June 8, 1795, to debate it. In Washington's view the treaty achieved two basic purposes. First, the treaty avoided war, which Washington believed would devastate the young nation. Second, Great Britain agreed to evacuate its forts on the Great Lakes by June 1, 1796. Coupled with Wayne's victory, the United States would be the major power in the northwest territory stretching to the Mississippi River and encompassing the Great Lakes and the Ohio River Valley. After two weeks of debate, the Senate approved the treaty by the necessary two-thirds majority, 20 votes to 10.

Washington's term closed with the passage of two other treaties. The Treaty of San Lorenzo between the United States and Spain granted U.S. citizens free and unlimited access to the Mississippi River all the way to New Orleans. During that period, New Orleans was controlled by Spanish authorities. The treaty also settled the western boundary of Spanish Florida.

A treaty with the nation of Algiers freed ten American sailors who had been in captivity since 1785. They had been captured by Barbary Coast pirates (see box) who had been operating off the coast of Algiers in the Mediterranean Sea since the 1400s. A ransom was paid. Those congressmen who were against paying ransom moved to halt appropriations (public funds) for six frigates (warships) that Washington had ordered for the U.S. Navy. Washington replied that such ships were needed to more forcefully address lawlessness at sea.

John Jay

Born in New York City in 1745, John Jay was elected to the Continental Congress in 1774 and in 1775. He drafted the first constitution of New York. He helped negotiate the Treaty of Paris with Great Britain, ending the American Revolution. With Alexander Hamilton and James Madison, Jay wrote the series of articles known as *The Federalist Papers,* which urged ratification of the U.S. Constitution. He was appointed the first chief justice of the Supreme Court by President Washington in 1789.

In 1794, Jay was appointed by Washington to negotiate a settlement with Great Britain. He concluded the agreement, known as Jay's Treaty. The treaty was vastly unpopular in the United States, but many historians believe that it accomplished as much as was possible during that time, when the United States was a much weaker nation than Great Britain. The treaty succeeded in defining boundaries between the United States and Canada and resolved some debts between the United States and Great Britain. However, the treaty did not allow the United States

John Jay. *Courtesy of the Library of Congress.*

to place restrictions at home on British trade, which was an advantage, of course, for Great Britain, and did not grant America access to trade with the West Indies, an area controlled by Great Britain.

While he was in England negotiating Jay's Treaty, Jay was elected governor of New York. He served in that post from 1795 to 1801. After 1801, Jay retired to private life at age fifty-five and lived until 1829.

As Washington's second term approached its end, he insisted on retiring. The precedent he set of serving a maximum of two terms was broken only once—by **Franklin D. Roosevelt** (1882–1945; see entry in volume 4), who was elected president four times. Washington had held together the young nation through the difficult early stages. Some of his decisions were unpopular, but all were made with the judgment that the actions would be in the best interest of the nation.

Washington returned to Mount Vernon to enjoy retirement with Martha, but their peace together did not last long. Washington was asked by his successor, John Adams, to lead American troops in case of war with France during a period of tense relations with that nation. Washington died in 1799. He had caught cold and, as was customary in those days, doctors bled him (took some of his blood), which was thought to help those who were ill. Instead, the loss of blood further weakened him and brought him to death.

Legacy

George Washington's legacy is enormous. His leadership as citizen, general, and president kept the fledgling (young and inexperienced) nation progressing through difficult times. As president, he set the example for using the authority of the highest elected official of the land while respecting the equal and balancing legislative powers of Congress and judicial powers of the Supreme Court.

Among his many precedents for presidential action, Washington established three patterns in the areas of treaty negotiation. First, after facing exhaustive debate with Congress over an early treaty with the Creek nation of Native Americans, Washington did not consult with Congress on later treaties. The Constitution mandated (commanded) that all treaties must be ratified by a two-thirds majority of the Senate. Washington recognized that the president alone had the power to negotiate treaties, whereas Congress had the power to accept or reject them. Second, Washington assigned aides to negotiate treaties, creating a model for presidential appointments that do not have to be approved by Congress. Third, during debate over appropriating (finding and budgeting) funds for Jay's Treaty, the House of Representatives demanded that Washington turn over all documents, including instructions and correspondence (letters) between the president and Jay regarding the treaty. Washington refused. The Constitution did not require him to do so, and he felt such an action would undermine the power of the presidency. That power of the presidency is called "executive privilege."

While maintaining progress among opposing factions, Washington's administration established national fi-

Barbary Pirates

Barbary Pirates controlled parts of the Mediterranean Sea from ports in present-day Algeria, Libya, and Tunisia (the Barbary coast). They demanded "tributes"—payment to keep them from attacking vessels passing on trade routes through the Mediterranean. When the pirates seized an American ship and took ten sailors hostage, the United States (then under the Articles of Confederation) had neither the naval power nor the unity needed to negotiate to free the hostages. President Washington paid a ransom to free them as part of the Algiers Treaty (1791), one of a series of treaties with the Barbary coast nations. That treaty was broken during the presidency of Thomas Jefferson and war followed.

The Barbary coast was dominated by pirates beginning in the sixteenth century. Many of the pirates were Muslims who preyed on vessels in the Mediterranean Sea. In the seventeenth century, the port city of Algiers, Algeria, was a pirate base from which pirate ships combed beyond the Mediterranean Sea to the Atlantic Ocean and even to the North Sea around Great Britain and Scandinavia. The use of steam engines in ships and the power of the British and American navies during the mid-eighteenth century helped put an end to piracy at sea. An act of piracy is considered an act against nations and subject to stiff penalties.

Buccaneers were another form of sea pirates. They came from western European nations and preyed on Spanish colonies in the New World, mostly during the second half of the seventeenth century.

nancial institutions. He used the authority of the federal government to stop a rebellion and to avoid what could have been a devastating war with England. He filled his administration with men representing various viewpoints. As he had done in the Revolutionary War, Washington helped hold together a group of inexperienced and idealistic revolutionaries through tough battles to progress toward a stronger union.

Where to Learn More

Cunliffe, Marcus. *George Washington and the Making of a Nation.* New York: American Heritage Publishing, 1966.

Emery, Noemie. *Washington, A Biography.* New York: Putnam, 1976.

A Selection of Washington Landmarks

George Washington Birthplace National Monument. 1732 Popes Creek Rd., Washington's Birthplace, VA 22443. (804) 224-1732. Plantation-style house from era of Washington's youth sits on site of Washington's birthplace. See http://www.nps.gov/gewa/ (accessed on May 30, 2000).

Mount Vernon. Mount Vernon, VA 22121. (800) 429-1520. Estate, gardens, and burial site of George and Martha Washington. See http://www.mountvernon.org/ (accessed on May 30, 2000).

Valley Forge National Historical Park. Box 122, Valley Forge, PA 19481-0122. (610) 782-0535. Site of Washington's Continental Army encampment during the winter of 1777–78. See http://www.ushistory.org/valleyforge/index.html (accessed on May 30, 2000).

Washington Crossing Historic Park. P.O. Box 103, Washington Crossing, PA 18977. (215) 493-4076. Site of where the Continental Army began its historic crossing of the Delaware River on Christmas night in 1776. Museum, graveyard, historic buildings. See http://www.spiritof76.com/wchp/index.html (accessed on May 30, 2000).

Washington Monument. The Mall, Washington, DC. 202-426-6841. The 555-foot obelisk is the most famous of all memorials to the nation's first president. See http://www.nps.gov/wamo/index2.htm (accessed on May 30, 2000).

George Washington's Mount Vernon Estate & Gardens. [Online] http://www.mountvernon.org/ (accessed on July 31, 2000).

Library of Congress. "George Washington Papers at the Library of Congress: 1741–1799." *American Memory.* [Online] http://lcweb2.loc.gov/ammem/gwhtml/gwhome.html (accessed on July 31, 2000).

Marrin, Albert. *The War for Independence: The Story of the American Revolution.* New York: Atheneum, 1988.

Osborne, Mary Pope. *George Washington: Leader of a New Nation.* New York: Dial Books for Young Readers, 1991.

Rosenburg, John. *First in War: George Washington in the American Revolution.* Brookfield, CT: Millbrook Press, 1998.

Martha Washington

Born June 2, 1731
Near Williamsburg, Virginia
Died May 22, 1802
Mount Vernon, Virginia

Helped establish the presidency
as a non-royal institution

Martha Washington was a gracious and unassuming (modest) woman who enjoyed private life. For the first fifteen years of her marriage to **George Washington** (1732–1799; see entry in volume 1), the couple lived quietly on his Virginia estate, Mount Vernon, as Washington settled into life as a planter. They often traveled to Williamsburg, then the capital of Virginia. She owned a home there, and Washington attended Virginia's House of Burgesses.

The Washingtons were both in their early forties when their calm lives suddenly changed. George Washington would spend more than seven years commanding American forces in the Revolutionary War (1775–83). After settling back into life in Virginia, the Washingtons spent eight years in New York and Philadelphia when Washington served as president of the United States. Even after he left office at the age of sixty-five, Washington was asked to command American forces in case war broke out with France.

Martha Washington preferred a quiet life, but she adapted to life's changing circumstances. She acted with the same tactfulness and cheerful spirit wherever their adventures led.

"I am fond of only what comes from the heart."

Martha Washington

Martha Washington.
Courtesy of the Library of Congress.

A young widow

Born Martha Dandridge on June 2, 1731, on a plantation near Williamsburg, she was the oldest daughter of wealthy planters John and Frances Dandridge. She had a modest amount of schooling—typical for an eighteenth-century girl. Martha enjoyed riding horses and embroidering while growing up and learning how to manage a household. At eighteen, she married Daniel Park Custis, a wealthy planter. She moved to his mansion, which he called the White House. During the next seven years, Martha bore four children, two of whom died in infancy. She became a widow when her husband died in 1757.

Martha was consoled by friends. In May of 1758, she was invited to stay with a nearby family, the Chamberlaynes. During her stay, Colonel Richard Chamberlayne was out walking when he met George Washington on the banks of the Pamunkey River. Washington had stopped to rest on his way to nearby Williamsburg. Washington, then twenty-six, had spent most of the previous six years as a military officer and was looking forward to civilian life.

Chamberlayne invited him to dinner, but Washington declined, wanting to continue on to Williamsburg. Chamberlayne persisted, promising to introduce Washington to "the prettiest and wealthiest widow in Virginia." Washington eventually accepted the invitation. The Old Man and Patsy (as they called each other) hit it off that evening. Washington followed up by sending letters to Martha as he completed his military service and returned to live on his estate, Mount Vernon. The couple married in January of 1759.

From Mount Vernon to Valley Forge

The next fifteen years were happy for the couple, except that Washington was growing increasingly frustrated with British rule in America. In addition to ever increasing taxes, Washington felt that American goods were being undersold by British agents. As rebellion began to spread throughout the colonies, Washington became commander of Virginia militia outfits in 1774. (A militia is a civilian military group organized for service during an emergency.) The fol-

lowing year, he was elected commander of the Continental Army when the American Revolution was underway.

During the war, Martha joined her husband whenever it was safe. She traveled to Cambridge, Massachusetts, after Washington assumed command of the army and held British forces under siege in nearby Boston. She was with him during the dreadful winter of 1777–78 when some twelve thousand American soldiers spent a frigid winter in terrible conditions at Valley Forge, about twenty miles northwest of Philadelphia, Pennsylvania.

Dispirited by defeats outside Philadelphia, which was held by British forces, the troops wintered at Valley Forge to protect Congress, in session at nearby York, Pennsylvania, from sudden British attack. Lacking supplies, food, and clothing and living in small huts they built, many soldiers died of starvation and cold. Doing what she could to help, Martha remained constantly busy—mending clothes, stitching blankets, nursing solders, and attempting to keep up morale.

George Washington and his family entertain General Lafayette at Mount Vernon.
Reproduced by permission of the Corbis Corporation.

After the hardships of Valley Forge, the Continental Army began having more success, but the war dragged on into 1782. With a climactic victory at Yorktown, Virginia, Washington received the surrender of British general Charles Cornwallis (1738–1805) not far from the estate where he first met Martha.

It was not until the end of 1784 when Washington officially ended his service with the Continental Army and returned to Mount Vernon. However, he and Martha were not able to resume their quiet lives. The weak, post-Revolution American government needed to be changed. Washington traveled to Philadelphia in 1787 to preside over debate about changes. The Convention succeeded in drawing up the American Constitution. It called for the creation of an executive branch of government (the administrative branch) that would be led by the nation's highest elected official, the president. In 1789, Washington was elected president. He was re-elected in 1792.

Busy in their sixties

The Washingtons lived in New York, the seat of government in 1789, and then in Philadelphia, the seat of government from 1790 to 1799. Martha did not enjoy her social role as first lady, but she made the best of it. She helped "the General" (as she now called her husband) establish formal and respectful social occasions. She helped keep a sense of ease at such gatherings to ensure that the presidency did not take on airs of royalty. "I am fond of only what comes from the heart," she stated while receiving guests politely and without fanfare. Whenever political topics were being discussed, she worked to change the subject to other areas, separating business and pleasure. She held her own weekly Friday receptions that the General would occasionally attend.

As conflicts between political factions began to grow during Washington's presidency, Martha turned cool toward those who were critical of presidential policies. Among them was Secretary of State **Thomas Jefferson** (1743–1826; see entry in volume 1). Nevertheless, there was never a loss of dignity in the social circles surrounding the president.

In 1797, the Washingtons, now in their mid-sixties, were finally able to return to Mount Vernon. Their happy time there included entertaining many visitors, but it was interrupted. Washington was asked by President **John Adams** (1735–1826; see entry in volume 1) in 1798 to prepare to command American forces in case tensions between America and France escalated into war. In 1799, Washington caught a nasty cold from which he never recovered. He died on December 14, 1799. Martha Washington lived on until May 22, 1802. The Washingtons were buried in a modest tomb at Mount Vernon.

Where to Learn More

Anderson, LaVere. *Martha Washington, First Lady of the Land.* Champaign, IL: Garrard, 1973. Reprint, New York: Chelsea Juniors, 1991.

Marsh, Joan F. *Martha Washington.* New York: Franklin Watts, 1993.

McPherson, Stephanie Sammartino. *Martha Washington: First Lady.* Springfield, NJ: Enslow Publishers, 1998.

Simon, Charnan. *Martha Dandridge Custis Washington, 1731–1802.* New York: Children's Press, 2000.

Articles of Confederation

Adopted on March 1, 1781; excerpted from
The Avalon Project **(Web site)**

*The first national American government
fails from lack of authority*

The Constitution of the United States was developed in 1787 and approved in 1789, shortly after **George Washington** (1732–1799; see entry in volume 1) became the nation's first president. The Constitution resulted from the failure of the nation's first attempt at a federal government, which was outlined in the Articles of Confederation. The idea for the Articles was proposed on July 12, 1776, by John Dickinson (1732–1808) to fellow members of the Second Continental Congress, who had just recently signed the Declaration of Independence. Because of various concerns among the thirteen colonies, the Articles of Confederation were not approved until 1781. Dickinson had proposed a strong central government with equal representation for the states and the power to levy taxes, but with no executive leader.

The failure of the Articles is important to understanding the Constitution and the office of president it established. Influenced by their experience of being controlled by the monarchy of Great Britain, Americans were reluctant to approve of a strong central government or a single powerful leader. Most delegates voting on the Articles favored a loose

"The said states hereby severally enter into a firm league of friendship with each other, for their common defence, the security of their Liberties, and their mutual and general welfare, binding themselves to assist each other. . . ."

From the Articles of Confederation

confederation of states, rather than a highly centralized national government.

In November of 1777, Congress voted to approve the Articles of Confederation and submitted it to the states for ratification. The Continental Congress was careful to give the states as much independence as possible and to specify limited functions for the federal government. Despite these precautions, several years passed before all the states ratified the Articles. In addition to being involved with the American Revolution, state officials disagreed over boundary lines. Other issues included conflicting decisions by state courts, various trade restrictions between states, the desire of small states to have equal representation in Congress, and concern by large states of having to pay most of the costs to support a federal government. The final major issue—claims on frontier land beyond the colonies—was settled when the states agreed to give control of western lands to the federal government.

Things to remember while reading the Articles of Confederation:

• Under the Articles, Congress was the only branch of the central government. Each state had one vote in Congress. Delegates to Congress were selected by state legislatures. A simple majority decided issues, except for some that required approval of nine of thirteen states. Each state could impose its own taxes on citizens, but there was no national tax. The authority of Congress included military matters, negotiating treaties and alliances, Indian relations, managing postal affairs, coining money, and settling disputes between states.

• The Articles created a loose confederation of independent states and gave limited powers to the central government. There was no independent executive. The federal government had no judicial branch, and the only judicial authority Congress had was the power to arbitrate disputes between states. Judicial proceedings in each state were to be honored by all other states.

Excerpt from the Articles of Confederation

Article I

*The **Stile** of this confederacy shall be "The United States of America."*

Article II

*Each state retains its **sovereignty**, freedom and independence, and every Power, Jurisdiction and right, which is not by this confederation expressly delegated to the United States, in Congress assembled.*

Article III

The said states hereby severally enter into a firm league of friendship with each other, for their common defence, the security of their Liberties, and their mutual and general welfare, binding themselves to assist each other, against all force offered to, or attacks made upon them, or any of them, on account of religion, sovereignty, trade, or any other pretence whatever.

Article IV

*The better to secure and perpetuate mutual friendship and intercourse among the people of the different states in this union, the free inhabitants of each of these states, paupers, vagabonds and fugitives from Justice excepted, shall be entitled to all privileges and immunities of free citizens in the several states; and the people of each state shall have free **ingress and regress** to and from any other state, and shall enjoy therein all the privileges of trade and commerce, subject to the same duties, impositions and restrictions as the inhabitants thereof respectively, provided that such restriction shall not extend so far as to prevent the removal of property imported into any state, to any other state of which the Owner is an inhabitant; provided also that no imposition, duties or restriction shall be laid by any state, on the property of the United States, or either of them.*

If any Person guilty of, or charged with treason, felony, or other high misdemeanor in any state, shall flee from Justice, and be found in any of the united states, he shall upon demand of the Governor or executive power, of the state from which he fled, be delivered up and removed to the state having jurisdiction of his offence.

Stile: Name.

Sovereignty: Freedom from external control.

Ingress and regress: Entering and leaving.

Full faith and credit shall be given in each of these states to the records, acts and judicial proceedings of the courts and magistrates of every other state.

Article V

For the more convenient management of the general interests of the United States, delegates shall be annually appointed in such manner as the legislature of each state shall direct, to meet in Congress on the first Monday in November, in every year, with a power reserved to each state, to recall its delegates, or any of them, at any time within the year, and to send others in their stead, for the remainder of the Year.

No state shall be represented in Congress by less than two, nor by more than seven Members; and no person shall be capable of being a delegate for more than three years in any term of six years; nor shall any person, being a delegate, be capable of holding any office under the united states, for which he, or another for his benefit receives any salary, fees or **emolument** of any kind.

Each state shall maintain its own delegates in a meeting of the states, and while they act as members of the committee of the states.

In determining questions in the United States, in Congress assembled, each state shall have one vote.

Freedom of speech and debate in Congress shall not be impeached or questioned in any Court, or place out of Congress, and the members of Congress shall be protected in their persons from arrests and imprisonments, during the time of their going to and from, and attendance on Congress, except for treason, felony, or breach of the peace.

Article VI

No state without the Consent of the United States in Congress assembled, shall send any embassy to, or receive any embassy from, or enter into any conference, agreement, or alliance or treaty with any King prince or state; nor shall any person holding any office of profit or trust under the United States, or any of them, accept of any present, emolument, office or title of any kind whatever from any king, prince or foreign state; nor shall the United States in Congress assembled, or any of them, grant any title of nobility.

No two or more states shall enter into any treaty, confederation or alliance whatever between them, without the consent of the united

Emolument: Compensation for service.

states in Congress assembled, specifying accurately the purposes for which the same is to be entered into, and how long it shall continue.

No state shall lay any **imposts** or duties, which may interfere with any stipulations in treaties, entered into by the United States in Congress assembled, with any king, prince or state, in pursuance of any treaties already proposed by congress, to the courts of France and Spain. . . .

Article VII

When land-forces are raised by any state for the common defence, all officers of or under the rank of colonel, shall be appointed by the legislature of each state respectively by whom such forces shall be raised, or in such manner as such state shall direct, and all vacancies shall be filled up by the state which first made the appointment.

Article VIII

All charges of war, and all other expenses that shall be incurred for the common defence or general welfare, and allowed by the United States in Congress assembled, shall be defrayed out of a common treasury, which shall be supplied by the several states, in proportion to the value of all land within each state, granted to or surveyed for any Person, as such land and the buildings and improvements thereon shall be estimated according to such mode as the united states in congress assembled, shall from time to time direct and appoint. The taxes for paying that proportion shall be laid and levied by the authority and direction of the legislatures of the several states within the time agreed upon by the United States in Congress assembled.

Article IX

The United States in congress assembled, shall have the sole and exclusive right and power of determining on peace and war, except in the cases mentioned in the sixth article—of sending and receiving ambassadors—entering into treaties and alliances, provided that no treaty of commerce shall be made whereby the legislative power of the respective states shall be restrained from imposing such imposts and duties on foreigners, as their own people are subjected to, or from prohibiting the exportation or importation of any species of goods or commodities whatsoever—of establishing rules for deciding in all cases, what captures on land or water shall be legal, and in what manner prizes taken by land or naval forces in the service of the United States shall be divided or appropriated—of granting let-

Imposts: Taxes.

ters of **marque** and reprisal in times of peace—appointing courts for the trial of piracies and felonies committed on the high seas and establishing courts for receiving and determining finally appeals in all cases of captures, provided that no member of Congress shall be appointed a judge of any of the said courts. . . .

Article X

The committee of the states, or any nine of them, shall be authorized to execute, in the recess of Congress, such of the powers of Congress as the United States in Congress assembled, by the consent of nine states, shall from time to time think expedient to vest them with; provided that no power be delegated to the said committee, for the exercise of which, by the articles of confederation, the voice of nine states in the Congress of the United States assembled is requisite.

Article XI

Canada **acceding** to this confederation, and joining in the measures of the United States, shall be admitted into, and entitled to all the advantages of this union: but no other colony shall be admitted into the same, unless such admission be agreed to by nine states.

Article XII

All bills of credit emitted, monies borrowed and debts contracted by, or under the authority of Congress, before the assembling of the United States, in pursuance of the present confederation, shall be deemed and considered as a charge against the United States, for payment and satisfaction whereof the said United States, and the public faith are hereby solemnly pledged.

Article XIII

Every state shall abide by the determinations of the United States in Congress assembled, on all questions which by this confederation are submitted to them. And the Articles of this confederation shall be inviolably observed by every state, and the union shall be perpetual; nor shall any alteration at any time hereafter be made in any of them; unless such alteration be agreed to in a Congress of the United States, and be afterwards confirmed by the legislatures of every state. . . . (The Avalon Project [Web site])

Marque: Retaliation.

Acceding: Giving consent.

What happened next . . .

By attempting to limit the power of the central government, the Articles did not provide one with sufficient power to govern effectively. Serious national and international problems ensued. The inability of the federal government to regulate trade and levy taxes, and the occasional refusal by states to give the government the money it needed, meant the government could not pay off the debts from the Revolution, including paying soldiers who had fought in the war and citizens who had provided supplies. Congress could not pass many measures that required a nine-state majority for approval. States often ignored Congress, which was powerless to enforce cooperation.

Internationally, some states started their own negotiations with foreign countries. In addition, the new nation was unable to defend its borders from British and Spanish encroachment because it could not pay for an army. Leaders like Alexander Hamilton (1755–1804; see box in **George Washington** entry in volume 1) of New York, **James Madison** (1751–1836; see entry in volume 1) of Virginia, and General George Washington began strongly suggesting that a better federal system was needed. On February 21, 1787, Congress called for a Constitutional Convention to revise the Articles. Between May and September of that year, the convention debated and eventually agreed to the Constitution of the United States.

The Constitution retains some of the features of the Articles of Confederation, but it gave considerably more power to the federal government. It provided for an executive branch and allowed the government to tax its citizens. Congress was expanded from one to two houses—the Senate and House of Representatives.

Did you know . . .

- The Articles contained a provision for the admission of Canada to the confederation. Americans had long hoped that the "oppressed Inhabitants of Canada," their neighbor to the north, but a British possession, would become a colony. They hoped that Canadians would want to escape what Americans considered to be British domination. In

1775, the Second Continental Congress told Canadians: "We yet entertain hopes of your uniting with us in the defence of our common liberty." But the Canadians were not interested in Congress's proposal. Congress asked again in 1777, and were once again turned down.

Where to Learn More

Giunta, Mary A., ed. *The Emerging Nation: A Documentary History of the Foreign Relations of the United States under the Articles of Confederation, 1780–1789.* Washington, D.C.: National Historical Publications and Records Commission, 1996.

Hoffert, Robert W. *A Politics of Tensions: The Articles of Confederation and American Political Ideas.* Boulder: University Press of Colorado, 1992.

Jensen, Merrill. *The New Nation: A History of the United States during the Confederation, 1781–1789.* New York: Knopf, 1950. Reprint, Boston: Northeastern University Press, 1981.

Yale Law School. "Articles of Confederation." *The Avalon Project.* [Online] http://www.yale.edu/lawweb/avalon/artconf.htm (accessed on June 22, 2000).

Washington's Farewell Address of 1796

Delivered on September 17, 1796; excerpted from
A Chronology of US Historical Documents (Web site)

The "Father of his Country"
warns about the dangers of political parties

During the presidency of **George Washington** (1732–1799; see entry in volume 1), some of the lingering conflicts among political leaders about the course of the new American government became more heated. Those who favored a strong central government to oversee the nation's defense, financial system, and other functions funded through tax revenues were called Federalists. They were opposed by anti-Federalists, a group who wanted limited federal government and more power for individual states.

The factions grew further apart as Washington's first term progressed. Washington had planned to serve only one term, but he was asked repeatedly to run for president again in 1792 to help keep the nation united. During Washington's second term, conflicts between Federalists and anti-Federalists worsened. In addition to their basic disagreement concerning the powers of the federal government, the two groups fought over whether the American economy should emphasize commerce and industry or agriculture. They differed sharply again when choosing sides in a war between France and England that flared up in 1793. As Washington's second

"The name of American, which belongs to you, in your national capacity, must always exalt the just pride of Patriotism, more than any appellation derived from local discriminations."

George Washington

term neared an end, the two groups had formed into political parties, the Federalists and the Democratic-Republicans.

Having presided over the Constitutional Convention in 1787, Washington was well aware of different views concerning the extent of the federal government's powers. But healthy debate—an essential element of democracy—had turned into a power struggle. Washington had selected men with varying views to work in his administration, but the growing division represented by political parties threatened to become imbalanced—where the stronger group pursues only its own interests.

Washington used the occasion of his Farewell Address in 1796 to express his pride in America and to warn about divisions that could break the nation apart. His Farewell Address remains important as a plea for unity over special interests.

Things to remember while reading an excerpt from President Washington's Farewell Address of 1796:

- Praising the federal government established by the Constitution, Washington compared it early in his speech to a fortress that offers security for the people. Later, he argued that the strong federal government established by the Constitution was a great advance over the weaker central government that was formed by the Articles of Confederation. He pleaded for Americans to continue to regard the Constitution with their highest respect.

- To provide an example of how government helps people, Washington cited "a treaty with Spain" (the Treaty of San Lorenzo) that granted U.S. citizens free and unlimited access to the Mississippi River all the way to Spanish-controlled New Orleans.

- Washington argued that political parties are a kind of natural occurrence where like-minded people form a group. However, he warned that such groups can create factions within the nation. The factions engage in conflict, with each group attempting to attain superiority. The more powerful group inevitably tries to weaken its opposition, which leads to counteraction (and even revenge) by other factions. That is one example he cited of how parties can promote special interests rather than the good of the nation.

Excerpt from President Washington's Farewell Address

*The unity of Government, which constitutes you one people, is also now dear to you. It is justly so; for it is a main pillar in the **edifice** of your real independence, the support of your tranquillity at home, your peace abroad; of your safety; of your prosperity; of that very Liberty, which you so highly prize. But as it is easy to foresee, that, from different causes and from different quarters, much pains will be taken, many **Artifices** employed, to weaken in your minds the conviction of this truth; as this is the point in your political fortress against which the **batteries** of internal and external enemies will be most constantly and actively (though often covertly and insidiously) directed, it is of infinite moment, that you should properly estimate the immense value of your national Union to your collective and individual happiness; that you should cherish a cordial, habitual, and immovable attachment to it; accustoming yourselves to think and speak of it as of the **Palladium** of your political safety and prosperity; watching for its preservation with jealous anxiety; **discountenancing** whatever may suggest even a suspicion that it can in any event be abandoned, and **indignantly** frowning upon the first dawning of every attempt to alienate any portion of our country from the rest or to enfeeble the sacred ties which now link together the various parts. . . .*

*For this you have every inducement of sympathy and interest. Citizens, by birth or choice, of a common country, that country has a right to concentrate your affections. The name of American, which belongs to you, in your national capacity, must always exalt the just pride of Patriotism, more than any **appellation** derived from local discriminations. With slight shades of difference, you have the same religion, manners, habits, and political principles. You have in a common cause fought and triumphed together; the Independence and Liberty you possess are the work of joint counsels, and joint efforts, of common dangers, sufferings, and successes. . . .*

In contemplating the causes, which may disturb our Union, it occurs as matter of serious concern, that any ground should have

Edifice: A large structure.

Artifices: Insincere manner.

Batteries: Pounding, battering.

Palladium: A reference to Greek mythology where the city of Troy was safe as long as a statue of Pallas was protected.

Discountenancing: Discouraging with a show of disapproval.

Indignantly: Showing anger at something unjust.

Appellation: Name.

been furnished for characterizing parties by Geographical discriminations, Northern and Southern, Atlantic and Western; whence designing men may endeavour to excite a belief, that there is a real difference of local interests and views. One of the expedients of party to acquire influence, within particular districts, is to misrepresent the opinions and aims of other districts. You cannot shield yourselves too much against the jealousies and heart-burnings, which spring from these misrepresentations; they tend to render alien to each other those, who ought to be bound together by **fraternal** affection. The inhabitants of our western country have lately had a useful lesson on this head; they have seen, in the negotiation by the Executive, and in the unanimous ratification by the Senate, of the treaty with Spain, and in the universal satisfaction at that event, throughout the United States, a decisive proof how unfounded were the suspicions propagated among them of a policy in the General Government and in the Atlantic States unfriendly to their interests in regard to the Mississippi; they have been witnesses to the formation of two treaties, that with Great Britain, and that with Spain, which secure to them every thing they could desire, in respect to our foreign relations, towards confirming their prosperity. Will it not be their wisdom to rely for the preservation of these advantages on the union by which they were **procured?** Will they not henceforth be deaf to those advisers, if such there are, who would sever them from their brethren, and connect them with aliens?

To the **efficacy** and permanency of your Union, a Government for the whole is indispensable. No alliances, however strict, between the parts can be an adequate substitute; they must inevitably experience the infractions and interruptions, which all alliances in all times have experienced. Sensible of this momentous truth, you have improved upon your first essay, by the adoption of a Constitution of Government better calculated than your former for an intimate Union, and for the efficacious management of your common concerns. This Government, the offspring of our own choice, uninfluenced and unawed, adopted upon full investigation and mature deliberation, completely free in its principles, in the distribution of its powers, uniting security with energy, and containing within itself a provision for its own amendment, has a just claim to your confidence and your support. Respect for its authority, compliance with its laws, acquiescence in its measures, are duties enjoined by the fundamental **maxims** of true Liberty. The basis of our political systems is the right of the people to make and to alter their Constitutions of Government. But the Constitution which at any time exists,

Fraternal: Brotherly.

Procured: Achieved.

Efficacy: Ability to produce the desired effect.

Maxims: Truths.

Complete American Presidents Sourcebook

till changed by an explicit and authentic act of the whole people, is sacredly obligatory upon all. The very idea of the power and the right of the people to establish Government presupposes the duty of every individual to obey the established Government.

*All obstructions to the execution of the Laws, all combinations and associations, under whatever plausible character, with the real design to direct, control, counteract, or awe the regular deliberation and action of the constituted authorities, are destructive of this fundamental principle, and of fatal tendency. They serve to organize faction, to give it an artificial and extraordinary force; to put, in the place of the delegated will of the nation, the will of a party, often a small but artful and enterprising minority of the community; and, according to the alternate triumphs of different parties, to make the public administration the mirror of the ill-concerted and **incongruous** projects of faction, rather than the organ of consistent and wholesome plans digested by common counsels, and modified by mutual interests.*

However combinations or associations of the above description may now and then answer popular ends, they are likely, in the course of time and things, to become potent engines, by which cunning, ambitious, and unprincipled men will be enabled to subvert the power of the people, and to usurp for themselves the reins of government; destroying afterwards the very engines, which have lifted them to unjust dominion.

Towards the preservation of your government, and the permanency of your present happy state, it is requisite, not only that you steadily discountenance irregular oppositions to its acknowledged authority, but also that you resist with care the spirit of innovation upon its principles, however specious the pretexts. One method of assault may be to effect, in the forms of the constitution, alterations, which will impair the energy of the system, and thus to undermine what cannot be directly overthrown. In all the changes to which you may be invited, remember that time and habit are at least as necessary to fix the true character of governments, as of other human institutions; that experience is the surest standard, by which to test the real tendency of the existing constitution of a country; that facility in changes, upon the credit of mere hypothesis and opinion, exposes to perpetual change, from the endless variety of hypothesis and opinion; and remember, especially, that, for the efficient management of your common interests in a country so extensive as ours a government of as much vigor as is consistent with the perfect security of liberty is indispensable. . . .

Incongruous: Uneven, disordered.

*I have already intimated to you the danger of parties in the state, with particular reference to the founding of them on geographical discriminations. Let me now take a more comprehensive view, and warn you in the most solemn manner against the **baneful** effects of the spirit of party, generally.*

This spirit, unfortunately, is inseparable from our nature, having its root in the strongest passions of the human mind. It exists under different shapes in all governments, more or less stifled, controlled, or repressed; but, in those of the popular form, it is seen in its greatest rankness, and is truly their worst enemy.

*The alternate domination of one faction over another, sharpened by the spirit of revenge, natural to party dissension, which in different ages and countries has perpetrated the most horrid enormities, is itself a frightful **despotism**. But this leads at length to a more formal and permanent despotism. The disorders and miseries, which result, gradually incline the minds of men to seek security and **repose** in the absolute power of an individual; and sooner or later the chief of some prevailing faction, more able or more fortunate than his competitors, turns this disposition to the purposes of his own elevation, on the ruins of Public Liberty.*

*Without looking forward to an **extremity** of this kind, (which nevertheless ought not to be entirely out of sight,) the common and continual mischiefs of the spirit of party are sufficient to make it the interest and duty of a wise people to discourage and restrain it. . . .*

In offering to you, my countrymen, these counsels of an old and affectionate friend, I dare not hope they will make the strong and lasting impression I could wish; that they will control the usual current of the passions, or prevent our nation from running the course, which has hitherto marked the destiny of nations. But, if I may even flatter myself, that they may be productive of some partial benefit, some occasional good; that they may now and then recur to moderate the fury of party spirit, to warn against the mischiefs of foreign intrigue, to guard against the impostures of pretended patriotism; this hope will be a full recompense for the solicitude for your welfare, by which they have been dictated. . . . (A Chronology of US Historical Documents [Web site])

Baneful: Seriously harmful.

Despotism: Rule by force and fear.

Repose: Rest.

Extremity: Extreme situation; in this case a worst-possible situation.

What happened next . . .

Washington's warnings about the dangers of the nation splitting into factions was soon borne out. In fact, party rivalries as well as factions within factions were displayed in the election of 1796. Within the Federalist Party, for example, Alexander Hamilton (1755–1804; see box in **George Washington** entry in volume 1) convinced some electors to vote for candidates other than **John Adams** (1735–1826; see entry in volume 1). With several candidates receiving votes, **Thomas Jefferson** (1743–1826; see entry in volume 1)—Hamilton's greatest rival and a member of the opposing Democratic-Republican Party—finished second to Adams and, thus, became the nation's vice president (as the rules mandated in those days).

President Adams faced challenges to his policies from both parties. Some Federalists took advantage of a possible war with France to pass anti-immigrant legislation as well as restrictions on free speech. That power play ended up costing the Federalists key support among voters. Jefferson was elected president in 1800, and never again would the Federalists win the presidency. The Democratic-Republican Party, in fact, won the next seven elections, including the 1824 vote that ended in victory for Adams's son, **John Quincy Adams** (1767–1848; see entry in volume 1).

Ironically, the Democratic-Republican Party was beset by factions beginning with the 1824 election. One group followed **Andrew Jackson** (1767–1845; see entry in volume 1), president from 1829 to 1837, to become the Democratic Party. The anti-Jackson faction did not become well-organized until 1836 as the Whig Party.

Washington also warned against promoting one's region over the concerns of the larger nation. That warning also went unheeded. Northern politicians consistently lobbied the federal government for favorable business policies. Southern politicians rallied against such policies and often promoted states' rights to protect their support for the institution of slavery. Such regional devisiveness, of course, contributed to the American Civil War (1861–65).

Washington correctly foresaw problems arising through special-interest, partisan politics and attitudes (where party, regional, and other loyalties overwhelm the best interests of the nation). Because special interests continue to influence the American political scene, Washington's speech remains important.

Did you know . . .

- George Washington was so popular and respected after the Revolutionary War that he could have become king, or a military dictator (a leader who rules with absolute power backed by a nation's military). He recognized the need for a strong, central government, but he wanted it to be fair and democratic. Called on to preside over the Constitutional Convention of 1787, Washington did not participate in debates that lasted throughout the summer. Instead, he concentrated on keeping the proceedings orderly.

- Washington did not relish the idea of becoming president. Before he left his home, Mount Vernon, to travel to New York for his inauguration, Washington told Henry Knox (1750–1806), who would become Washington's secretary of war, that he felt like a felon on his way to be hanged. His humbleness, as well as his ability to be forceful, provided Washington with the balanced judgment necessary to steer the new nation through tough times. He planned to serve only one term, but he again answered the call when the troubled nation looked to him for continued leadership.

Where to Learn More

Flexner, James Thomas. *George Washington: Anguish and Farewell, 1793–1799.* Boston: Little Brown & Company, 1972.

Meltzer, Milton. *George Washington and the Birth of Our Nation.* New York: Franklin Watts, 1986.

Spalding, Matthew, and Patrick J. Garrity. *A Sacred Union of Citizens: George Washington's Farewell Address and the American Character.* Lanham, MD: Rowman & Littlefield, 1996.

University of Oklahoma Law Center. "The Farewell Address of President George Washington." *A Chronology of US Historical Documents.* [Online] http://www.law.ou.edu/washbye.html (accessed on June 21, 2000).

John Adams
Second president (1797–1801)

John Adams

Born October 13, 1735
Braintree, Massachusetts
Died July 4, 1826
Quincy, Massachusetts

Second president of the United States
(1789–1797)

His words and actions trumpeted the
importance of a government composed of
strong independent branches.

As one of the nation's Founding Fathers, John Adams enjoyed a long and distinguished career as a public servant. He was a delegate from Massachusetts to the Continental Congress and was a member of the Continental Congress team that drafted the Declaration of Independence in 1776. (The Declaration of Independence is the document through which the American colonies declared independence from Great Britain.) Adams served as a diplomat in England, the Netherlands, and France. He also helped lead the Massachusetts State Constitutional Convention (1779). He served eight years as the first vice president of the United States.

Adams was unable to forge a coalition (partnership) of support during his own presidency, despite having worked with American leaders for decades. He faced bickering within his own Federalist party and dissension (disagreement) from some of the sixteen states of the Union as well. He was the first incumbent president (president currently in office) to lose reelection. Nevertheless, Adams remains a significant figure among the nation's Founding Fathers. He left behind a large body of writings. His words show a great deal of insight

Independence Day "ought to be solemnized with pomp and parade, with shows, games, sports, guns, bells, bonfires, and illuminations, from one end of this continent to the other, from this time forward forevermore."

John Adams

John Adams.
Courtesy of the Library of Congress.

55

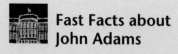

Fast Facts about John Adams

Full name: John Adams

Born: October 30, 1735

Died: July 4, 1826

Burial site: First Unitarian Church, Quincy, Massachusetts

Parents: John and Susanna Boylston Adams

Spouse: Abigail Smith (1744–1818; m. 1764)

Children: Abigail Amelia (1765–1813); John Quincy (1767–1848); Susanna (1768–1770); Charles (1770–1800); Thomas Boylston (1772–1832)

Religion: Unitarian

Education: Harvard College (B.A., 1755)

Occupations: Farmer; teacher; attorney

Government positions: Continental congressman; minister to France, the Netherlands, and England; vice president under George Washington

Political party: Federalist

Dates as president: March 4, 1797– March 4, 1801

Age upon taking office: 61

into the exciting times in which he lived. His writing also reveals his warm, witty, and sometimes cantankerous (cranky) personality.

A Puritan legacy

John Adams was born on October 30, 1735, and raised in Braintree, Massachusetts. (Braintree became Quincy [KWIN-zee], Massachusetts.) His father's family had settled there about a century before. He grew up in a Puritan household. Puritans believed in simple religious ceremonies and creeds and strict religious discipline. The Adams family belonged to a Congregationalist church. In Congregationalism, a form of church government used by the Puritans, each local congregation (a group of people who gather for religious worship) is self-governing. Both his mother, Susanna, and his father, John—a Congregationalist church deacon, farmer, and local elected official—had forceful personalities.

A talkative boy who loved the outdoors, Adams despised school as a youngster. When he was not cutting class to hunt, fish, or skate in the woods and ponds surrounding Braintree, Adams studied classical languages, logic (the study of principles of reasoning), and rhetoric (the study of the art of speaking and writing). One day, he informed his father that his education was an unnecessary expense, for he planned to become a farmer. The elder Adams then forced his son to spend an entire day, sunrise to sunset, alongside him at work. Exhausted but prideful, Adams refused to admit that farming involved backbreaking work. His father nevertheless settled the question for him and sent him to class the next day.

Adams entered Harvard College at the age of fifteen in the fall of 1751. He was expected to follow in the footsteps of his uncle, who had studied there to become a minister. Although he excelled as a student, Adams began to have doubts about his suitability for a religious figure's life. After graduating third in his class of the year 1755, Adams decided to teach school while thinking about his goals for the future.

Prominent Boston attorney

Adams decided to become a lawyer. He studied with a Worcester, Massachusetts, attorney for two years before he was admitted to the Massachusetts bar (the legal profession) in 1758. Beginning his practice in Braintree, Adams rose to a position of importance locally within a few years. He traveled frequently to Boston to argue cases. Becoming financially secure, he began courting Abigail Smith (1744–1818; see entry on **Abigail Adams** in volume 1), the seventeen-year-old daughter of a well-to-do minister in nearby Weymouth. They were wed on October 25, 1764, after a three-year courtship. Over the next decade, they had five children.

Adams grew increasingly involved in colonial politics. He forged ties with a number of emerging patriots who rallied (united) against the English Parliament's Stamp Act of 1765. The Stamp Act was a law passed by the British government that required the payment of a tax to Great Britain on papers and documents produced in the colonies. The tax caused considerable public outcry and even riots. Adams authored Braintree's official protest of the act and wrote diatribes (strong,

 John Adams Timeline

1755: Born in Massachusetts

1755–1758: Teaches grammar school

1756: Begins studying law

1758: Admitted to the bar of the State of Massachusetts

1773: Serves in Massachusetts state legislature

1774: Serves as delegate to First Continental Congress and to Second Continental Congress (1775)

1779: Elected to Massachusetts Constitutional Convention and authors the state constitution

1780–85: Serves as U.S. envoy in France and the Netherlands; member of negotiation committee for the Treaty of Paris, 1783

1785–88: Serves as U.S. minister to Britain

1789–97: Serves as vice president under George Washington

1796–1801: Serves as second U.S. president

1826: Dies in Massachusetts

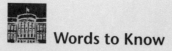

Words to Know

Anti-Federalists: A group who wanted a limited federal government and more power for individual states.

Bar: A term that encompasses all certified lawyers—those who have passed all official requirements (the bar exam) to be certified as lawyers.

Checks and balances: The system within which the three branches of the U.S. government can review and dismiss acts passed by one of the other branches.

Continental Army: The army formed by the Continental Congress during the Revolutionary War. The army included militias (civilian emergency forces) from the individual colonies as well as new recruits.

Continental Congress: An assembly of delegates representing the colonies. The assembly first met in 1774. When they met again in 1775, the Revolutionary War (1775–83) was underway. The Con-

tinental Congress evolved into the revolutionary government.

Federalists: Members of a major political party in the early United States. Federalists believed in a strong, centralized federal government.

Incumbent: The official currently holding an office.

Loyalists: Americans who remained loyal to Great Britain during the Revolutionary War (1775–83).

Midterm elections: Congressional elections that occur halfway through a presidential term and can affect the president's dealing with Congress. A president is elected every four years; representatives, every two years; and senators, every six years.

Platform: A declaration of policies that a candidate or political party intends to follow if elected.

even bitter, criticism) against it for the *Boston Gazette*. The rights of Englishmen, he declared, came from God, not the Crown or Parliament (the British national legislative body). The colonists, as equals of English citizens, he added, should not be forced to accept unfair laws.

A revolutionary spirit

In 1770, Adams was elected to the General Court (the Massachusetts state legislature). By 1773, he was firmly convinced that the colonies could benefit by breaking ties with England. War seemed imminent. Adams was selected as a delegate to the first Continental Congress, held in Philadelphia, Pennsylvania, in 1774. When war broke out in 1775, the Second Continental Congress convened (met formally). During those sessions, the Congress established the Continental Army from state militias (emergency civilian forces) and new recruits. Adams nominated **George Washington** (1732–1799; see entry in volume 1) as commander-in-chief. Recognizing the need for some type of federated framework for the colonies should independence be achieved, Adams wrote *Thoughts on Government* (see **John Adams** primary source entry in volume 1). The essay presented a detailed plan for a government with three branches—an executive branch, a legislative branch, and a judicial branch.

Adams was involved in the Continental Congress of 1776 at which the Declaration of Independence was ratified. With war and American independence declared, Adams was finally able to return to his family in Braintree. Late the following year, however, he sailed with his ten-year-old son, **John Quincy Adams** (1767–1848; see entry in volume 1), for France. Sent with the task of negotiating a treaty of alliance, the senior Adams remained there for two years as a diplomat. Returning home in 1779, he was elected a delegate to the Massachusetts Constitutional Convention, and he wrote the document supporting statehood. Adams returned to France when the end to the Revolutionary War (1775–83) seemed close at hand. Representing his country, Adams signed the Treaty of Paris in 1783. This treaty formally ended the Revolutionary War.

Remaining in Europe, Adams was named minister to Britain in 1785. He lived in London for three years and forged a close friendship with **Thomas Jefferson** (1743–1826; see entry in volume 1), who was minister to France. During this time, Adams wrote *Defence of the Constitutions of Government of the United States of America*. In this work, Adams urged the formation of an American government with three branches that could review and dismiss acts passed by one of the other branches, thus creating a system of checks and balances. (One branch could review what another was doing, providing a balanced view, if needed.) Adams's version of government included an upper legislative chamber made up of "the rich, the wellborn and the able." This kind of aristocratic pretension caused some members of the Constitutional Convention (1787) to dismiss Adams as a potential leader of the new nation.

First vice president

When it came time to elect the nation's first president in 1789, electors unanimously favored George Washington. Under the terms of the new Constitution, Adams became vice president when he finished second in voting to Washington. Alexander Hamilton (1755–1804; see box in **George Washington** entry in volume 1), a younger political figure, did not like Adams and had lobbied against him during the balloting. It was the beginning of a long battle between the two men, especially as Hamilton—as secretary of the treasury—became the most trusted of Washington's cabinet officials.

As Washington's vice president for two terms, Adams began to despise the position. He had very few duties or official roles, other than to serve as the tiebreaker vote for the Senate. He called the vice presidency "the most insignificant office that ever the invention of man contrived or his imagination conceived." His frustration was compounded by the growing political unrest among the patriots of 1776.

Those who favored a strong central government, life terms for senators, and a political system that encouraged trade and commerce became known as Federalists. Hamilton became the unofficial leader of the group. The Federalists were opposed by a group called anti-Federalists, led by Thomas Jefferson, who believed that a strong federal government would lead to a corrupt ruling class. They were distrustful of the advantages that a Federalist agenda seemed to give New England's merchant and industrial class over the nation's farmers.

Adams, widely viewed as Washington's successor, did not wholeheartedly support the Federalist platform (a declaration of policies that a candidate or political party intends to follow if elected). Adams disagreed with Hamilton's arguments for the creation of a national bank and a large standing army. Moreover, he was wary about the large number of former Loyalists (Americans loyal to Britain) among the Federalist ranks. Opposition to Federalists centered around Jeffer-

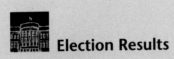

Election Results

1796

Presidential / Vice presidential candidates	Popular votes	Electoral votes
John Adams (Federalist)	—	71
Thomas Jefferson (Democratic-Republican)	—	68
Thomas Pinckney (Federalist)	—	59
Aaron Burr (Democratic-Republican)	—	30
Others	—	48

Popular votes were not yet part of the presidential election of 1796. (The public at large did not vote.) Adams received a majority of the total electoral votes, making him the president. Under the system then in place, the person with the second highest number of electoral votes became the vice president.

son and the emerging Democratic-Republican Party, which championed increased states' rights and limited terms for elected officials.

The election of 1796 would be the first true contest between political ideologies (ideas) in the new nation. Adams became the Federalist candidate after Washington announced his retirement from politics. With no media except newspapers, the campaign was largely carried out as a press war fought in opinionated broadsheets loyal to one side or another. Broadsheets were newspapers with large-sized pages.

Hamilton worked against Adams by convincing some Federalist electors to vote for Adams's vice presidential candidate, fellow Federalist Thomas Pinckney (1750–1828), but not for Adams. In the nation's first few presidential elections, each state was represented by electors. The number of electors for each state was determined by its population. Electors each voted for two candidates. The person who received the most votes became president. The runner-up became vice president.

Hamilton's ploy (trick) backfired. Enough delegates withheld votes from Pinckney to cause Jefferson to finish second and become Adams's vice president. For the only time in American history, the two offices were held by members of opposing parties. (In the 1864 election, Republican incumbent president **Abraham Lincoln** [1809–1865; see entry in volume 2] chose Democrat **Andrew Johnson** [1808–1875; see

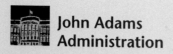 **John Adams Administration**

Administration Dates
March 4, 1797–March 4, 1801

Vice President
Thomas Jefferson (1797–1801)

Cabinet
Secretary of State
Timothy Pickering (1797–1800)
John Marshall (1800–1801)

Secretary of the Treasury
Oliver Wolcott Jr. (1797–1801)
Samuel Dexter (1801)

Secretary of War
James McHenry (1797–1800)
Samuel Dexter (1800–1801)

Attorney General
Charles Lee (1797–1801)

Secretary of the Navy (created in 1798)
Benjamin Stoddert (1798–1801)

Postmaster General
Joseph Habersham (1797–1801)

entry in volume 2] as his vice presidential running mate, but in the spirit of "national union" during the troubled Civil War era, the Republican Party temporarily changed its name to the National Union Party. Thus, in this case—unlike in the Adams-Jefferson case—opposing party members willingly joined forces to run on a national ticket and won.) Elected by a margin of just three votes, Adams was inaugurated (ceremonially installed in office) on March 4, 1797, at Congress Hall in Philadelphia. In his first speech as president, Adams called for national unity and an end to domestic (internal) disagreements. He stressed the need to maintain peace with all nations and to remain free from any difficult situations with other powers.

The nation's second president

Adams was the first president to succeed another. There was no precedent (previous example) on how he might proceed. His fatal error, according to both himself and later political analysts, was to keep Washington's Cabinet. These advisers were dominated by men faithful to Hamilton. Another mistake was Adams's habit of spending much of his time in Braintree. He was not present to witness how slowly or incorrectly his directives were carried out by men loyal to Hamilton.

The Adams administration was dominated by the threat of war with France. The Revolution of 1789 had overthrown the French monarchy. France's new leaders eagerly exploited political unrest across Europe. They sought to spread France's revolutionary spirit across the European continent through armed conflict. Under President Washington, the United States declared itself neutral (showing allegiance

John Adams, reflecting on his missions to France said, "I desire no other inscription over my gravestone than: 'Here lies John Adams, who took upon himself the responsibility of peace with France in the year 1800.'" *Courtesy of the Library of Congress.*

to neither side) in France's war with England. However, both nations stopped American ships at sea and seized cargoes they believed were destined for their enemies. By the time Adams took office, France had seized nearly three hundred merchant vessels.

In the summer of 1797, Adams sent a team of diplomats—Massachusetts politician Elbridge Gerry (1744–1814),

John Marshall

John Marshall was a key adviser to the nation's first two presidents and the chief justice of the Supreme Court for thirty-five years. Marshall, born on September 24, 1755, spent his early years working on the family farm in Virginia. At age fourteen, Marshall briefly attended a nearby academy. Swept up in the growing colonial rebelliousness toward Great Britain in the early 1770s, Marshall began reading law books. By age twenty, he intended to make law his career.

When the American Revolution broke out in 1775, Marshall enlisted in the Continental Army. Marshall participated in several major battles and was with General George Washington at Valley Forge, Pennsylvania, during the miserable winter of 1776–77. With his persuasive personality and strong leadership ability, Marshall received many promotions. Still interested in the law, Marshall attended lectures on law at the College of William and Mary.

After the war, Marshall moved to Richmond, Virginia. Though a relatively untrained lawyer, Marshall quickly demonstrated the qualities that would make him one of the country's most respected leaders. His ability to gather bits of evidence into a logical and convincing argument soon earned him a place among the great lawyers of the day and a position in the Virginia legislature. Marshall was among many dissatisfied with the government established in 1781 by the Articles of Confederation. He supported adoption of the Constitution as a protection of human rights and as a base for a strong federal government.

Almost immediately after the Constitution was ratified in 1789, Marshall helped define the roles of various government officers. In 1796 and 1799, he supported the president's right to negotiate with foreign countries. President Washington offered Marshall the position of attorney general, but he declined. He also turned down the offer of John Adams to become either secretary of war or minister to France. Though he supported Adams—and served as Adams's secretary of state in 1800–1801—Marshall opposed the Alien and Sedition Acts (1798). When Adams was soundly defeated by Thomas Jefferson in the presidential election of 1800, the decline of the Federalist Party (of which Adams and Marshall were leaders) was underway. Hoping to salvage some power, Adams appointed numerous Federalists as judges before he left office. In one of his last acts as president, Adams nominated Marshall for chief justice of the Supreme Court. The lame-duck Federalist-controlled Senate confirmed the nomination.

As chief justice, Marshall quickly won the respect of the other justices. His first major case was *Marbury v. Madison* (1803). Just before Adams left office, he had nominated William Marbury to be justice of the peace of Washington, D.C. His appointment had been confirmed by the Senate, but Adams had left office before the official papers could be delivered to

John Marshall.
Courtesy of the Library of Congress.

Marbury. President Jefferson ordered Secretary of State James Madison not to deliver the appointment. Marbury petitioned the Supreme Court for a *writ of mandamus* (a command placed on an official to perform his duty). Jefferson, a supporter of states' rights, favored a weak Supreme Court. Marshall, on the other hand, favored a strong central government. If the judgment were based on politics, Marshall would have ruled in favor of Marbury.

Marshall, however, was committed to making the Constitution serve as a guide for the United States. Ruling that Congress had no authority to pass the part of a law in 1789 upon which Marbury based his claim, Marshall declared the act unconstitutional because it gave the Supreme Court powers that the Constitution had not in-

tended. The Court refused to hear *Marbury v. Madison.* It was a brilliant decision for the Court. Marshall had established an important pattern. All federal laws had to be in keeping with the Constitution, and the Court would serve to judge them.

Three years later, in the trial of U.S. senator Aaron Burr, Marshall again showed sound judgment. Burr had embarked on a mysterious trip down the Ohio and Mississippi rivers, gathering followers and arming them for some unspecified reason. Pursued by the military, Burr was arrested for treason, accused of attempting to establish a new country in the Louisiana Territory and Mexico. An angry Jefferson called for Burr's prosecution. But in the trial, Marshall insisted on the principle of "innocent until proven guilty," stating that *talking* about rebellion and *carrying out* a rebellion were two different issues. He ruled that it was necessary to prove an act of treason by the testimony of at least two witnesses. Since Burr had not engaged in an act of war witnessed by at least two people, Marshall refused to try him on the charge of treason. Instead, Burr was tried on a lesser charge, and he was found not guilty. Marshall had again identified the Supreme Court as interpreter of the Constitution and limited in its powers by that document.

Through the years Marshall went on to write forty-four decisions, many of them laying the groundwork for the form of government still in operation in the United States. Marshall died in 1835.

Virginia Federalist leader John Marshall (1755–1835), and former minister to France Charles C. Pinckney (1746–1825)—to negotiate with French foreign minister Charles-Maurice de Talleyrand-Périgord (1754–1838). Talleyrand-Périgord refused to meet with the American emissaries, however, so he sent three aides instead. Talleyrand-Périgord's representatives immediately asked for a bribe of $250,000 for Talleyrand-Périgord, a loan for France, and an apology from Adams. Because overseas communication took a long time in this era before electronic transmissions, Adams did not learn of the demands until a dispatch arrived on his desk in March of 1798. Some members of his cabinet urged a declaration of war with France. Others urged an alliance with England. Adams decided to continue to negotiate for peace but to prepare for war. Congress demanded that the details be made public. Adams did so in April of 1798, but he kept secret the names of the French envoys, and referred to them only as X, Y, and Z. The incident became known as the XYZ Affair.

The public was outraged. War fever immediately swept the country. Adams, like Washington, felt that the United States was not prepared to do battle against one of Europe's mightiest powers. He acted with restraint. Throughout 1798 and the next year, an unofficial war, known as the Quasi-War, would be carried on by American and French ships on Atlantic seas. Adams won funds from Congress to enlarge the army and to create a separate naval force that would be administered by a new Cabinet post, secretary of the navy. Adams asked George Washington to head the army and Benjamin Stoddert (1751–1813) to be the secretary of the navy. While Adams was in Massachusetts, his Cabinet voted to make Hamilton second in command to Washington. Hamilton's call for war with both France and Spanish America greatly concerned Adams. He felt that a seditious government takeover by the army, under Hamilton's leadership, was entirely possible. (Sedition is conduct or language that incites others to rebel against the state.)

Alien and Sedition Acts

Two factions (groups) in the country emerged: pro-French and pro-British. Federalists were anti-France. The Federalists believed that there were many French spies among the United States' rapidly increasing immigrant population. Federalists were also concerned about Irish Americans, many of whom were longtime enemies of the British. Jefferson's anti-British Democratic-Republicans were concerned that Adams was planning to establish a monarchy (a system where one person rules a country for life). Democratic-Republican newspapers of the day, especially the *Aurora*, referred to Adams as the "Duke of Braintree." The president was criticized for appointing his son, John Quincy Adams, as minister to Prussia. Rumors were spread that the family was enriching its fortunes at the public's expense. Meanwhile, Hamilton and the Federalists won a Congressional majority in the midterm elections (elections that occur halfway through a president's term) of 1798. They saw an opportunity to forcibly defeat their opposition.

French foreign minister Charles-Maurice de Talleyrand-Périgord (above) refused to negotiate with President Adams's emissaries unless the United States paid a $250,000 bribe.
Courtesy of the Library of Congress.

In the tense summer of 1798, Congress quickly passed four bills. President Adams then signed the bills against his better judgment. The Naturalization Act, the Alien Act, the Alien Enemies Act, and the Sedition Act aroused a tremendous public outcry. The Naturalization Act extended from five to fourteen years the waiting period before citizenship—and with it, the right to vote—could be obtained by new immigrants. The Alien acts gave the president the right to deport or jail foreign citizens he judged as a threat to the nation's stability, especially during wartime. The Sedition Act criminalized criticism of the government. To write or publish views that ridiculed the administration was punishable by harsh fines and jail terms. In all, twenty-five people were arrested and ten convicted. All of them were journalists, including Benjamin Franklin Bache (1769–1798), the publisher of the *Aurora* and the grandson of Benjamin Franklin (1706–1790).

The Alien and Sedition Acts

The Alien Act (June 25, 1798)

The excerpts below highlight the most controversial parts of the Alien Act and the Sedition Act. The Alien Act gave the president power to deport any non-citizen considered dangerous. The Sedition Act made it a criminal offense to publish "false, malicious, or scandalous" statements about the federal government and its officials. Two other acts were part of the four laws collectively known as the Alien and Sedition Acts. The Naturalization Act raised the age from five to fourteen the number of years an immigrant had to reside in the United States before he or she could become a citizen. The Alien Enemies Act allowed government officials to arrest and deport any citizen of a foreign nation at war with the United States.

An Act concerning Aliens.

Sec. 1. Be it enacted . . ., That it shall be lawful for the President of the United States at any time during the continuance of this act, to order all such aliens as he shall judge dangerous to the peace and safety of the United States, or shall have reasonable grounds to suspect are concerned in any treasonable or secret machinations against the government thereof, to depart out of the territory of the United States, within such time as shall be expressed in such order, which order shall be served on such alien by delivering him a copy thereof, or leaving the same at his usual abode, and returned to the office of the Secretary of State, by the marshal or other person to whom the same shall be directed. And in case any alien, so ordered to depart, shall be found at large within the United States after the time limited in such order for his departure, and not having obtained a license from the President to reside therein, or having obtained such license shall not have conformed thereto, every such alien shall, on conviction thereof, be imprisoned for a term not exceeding three years, and shall never after be admitted to become a citizen of the United States. Provided always, and be it further enacted, that if any alien so ordered to depart shall prove to the satisfaction of the President, by evidence to be taken before such person or persons as the President shall direct, who are for that purpose hereby authorized to administer oaths, that no injury or danger to the United States will arise from suffering such alien to reside therein, the President may grant a license to such alien to remain within the United States for such time as he shall judge proper, and at such place as he may designate. And the President may also require of such alien to enter into a bond to the United States, in such penal sum as he may direct, with one or more sufficient sureties to the satisfaction of the person authorized by the President to take the same, conditioned for the good behavior of such alien during his residence in the United States, and not violating his license, which license the President may revoke, whenever he shall think proper.

Sec. 2. And be it further enacted, That it shall be lawful for the President of the United States, whenever he may deem it necessary for the public safety, to order to be removed out of the territory thereof, any alien who may or shall be in prison in pursuance of this act; and to cause to be arrested and sent out of the United States such of those aliens as shall have been ordered to depart therefrom and shall not have obtained a license as aforesaid, in all cases where, in the opinion of the President, the public safety requires a speedy removal. And if any alien so removed or sent out of the United States by the President shall voluntarily return thereto, unless by permission of the President of the United States, such alien on conviction thereof, shall be imprisoned so long as, in the opinion of the President, the public safety may require. . . .

Sec. 6. And be it further enacted, That this act shall continue and be in force for and during the term of two years from the passing thereof.

The Sedition Act (July 14, 1798)

An Act in addition to the act, entitled "An act for the punishment of certain crimes against the United States."

Sec. 1. Be it enacted . . ., That if any persons shall unlawfully combine or conspire together, with intent to oppose any measure or measures of the government of the United States, which are or shall be directed by proper authority, or to impede the operation of any law of the United States, or to intimidate or prevent any person holding a place or office in or under the government of the United States, from undertaking, performing or executing his trust or duty; and if any person or persons, with intent as aforesaid, shall counsel, advise or attempt to procure any insurrection, riot, unlawful assembly, or combination, whether such conspiracy, threatening, counsel, advice, or attempt shall have the proposed effect or not, he or they shall be deemed guilty of a high misdemeanor, and on conviction, before any court of the United States having jurisdiction thereof, shall be punished by a fine

not exceeding five thousand dollars, and by imprisonment during a term not less than six months nor exceeding five years; and further, at the discretion of the court may be holden to find sureties for his good behaviour in such sum, and for such time, as the said court may direct.

Sec. 2. That if any person shall write, print, utter, or publish, or shall cause or procure to be written, printed, uttered or published, or shall knowingly and willingly assist or aid in writing, printing, uttering or publishing any false, scandalous and malicious writing or writings against the government of the United States, or either house of the Congress of the United States, or the President of the United States, with intent to defame the said government, or either house of the said Congress, or the said President, or to bring them, or either of them, into contempt or disrepute; or to excite against them, or either or any of them, the hatred of the good people of the United States, or to stir up sedition within the United States, or to excite any unlawful combinations therein, for opposing or resisting any law of the United States, or any act of the President of the United States, done in pursuance of any such law, or of the powers in him vested by the constitution of the United States, or to resist, oppose, or defeat any such law or act, or to aid, encourage or abet any hostile designs of any foreign nation against the United States, their people or government, then such person, being thereof convicted before any court of the United States having jurisdiction thereof, shall be punished by a fine not exceeding two thousand dollars, and by imprisonment not exceeding two years.

Source: *United States Statutes At Large.* Vol. 1, Washington, D.C.: Government Printing Office.

Vehemently (forcefully and expressively) opposed to the Alien and Sedition Acts (as the four acts were called), Vice President Jefferson argued that they were unconstitutional. The Sedition Act, in particular, he viewed as a violation of the First Amendment guarantee of the right to free speech. This became the first challenge to the Constitution in American history. With former U.S. representative **James Madison** (1751–1836; see entry in volume 1), Jefferson authored the Kentucky and Virginia Resolutions, passed by the legislatures of those states. The resolutions (formal statements) challenged federal authority to enact such laws. Furthermore, the Kentucky Resolution asserted that states had the right to reject federal laws.

Move to Washington

Adams, not surprisingly, was miserable in his single term as president. The outcry against the Alien and Sedition Acts was great, but he was forced to defend them. The undeclared war with France still dragged on, but much of Europe was now uniting against France. Adams felt the prospects for a new peace accord were promising. Early in 1799, he sent a new minister to France to renew negotiations. This decision caused a furor in the Senate, which was packed with pro-war Federalists. Cabinet members loyal to Hamilton attempted to delay the mission by slowing correspondence and instructions. Despite these obstacles, the Convention of 1800 was concluded in September of that year. Adams took credit and was justly proud of his avoidance of full-scale battle. "I desire no other inscription over my gravestone than: 'Here lies John Adams, who took upon himself the responsibility of the peace with France in the year 1800,'" he would write later.

The seat of government moved to Washington, D.C., in 1800. Adams made the journey that autumn to what New Englanders viewed as a muddy, malarial swamp in the middle of nowhere. A carriage carrying Abigail Adams there for the first time became lost in the woods. The White House, then called the President's Palace, was still unfinished and quite damp. The draftiness permanently aggravated Abigail Adams's chronic rheumatism (a condition that causes joint and muscle pain and disability). Their son Charles, an alcoholic, died that year. Adams somewhat halfheartedly agreed to run for a second term.

By the time the election of 1800 neared, the power of the Federalists was rapidly disintegrating. Congressional debate over ratification of a treaty with France split them further. Hamilton attacked Adams in a harsh fifty-page document. Hamilton called Adams unfit to hold the presidency and a leader who had humiliated the nation. Meanwhile, Democratic-Republicans had gained political strength in several states. Adams and his running mate Pinckney were bested by fewer than a dozen electoral votes apiece by Jefferson and Aaron Burr (1756–1836; see box). Responding to his loss in 1800 to Jefferson, Adams created over two hundred new judicial positions during the last days of his term. He filled the posts with Federalists in what became known as the Midnight Appointments.

John Adams and Thomas Jefferson (above) had an up-and-down relationship through the years. In their retirement years, they were good friends, frequently writing letters to each other. Each man died on July 4, 1826.
Courtesy of the Library of Congress.

Retirement

When Jefferson was inaugurated, Adams refused to formally greet him at the ceremony. He left early that morning for his family estate in the section of Braintree that was renamed Quincy in 1792. Adams spent the next quarter-century roaming its lands once again. He spent time reading, writing, and when his eyesight failed, listening to his grandchildren read aloud to him. He and his longtime enemy, Jefferson, eventually made peace in 1812. They corresponded regularly after that. Widowed in 1818, Adams had the honor of watching his son, John Quincy Adams, sworn in as the sixth president in 1825.

Adams lived to be ninety years old. He died in Quincy on July 4, 1826. On the same day, the nation celebrated

A Selection of Adams Landmarks

Abigail Adams Historic Birthplace. 180 Norton St., Weymouth, MA 02188. (781) 335-4205. Birthplace of the first lady. See http://southshoreserver.com/abigailadams/ (accessed on June 5, 2000).

Adams National Historic Site Visitors Center. 1250 Hancock St., Quincy, MA. 02169. (617) 773-1177. Videos, slide shows, and exhibits about the Adams family. The historic site includes three Adams houses: the birth site of President John Adams at 133 Franklin Street, the birth site of President John Quincy Adams at 141 Franklin Street, and "Peacefield," a home owned by John Adams at 135 Adams Street. See http://www.nps.gov/adam/ (accessed on June 5, 2000).

United First Parish Church. 1306 Hancock St. (Quincy Center), Quincy, MA 02169. (617) 773-1290. President and Mrs. Adams, as well as their son, President John Quincy Adams, and his wife, are entombed in the family crypt in the church's basement. See http://www.ufpc.org/ (accessed on June 5, 2000).

the fiftieth anniversary of the Declaration of Independence. Adams's famous last words were, "Jefferson still survives." But Adams was unaware that Jefferson had died in Virginia earlier that same day.

Legacy

John Adams was a major influence during the period when the colonies were transformed into the United States of America. His political views, combined with his sense of public service, helped shape the nation's early history and affirm American sovereignty (independence and self-government). His contributions to the Declaration of Independence and the Constitution were especially notable.

As president, Adams was justly proud of his major accomplishment—avoiding full-scale conflict with France. Despite the excited public cries for war and the determined militarism of his own Federalist party, Adams kept the new, unsteady nation out of battle against a far more powerful foe. He became the first president to achieve a major, lasting peace agreement with a foreign power. Yet the pro-war attitude of many Americans had made him fearful. Some Federalists cautioned that an unruly mob might execute the First Family, in the style of the French Revolution. Adams was outraged by the attacks in the press on him, his administration, and his family. As a result, he signed into law the repressive Sedition Act, which borrowed its harsh measures from the restrictive decrees (pronouncements) common to the monarchies of Europe.

The Sedition Act was set to expire on the day that Adams left office. In the meantime, his own vice president—Thomas Jefferson—authored a resolution condemning it. Jefferson's challenge asserted that the federal government did not possess the right to exercise powers not entrusted to it by the terms of Constitution. The Kentucky Resolution, furthermore, declared that states had the right to nullify (negate) objectionable federal laws. Debate over that question become more pronounced during the next six decades of American politics and history.

The Midnight Appointments by Adams were challenged by President Jefferson, who refused to honor the decrees when he took office. The debate over this issue eventually led to the 1803 Supreme Court decision *Marbury v. Madison*. This case marked the high court's first invalidation of a law passed in Congress. John Marshall, the chief justice of the Supreme Court during the *Marbury v. Madison* case, was appointed by Adams. He went on to a distinguished tenure on the Court that helped define its place in American government.

The awkwardness that existed throughout Adams's term due to his vice president being from a different party never occurred again after passage of the Twelfth Amendment to the Constitution in 1804. The Twelfth Amendment revised the electoral process, separating the election of president and vice president.

Where to Learn More

Adams, Charles Francis, ed. *The Works of John Adams, Second President of the United States.* Boston: Little, Brown, 1850–56. Reprint, New York: AMS Press, 1971.

Butterfield, L. H., ed. *The Earliest Diary of John Adams.* Cambridge, MA: Harvard University Press, 1966.

Butterfield, L. H., Marc Friedlander, and Mary-Jo Kline, eds. *The Book of Abigail and John: Selected Letters of the Adams Family, 1762–1784.* Cambridge, MA: Harvard University Press, 1975. Reprint, Bridgewater, NJ: Replica Books, 1997.

Cappon, Lester J., ed. *The Adams-Jefferson Letters.* Chapel Hill: University of North Carolina Press, 1959. Reprint, 1988.

Ferling, John E. *John Adams: A Life.* Knoxville: University of Tennessee Press, 1992. Reprint, New York: Henry Holt, 1996.

Shepherd, Jack. *The Adams Chronicles: Four Generations of Greatness.* Boston: Little, Brown, 1975.

Abigail Adams

Born November 1744
Weymouth, Massachusetts
Died October 28, 1818
Quincy, Massachusetts

One of America's earliest advocates for women's rights

The wife of one president and mother of another, Abigail Adams was an intelligent, independent woman. While her husband **John Adams** (1735–1826; see entry in volume 1) traveled on diplomatic assignments, she was left to fend for herself and her young children for several years. She corresponded with him frequently. The ideas and impressions she expressed have been published and add greatly to official sources from this era.

An early champion of equal rights for women, Abigail urged her husband to put his fair-minded practices into law. "I desire you would remember the ladies and be more generous and favorable to them than your ancestors. Do not put such power into the hands of the Husbands," Adams urged him in 1776 while he was away in Philadelphia, helping with the Declaration of Independence. "Remember," she added, "all Men would be tyrants if they could."

Parson's daughter

Abigail Smith Adams was born in November of 1744, in Weymouth, Massachusetts, a seaport fourteen miles out-

"I desire you would remember the ladies and be more generous and favorable to them than your ancestors."

Abigail Adams, in a letter to her husband, John Adams

Abigail Adams.
Reproduced by permission of the National Portrait Gallery, Smithsonian Institution.

side of Boston. Her mother, Elizabeth Quincy, was descended from one of Massachusetts's oldest and most prominent families. Her father, William Smith, was a Harvard-trained Congregationalist minister who taught his three daughters to read. Each local Congregationalist church was self-governing. Though she had no formal schooling, Abigail read avidly during her youth and came to possess a sharp, independent cast of mind.

Abigail met her future husband through an introduction by her older sister's fiancé. Eleven years older than her, John Adams was a Harvard graduate working as a lawyer in Braintree, Massachusetts. He was clearly enchanted by her intelligence and opinions. In letters from this period, he called her "Miss Jemima" and once wrote a "Catalogue of your Faults," pointing out in endearing terms that she was bad at cards, couldn't sing, and walked pigeon-toed. He often noted that she kept her head downcast—a habit that stemmed, he said, from her frequent reading.

They married in 1764 and moved to property that he owned in Braintree. Their first child, a daughter named after her mother but called "Nabby," was born in 1765. A son, **John Quincy Adams** (1767–1848; see entry in volume 1), arrived two years later. By the time their fifth child, Thomas, was born in 1772, the political climate in New England was increasingly tense. John Adams was one of a number of young, educated colonial lawyers and activists who were advocating independence from England. To protest a tax on tea, upset colonists disguised as Native Americans dumped the unloaded tea from three ships in Boston Harbor in 1773. This event became known as the Boston Tea Party. Not long after, John Adams departed for Philadelphia to take part in the Continental Congress.

Abigail was left to run the family estate and to care for four children (a fifth child had died in 1770) in an atmosphere of uncertainty and political violence. Her husband returned home on occasion, but when war broke out in earnest in April of 1775, John Adams left again for Philadelphia. The letters she wrote him reveal much about the fears faced by ordinary New Englanders during this period. Enemy soldiers were often perilously near. Outbreaks of infectious diseases like smallpox and dysentery felled many, including her mother. Cannons sometimes boomed through the night. With her son John Quincy, then just seven years old, she watched the battle of Bunker Hill from a far hilltop. Like other homeowners in the area, Abigail was expected to occasionally house militiamen (civilian emergency troops). One day, she melted pewter spoons in a kettle in her kitchen, helping to make bullets for John Adams's brother Elihu, a Minuteman. (Minuteman was a name for a Revolutionary War militiaman from Massachusetts who was ready to fight on a moment's notice.)

Reunited

Boston was liberated from the British in March of 1776. The thirteen colonies signed the Declaration of Independence in July. Beginning in early 1778, John Adams served in England as a diplomat. In the summer of 1784, Abigail and daughter Nabby sailed for London to join him. It was the first time she had seen her husband in nearly five years. From there the family went to Paris as John Adams began his duties as the U.S. minister to France. Abigail Adams was shocked by what she felt were rather indecent French manners. She delighted, however, in attending the theater and ballet, both of which were nonexistent in New England. From 1785 to 1787, the family lived in London after her husband was made the first U.S. minister to the Court of St. James. Irritated by the complexities of running a diplomatic residence with its customary dinners—Congress provided no funds for their household—Abigail Adams feared she and her husband would be financially ruined. London newspapers poked fun at her frugal (thrifty) ways.

Abigail was happy to return to Massachusetts in 1788. Shortly after, her husband was elected to the office of vice president, serving under **George Washington** (1732–1799; see entry in volume 1). She could not attend the New York

In 1773, colonists protested the British tea tax by dumping fifteen thousand pounds of tea into Boston Harbor in what became known as the Boston Tea Party.
Lithograph by Sarony and Major. Courtesy of the National Archives and Records Administration.

City inauguration (installation to office in a formal ceremony) because of bad roads in late winter. Facing another long separation, John Adams urged his wife to join him. They rented a house in the Richmond Hill section of the city. After accompanying him when the nation's capital moved to Philadelphia in 1790, she hosted an open house every Monday and a formal dinner each Wednesday. She also became a close friend of first lady **Martha Washington** (1732–1802; see entry in volume 1).

As she approached her fiftieth birthday, Abigail's health began to decline. She returned to Braintree and corresponded steadily with her husband. Adams wrote back extensively on political matters, such as debates in Congress. In turn, she provided him with her accounts of the local political mood in Massachusetts. Both delighted when they expressed the same opinion in letters that crossed in the mail. Their children were marrying and beginning families of their own. At various times, the children lived with her or sent grandchildren to stay for an extended period.

America's second first lady

In February of 1797, John Adams became the second president of the United States. Again, Abigail did not attend the inauguration ceremony because of the difficult trek in winter. Soon the chief executive was pleading in letters for his wife to join him. "The times are critical and dangerous, and I must have you here to assist me," he wrote. "I can do nothing without you." Abigail arrived in Philadelphia in the spring of 1797. She took over her duties as wife of the president, which involved supervising a staff, planning menus for official dinners, and receiving callers. She also assisted her husband in other matters: She offered her opinions on policy issues, helped him draft correspondence, and relayed discussions she had with members of Congress and other officials. Abigail was sometimes called a "minister without portfolio," or a Cabinet secretary without a department. Whenever possible, the Adamses returned to Braintree.

When her husband's popularity declined as he refused to go to war with France, Abigail grew frustrated by newspaper attacks on him. Although she supported the idea of a free press, she was strongly opposed to its penchant (strong liking) for libelous statements (statements meant to damage a person's reputation or to expose a person to public ridicule) and attacks upon her family. In a letter to her sister, Abigail stated her support for a sedition bill pending in Congress, which eventually passed. Under its harsh terms, several newspaper editors were jailed. The resulting uproar contributed to the downfall of her husband's administration.

The "Presidential Palace"

When the nation's capital was moved to the District of Columbia in the fall of 1800, President Adams left for the new "Federal City" without his wife. On the way back to Braintree from Philadelphia, she stopped in New York to visit her ailing son Charles. His alcoholism and gambling had long grieved his parents. She was at his side when he died.

When the "Presidential Palace" (the new building was not yet called the White House) was ready for occupancy, Abigail made the trip south. Washington, D.C., was still virtually an isolated, unpopulated swamp tending to promote outbreaks of yellow fever. She found the palace unfinished, damp, and drafty. These circumstances aggravated her rheumatism (a condition that causes joint and muscle pain and disability). With little space available, she ordered the family's laundry to be hung in what became known as the East Room. Nevertheless, she entertained as was expected, hosting the first reception on New Year's Day of 1801 in what would become the Oval Room of the White House.

Together at last

John Adams lost his bid for reelection in 1800 to **Thomas Jefferson** (1743–1826; see entry in volume 1). Adams returned to Massachusetts and to his wife, who had left Washington, D.C., a month earlier. Their home was now located in Quincy (KWIN-zee), renamed from Braintree in 1792 in honor of her grandfather, John Quincy. The ex-president and ex–first lady spent the next seventeen years together, the longest continuous period of each other's company in their marriage. The retirement, however, was marked by more family tragedy. Nabby was diagnosed with breast cancer. Medical treatment for cancer was very primitive in this time. Nabby underwent a mastectomy without anesthesia in the home of her parents. She suffered terribly but went into remission (a cancer-free period) for another two years. Sadly, she had married an undependable husband, who left her for long periods of time and often with no funds. Nabby once again became ill and returned to Quincy with her two children so that she could die at her parents' home.

Abigail Adams outlived three of her own children, as well as her younger and older sisters. Just a few weeks before her seventy-fourth birthday, she contracted typhoid fever. She died at home on October 28, 1818. The entire town of Quincy mourned her passing. Both the governor of Massachusetts and the president of Harvard College were among her pallbearers (persons who carry the casket at a funeral). Her husband remarked that a part of him died with her. Son John Quincy wrote to his brother Thomas that their mother's life "gave the lie to every libel on her sex that was ever written."

Where to Learn More

Akers, Charles W. *Abigail Adams: An American Woman.* Second edition. New York: Longman, 2000.

Bober, Natalie S. *Abigail Adams: Witness to a Revolution.* New York: Atheneum Books for Young Readers, 1995.

Butterfield, L. H., Marc Friedlander, and Mary-Jo Kline, eds. *The Book of Abigail and John: Selected Letters of the Adams family, 1762–1784.* Cambridge, MA: Harvard University Press, 1975. Reprint, Bridgewater, NJ: Replica Books, 1997.

Diller, Daniel C. *The Presidents, First Ladies, and Vice Presidents: White House Biographies, 1789–1997.* Washington, D.C.: Congressional Quarterly, 1997.

Nagel, Paul C. *The Adams Women: Abigail and Louisa Adams, Their Sisters and Daughters.* New York: Oxford University Press, 1987.

Adams's "Thoughts on Government"

Written in January 1776; excerpted from
A Hypertext on American History **(Web site)**

One of the nation's Founding Fathers envisions an American Republic as the colonies fight for independence from England

J ohn Adams (1735–1826; see entry in volume 1) made contributions to the Declaration of Independence (1776) and the American Constitution (1787). His ideas influenced the kind of government that was adopted by the state of Massachusetts in 1779 and the United States with ratification of the Constitution in 1789. Adams and several other American leaders formed similar ideas about how government can operate. The unique American system was developed by a group that drew on personal experiences as well as examples of past political structures.

Having endured what they considered unjust laws and actions by an authority, Great Britain, that acted primarily to protect its own best interests across an ocean, Adams and American patriots understood that the governed must be represented in their government. In their view, the happiness of society is the object of government. That sentiment is expressed in the Declaration of Independence—that all human beings " are endowed by their Creator with certain unalienable rights, that among them are life, liberty and the pursuit of happiness."

"The form of government which communicates ease, comfort, security, or, in one word, happiness, to the greatest number of persons, and in the greatest degree, is the best."

John Adams

With the beginning of the American Revolution in 1775, the prospect of American independence became possible. Having rallied against what they viewed as excessive authority of the British government, Americans faced the issue of what kind of government would best serve such ideals as individual liberty and representation, and what kind of government would foster the pursuit of happiness.

Adams was asked those questions by George Wythe (1726–1806), a patriot and judge from Virginia and a signer of the Declaration of Independence. In January of 1776, Adams responded in a letter to Wythe. Many of his ideas in that letter became reality as newly independent states formed their individual governments in the late 1770s and early 1780s, and when the U.S. government was formed with the Constitution in 1787.

Things to remember while reading an excerpt from "Thoughts on Government":

- The American Revolution (1775–83) was already underway when Adams wrote the letter to Wythe. Americans were fighting for independence, but there was as yet no plan for establishing a new form of government if and when America gained its independence.

- Early in the letter, Adams developed two central themes that would be addressed later in the Declaration of Independence and the Constitution. First, he argued that the primary goal of government is to promote happiness. That idea forms one of the principles in the Declaration of Independence that explain why the colonies felt justified in declaring independence; the Declaration lists a series of wrongs perpetrated by Great Britain. Secondly, Adams argued for a republican government: in a republican form of government, supreme power resides with citizens who elect their leaders and have the power to change their leaders.

- Adams stressed the necessity for having a legislative body that would represent the people. He listed six reasons why it was important that such a representative assembly comprise two parts: such an arrangement would ensure that the assembly would not grow too powerful—each legislative body (one elected by state legislators, another by citizens) could balance the other.

- The judiciary forms the third branch in Adams's conception of government. Unlike the other two branches, where officials are elected, Adams argued that judges should be appointed and hold their position for life. Adams defended those differences by noting that it takes expertise in law to act as a judge. He also provided a means for impeaching (removing) judges who betray the principles of law.

- The letter ended on a personal note. Adams expresses his delight that he and Wythe ("my dear friend") were living in such a wonderful time when they had an opportunity to form a new government—"the wisest and happiest government that human wisdom can contrive." Adams ended the letter by quoting English poet John Milton (1608–1674). Throughout the letter, Adams's wide reading is evident: he makes references to Greek and Chinese philosophers, religious leaders of the Middle East, and political philosophers.

Virginia judge George Wythe. In a letter to Wythe, John Adams gave his opinions on how a federal government should operate. *Courtesy of the Library of Congress.*

Excerpt from "Thoughts on Government"

*We ought to consider what is the **end** of government, before we determine which is the best form. Upon this point all speculative politicians will agree, that the happiness of society is the end of government, as all **divines** and moral philosophers will agree that the happiness of the individual is the end of man. From this principle it will follow, that the form of government which communicates ease,*

End: A goal, a final outcome.

Divines: Holy people.

comfort, security, or, in one word, happiness, to the greatest number of persons, and in the greatest degree, is the best.

All **sober** inquirers after truth, ancient and modern, pagan and Christian, have declared that the happiness of man, as well as his dignity, consists in **virtue. Confucius, Zoroaster, Socrates, Mahomet,** not to mention authorities really sacred, have agreed in this.

If there is a form of government, then, whose principle and foundation is virtue, will not every sober man acknowledge it better calculated to promote the general happiness than any other form?

Fear is the foundation of most governments; but it is so sordid and brutal a passion, and renders men in whose breasts it predominates so stupid and miserable, that Americans will not be likely to approve of any political institution which is founded on it.

Honor is truly sacred, but holds a lower rank in the scale of moral excellence than virtue. Indeed, the former is but a part of the latter, and consequently has not equal pretensions to support a frame of government productive of human happiness.

The foundation of every government is some principle or passion in the minds of the people. The noblest principles and most generous affections in our nature, then, have the fairest chance to support the noblest and most generous models of government.

A man must be indifferent to the sneers of modern English men, to mention in their company the names of **Sidney, Harrington, Locke, Milton, Nedham, Neville, Burnet, and Hoadly.** No small **fortitude** is necessary to confess that one has read them. The wretched condition of this country, however, for ten or fifteen years past, has frequently reminded me of their principles and reasonings. They will convince any candid mind, that there is no good government but what is **republican.** That the only valuable part of the British constitution is so; because the very definition of a republic is "an empire of laws, and not of men." That, as a republic is the best of governments, so that particular arrangement of the powers of society, or, in other words, that form of government which is best contrived to secure an impartial and exact execution of the laws, is the best of republics.

Of republics there is an inexhaustible variety, because the possible combinations of the powers of society are capable of innumerable variations.

As good government is an empire of laws, how shall your laws be made? In a large society, inhabiting an extensive country, it is im-

Sober: Serious.

Virtue: Moral strength and excellence; good.

Confucius, Zoroaster, Socrates, Mahomet: Ancient philosophers and religious leaders.

Sidney, Harrington, Locke, Milton, Nedham, Neville, Burnet, and Hoadly: A group of famous Englishmen that includes two philosophers, two political figures, a poet, a journalist, and two clergymen.

Fortitude: Strength to bear hardship.

Republican: Government (republic) in which leaders are elected.

possible that the whole should assemble to make laws. The first nec-
*essary step, then, is to **depute** power from the many to a few of the*
most wise and good. But by what rules shall you choose your repre-
sentatives? Agree upon the number and qualifications of persons
*who shall have the benefit of choosing, or **annex** this privilege to the*
inhabitants of a certain extent of ground.

The principal difficulty lies, and the greatest care should be em-
ployed, in constituting this representative assembly. It should be in
miniature an exact portrait of the people at large. It should think,
feel, reason, and act like them. That it may be the interest of this as-
sembly to do strict justice at all times, it should be an equal represen-
tation, or, in other words, equal interests among the people should
have equal interests in it. Great care should be taken to effect this,
and to prevent unfair, partial, and corrupt elections. Such regula-
tions, however, may be better made in times of greater tranquillity
than the present; and they will spring up themselves naturally, when
all the powers of government come to be in the hands of the people's
friends. At present, it will be safest to proceed in all established
modes, to which the people have been familiarized by habit.

A representation of the people in one assembly being obtained,
a question arises, whether all the powers of government, legislative,
executive, and judicial, shall be left in this body? I think a people
cannot be long free, nor ever happy, whose government is in one as-
sembly. My reasons for this opinion are as follow:

1. A single assembly is liable to all the vices, follies, and frailties
of an individual; subject to fits of humor, starts of passion, flights of
enthusiasm, partialities, or prejudice, and consequently productive
of hasty results and absurd judgments. And all these errors ought to
be corrected and defects supplied by some controlling power.

*2. A single assembly is apt to be **avaricious**, and in time will not*
scruple** to exempt itself from burden which it will lay, without **com-
***punction**, on to its constituents.*

3. A single assembly is apt to grow ambitious, and after a time
*will not hesitate to vote itself **perpetual**. . . .*

4. A representative assembly, although extremely well qualified,
and absolutely necessary, as a branch of the legislative, is unfit to
exercise the executive power, for want of two essential properties, se-
*crecy and **despatch**.*

Depute: Delegate; assign responsibility.

Annex: Add to.

Avaricious: Greedy.

Scruple: Act with best intentions.

Compunction: Stress relating to awareness of guilt.

Perpetual: Continuing, never-ending.

Despatch: Dispatch; speedy transmission.

5. A representative assembly is still less qualified for the judicial power, because it is too numerous, too slow, and too little skilled in the laws.

6. Because a single assembly, possessed of all the powers of government, would make arbitrary laws for their own interest, execute all laws arbitrarily for their own interest, and **adjudge** all controversies in their own favor.

But shall the whole power of legislation rest in one assembly? Most of the foregoing reasons apply equally to prove that the legislative power ought to be more complex; to which we may add, that if the legislative power is wholly in one assembly, and the executive in another, or in a single person, these two powers will oppose and encroach upon each other, until the contest shall end in war, and the whole power, legislative and executive, be **usurped** by the strongest.

The judicial power, in such case, could not mediate, or hold the balance between the two contending powers, because the legislative would undermine it. And this shows the necessity, too, of giving the executive power a negative upon the legislative, otherwise this will be continually encroaching upon that.

To avoid these dangers, let a distinct assembly be constituted, as a mediator between the two extreme branches of the legislature, that which represents the people, and that which is vested with the executive power.

Let the representative assembly then elect by ballot, from among themselves or their constituents, or both, a distinct assembly, which, for the sake of **perspicuity**, we will call a council. It may consist of any number you please, say twenty or thirty, and should have a free and independent exercise of its judgment, and consequently a negative voice in the legislature.

These two bodies, thus constituted, and made integral parts of the legislature, let them unite, and by joint ballot choose a governor, who, after being stripped of most of those badges of domination, called prerogatives, should have a free and independent exercise of his judgment, and be made also an integral part of the legislature. This, I know, is liable to objections; and, if you please, you may make him only president of the council, as in Connecticut. But as the governor is to be invested with the executive power, with consent of council, I think he ought to have a negative upon the legislative. If he is annually elective, as he ought to be, he will always have so

Adjudge: Judge.

Usurped: Authority taken over illegally.

Perspicuity: Clear understanding.

Complete American Presidents Sourcebook

much reverence and affection for the people, their representatives and counsellors, that, although you give him an independent exercise of his judgment, he will seldom use it in opposition to the two houses, except in cases the public utility of which would be conspicuous; and some such cases would happen.

In the present **exigency** of American affairs, when, by an act of Parliament, we are put out of the royal protection, and consequently discharged from our allegiance, and it has become necessary to assume government for our immediate security, the governor, lieutenant-governor, secretary, treasurer, commissary, attorney-general, should be chosen by joint ballot of both houses. And these and all other elections, especially of representatives and counsellors, should be annual, there not being in the whole circle of the sciences a **maxim** more infallible than this, "where annual elections end, there slavery begins.". . .

The dignity and stability of government in all its branches, the morals of the people, and every blessing of society depend so much upon an upright and skillful administration of justice, that the judicial power ought to be distinct from both the legislative and executive, and independent upon both, that so it may be a **check** upon both, as both should be checks upon that. The judges, therefore, should be always men of learning and experience in the laws, of exemplary morals, great patience, calmness, coolness, and attention. Their minds should not be distracted with jarring interests; they should not be dependent upon any man, or body of men. To these ends, they should hold **estates** for life in their offices; or, in other words, their commissions should be during good behavior, and their salaries ascertained and established by law. For misbehavior, the grand inquest of the colony, the house of representatives, should **impeach** them before the governor and council, where they should have time and opportunity to make their defence; but, if convicted, should be removed from their offices, and subjected to such other punishment as shall be thought proper. . . .

If the colonies should assume governments separately, they should be left entirely to their own choice of the forms; and if a continental constitution should be formed, it should be a congress, containing a fair and adequate representation of the colonies, and its authority should sacredly be confined to these cases, namely, war, trade, disputes between colony and colony, the post office, and the **unappropriated lands of the crown,** as they used to be called. These colonies, under such forms of government, and in such a

Exigency: Situation requiring immediate action.

Maxim: Truth.

Check: Power to evaluate and approve or deny an action.

Estates: Positions.

Impeach: Accuse an official of misbehavior in order to bring them to trial.

Unappropriated lands of the crown: Territories claimed by a nation but having no form of government ruling over them.

union, would be unconquerable by all the monarchies of Europe. You and I, my dear friend, have been sent into life at a time when the greatest lawgivers of **antiquity** *would have wished to live. How few of the human race have ever enjoyed an opportunity of making an election of government, more than of air, soil, or climate, for themselves or their children! When, before the present* **epocha,** *had three millions of people full power and a fair opportunity to form and establish the wisest and happiest government that human wisdom can contrive? I hope you will avail yourself and your country of that extensive learning and* **indefatigable** *industry which you possess, to assist her in the formation of the happiest governments and the best character of a great people. For myself, I must beg you to keep my name out of sight; for this feeble attempt, if it should be known to be mine, would oblige me to apply to myself those lines of the immortal John Milton, in one of his sonnets:*

> *I did but prompt the age to quit their clogs*
> *By the known rules of ancient liberty,*
> *When straight a barbarous noise environs me*
> *Of owls and cuckoos, asses, apes, and dogs*

(A Hypertext on American History [Web site])

What happened next . . .

Beginning in May of 1776, delegates from the thirteen colonies met in Philadelphia at the Colonial Convention. They agreed that a resolution was needed to announce their reasons for seeking independence from Great Britain. By this time, the Revolutionary War (1775–83) had been underway for over a year. The Convention turned to Virginia delegate **Thomas Jefferson** (1743–1826; see entry in volume 1) to write such a resolution. John Adams and Pennsylvania statesman Benjamin Franklin (1706–1790) looked over the document Jefferson composed and suggested minor changes. The document—the Declaration of Independence—was then presented to the Convention. After debate and a few more changes, the Declaration was signed by those present and made public on July 4, 1776.

Antiquity: Ancient times.

Epocha: Time period, era, epoch.

Indefatigable: Untiring.

A similar form to the tripartite (three part) system of government that Adams spelled out in the letter was adopted in the American Constitution, which was drafted in 1787 and ratified by the states in 1789. Much of what Adams proposed in the letter was realized in the Constitution. The major difference was that the two houses of Congress would form one branch of government; a court would form a second branch; and a chief executive—an element missing from Adams's plan—would form the third branch.

Debates among American leaders and citizens with similar and different ideas for government occurred during the 1770s and 1780s, as states formed their governments. The federal government blends the ideas of many people in its attempt, as the Constitution states, "to form a more perfect union." That the Constitution says "more perfect," rather than "perfect," shows that there will always be room for debate and improvement.

Did you know . . .

- Because he was often away from home on diplomatic missions, John Adams maintained frequent correspondences with his wife, **Abigail Adams** (1744–1818; see entry in volume 1). An independent thinker and proponent for the rights of women, she often suggested that her husband include women in his ideas and proposals for fair and equal government. Two months after Adams wrote his letter to Wythe, for example, Abigail wrote to her husband, "In the new code of laws which I suppose it will be necessary for you to make I desire you would remember the ladies and be more generous and favorable to them than your ancestors (were)."

Where to Learn More

Santrey, Laurence. *John Adams, Brave Patriot*. Mahwah, NJ: Troll Associates, 1986.

Thompson, C. Bradley. *John Adams and the Spirit of Liberty*. Lawrence: University Press of Kansas, 1998.

University of Groningen, Department of Alta-Informatica. "John Adams: Thoughts on Government." *A Hypertext on American History*. [Online] http://odur.let.rug.nl/~usa/P/ja2/writings/tog.htm (accessed on June 21, 2000).

Thomas Jefferson
Third president (1801–1809)

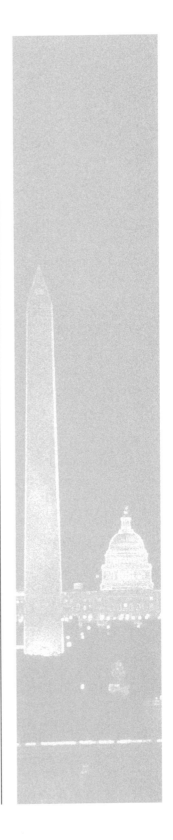

Thomas Jefferson

Born April 13, 1743
Goochland (now Albemarle) County, Virginia
Died July 4, 1826
Charlottesville, Virginia

Third president of the United States (1801–1809)

**Belief that a government should
not interfere with life, liberty, and the
pursuit of happiness was reflected in the
Declaration of Independence that he authored**

"The God who gave us life, gave us liberty at the same time."

Thomas Jefferson

Thomas Jefferson.
Reproduced by permission of the National Portrait Gallery, Smithsonian Institution.

President **John F. Kennedy** (1917–1963; see entry in volume 5) once hosted a White House dinner attended by many Nobel Prize winners. Looking out on the gathering of famous scientists, physicians, and writers, he remarked that it was "the most extraordinary collection of talent" that had "ever been gathered together at the White House—with the possible exception of when Thomas Jefferson dined alone." His remark was meant to be respectful. Jefferson was an accomplished writer, architect, naturalist, inventor, diplomat, and educator, among his many talents.

Jefferson was of great service to his state, Virginia, and his country. He helped draft the original documents when Virginia established its post-colonial government in 1781. He wrote an internationally-acclaimed book, *Notes on the State of Virginia,* that was published in 1785. His Act for Establishing Religious Freedom was adopted by the state in 1786. He founded the University of Virginia. In service to his country, Jefferson authored the Declaration of Independence and served as a diplomat, secretary of state, vice president, and president. He continually fought for America's most cher-

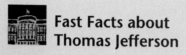

Fast Facts about Thomas Jefferson

Full name: Thomas Jefferson

Born: April 13, 1743

Died: July 4, 1826

Burial site: Monticello, Charlottesville, Virginia

Parents: Peter and Jane Randolph Jefferson

Spouse: Martha Wayles Skelton (1748–1782; m. 1772)

Children: Martha Washington (1772–1836); Jane Randolph (1774–1775); Infant son (1777–1777); Mary (1778–1804); Lucy Elizabeth (1780–1781); Lucy Elizabeth (1782–1784); in addition, scientific evidence strongly suggests that Jefferson fathered at least one and as many as six children by slave Sally Hemings

Religion: Deism

Education: Attended College of William and Mary

Occupations: Farmer; lawyer

Government positions: Virginia House of Burgesses delegate; Continental Congress member; Virginia governor; minister to France; secretary of state under George Washington; vice president under John Adams

Political party: Democratic-Republican

Dates as president: March 4, 1801–March 4, 1805 (first term); March 4, 1805–March 4, 1809 (second term)

Age upon taking office: 57

ished ideals of liberty—that human beings are born with natural rights, rather than having rights bestowed upon them by a government, and that governments govern by consent of the people, rather than by imposing (forcing) their will upon the people.

Always doing something

Thomas Jefferson was born in a log cabin in Goochland (now Albemarle) County, Virginia, on April 13, 1743. His father, Peter, had recently acquired 400 acres in an undeveloped area of Virginia. The cabin was the beginning of an estate (a large piece of rural land, usually with a house) called Shadwell that Peter was building. Jefferson's mother, Jane Randolph Jefferson, was a descendant of original English settlers in Virginia.

A farmer and a surveyor (person who measures the earth's surface by means of taking angles and distances), Peter became a justice of the peace (a legal official empowered to hear minor cases of law, to preside over wedding ceremonies, and to administer oaths of office), a judge, and a militia leader (leader of a civilian emergency military force) as the area around him formed into Albemarle County in 1744. The following year, he took on additional responsibilities upon the death of his friend and his wife's cousin, William Randolph. The Jefferson family moved to Randolph's home, Tuckahoe, for a short time. Peter managed the estate and supervised the education of the four Randolph children as well as his own. (Jefferson had two older sisters at the time, and he would soon have three younger sisters and a brother.)

Jefferson began receiving private tutoring at age five. Over the next few years, he developed into an excellent student, learning Latin and Greek, reading classical texts and modern literature, and studying geography and the natural sciences. Red-haired and tall (he would grow to be well over six feet), Jefferson played the violin and enjoyed riding horses and dancing. Jefferson entered the College of William and Mary in 1760 and graduated in 1762. For the next five years, he studied law and continued to read widely.

In 1767, Jefferson was certified (had approval in written form) to practice law in the state of Virginia. By this time, he was more interested in improving the Shadwell estate. He began planning his own estate based on classical (Greek and Roman) styles of architecture. Always busy, he observed and wrote about wildlife and plants. He practiced crop rotation, the farming technique of switching back and forth between crops for the purpose of improving the soil. He pursued an interest in new medicines. (He even traveled to Philadelphia, Pennsylvania, to receive a newly developed smallpox vaccination.) He began tinkering with ways to improve farming and home life. He applied scientific methods to every aspect of his life, keeping detailed records of everything from the daily temperature and weather to expenses and recipes.

Thomas Jefferson Timeline

1743: Born in Virginia

1762: Graduates from College of William and Mary

1769–74: Serves in Virginia House of Burgesses

1776: Authors the Declaration of Independence

1779–81: Serves as governor of Virginia

1785–89: Serves as minister to France

1790–93: Serves as secretary of state

1797–1801: Serves as vice president

1801–9: Serves as third U.S. president

1803: Louisiana Territory is purchased from France for $15 million dollars

1804: Lewis and Clark expedition begins

1807: Embargo Act forbids American ships to leave American waters

1819: University of Virginia is founded

1826: Dies in Virginia

Writer and politician

Jefferson was elected to Virginia's House of Burgesses in 1768 at the age of twenty-five. Two of his lasting political traits

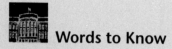

Words to Know

Alien and Sedition Acts: Four bills—the Naturalization Act, Alien Act, Alien Enemies Act, and Sedition Act—passed by Congress in 1798 and signed into law by President Adams. The Naturalization Act extended from five to fourteen years the waiting period before citizenship—and with it, the right to vote—could be obtained by new immigrants. The two Alien acts gave the president the right to deport or jail foreign citizens he deemed a threat to the nation's stability, especially during wartime. The Sedition Act criminalized criticism of the government. To write or publish views that disparaged the Administration was punishable by harsh fines and jail terms.

Anti-Federalists: A group who wanted a limited federal government and more power for individual states.

Articles of Confederation: From March 1, 1781, to June 21, 1788, the Articles served as the equivalent of the Constitution (1787). The Constitution replaced the Articles, which had failed to produce a strong central government, and the present-day United States was formed.

Democratic-Republicans: Supporters of a political party in the United States led by Thomas Jefferson and James Madison in the 1790s to oppose the Federalist Party and close ties with Great Britain. Also called the Republican Party and the Jeffersonian Republican Party at the time, but the term Democratic-Republican helps distinguish that early political group from the Democratic and Republican parties that were formed later. The Democratic-Republican Party dissolved in the 1820s. Many former members began supporting the formation of the Democratic Party led by Andrew Jackson, who was elected president in 1828 and 1832. The modern-day Republican Party was formed in 1854.

Federalist: A proponent for a strong national (federal) government.

First Continental Congress: A group of representatives from the thirteen colonies who met in Philadelphia in 1774 to list grievances (complaints) against England.

House of Burgesses: A representative body of the Virginia colony made up of colonists but under the authority of British rule.

Lame duck: An expression used to describe an official who has lost an election and is filling out the remainder of his or her term.

Monarchy: A form of government in which a single person (usually a king or queen) has absolute power.

Republican government: A form of government in which supreme power resides with citizens who elect their leaders and have the power to change their leaders.

Second Continental Congress: A group of representatives from the thirteen colonies who began meeting in Philadelphia in 1775 and effectively served as the American government until the Constitution was adopted in 1787.

surfaced immediately. First, against the influence of wealthy landowners, he championed the cause of the more modest, self-made man (a person who becomes successful through hard work and without the financial help of others). Second, although he was not a skilled speaker, Jefferson was an excellent writer to whom others turned to express ideas and policies.

In 1769, Jefferson began construction on the estate he designed. He called it Monticello (Italian for "small mountain"). On January 1, 1772, he married Martha Wayles Skelton (1748–1782; see entry on **Martha Jefferson** in volume 1), a twenty-four-year-old widow. "Patsy," as Jefferson called her, shared his love of music. She played harpsichord and organ. They had six children, but only two daughters survived into adulthood.

Jefferson was swept into growing rebellious fervor (intensity of emotion) against a series of taxes imposed on the colonies by British authority. Appeals spread from Massachusetts to the other colonies to unite in a boycott of British goods. The growing rebelliousness of Virginia's House of Burgesses led British authorities to dissolve it. Nevertheless, Virginians leading an anti-British crusade, including Jefferson and fellow House of Burgesses delegate **George Washington** (1732–1799; see entry in volume 1), met secretly in the Raleigh Tavern in Williamsburg (then the capital of Virginia) on May 27, 1774. The legislators voted to express sympathy towards Massachusetts for refusing to recognize commercial limitations (limits on trade) imposed by the British. Patrick Henry (1736–1799; see box) and Richard Henry Lee (1732–1794; see box) were two other Virginians supporting the colonial resistance. Jefferson, Henry, and Lee together organized a protest after British authorities planned to take to England and execute colonists they held responsible for burning a British ship off the coast of Rhode Island.

Jefferson was elected delegate to a Virginia convention responsible for establishing a plan of action for that colony. He wrote *A Summary of the Rights of British America,* a manifesto (a public declaration of political principles or positions) that declared that the English parliament had no authority over the colonies and that its acts were attempts to smother basic colonial freedom. He accused the British of rejecting colonial laws and of preventing the colonies from outlawing slavery. A major theme in the *Summary* would become central to the American cause: human rights are derived from the laws of nature, not granted as gifts from monarchs (kings and queens).

Jefferson fell ill and could not attend the Virginia convention. His *Summary* was read and applauded by delegates, but many of its statements were rewritten so as not to offend British authorities. Another Virginia convention met in 1775 to discuss resolutions of the First Continental Congress (1774), a group of representatives from each of the colonies who had met in Philadelphia. The Congress had resolved to unite against British authority. Patrick Henry best represented the Virginia convention's support for the Congress when he stated, "Give me liberty, or give me death."

The Declaration of Independence

Jefferson spoke before the Second Continental Congress in Philadelphia in June 1775. The Second Congress consisted of colonial representatives who met and thereafter served as the American government until the Constitutional Convention in 1787. Jefferson was asked to write a summary of his views. But, again, his statements were edited and effectively watered down.

The Congress met again the following year. With the Revolutionary War (1775–83) well underway, the Congress wanted to issue a proclamation. After Richard Henry Lee called for a resolution to end the colonies' allegiance with Great Britain, Jefferson was asked to write such a declaration. "I will do as well as I can," he replied. His draft was looked over by Massachusetts delegate **John Adams** (1735–1826; see entry in volume 1) and Pennsylvania statesman Benjamin Franklin (1706–1790; see box in **George Washington** entry in volume 1), who suggested only minor changes. The declaration was approved on July 2, 1776. After a few more changes, including the removal of a paragraph denouncing slavery, the Declaration of Independence was officially issued on July 4, 1776. (See **Thomas Jefferson** primary source entry in volume 1.) A justification (basis) for American independence, its major themes—that humans enjoy natural rights provided by a creator, not by monarchs, and that governments govern by consent of the people, not by forcing government on the peo-

Patrick Henry

Born in Hanover County, Virginia, in 1736, Patrick Henry was self-educated. After failing as a storekeeper and a farmer, Henry studied and became a lawyer in 1760.

In 1765, he became a member of the House of Burgesses, the colonial legislature of Virginia. Fiercely rebellious, he led protests against British taxes imposed on the colonies. In 1769, he urged a break from Great Britain. Henry was chairman of a committee that prepared a defense plan for Virginia during the American Revolution (1775–83) and helped draft the Virginia Constitution. He was governor of Virginia (1776–79, 1784–86) and a delegate to the Virginia convention (1788) for the ratification of the U.S. Constitution. Believing the Constitution did not safeguard the rights of states and of individuals, he led support for the Bill of Rights—the first ten amendments to the Constitution. After declining

Patrick Henry.
Reproduced by permission of the National Portrait Gallery, Smithsonian Institution.

several government positions, he was elected to the Virginia legislature in 1799, but died before his term began.

ple—were familiar Jeffersonian ideals. They were influenced by British philosopher John Locke (1632–1704; see box). Copies of the new declaration spread throughout the colonies and were received with great enthusiasm.

Representing his state

Jefferson then resigned from the Continental Congress to return to Virginia. He wanted to take part in drafting a form of republican government for that colony. In a republican government, power is in the hands of the citizens, who choose their leaders in elections. Jefferson's ideas for placing few restrictions on individuals and expanding voting rights to

Richard Henry Lee

Richard Henry Lee was born on January 20, 1732, into a family long prominent in Virginia's history. He had private tutors at home and went on to Wakefield Academy in England. By the age of 26, he was already a justice of the peace in Westmoreland County and a member of the colony's legislature, the House of Burgesses. He established his reputation as a speechmaker second only to Patrick Henry, with whom he shared leadership of the "progressive" faction in the House and led the colony's vigorous opposition to new British tax measures after 1764.

Between 1766 and 1776, Lee developed a reputation throughout the colonies as the "Son of Liberty." In addition to writing protests against what he felt were unjust measures by England, Lee organized a boycott against stamps after their prices were raised. He also led an armed party against the local stamp distributor. Lee was one of the most active and influen-tial members of the First and Second Continental Congresses, serving on the committees that drew up declarations against acts by England. In July 1775, he proposed an economic declaration of independence, throwing open American ports to the trade of the world; but Congress did not act on Lee's suggestion until almost a year later, when it also recommended the formation of independent state governments, an action Lee had already urged upon Virginia. Lee's three famous resolutions of June 7, 1776, followed logically: American independence, an alliance with France, and a plan of interstate confederation.

Lee resisted efforts to give Congress the power to regulate commerce and to impose customs duties. He believed that social happiness was to be found in "a wise and free republic and a virtuous people." For these reasons, he viewed the Constitutional Convention of 1787 with suspicion and declined to serve as a delegate. Lee wrote the

include small landowners were adopted. A milder form of his stand on religious freedom and separation of church was accepted. Not accepted was his provision (discussion of a certain subject in a document) to guarantee public education for all children, regardless of economic background.

Through 1779, Jefferson occupied himself primarily by building and refining the estate of Monticello. During his years there, he introduced olive trees to North America. He experimented with introducing other tree species not indigenous (native) to Virginia, including orange trees. He perfected

Richard Henry Lee.
Source unknown.

most thoughtful, skillful, and powerful views against Federalist policies that supported a strong central government. His "Letters from the Federal Farmer" (1787) voiced fears about the consolidated government outlined by the Constitution and the "formi-dable combination of power" vested in the president and Senate; Lee also protested the inadequacy of representation of all interests in the House and the absence of a bill of rights. Lee saw the issue as a contest against aristocracy by the vast majority of "men of middling property."

In the end, Lee accepted the Constitution because it was "this or nothing," and he served as one of Virginia's first senators in the new government. He died on June 19, 1794, never quite reconciled to the Constitution despite the Bill of Rights, which he had helped to add. Arguing that the Constitution infringed on states' rights, he became largely responsible for the Tenth Amendment: "The powers not delegated to the United States by the Constitution, nor prohibited by it to the States, are reserved to the States respectively, or to the people."

an improved plow. He invented such home implements as the swivel chair (a chair that turns and allows great freedom of movement), the dumb-waiter (a small elevator for home use), and a copying machine (in this case, a machine that connected the motion of one handheld pen with another; the second pen created the copy as the writer moved the first pen). Jefferson tinkered with clocks, steam engines, and central heating, drew designs for cities, and read and collected books.

Jefferson was elected governor of Virginia in 1779. By that time, fighting in the Revolution had spread from New

John Locke

John Locke was an English philosopher who emphasized the importance of experience of the senses in pursuit of knowledge rather than instinctive speculation or deduction. This philosophy is called empiricism (from the word "empirical," meaning based on observation or experience). Locke's doctrine was expressed in *Essay Concerning Human Understanding* (1690). He regarded the mind of a person at birth as a *tabula rasa* (a blank slate) upon which experience created and stored knowledge, just as a person can write facts on a chalkboard (or today, more likely, store information in a computer). Locke held that all persons are born good, independent, and equal.

In his *Two Treatises of Government* (1690), Locke attacked the theory of divine right of kings. He argued that sovereignty (supreme authority) resided with the people. He further stated that the state is bound by civil law (law decided on by citizens of a country) and natural law (principles that come from nature but are applicable to human beings). Locke argued that revolution was not only a right but often an obligation (duty) whenever natural rights (life, liberty, and property) are threatened. In other words, people have an obligation to defend their life and liberty. "Property" is defined as a person's body and all things that the person legally possesses under civil law.

Locke died in 1704, but his works were highly influential during the eighteenth century. His impact on Jefferson and other American leaders is reflected in both

England to the southern states. Georgia and the Carolinas fell under British control, and British troops moved into Virginia, setting up headquarters in Yorktown. Military shrewdness was not among Jefferson's talents. Virginia fell as he responded too slowly to the British advance. He barely escaped an attack on Monticello. He declined reelection in 1781 in favor of someone with a military background. His conduct during the war was investigated by the Virginia legislature in 1781, but a newly elected legislature in 1782 cleared him of all charges.

Jefferson continued to study, tinker, and write. He wrote an internationally acclaimed book, *Notes on the State of Virginia,* that was published in 1785. The book contained observations on the natural history, geography, climate, agriculture, and economy of the state. The book also included in-

John Locke.
Reproduced by permission of the Corbis Corporation.

the Declaration of Independence and the Constitution. The Declaration of Independence is a justification for American rebellion: natural rights, life, and liberty had been violated by Great Britain (the violations are listed in the document), and after attempts to address those wrongs had failed, Americans felt impelled to declare independence. Locke's belief that governments should follow majority rule is reflected in the Constitution. Locke had proposed a government consisting of three branches, each of which could check and balance the actions of the other branches (but Locke's system called for a more powerful legislative branch than the Constitution outlines). Locke's writings helped American leaders to form their ideas on human rights and to establish a system of government that reflected the will of the people.

sights on Native Americans of the region, Jefferson's views on balance of powers in government, and an essay denouncing slavery. His Act for Establishing Religious Freedom was adopted in Virginia in 1786.

But that period was sad for Jefferson as well. His wife Patsy died on September 6, 1782. They had been married for ten years. Two of their daughters and a son had died as infants. Another daughter, Elizabeth, born shortly before Patsy's death, died in 1784. Jefferson remained in seclusion (willingly staying apart from others) for several months following his wife's death. He reemerged in 1783 when he was elected to the Congress established by the Articles of Confederation (a document that served basically as the first American constitution from 1781 to 1788). He issued sever-

Sally Hemings

In colonial America, the status of the mother—free or slave—determined the status of the child. Sally Hemings's father, John Wayles, was white but her mother, Elizabeth Hemings, was a mulatto slave—the child of a white father and a full-blooded African mother. Elizabeth Hemings was Wayles's slave from birth, and after the death of Wayles's wife, she became his mistress. Together they had six children.

Wayles died in 1773, the same year Sally was born a slave. Sally, her mother, and her five siblings (along with about 125 other slaves and 11,000 acres of land), were inherited by Martha Wayles Jefferson, wife of Thomas Jefferson (then a wealthy Virginia planter). Sally Hemings was Martha's half-sister, both having been fathered by the same man. Since Martha was born in wedlock, she had rights to the family estate. The Hemingses were brought to Monticello, Jefferson's Virginia farming estate, and made house slaves.

Martha Jefferson died in September of 1782, leaving Thomas Jefferson a widower and the father of two girls. In 1784, the forty-one-year-old Jefferson was sent as a diplomat to France by the American colonial government. Jefferson's eldest daughter, Martha, joined him in Paris a short time later to attend school. In 1787, Jefferson sent for his other daughter, Maria, who travelled with Hemings.

Historians are not certain exactly what happened in Paris between Thomas Jefferson and Sally Hemings. Legally, Hemings was a free person in Paris, as slavery had been abolished in France. In the fall of 1789, Jefferson and his two daughters, as well as Sally and James Hemings, returned to America. (James was in Paris working for Jefferson and then apprenticing as a chef.)

By all accounts, Hemings was visibly pregnant upon her arrival at Monticello. Many years later, in 1873, Madison Hemings (1805-1877), the sixth child of Sally Hemings, spoke of his mother's return from Paris in the *Pike County Republican,* an Ohio newspaper. During her time in Paris, he said, "my mother became Mr. Jefferson's concubine [unmarried lover], and when he was called back home she was

al papers expressing his ideas. One paper recommended that American currency should be based on the decimal system, a numbering system based on the number ten. The penny and the dime were later established from this suggestion.

In 1784, Jefferson was appointed diplomat to France, where he joined his friends John Adams and Benjamin Franklin. Franklin retired the following year, and Adams returned to England to represent American interests there. Jef-

[pregnant] by him." He said his mother balked at returning to America, because "in France she was free, while [in] Virginia she would be re-enslaved." Madison Hemings said that Jefferson "promised her extraordinary privileges, and made a solemn pledge that her children should be freed at the age of twenty-one years" if Sally left Paris. "Soon after their arrival, [my mother] gave birth to a child, of whom Thomas Jefferson was the father."

Between 1790 and 1808, Sally Hemings gave birth to seven children, all the time while residing at Monticello. Two children were listed as "runaways" in Jefferson's personal records from 1822. The reality was that they were allowed to walk away. They were able to blend into the free white world of Washington, D.C., because of their light-colored skin. Two other children were freed in Jefferson's will at his death in 1826. Jefferson's daughter, Martha, freed Sally Hemings. Hemings died in 1835.

The public first learned of Sally Hemings in 1802, during the second year of Jefferson's presidency, when the *Rich-mond Recorder* published an article that speculated on a relationship between Hemings and the president. The possibility that Jefferson had fathered Hemings's children caused great controversy. At the time, the charge was proven neither true nor false; the president himself never denied or confirmed the relationship.

Historians argued for years about the Jefferson-Hemings relationship.

But the results of a 1998 DNA test on known descendants of both Jefferson and Hemings added great weight to the historical evidence for a Jefferson-Hemings connection. The complex study compared genes of Jefferson descendents and Hemings descendents. The results showed a definite genetic link between the two families, but could only confirm that *a Jefferson*, not necessarily *Thomas* Jefferson, fathered a child with Sally Hemings. (The president's brother, Randolph, and his two sons, spent some time at Monticello.) More tests will be needed before any definitive scientific findings can prove Jefferson's paternity one way or another.

ferson helped negotiate treaties with European nations. He became a great favorite in France and was charmed by the country as well. The widower Jefferson likely began a romance while in France with Sally Hemings (1773–1835; see box), one of Jefferson's slaves.

As political struggles developed in France late in the 1780s, Jefferson hoped for a peaceful revolution that would transform France from a monarchy (a government headed by

Jefferson enjoyed experimenting with agriculture. He introduced olive trees to North America and developed a rice-growing technique that helped make the United States a major rice producer.

a king or a queen) to a republican government. The extremely violent French Revolution (1789–1803) occurred instead. While he was in France, Jefferson was sent a copy of the Constitution. The Constitution was accepted by a 1787 convention in Philadelphia attended by representatives from all of the thirteen states. Jefferson wrote to fellow Virginian **James Madison** (1751–1836; see entry in volume 1), a delegate of the Convention, that he approved of the document, but he recommended a bill of rights for citizens. He also expressed fear that no provision was made that could stop a president from being continually reelected. As a congressman in the newly formed United States, Madison fought for the Bill of Rights, which became the first ten amendments to the U.S. Constitution in 1791. Jefferson, meanwhile, was called back to the United States in 1789 and was asked to serve as secretary of state for the nation's first president, George Washington.

Jefferson and Hamilton

During Washington's administration, Jefferson and Alexander Hamilton (1755–1804; see box in **George Washington** entry in volume 1), secretary of the treasury, led different approaches to the federal government. Favoring few federal laws and an agrarian-based (farm-based) economy that valued small landowners, Jefferson clashed with Hamilton's Federalist plans for a strong central government and an economy led by commerce and industry. Washington often sided with Hamilton, though he encouraged and respected varying views.

Jefferson's views were represented in Congress by Madison and others who became known as Anti-Federalists. The Anti-Federalists opposed a strong central government. They opposed the Federalist plan for introducing taxes and creating a national bank. Taxes were needed, argued Hamilton, for such things as paying off the nation's debt and funding federal programs. Anti-Federalists countered that tax revenues would fuel a large-scale federal government that would supersede (override) the powers of individual states. They were also against the creation of a national bank system, believing it would foster an economy that rewarded lenders and merchants as opposed to producers of goods, like farmers and artisans (craftsmen).

Jefferson called the Federalists' bank measure unconstitutional, arguing that Congress was not authorized to charter a national bank (see **Thomas Jefferson** primary source entry in volume 1). In his counterargument, Hamilton noted that Congress was granted by the Constitution the right to levy (collect) taxes, coin money, and pay the nation's debts—all of which would be functions of a national bank.

The dispute between Federalists and anti-Federalists widened as Great Britain and France went to war in 1793. President Washington wanted to protect the young nation by staying out of the conflict. Hamilton, meanwhile, favored maintaining ties with Great Britain to continue receiving trade revenue from that nation. Jefferson and his followers favored France, noting that the French had formed an alliance with America that helped win independence. Washington again sided with Hamilton and the Federalists.

The disputes between Hamilton and Jefferson led to the formation of opposing political parties, the Federalists and the Democratic-Republicans. Those parties were much less organized than modern-day American political parties that emerged in the 1830s. Federalists generally included those in favor of a strong central government, Hamilton's economic system, and flexible (changeable) interpretation of the Constitution. Democratic-Republicans, on the other hand, wanted to limit national government to emphasize states' rights. Called "constructionists," they argued that if the Constitution was to remain meaningful it must be followed literally (exactly). Others, like Hamilton, contended that the document served as a framework and guide. They agreed that its basic principles must be followed but believed that the Constitution was open to interpretation.

Jefferson grew increasingly frustrated in Washington's administration. Washington had planned to serve only one term, but the nation was growing apart. For the sake of maintaining unity, Washington ran for a second term. He asked Jefferson to continue in his role as secretary of state. Washington won reelection in 1792, and Jefferson remained in the administration until 1794. He returned to Monticello, but he stayed politically active by writing commentary in various journals. He became president of the American Philosophical Society in 1797.

Jefferson and Adams

As Washington's second term approached its end, Jefferson was a candidate for president in 1796. In the first few presidential elections, each state had a certain number of electors based on that state's population. Each elector voted for two candidates. The candidate with the most votes became president, and the runner-up became vice president. John Adams edged Jefferson by three electoral votes to claim the presidency in 1796. As vice president, Jefferson was back in Philadelphia (the seat of government from 1790 to 1800) serving an administration whose policies countered his beliefs.

Shortly after he became president, Adams sent diplomats to France. Three French agents told the diplomats that bribes (money or property offered to influence or persuade) were expected from Americans before negotiations could begin. In 1798, Adams made public the French demands, identifying the three French agents as simply X, Y, and Z. The American public was outraged toward France over the XYZ Affair. Ex-president and ex-general Washington was alerted to remain on call if needed to command American troops in a possible war with France.

To prepare for war, the American army and navy were expanded and the Department of the Navy was created. Those actions furthered the power of the federal government, to which Jefferson objected. He became further incensed when Federalists passed the Alien and Sedition Acts in 1798, four bills passed by Congress in 1798 and signed into law by President Adams. For new immigrants, the Naturalization Act extended the waiting period for citizenship and the right to vote from five to fourteen years. The Alien Acts gave the president the right to deport or jail foreign citizens he thought were a threat to the nation's stability, especially during wartime. Intended to prohibit criticism of the federal government, the Sedition Act made it a criminal offense to print or publish false, malicious (intentionally harmful), or scandalous (reputation-damaging) statements directed against the U.S. government, the president, or Congress. To write or publish views that disparaged (put down) the Administration was punishable by harsh fines and jail terms. The Sedition Act was an attempt by Federalists to curb newspapers that supported the Democratic-Republican Party.

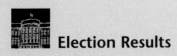

Election Results

1800

Presidential / Vice presidential candidates	Popular votes	Presidential electoral votes
Thomas Jefferson (Democratic-Republican)	—	73
Aaron Burr (Democratic-Republican)	—	73
John Adams (Federalist)	—	65
Charles C. Pinckney (Federalist)	—	64
John Jay (Federalist)	—	1

Popular votes were not yet part of the presidential election of 1800. (The public at large did not vote.) Under the system then in place, the person with the highest number of electoral votes became president; the person in second place became the vice president. Because both Jefferson and Burr received 73 votes, the vote went to the U.S. House of Representatives. There, each state had a single vote. On the thirty-sixth ballot, Jefferson received ten votes, Burr received four, and two states abstained. Thus, Jefferson became president and Burr became vice president.

1804

Presidential / Vice presidential candidates	Popular votes	Presidential electoral votes
Thomas Jefferson / George Clinton (Democratic-Republican)	—	162
Charles C. Pinckney / Rufus King (Federalist)	—	14

Popular votes were not yet part of the presidential election of 1804. (The public at large did not vote.) The 1804 election was the first election held under the Twelfth Amendment to the U.S. Constitution, which requires electors to cast separate ballots for president and vice president during the nomination process.

Jefferson and Madison were the most outspoken opponents of the acts. To protest Federalist violations of civil liberties and the freedom of the press, Jefferson worked through the Kentucky legislature and Madison through Virginia's legislature. The two states passed resolutions declaring that states had a right to nullify (negate) federal laws they considered excessive. Although the resolutions accomplished little at the time, they were part of a larger, negative response to the Federalist-dominated government. Adams became hugely unpopular after the acts went into effect. The backlash against the Federalists was the beginning of the downfall of the party.

Actions versus ideology

Political power in the United States changed from the Federalists to the Democratic-Republicans with the election of

District of Columbia

Bills passed by the U.S. Congress in 1790–91 created the district on a tract of land ceded (given up) by Maryland and Virginia. The area contained the communities of Alexandria and Washington. The cornerstone of the U.S. Capitol building was laid in 1793. In 1800, Congress moved there from its temporary headquarters in Philadelphia. In 1847, Alexandria and the remainder of the district on the western bank of the Potomac were returned to the state of Virginia by an act of Congress. Georgetown held the status of a separate town within the district from 1878 to 1895, when it was merged with Washington.

1800. Jefferson and Aaron Burr (1756–1836; see box), another Democratic-Republican, both finished ahead of Adams in votes by electors. There was only one problem: Jefferson and Burr tied with 73 electoral votes. Each elector voted for two candidates, but the electors were not required to specifically name which of the two they favored for president. It was assumed all along that Jefferson was the presidential candidate, but the Constitution mandates (commands) that if no candidate receives a majority of electoral votes, the election is to be decided in the House of Representatives, with each state having one vote.

The House voted thirty-six times without resolving the election, with Federalists doing all they could to block Jefferson's election. He was viewed by them as a radical. Finally, on the thirty-seventh ballot, Jefferson prevailed 10 votes to 4, with two states voting for other candidates. Jefferson was the first president to be inaugurated in the nation's new capital, the District of Columbia. Jefferson regarded his victory as a "revolution" representing the will of common people. However, he made an attempt to bring together the nation with a conciliatory (calming and unifying) and modest inaugural address. "We are all Federalists, we are all Republican," he stated.

Differences between Adams and Jefferson were so strained that Adams did not attend the inauguration. The two men, who had worked together on the Declaration of Independence and as diplomats in France, did not speak again for many years. After the election, while serving out his term, Adams and lame duck Federalists (Federalist politicians who had lost their elections and were waiting out the rest of their time in office) in Congress created some two hundred new judicial posts (positions pertaining to a court of justice) and stocked them with Federalist sympathizers. With influence in the presidency and Congress lost, Federalists wanted to maintain power through the federal court system.

Upon taking office, Jefferson immediately instructed his secretary of state, James Madison, to withhold all judicial appointments that had not yet been commissioned. Judge William Marbury, one of those affected by Jefferson's actions, sued to have the Supreme Court intervene in (step in to change) the president's actions. In the historic *Marbury v. Madison* ruling of 1803, Chief Justice John Marshall (1755–1835; see box in **John Adams** entry in volume 1), himself a Federalist, ruled that the law passed by Congress (part of the Judiciary Act of 1789) allowing Marbury to sue was unconstitutional. At the same time, he took the opportunity to severely criticize the actions of Jefferson and Madison. The case set a precedent (a model for future occurrences) for judicial review—meaning that the Supreme Court, if petitioned, could serve to determine the constitutionality of actions undertaken by the other two branches of the federal government.

Jefferson faced war soon after taking office. Barbary pirates (see box in **George Washington** entry in volume 1) controlled parts of the Mediterranean Sea from ports in present-day Algeria, Libya, and Tunisia (the Barbary coast). The pirates demanded "tributes"—payment to keep them from attacking vessels passing along trade routes through the Mediterranean. Jefferson refused to pay these bribes. The conflict eventually led to a series of naval battles in which the United States prevailed in 1805.

Meanwhile, American diplomats were negotiating with French emperor Napoleon (1769–1821; see box in **James Monroe** entry in volume 1) to purchase the port city of New Orleans. The city was about to return from Spanish to French

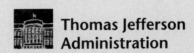

Thomas Jefferson Administration

Administration Dates
March 4, 1801–March 4, 1805
March 4, 1805–March 4, 1809

Vice President
Aaron Burr (1801–5)
George Clinton (1805–9)

Cabinet
Secretary of State
James Madison (1801–9)

Secretary of the Treasury
Samuel Dexter (1801)
Albert Gallatin (1801–9)

Secretary of War
Henry Dearborn (1801–9)

Attorney General
Levi Lincoln (1801–5)
John Breckinridge (1805–6)
Caesar A. Rodney (1807–9)

Secretary of the Navy
Benjamin Stoddert (1801)
Robert Smith (1801–9)

Postmaster General
Joseph Habersham (1801)
Gideon Granger (1801–9)

The Louisiana Purchase—the largest real estate deal in history—was a bargain. The cost works out to about three cents per acre for the 512-million-acre acquisition.

control. In 1803, Napoleon expanded his offer to include the entire French colony of Louisiana—an area of more than eight hundred thousand square miles west of the Mississippi River.

Ideologically, Jefferson was a strict constructionist of the Constitution. Land acquisitions are not covered by the U.S. Constitution. Jefferson considered proposing an amendment in order to make the purchase. But when Napoleon began indicating that he was having second thoughts about his offer, Jefferson approached Congress and asked for immediate ratification (approval) by considering the purchase a treaty. (Treaties are negotiated by the executive branch but are subject to ratification by a two-thirds majority of the Senate.) On October 20, 1803, the Louisiana Purchase—the largest real estate transaction in history—became official. The $15 million dollar purchase doubled American territory.

Spain, however, indicated that it was still considering whether or not to cede (formally surrender possession of) New Orleans. Jefferson responded by sending military troops to the city and Spain ceded it. The American flag was raised for the first time in New Orleans on December 20, 1803.

The Louisiana Purchase, Jefferson's anti-Federalist actions, and his shows of military strength made him a popular president. His style was also embraced—at least at home. Jefferson refused all examples of pomp (showy display) and formality. Dinners were casual, even state dinners. Instead of pre-assigned seating, guests could expect a first-come, first-served arrangement. Foreign diplomats were not officially greeted or announced. Jefferson often received diplomats while dressed casually and wearing slippers. British and Spanish officials in the capital began a kind of social war with American diplomats. Each side began to slight the other officials; that is to ignore or insult the opposite side, without regard for the conventional manners of the time.

During his first term Jefferson established the Lewis and Clark expedition (see box) to explore and report on western North America. Meriwether Lewis (1774–1809) and William Clark (1770–1838) were charged by the president with reporting on physical features, climate, wildlife, and Native American customs and languages. They began their journey at the headwaters of the Missouri River around St. Louis, Missouri, on May 4, 1804. They reached the Pacific Ocean in

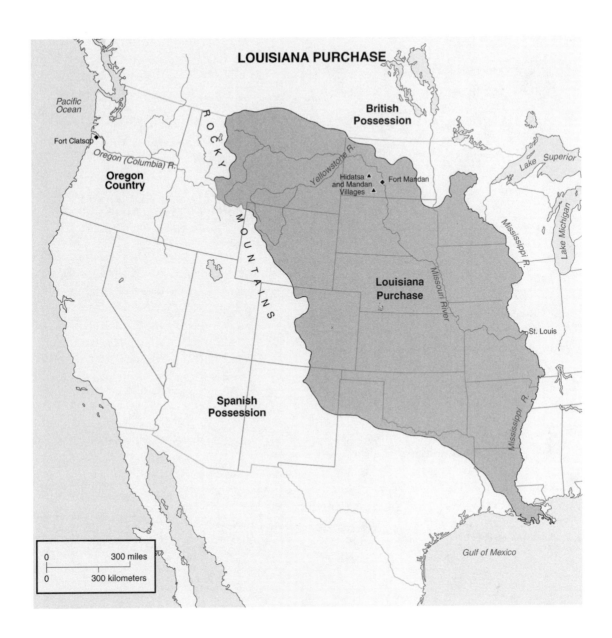

LOUISIANA PURCHASE

Pacific Ocean

Fort Clatsop

Oregon (Columbia) R.

Oregon Country

ROCKY MOUNTAINS

British Possession

Yellowstone R.

Hidatsa and Mandan Villages

Fort Mandan

Lake Superior

Lake Michigan

Mississippi R.

Louisiana Purchase

Missouri River

St. Louis

Spanish Possession

Mississippi R.

Gulf of Mexico

| 0 | 300 miles |
| 0 | 300 kilometers |

January of 1807. In addition to bringing back invaluable information on the frontier, the expedition allowed the United States to make a claim on western area beyond the Louisiana Purchase, which was called the Oregon Territory.

Several other expeditions were also authorized by Jefferson. An 1804 trek traced the Red River, the southernmost of the larger tributaries of the Mississippi River, to its source

Map shows the area encompassing the Louisiana Purchase. This territory, bought from France in 1803 for $15 million, doubled the size of the United States. *The Gale Group.*

Lewis and Clark Expedition

Meriwether Lewis (1774–1809) was born in Albemarle County, Virginia—the same county in which Thomas Jefferson was born in 1743. Lewis appeared destined for the life of a Virginia gentleman farmer, but in 1794, when Pennsylvania insurgents (people revolting against an authority) brought on the Whiskey Rebellion, Lewis answered President George Washington's call for militia volunteers. The campaign was bloodless, but Lewis enjoyed himself. He wrote his mother, "I am quite delighted with a soldier's life."

While on frontier duty, Lewis met William Clark (1770–1838), who was commanding the special company of sharpshooters to which Lewis was transferred. After service on the Mississippi River, Lewis was asked by his old Virginia friend Thomas Jefferson, now president of the United States, to become his confidential White House secretary. While Lewis served in that capacity from 1801 until 1803, the president discussed with him his dream of sending an exploring expedition to the Pacific

via the Missouri River. When Jefferson offered him leadership of the expedition, Lewis accepted, choosing Clark as his associate. Lewis took a "crash" course in science from scholars of the American Philosophical Society, since he was to make scientific reports on the West.

William Clark was born in Caroline County, Virginia. He joined militia companies fighting local tribes in the Ohio country in 1789 and three years later won a lieutenant's commission in the U.S. infantry. He served in the campaign of General "Mad Anthony" Wayne (1745–1796). The campaign ended with a victory over the Native Americans in the Battle of Fallen Timbers (1794).

Clark led the expedition's fleet of boats upriver on May 14, 1804. Lewis joined Clark, and the two officers then led their men up the Missouri to the territory of the Mandan Native American tribe, in what is now North Dakota. They wintered there before continuing in the spring of 1805.

in present-day Oklahoma. (Tributaries are smaller rivers that feed into larger rivers.) Adventurer Zebulon Pike (1779–1813) led an 1805 journey to the source of the Mississippi River. In 1806, Pike traced the Arkansas River from its headwaters at the Mississippi River to present-day Colorado.

Quarrelsome second term

Jefferson was at the height of his national popularity around election time in 1804. Following the contested election

Indian guide Sacajawea helps explorers Meriwether Lewis and William Clark on their famous expedition in the early 1800s.
Reproduced by permission of the Corbis Corporation.

out to be nearly worthless but his wife, Sacajawea (c. 1786–1812), was a helpful guide. Sacajawea was the sister of the chief of the Shoshone tribe. Through her, Lewis got the horses he needed to cross the Rocky Mountains. Once across, the explorers drifted in new canoes down the Clearwater and Snake rivers and continued down the Columbia River to the Pacific Ocean. Winter quarters were built at Ft. Clatsop, south of the mouth of the Columbia on the Oregon coast. Lewis decided to split the party on its return to Missouri. He sent Clark to explore the Yellowstone River while he made a first exploration of the Marias River. Clark's wilderness and leadership skills contributed to the success of the expedition. Clark got along better with the men and was a fine mapmaker. Both men kept diaries of the journey.

Sacajawea was honored by the U.S. Mint when her likeness was selected to appear on the new dollar coin. The coin went into circulation in 2000.

By August, the Missouri River had dwindled to a series of shallow tributaries that canoes could not negotiate. Luckily, Lewis had hired Toussaint Charbonneau as an interpreter-guide. Charbonneau turned

of 1800, the Twelfth Amendment to the Constitution was adopted. The amendment provided for separate elections for president and vice president. Jefferson won in a landslide, 162 electoral votes to 14 votes for Federalist candidate Charles C. Pinckney (1746–1825). George Clinton (1759–1812), a six-term governor of New York, replaced Aaron Burr as vice president.

Burr remained in the public eye, however. After losing his bid to succeed Clinton as governor of New York in 1804, Burr challenged Alexander Hamilton to a duel and killed him. Hamilton had spoken out vigorously against Burr during the

Aaron Burr

Born in Newark, New Jersey, on February 6, 1756, Aaron Burr graduated from the College of New Jersey in 1772 and began to study law. Attracted by the Revolutionary War, Burr joined the Continental Army and served effectively in a variety of posts until March 1779. After establishing a successful legal practice in the booming town of Albany, New York, Burr moved in 1783 to New York City and developed a substantial reputation and income.

In 1791, Burr was elected to the U.S. Senate, defeating Philip Schuyler (1733–1804), Alexander Hamilton's father-in-law. Burr and Hamilton had been political and professional rivals for some time. From 1797 to 1799, Burr served in the New York legislature. Burr was defeated by Thomas Jefferson in the 1800 presidential election, partly due to Hamilton's support for Jefferson. As the second-place vote-getter, Burr served as Jefferson's vice president until 1805. In 1804, he failed to be renominated and also lost in a bid to become governor of New York. Hamilton, his longtime political foe, publicly opposed Burr's candidacy. Burr eventually challenged him to a duel. On July 11, 1804, Burr shot Hamilton once, and Hamilton died the next day.

Burr soon became involved in a scheme called the Burr Conspiracy. From land he acquired in the Louisiana Territo-

Aaron Burr.
Courtesy of the Library of Congress.

ry, Burr planned to invade Spanish territory. James Wilkinson (1757–1825), one of Burr's associates, denounced him to Jefferson (went to Jefferson and formally accused him). Jefferson had Burr arrested. After being acquitted on charges of treason on September 1, 1807, Burr went to Europe and lobbied for European assistance for his scheme. Financially strapped, he returned to New York City in 1812 to practice law. In 1833, he married a wealthy widow, Eliza Brown Jumel, who soon divorced him because he demanded to use most of her money for his debts and plans.

campaign. Shortly after, Burr became involved in a conspiracy on the frontier. With a small military force, he planned either to take possession of part of the Louisiana territory or to invade Mexico. He was captured and brought to trial on charges of treason in 1807.

Jefferson was so outraged by Burr's action that he overstepped his authority as president as well as his ideals. He demanded that Burr be found guilty even before the trial began. Chief Justice John Marshall presided over the case. Despite Jefferson's protests, Marshall disallowed many pieces of evidence presented by the government. The remaining evidence was insufficient for a guilty verdict, and Burr was set free. Jefferson's impulsiveness helped weaken the case against Burr.

Meanwhile, Great Britain and France were at war again. Each side forbade any nation to trade with its opponent. Jefferson replied by pushing the Embargo Act (1807) through Congress. The act banned trade with both nations in

After years of being political enemies, Vice President Aaron Burr challenged former secretary of the treasury Alexander Hamilton to a duel. Burr's shot killed Hamilton.
Courtesy of the Library of Congress.

an attempt to have them respect America's neutral rights and to show the importance of trade with the United States. An effort to punish both nations, the embargo had the opposite effect. With the absence of American trade competition, both nations prospered in international markets. The loss of tariff revenue (income) was costly to the federal treasury and those flourishing from trade—from northern industrialists to southern farmers. Smuggling increased dramatically.

The embargo was extremely unpopular and even considered unconstitutional. Jefferson maintained it until just before he left office in 1809. By then he had lost the great support he had enjoyed when elected to his second term. Nevertheless, Jefferson was invited by Democratic-Republicans to run again. He would have likely won the election of 1808. Following the precedent set by George Washington of serving only a maximum of two terms, however, Jefferson declined to run again. James Madison, his longtime friend and political ally, followed him as president.

The Sage of Monticello

Jefferson retired to Monticello after his second term concluded. He restored the gardens and refurbished the interior of his home with furniture and inventions. Known as the Sage of Monticello, Jefferson frequently received guests, many of whom stayed overnight and for several days. He doted on his grandchildren. After the Library of Congress was burned during the British occupation of Washington, D.C., during the War of 1812 (1812–15; fought between the United States and Great Britain), Jefferson sold sixty-five hundred books to the library to begin a new national collection.

Jefferson founded the University of Virginia and became its rector (president) in 1819. He designed the campus and watched the progress of construction through a telescope perched on his "little mountain" that overlooks the campus. He helped select professors and the school's curriculum (courses of study). He instituted another of his cherished ideals: The university was founded to accept students based on merit, rather than wealth.

Jefferson renewed his friendship with John Adams during the last decade of his life. The two men, who had worked together on the Declaration of Independence, both died on July 4, 1826—fifty years to the day that the declaration was officially made public. Approaching death, Jefferson wrote his own epitaph (inscription for his tombstone), revealing what he considered his three greatest accomplishments:

> Here was buried
> Thomas Jefferson
> Author of the Declaration of American Independence
> Of the Statute of Virginia for Religious Freedom
> And Father of the University of Virginia.

Legacy

As a man of many achievements, Thomas Jefferson proved versatile and resourceful. He was able to learn and achieve most everything he set his mind to. These attributes served him well as president. Although he favored limited power for the federal government and was a constructionist (a literalist) in regard to the Constitution, some of his most noteworthy actions as president came when he showed flexibility or used his presidential power. The timing of the Louisiana Purchase, for example, made it important for him to act quickly, decisively, and forcefully—even if his actions were constitutionally questionable. His use of the military—to confront pirates in the Mediterranean sea, and to ensure that Spain would hand over New Orleans as promised—were successful.

Jefferson's quick actions in some other areas proved unsuccessful. His challenge upon taking office to his predecessors' judicial appointments led to the *Marbury v. Madison* case. The decision brought a needed balance of powers (but less presidential power) through which the Supreme Court could decide the constitutionality of acts of Congress and the executive branch. Jefferson's insistence that his former vice president, Aaron Burr, be found guilty of treason went against his own principles of justice and fair trial. The Embargo of 1807 ended up hurting America though it was meant to punish Great Britain and France.

A Selection of Jefferson Landmarks

Declaration (Jacob Graff) House. Seventh and Market Sts., Philadelphia, PA 19106. (215) 597-8974. Jefferson rented this house while he worked on the draft of the Declaration of Independence. Display reconstructs the history of the Declaration. See http://www.ushistory.org/tour/_graff.html (accessed on June 7, 2000).

Monticello. Box 316, Charlottesville, VA 22902. (804) 984-9800. Museum, house, plantation, gardens, and burial site of Thomas and Martha Jefferson. See http://www. monticello.org/ (accessed on June 7, 2000).

Poplar Forest. Box 419, Forest, VA 24551-0419. (804) 525-1806. Jefferson built an octagonal-shaped house on this 4800-acre plantation. See http://www.poplarforest.org/ (accessed on June 7, 2000).

Thomas Jefferson Memorial. Tidal Basin (south bank), Washington, DC. (202) 619-7275. Inspirational circular structure that includes inscriptions of Jefferson's writings on the interior walls. While president, Franklin D. Roosevelt had two trees removed that blocked the view of the memorial from the White House. See http://www.nps.gov/thje/index2. htm (accessed on June 7, 2000).

Where to Learn More

Bishop, Arthur, ed. *Thomas Jefferson, 1743–1826.* Dobbs Ferry, NY: Oceana Publications, 1971.

Bober, Natalie. *Thomas Jefferson: Man on a Mountain.* New York: Atheneum, 1988. Reprint, New York: Aladdin Paperbacks, 1997.

Bruns, Roger, ed. *Thomas Jefferson.* New York: Chelsea House, 1986.

Library of Congress. "Thomas Jefferson Papers at the Library of Congress." *American Memory.* [Online] http://lcweb2.loc.gov/ammem/gwhtml/ gwhome.html (accessed on July 31, 2000).

Nardo, Don. *Thomas Jefferson.* San Diego: Lucent Books, 1993.

Old, Wendie C. *Thomas Jefferson.* Springfield, NJ: Enslow, 1997.

Public Broadcasting System. "Thomas Jefferson Online." *PBS Online.* [Online] http://www.pbs.org/jefferson/ (accessed on July 31, 2000).

University of Virginia Library. *Thomas Jefferson Online Resources at the University of Virginia.* [Online] http://etext.virginia.edu/jefferson/ (accessed on July 31, 2000).

Martha Jefferson

Born October 19, 1748
Charles City County, Virginia
Died September 6, 1782
Charlottesville, Virginia

Music lover died almost twenty years
before her husband became president

W hen **Thomas Jefferson** (1743–1826; see entry in volume 1) took office as president in 1801, he had been a widower for nearly twenty years. His daughter, Patsy, teamed with future first lady **Dolley Madison** (1768–1849; see entry in volume 1), the spirited wife of Jefferson's secretary of state **James Madison** (1751–1836; see entry in volume 1), to help host social occasions.

Festivities at the Presidential Palace (as the White House was called back then) under Jefferson did not demand much effort from the host and hostesses. Jefferson was quite informal, sometimes greeting foreign dignitaries in casual clothes and slippers. Guests at social functions were not formally announced. They were sure to arrive as early as possible: Seating at many dinners was not prearranged, often leaving guests to scramble in a first-come, first-served format.

Things probably would have been different had Martha Wayles Skelton Jefferson lived to see her husband become president. The Presidential Palace would certainly have been filled with music. Jefferson and Martha (he called her

"[Martha was] the cherished companion of my life, in whose affections . . . I have lived . . . the last ten years of my life in unchequered happiness."

Thomas Jefferson

"Patsy") first found romantic harmony by playing music to-gether—he on the violin, and she on the harpsichord.

A duet

Not much is known about Patsy. Jefferson was deeply grieved by her death and rarely wrote or spoke about her af-terwards. About her death, he mourned the loss of "the cher-ished companion of my life, in whose affections, unabated on both sides, I have lived the last ten years of my life in unche-quered happiness."

Patsy was born Martha Wayles on October 19, 1748, in Charles City County, Virginia. At the age of eighteen, she married Bathurst Skelton, a young attorney who died when she was twenty. As a pretty and lively young widow, Martha soon had a few suitors. Among them was Thomas Jefferson. He was an attorney, but most of Jefferson's attention was con-centrated on constructing an estate he had designed. He called it Monticello (Italian for "small mountain").

Jefferson met Patsy when he was in Williamsburg, then the capital of Virginia, serving in the House of Burgess-es—the colony's legislative assembly. She lived nearby on the estate she inherited from Skelton called "The Forest."

When Jefferson began to be interested in Patsy, he wooed her with music. According to some accounts, she was being courted by two other gentleman who showed up at her home one day. Jefferson was already there. He was playing vi-olin, she was playing harpsichord, and they both were singing merrily. The two suitors gave up. Jefferson presented Patsy with a piano during their courtship. The two enjoyed dancing as well.

They were a happy couple. Their wedding was held at The Forest on January 1, 1772. Several days of festivities fol-lowed. Then they made the one-hundred-mile ride to Monti-cello by carriage through increasingly wintry conditions. At the foot of Monticello, they discovered that they could not get through. The roads were impassable for the carriage. Not discouraged, the newlyweds mounted horses and slowly wound their way up to their new home. Because of the storm, no one was there to greet them. The house was cold, empty and dark, but they soon had a fire going and found a bottle of wine to toast their new life together.

"Time wastes too fast . . . "

An evening alone together would be rare over the next ten years. Jefferson was increasingly involved in the American Revolution (1775–83) and in the establishment of the post-colonial state of Virginia. Patsy bore six children during that period. Their oldest daughter, Martha, was born in September 1772. Of their six children, only two survived into adulthood—Martha, called Patsy like her mother, and Mary, who was more often called Maria or Polly.

Jefferson, meanwhile, continued to serve in the increasingly rebellious House of Burgesses, which was dissolved by British authorities in 1774. He wrote books and served as a delegate to the Continental Congress. In 1776, he penned the Declaration of Independence. From 1777 to 1779, he continually improved Monticello. He was elected governor of Virginia in 1779.

Patsy was growing frail (sickly) from her frequent pregnancies. Jefferson turned down an appointment to serve as a diplomat in France, wanting to stay near his ill wife. Meanwhile, the Revolutionary War spread to Virginia with a British invasion. In January 1781, Patsy was in Richmond, Virginia, with her newborn daughter, Lucy Elizabeth, and had to flee an oncoming British attack. Lucy died in April. In June, the Jefferson family barely escaped when British soldiers stormed Monticello.

The strain of bearing another child in May of 1782 further weakened Patsy, and she never recovered. She died on

Monticello, home of Thomas and Martha Jefferson.
Reproduced by permission of the Corbis Corporation.

September 6, 1782. Jefferson was at her side during her illness. Near her death, Patsy was reading a book by one of her (and Jefferson's) favorite contemporary novelists, Laurence Sterne (1713–1768). From his novel *Tristam Shandy*, Patsy began copying a passage that began "Time wastes too fast . . . ." When she grew too tired to continue writing, Jefferson finished the passage for her: "Every time I kiss thy hand to bid adieu, every absence which follows it, are preludes to that eternal separation we are shortly to make."

White House child

When Jefferson became president, his daughter Patsy (Mrs. Thomas Mann Randolph Jr.) was the lady of the house in the winter of 1802–3 and in 1805 and 1806. She gave birth to a son—the first child born in the White House—and named it James, in honor of family friend and Secretary of State James Madison. After his presidency ended in 1809, Jefferson retired to Monticello, where he lived happily for seventeen more years. Daughter Patsy and her family lived there as well, allowing Jefferson—now called the Sage of Monticello—to dote on his grandchildren while attending to his estate. He received many visitors there until his death in 1826. Both he and his beloved wife, Patsy, are buried at Monticello.

Where to Learn More

Anthony, Carl Sferrazza. *First Ladies: The Saga of the Presidents' Wives and Their Power, 1789–1961.* New York: William Morrow, 1990.

Bober, Natalie. *Thomas Jefferson: Man on a Mountain.* New York: Atheneum, 1988. Reprint, New York: Aladdin Paperbacks, 1997.

The Declaration of Independence

**Issued on July 4, 1776;
excerpted from *The Exhibit Hall* (Web site)**

Jefferson's justification for rebellion

The Second Continental Congress first met in May of 1775. A previous convention of delegates representing the thirteen colonies met in 1774 and sent to King George III (1738–1820) of England a list of grievances against British authority in the colonies they wanted the king to remove. By the time the Second Continental Congress met, King George had not responded, and the first battles of the American Revolution (1775–83) had occurred. The Congress, which would essentially serve as the national government from 1775 to 1788 (when it was replaced by the Constitution), established the Continental Army and a national currency.

By the summer of 1776, colonial sentiment clearly favored independence from Great Britain. England had already declared that American colonists were engaging in "open and avowed rebellion," and England had hired German mercenaries (soldiers hired to serve a foreign country) to fight in America. On June 7, 1776, Richard Henry Lee (1732–1794; see box in **Thomas Jefferson** entry in volume 1), a delegate from Virginia, proposed a resolution to the Congress: "Resolved: That these United Colonies are, and of right ought to be, free and

"We . . . do, in the Name, and by Authority of the good People of these Colonies, solemnly publish and declare, That these United Colonies are, and of Right ought to be Free and Independent States; that they are Absolved from all Allegiance to the British Crown. . . ."

From the Declaration of Independence

independent states, that they are absolved from all allegiance to the British crown."

Congress began debating whether or not to support such a resolution. A group of men—the Committee of Five, as they were called—was appointed to draft an official statement that would present to the world the case for independence on the part of the colonies. The Committee consisted of **John Adams** of Massachusetts (1735–1826; see entry in volume 1), Roger Sherman of Connecticut (1721–1793), Benjamin Franklin of Pennsylvania (1706–1790), Robert Livingston of New York (1746–1813), and **Thomas Jefferson** (1743–1826; see entry in volume 1) of Virginia. The Committee voted unanimously for Jefferson to write the statement. He showed the completed text to Adams and Franklin, who suggested only minor changes. The Committee presented the document—The Declaration of Independence—to Congress, which approved it on July 2. A few more changes were made, and then the Declaration of Independence was printed and made public on July 4, 1776.

Jefferson explained later that the purpose of the Declaration was "not to find out (express) new principles, or new arguments, never before thought of . . . but to place before mankind the common sense of the subject, in terms so plain and firm as to command their assent, and to justify ourselves in the independent stand we are compelled to take."

Things to remember while reading the Declaration of Independence:

- The Declaration of Independence can be divided into five parts: the introduction (the first paragraph), which states that the document will declare the causes that make it necessary for the colonies to break from England; the preamble (second paragraph), which presents "self-evident" (obvious to everyone) principles—when those principles are violated by a government, those violated have the right to abolish that form of government; the main body, where specific grievances against King George III are listed; a second part of the main body (the next to last paragraph), which announces that colonists have appealed in vain to the British people to stop unfair actions; and the conclusion (final paragraph), which announces that the connection of the colonies and England "is and ought to be totally dissolved."

- The introduction consists of one long sentence that presents the American cause in an historic framework—within "the course of human events"—to show its significance. The purpose of the Declaration is to declare publicly the "causes" for people to institute a new government: under those terms, revolution is not simply preferable, it is inevitable and unavoidable. In fact, it becomes necessary when alternatives for settling differences have been exhausted. The introduction distinguishes between "One people" (Americans) and "another" (the British) to reinforce the necessity of breaking "political bands" and to show that the conflict is not a civil war.

George III, king of England during the Revolutionary Era.
Painting by Benjamin West, mezzotint by E. Fisher. Courtesy of the National Archives and Records Administration.

- The preamble presents a philosophy of government where revolution is justified when "self-evident" truths ("that all men are created equal, that they are endowed by their Creator with certain unalienable Rights") are violated. The preamble progresses from the creation of humankind, to the institution of government, to the right to abolish governments that fail to protect people's unalienable rights, to creating a new government that will secure safety and happiness. The word "happiness" had a distinctive meaning to people of that period: happiness was equated with virtue, or moral goodness—people felt happy when they acted with virtue.

- The preamble ends by identifying King George for the first time as the source of injustice. Then, the main body provides proof—"To prove this, let Facts be submitted to a candid world." A candid world refers to readers who are impartial, like a jury. Twenty-seven facts are submitted as evidence. They include abuses of the king's power (1–12), examples of the king combining with "others" (England's Parliament) to enact unfair measures (13–22), and charges of violence and cruelty by the king in waging war against his American subjects (23–27). The presentation of these charges gradually changes in tone: it begins moderately and ends with more aggressive and emotional verbs ("plundered," "ravaged," "destroyed") .

- The final two paragraphs climax and conclude the Declaration. After the final charge against the king, the paragraph beginning "Nor" shifts attention to the colonists' failed appeal to their "British brethren." The final paragraph declares independence. The Declaration, which began in an impersonal tone, concludes with gusto—"we mutually pledge to each other our Lives, our Fortunes, and our sacred Honor."

The Declaration of Independence

IN CONGRESS, July 4, 1776.

The unanimous Declaration of the thirteen united States of America,

*When in the Course of human events, it becomes necessary for one people to dissolve the political bands which have connected them with another, and to assume among the powers of the earth, the separate and equal station to which the **Laws of Nature** and of Nature's God entitle them, a decent respect to the opinions of mankind requires that they should declare the causes which impel them to the separation.*

*We hold these truths to be **self-evident**, that all men are created equal, that they are endowed by their Creator with certain **unalienable** Rights, that among these are Life, Liberty and the pursuit of Happiness.—That to secure these rights, Governments are instituted among Men, deriving their just powers from the consent of the governed, —That whenever any Form of Government becomes destructive of these ends, it is the Right of the People to alter or to abolish it, and to institute new Government, laying its foundation on such prin-*

Laws of Nature: What exists outside of human influence (gravity, for instance). Jefferson viewed his famous "all men are created equal" philosophy as a law of nature.

Self-evident: Obvious to all.

Unalienable: That which cannot be taken away.

ciples and organizing its powers in such form, as to them shall seem most likely to effect their Safety and Happiness. **Prudence,** indeed, will dictate that Governments long established should not be changed for light and **transient** causes; and accordingly all experience hath **shewn,** that mankind are more disposed to suffer, while evils are sufferable, than to right themselves by abolishing the forms to which they are accustomed. But when a long train of abuses and **usurpations,** pursuing invariably the same Object evinces a design to reduce them under absolute **Despotism,** it is their right, it is their duty, to throw off such Government, and to provide new Guards for their future security.—Such has been the patient sufferance of these Colonies; and such is now the necessity which constrains them to alter their former Systems of Government. The history of the present King of Great Britain is a history of repeated injuries and usurpations, all having in direct object the establishment of an absolute Tyranny over these States. To prove this, let Facts be submitted to a candid world.

He has refused his Assent to Laws, the most wholesome and necessary for the public good.

He has forbidden his Governors to pass Laws of immediate and pressing importance, unless suspended in their operation till his Assent should be obtained; and when so suspended, he has utterly neglected to attend to them.

He has refused to pass other Laws for the accommodation of large districts of people, unless those people would relinquish the right of Representation in the Legislature, a right inestimable to them and formidable to tyrants only.

He has called together legislative bodies at places unusual, uncomfortable, and distant from the **depository** of their public Records, for the sole purpose of fatiguing them into compliance with his measures.

He has dissolved Representative Houses repeatedly, for opposing with manly firmness his invasions on the rights of the people.

He has refused for a long time, after such dissolutions, to cause others to be elected; whereby the Legislative powers, incapable of **Annihilation,** have returned to the People at large for their exercise; the State remaining in the mean time exposed to all the dangers of invasion from without, and convulsions within.

He has endeavoured to prevent the population of these States; for that purpose obstructing the Laws for **Naturalization** of Foreign-

Prudence: Wisdom.

Transient: Temporary.

Shewn: Shown.

Usurpations: Illegal acts against authority.

Despotism: Tyranny; ruling with unlimited power.

Depository: Storage place.

Annihilation: Utter destruction.

Naturalization: The process of becoming a citizen.

ers; refusing to pass others to encourage their migrations hither, and raising the conditions of new Appropriations of Lands.

He has obstructed the Administration of Justice, by refusing his Assent to Laws for establishing Judiciary powers.

He has made Judges dependent on his Will alone, for the tenure of their offices, and the amount and payment of their salaries.

He has erected a multitude of New Offices, and sent hither swarms of Officers to harrass our people, and eat out their **substance.**

He has kept among us, in times of peace, Standing Armies without the Consent of our legislatures.

He has affected to render the Military independent of and superior to the Civil power.

He has combined with others to subject us to a jurisdiction foreign to our constitution, and unacknowledged by our laws; giving his Assent to their Acts of pretended Legislation:

For Quartering large bodies of armed troops among us:

For protecting them, by a mock Trial, from punishment for any Murders which they should commit on the Inhabitants of these States:

For cutting off our Trade with all parts of the world:

For imposing Taxes on us without our Consent:

For depriving us in many cases, of the benefits of Trial by Jury:

For transporting us beyond Seas to be tried for pretended offences

For abolishing the free System of English Laws in a neighbouring Province, establishing therein an Arbitrary government, and enlarging its Boundaries so as to render it at once an example and fit instrument for introducing the same absolute rule into these Colonies:

For taking away our Charters, abolishing our most valuable Laws, and altering fundamentally the Forms of our Governments:

For suspending our own Legislatures, and declaring themselves invested with power to legislate for us in all cases whatsoever.

He has abdicated Government here, by declaring us out of his Protection and waging War against us.

Substance: Essence.

He has plundered our seas, ravaged our Coasts, burnt our towns, and destroyed the lives of our people.

He is at this time transporting large Armies of foreign **Mercenaries** to compleat the works of death, desolation and tyranny, already begun with circumstances of Cruelty & **perfidy** scarcely paralleled in the most barbarous ages, and totally unworthy the Head of a civilized nation.

He has constrained our fellow Citizens taken Captive on the high Seas to bear Arms against their Country, to become the executioners of their friends and Brethren, or to fall themselves by their Hands.

He has excited **domestic insurrections** amongst us, and has endeavoured to bring on the inhabitants of our frontiers, the merciless Indian Savages, whose known rule of warfare, is an undistinguished destruction of all ages, sexes and conditions.

In every stage of these Oppressions We have Petitioned for **Redress** in the most humble terms: Our repeated Petitions have been answered only by repeated injury. A Prince whose character is thus marked by every act which may define a Tyrant, is unfit to be the ruler of a free people.

Nor have We been wanting in attentions to our British brethren. We have warned them from time to time of attempts by their legislature to extend an **unwarrantable** jurisdiction over us. We have reminded them of the circumstances of our emigration and settlement here. We have appealed to their native justice and **magnanimity**, and we have conjured them by the ties of our common kindred to disavow these usurpations, which, would inevitably interrupt our connections and correspondence. They too have been deaf to the voice of justice and of **consanguinity**. We must, therefore, acquiesce in the necessity, which denounces our Separation, and hold them, as we hold the rest of mankind, Enemies in War, in Peace Friends.

We, therefore, the Representatives of the united States of America, in General Congress, Assembled, appealing to the Supreme Judge of the world for the **rectitude** of our intentions, do, in the Name, and by Authority of the good People of these Colonies, solemnly publish and declare, That these United Colonies are, and of Right ought to be Free and Independent States; that they are Absolved from all Allegiance to the British Crown, and that all political connection between them and the State of Great Britain, is and ought to be totally dissolved; and that as Free and Independent

Mercenaries: Hired soldiers with no natural allegiance.

Perfidy: Treacherousness and cruelty.

Domestic insurrections: Riots.

Redress: Removal.

Unwarrantable: Unreasonable, unjustified.

Magnanimity: Generosity.

Consanguinity: Of the same origin; related by blood.

Rectitude: Moral integrity.

States, they have full Power to levy War, conclude Peace, contract Alliances, establish Commerce, and to do all other Acts and Things which Independent States may of right do. And for the support of this Declaration, with a firm reliance on the protection of divine Providence, we mutually pledge to each other our Lives, our Fortunes and our sacred Honor.

[The Declaration of Independence was signed by fifty-six representatives of the thirteen colonies. In alphabetical order by state, they were:

Connecticut: Samuel Huntington, Roger Sherman, William Williams, and Oliver Wolcott; Delaware: Thomas McKean, George Read, and Caesar Rodney; Georgia: Button Gwinnett, Lyman Hall, and George Walton; Maryland: Charles Carroll, Samuel Chase, William Paca, and Thomas Stone; Massachusetts: John Adams, Samuel Adams, Elbridge Gerry, John Hancock, and Robert Treat Paine; New Hampshire: Josiah Bartlett, Matthew Thornton, and William Whipple; New Jersey: Abraham Clark, John Hart, Francis Hopkinson, Richard Stockton, and John Witherspoon; New York: William Floyd, Francis Lewis, Philip Livingston, and Lewis Morris; North Carolina: Joseph Hewes, William Hooper, and John Penn; Pennsylvania: George Clymer, Benjamin Franklin, Robert Morris, John Morton, George Ross, Benjamin Rush, James Smith, George Taylor, and James Wilson; Rhode Island: William Ellery and Stephen Hopkins; South Carolina: Thomas Heyward Jr., Thomas Lynch Jr., Arthur Middleton, and Edward Rutledge; and Virginia: Carter Braxton, Benjamin Harrison, Thomas Jefferson, Francis Lightfoot Lee, Richard Henry Lee, Thomas Nelson Jr., and George Wythe. (*The Exhibit Hall* [Web site])

What happened next . . .

Church bells rang throughout Philadelphia, Pennsylvania, on the afternoon of July 4, 1776, to signal that the Declaration of Independence had been ratified by the Continental Congress. Copies were published the following day for distribution, while the actual original document remained with the Congress. The Declaration was cheered throughout

the colonies, where the Revolutionary War had been going on for over a year.

Many of the charges against King George were challenged or refuted by John Lind, acting on behalf of the English government. He wrote a 118-page response to the one-page Declaration. Nevertheless, the Declaration of Independence was regarded then, as it is now, as a well-reasoned and impassioned expression of liberty and the right to overthrow tyranny.

The Declaration of Independence Committee (left to right): Thomas Jefferson, Roger Sherman, Benjamin Franklin, Robert R. Livingston, and John Adams. *Courtesy of the Library of Congress.*

Did you know . . .

Fifty-eight members of the Continental Congress signed the Declaration of Independence, but the July 4 printing only included the names of Congress president John Hancock (1737–1793) and Congress secretary Charles Tomlinson. Others were omitted to protect them from possible reprisals by the British. In January of 1777, the original document was in Baltimore, Maryland, with the Congress, which had relocated there from Philadelphia to avoid British attack. On January 18, 1777, prints were made from the original document and featured all of the fifty-eight signatures. By then, the Continental Army was fighting well enough to foster hope that the British could be defeated.

Where to Learn More

Bober, Natalie. *Thomas Jefferson: Man on a Mountain.* New York: Atheneum, 1988. Reprint, Aladdin Paperbacks, 1997.

Bruns, Roger, ed. *Thomas Jefferson.* New York: Chelsea House, 1986.

"Declaration of Independence." Surfing the Net with Kids. [Online] http://surfnetkids.com/declaration.htm (accessed on June 8, 2000).

Meltzer, Milton. *Thomas Jefferson: The Revolutionary Aristocrat.* New York: Franklin Watts, 1991.

Morse, John T., Jr. *Thomas Jefferson* (American Statesmen Series, Vol. 11). New York: Chelsea House, 1997.

Nardo, Don. *The Importance of Thomas Jefferson.* San Diego: Lucent Books, 1993.

National Archives and Records Administration. "The Declaration of Independence." *The Exhibit Hall.* [Online] http://www.nara.gov/exhall/charters/declaration/decmain.html (accessed on June 22, 2000).

Rayner, B. L. *Life of Thomas Jefferson.* Revised and edited by Eyler Robert Coates Sr. [Online] http://www.geocities.com/Athens/Forum/1683/ljindex.htm (accessed on June 23, 2000).

Jefferson's Opinion on the Constitutionality of a National Bank

Issued in 1791; excerpted from *The Avalon Project* (Web site)

An American statesman argues against powers being assumed by the federal government

A major issue that has been a frequent source of debate in the United States is the extent of power the federal government should wield. The failure of the central government created under the Articles of Confederation (see **George Washington** primary source entry in volume 1) led to the Constitutional Convention of 1787. Even after the Constitution was completed, a year passed before the two-thirds majority of states (nine of thirteen) approved the document that formed the United States.

Many noted American statesmen, including future presidents **Thomas Jefferson** (1743–1826; see entry in volume 1) and **James Monroe** (1758–1831; see entry in volume 1), were concerned that the federal government outlined in the Constitution could overwhelm the power of individual states. They were joined by another future president, **James Madison** (1751–1836; see entry in volume 1), who was later called "the Father of the Constitution" for his contributions to the document and its ratification. Together, they formed a group known as anti-Federalists. Their views were countered by Federalists, including **George Washington** (1732–1799; see entry in volume 1) and Alexander Hamilton (see box in

"The incorporation of a bank, and the powers assumed by this bill, have not, in my opinion, been delegated to the United States, by the Constitution."

Thomas Jefferson

George Washington entry in volume 1), who believed the federal government needed to have certain broad powers above those of states in order to be effective.

Jefferson and Madison opposed several actions by the Washington administration that enhanced the power of the federal government. Among those was the proposal for a national bank. As presented by Hamilton, Washington's secretary of the treasury, the national bank would store government funds, help collect taxes, and regulate currency. Madison, a representative from Virginia, opposed the national bank bill in Congress, arguing that it was unconstitutional. He was joined by Jefferson, Washington's secretary of state. Jefferson wrote his Opinion on the Constitutionality of a National Bank in 1791.

Things to remember while reading an excerpt from Jefferson's Opinion on the Constitutionality of a National Bank:

- Jefferson was a Constitutional constructionist—a term that describes an American politician who believes the federal government can only act in a manner specifically defined by the Constitution. Jefferson drew on his constructionist principles and concern for the rights of states in the first paragraph of the excerpt to argue that a national bank is unconstitutional. Jefferson quoted the tenth amendment to the Constitution to base his argument that since the bank's powers were not specifically authorized by the Constitution, those powers belonged to the states.

- In addition to the broad question of whether the Constitution allows for the creation of a national bank, Jefferson debated particular items in the bank bill. At the time he published this essay, the bank bill was being debated in Congress. In point #3 of section I of his essay, Jefferson challenged the idea that a national bank should be established with the power to regulate commerce. Jefferson noted that creating a bank and regulating commerce are different things. "To make a thing which may be bought or sold," he stated, "is not to prescribe regulations for buying and selling."

- Jefferson's constructionist principles were evidenced in his argument in point #1 of section II. Jefferson believed the Constitution listed the only areas of authority for the federal government. For example, he stated that the Constitution "laced" (tied down) Congress with few specific powers, and Congress was not to decide issues outside of its powers. To do so, Jefferson continued, would mean that Congress could address any issue under the pretense that it was debating what was good for the people.

- The debate over the national bank brought to the forefront a major issue concerning the Constitution: is it meant to be taken literally, as constructionists believed, or is it open to interpretation and meant to serve as a guide? That debate has enriched the United States, even as the Constitution continues to firmly guide the nation.

Jefferson's Opinion on the Constitutionality of a National Bank

I consider the foundation of the Constitution as laid on this ground: That "all powers not delegated to the United States, by the Constitution, nor prohibited by it to the States, are reserved to the States or to the people." To take a single step beyond the boundaries thus specially drawn around the powers of Congress, is to take possession of a boundless field of power, no longer susceptible of any definition.

The incorporation of a bank, and the powers assumed by this bill, have not, in my opinion, been delegated to the United States, by the Constitution.

*I. They are not among the powers specially **enumerated**: for these are:*

1. A power to lay taxes for the purpose of paying the debts of the United States; but no debt is paid by this bill, nor any tax laid. Were it a bill to raise money, its origination in the Senate would condemn it by the Constitution.

*2. "To borrow money." But this bill neither borrows money nor ensures the borrowing of it. The **proprietors** of the bank will be just*

Enumerated: Listed consecutively.

Proprietors: Owners and operators.

as free as any other money holders, to lend or not to lend their money to the public. The operation proposed in the bill first, to lend them two millions, and then to borrow them back again, cannot change the nature of the latter act, which will still be a payment, and not a loan, call it by what name you please.

3. To "regulate commerce with foreign nations, and among the States, and with the Indian tribes." To erect a bank, and to regulate commerce, are very different acts. He who erects a bank, creates a subject of commerce in its bills, so does he who makes a bushel of wheat, or digs a dollar out of the mines; yet neither of these persons regulates commerce thereby. To make a thing which may be bought and sold, is not to prescribe regulations for buying and selling. Besides, if this was an exercise of the power of regulating commerce, it would be void, as extending as much to the internal commerce of every State, as to its external. For the power given to Congress by the Constitution does not extend to the internal regulation of the commerce of a State, (that is to say of the commerce between citizen and citizen,) which remain exclusively with its own legislature; but to its external commerce only, that is to say, its commerce with another State, or with foreign nations, or with the Indian tribes. Accordingly the bill does not propose the measure as a regulation of trade, but as "of considerable advantages to trade." Still less are these powers covered by any other of the special enumerations.

II. Nor are they within either of the general phrases, which are the two following:

*1. To lay taxes to provide for the general welfare of the United States, that is to say, "to lay taxes for the purpose of providing for the general welfare." For the laying of taxes is the power, and the general welfare the purpose for which the power is to be exercised. They are not to lay taxes **ad libitum** for any purpose they please; but only to pay the debts or provide for the welfare of the Union. In like manner, they are not to do anything they please to provide for the general welfare, but only to lay taxes for that purpose. To consider the latter phrase, not as describing the purpose of the first, but as giving a distinct and independent power to do any act they please, which might be for the good of the Union, would render all the preceding and subsequent enumerations of power completely useless.*

It would reduce the whole instrument to a single phrase, that of instituting a Congress with power to do whatever would be for the good of the United States; and, as they would be the sole judges of the good or evil, it would be also a power to do whatever evil they please.

Ad libitum: Freedom to act or not act, as opposed to being obligated.

Complete American Presidents Sourcebook

*It is an established rule of construction where a phrase will bear either of two meanings, to give it that which will allow some meaning to the other parts of the instrument, and not that which would render all the others useless. Certainly no such universal power was meant to be given them. It was intended to lace them up straitly within the enumerated powers, and those without which, as means, these powers could not be carried into effect. It is known that the very power now proposed as a means was rejected as an end by the Convention which formed the Constitution. A proposition was made to them to authorize Congress to open canals, and an **amendatory** one to empower them to incorporate. But the whole was rejected, and one of the reasons for rejection urged in debate was, that then they would have a power to erect a bank, which would render the great cities, where there were prejudices and jealousies on the subject, **adverse** to the reception of the Constitution.*

2. The second general phrase is, "to make all laws necessary and proper for carrying into execution the enumerated powers." But they can all be carried into execution without a bank. A bank therefore is not necessary, and consequently not authorized by this phrase.

*It has been urged that a bank will give great facility or convenience in the collection of taxes, Suppose this were true: yet the Constitution allows only the means which are "necessary," not those which are merely "convenient" for effecting the enumerated powers. If such a latitude of construction be allowed to this phrase as to give any non-enumerated power, it will go to everyone, for there is not one which ingenuity may not torture into a convenience in some instance or other, to some one of so long a list of enumerated powers. It would swallow up all the delegated powers, and reduce the whole to one power, as before observed. Therefore it was that the Constitution restrained them to the necessary means, that is to say, to those means without which the grant of power would be **nugatory**. . . .*

It may be said that a bank whose bills would have a currency all over the States, would be more convenient than one whose currency is limited to a single State. So it would be still more convenient that there should be a bank, whose bills should have a currency all over the world. But it does not follow from this superior conveniency, that there exists anywhere a power to establish such a bank; or that the world may not go on very well without it.

Can it be thought that the Constitution intended that for a shade or two of convenience, more or less, Congress should be au-

Amendatory: Additional.

Adverse: Having a negative effect.

Nugatory: Of little or no consequence.

thorized to break down the most ancient and fundamental laws of the several States; such as those against **Mortmain**, the laws of **Alienage**, the rules of descent, the acts of distribution, the laws of **escheat and forfeiture**, the laws of **monopoly?** Nothing but a necessity invincible by any other means, can justify such a prostitution of laws, which constitute the pillars of our whole system of jurisprudence. Will Congress be too strait-laced to carry the Constitution into honest effect, unless they may pass over the foundation-laws of the State government for the slightest convenience of theirs?

The **negative of the President** is the shield provided by the Constitution to protect against the invasions of the legislature: 1. The right of the Executive. 2. Of the Judiciary. 3. Of the States and State legislatures. The present is the case of a right remaining exclusively with the States, and consequently one of those intended by the Constitution to be placed under its protection, It must be added, however, that unless the President's mind on a view of everything which is urged for and against this bill, is tolerably clear that it is unauthorized by the Constitution; if the pro and the con hang so even as to balance his judgment, a just respect for the wisdom of the legislature would naturally decide the balance in favor of their opinion. It is chiefly for cases where they are clearly misled by error, ambition, or interest, that the Constitution has placed a check in the negative of the President. (The Avalon Project [Web site])

What happened next . . .

The bank bill passed Congress and was signed into law by President Washington on February 25, 1791. The concerns of Jefferson and Madison were weighed by Washington. However, Washington finally sided with Hamilton, who wrote an essay, "Defense of the Constitutionality of the Bank," in which he argued that an economic collapse would occur without such a bank. Hamilton further stated that the Constitution provided for "implied powers"—those not specifically listed, but which the government can deem necessary. Washington was concerned that the new government might be too weak, similar to the one established by the Articles of Confederation.

Mortmain: Property or gifts given to an organization for perpetuity.

Alienage: The status of an alien.

Escheat and forfeiture: The return of lands to a state when there are no heirs to the property owner.

Monopoly: An organization that enjoys complete control over a business sector.

Negative of the President: The power of veto.

Complete American Presidents Sourcebook

Debate over the bank bill crystallized opposing factions—Federalists and anti-Federalists—into political parties. Lively debate between the two occurred throughout the 1790s. With the election of Jefferson to the presidency in 1800, Federalists began losing power and virtually disappeared by 1820. Jefferson's constructionist principles were put to the test during his own presidency, and he proved to have a more flexible view of the Constitution during his presidency than he had previously.

The question of the constitutionality of the national bank was not over after it was established in 1791. A revised national bank (the Second National Bank) was created in 1816 and chartered for twenty years. In 1832, President **Andrew Jackson** (1767–1845; see entry in volume 1) vetoed a bill that would recharter the Second National Bank, creating a whole new debate over the national bank issue (see **Andrew Jackson** primary source entry in volume 1).

Did you know . . .

- The Bank of the United States was chartered (approved) for twenty years by the federal government and established in Philadelphia in 1791. The bank was authorized to issue as legal tender bank notes exchangeable for gold. The bank's charter was not renewed in 1811, but the Second Bank of the United States was in 1816. It served well, but President Andrew Jackson vetoed the charter renewal in 1832. Despite being successful, the national bank continued to be opposed by those believing it impinged upon states' rights.

- The Independent Treasury System, a network of government offices, was established in 1846. The system proved inadequate during the Civil War (1861–65) and the tremendous economic growth of the second half of the nineteenth century. Numerous banking acts addressed problems until the Federal Reserve Act (1913) created a new centralized reserve (savings) system. That system was still in place at the turn of the century, although it was amended several times to address banking problems during the twentieth century.

Where to Learn More

Bowers, Claude G. *Jefferson and Hamilton: The Struggle for Democracy in America.* New York: Houghton-Mifflin, 1925. Reprint, 1972.

Knox, John Jay. *A History of Banking in the United States.* New York: B. Rhodes, 1900. Reprint, New York: A. M. Kelley, 1969.

Taus, Esther Rogoff. *Central Banking Functions of the United States Treasury, 1789–1941.* New York: Columbia University Press, 1943. Reprint, New York: Russell & Russell, 1967.

Yale Law School. "Jefferson's Opinion on the Constitutionality of a National Bank, 1791." *The Avalon Project.* [Online] http://www.yale.edu/lawweb/avalon/amerdoc/bank-tj.htm (accessed on June 22, 2000).

James Madison

Fourth president (1809–1817)

James Madison

Born March 16, 1751
Port Conway, Virginia
Died June 28, 1836
Montpelier, Virginia

Fourth president of the United States (1809–1817)

Led the United States in its first war in defense of the national interest against Great Britain—the War of 1812

James Madison is remembered as "the Father of the Constitution." He helped arrange the convention of 1787 at which the Constitution was written. He was a leading promoter and defender of the document during the ratification process, when it had to be formally approved by nine of the thirteen states in order to go into effect. He championed the first ten amendments that form the Bill of Rights (see **James Madison** primary source entry in volume 1).

Madison's efforts with the Constitution reflected his particular strengths. Skillful in debate and level-headed, he was able to balance ideals and realities, conviction and compromise. Standing just five feet, four inches tall and weighing around 100 pounds, he was the smallest of all U.S. presidents. Small in stature but large in character, he helped find practical ways to establish a republican form of government that represented the will of the people and could improve on its own imperfections. In a republican government, supreme power resides with citizens who elect their leaders and have the power to change their leaders.

"Every word of the Constitution decides a question between power and liberty."

James Madison

James Madison.
Portrait by Stuart Gilbert. Courtesy of the National Archives and Records Administration.

145

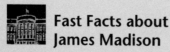

Fast Facts about James Madison

Full name: James Madison

Born: March 16, 1751

Died: June 28, 1836

Burial site: Family cemetery, Montpelier, Virginia

Parents: James and Eleanor Rose Conway Madison

Spouse: Dolley Dandridge Payne Todd (1768–1849; m. 1794)

Children: None

Religion: Episcopalian

Education: College of New Jersey (now Princeton University; B.A., 1771)

Occupations: Politician; farmer

Government positions: Virginia Constitutional Convention member; Continental congressman; Virginia state delegate; U.S. Constitutional Convention member; U.S. representative from Virginia; secretary of state under Thomas Jefferson

Political party: Democratic-Republican

Dates as president: March 4, 1809–March 4, 1813 (first term); March 4, 1813–March 4, 1817 (second term)

Age upon taking office: 57

Madison was elected president in 1808 during troubling times. Great Britain and France were at war. Neither side respected America's shipping rights. Both sides ignored the young nation's attempts to assert its rights through diplomacy. Madison steered the nation into the War of 1812 (1812–15) with Great Britain, a conflict for which the nation was ill prepared. The war ended without victory for either side. American spirits were bolstered, however, by having simply survived the war. Additionally, land and naval victories in the Great Lakes region secured the frontier area north of the Ohio River and west to the Mississippi River for settlement. When Madison left office, the United States was emerging as an equal among the most powerful nations.

Political and other fevers

James Madison was born on March 16, 1751, in the home of his maternal grandparents (the grandparents on his mother's side of the family) along the Rappahannock River in Port Conway, Virginia. Madison was taken home to a five-thousand-acre estate called Montpelier, where he grew up and which he eventually inherited. Madison's father, also named James, was a tobacco grower.

Madison was schooled primarily at home and prepared to attend college. He studied history, government, and law at the College of New Jersey (later Princeton University), graduating in 1771. At the time, American colonists were growing increasingly rebellious against British rule. Madison remained awhile in New Jersey, trying to decide between a career as a clergyman or as a lawyer. Meanwhile, he caught political fever during meetings with a local group that debated issues of the day, like the future course of America.

Six months after graduation, Madison returned to Montpelier in ill health and spent over a year recuperating. Historians generally agree that as a young man Madison was a hypochondriac—a person who claims repeated illnesses but shows few real physical symptoms. He spent much of his recuperation period reading and forming ideas for a republican form of government. By 1774, Madison was feeling better and was determined to participate in pro-independence movements in the colonies. As the people's rebelliousness grew, he was appointed to the Committee of Safety, a local Virginia defense group.

In 1776, Madison was a member of the Virginia Convention. This assembly formed the state's constitution. He worked to promote religious freedom with another Virginia delegate, **Thomas Jefferson** (1743–1826; see entry in volume 1). Jefferson had recently returned from Philadelphia, Pennsylvania, where he had authored the Declaration of Independence (see **Thomas Jefferson** primary source entry in volume 1). Madison then served on the state executive council from 1777 to 1778 under Virginia governor Patrick Henry (1736–1799; see box in **Thomas Jefferson** entry in volume 1). In 1779, Madison was elected to the Continental Congress. At age twenty-nine, he was the youngest congressman.

Reserved at first, Madison gradually began to participate in the proceedings. He became an effective debater and legislator. Like fellow Virginian **George Washington**

 James Madison Timeline

1751: Born in Virginia

1771: Graduates from the College of New Jersey (now Princeton University)

1776: Serves as member of Virginia Constitutional Convention

1780–83: Serves as member of Continental Congress

1787: Serves as member of Constitutional Convention

1789–97: Serves in U.S. House of Representatives

1801–9: Serves as secretary of state under Thomas Jefferson

1809–17: Serves as fourth U.S. president

1812: War of 1812 begins

1814: Washington, D.C., captured and burned by British; Francis Scott Key writes "The Star-Spangled Banner"

1836: Dies in Virginia

Words to Know

Alien and Sedition Acts: Four bills—the Naturalization Act, Alien Act, Alien Enemies Act, and Sedition Act—passed by Congress in 1798 and signed into law by President John Adams. The Naturalization act extended from five to fourteen years the waiting period before citizenship—and with it, the right to vote—could be obtained by new immigrants. The two Alien Acts gave the president the right to deport or jail foreign citizens he deemed a threat to the nation's stability, especially during wartime. The Sedition Act criminalized criticism of the government. To write or publish views that disparaged the Administration was punishable by harsh fines and jail terms.

Anti-Federalists: A group who wanted a limited federal government and more power for individual states.

Articles of Confederation: From March 1, 1781, to June 21, 1788, the Articles served as the equivalent of the Constitution (1787). The Constitution replaced the Articles, which had failed to produce a strong central government. Thus was formed the present-day United States.

Checks and balances: In the American system of government, the three branches have powers to evaluate and approve or deny an action taken by another branch. For example, a president can veto legislation passed by Congress.

Confederacies: A group of persons, states, or nations that form an alliance.

Democratic-Republicans: Supporters of a political party in the United States led by Thomas Jefferson and James Madison in the 1790s to oppose the Federalist Party and close ties with Great Britain. Also called the Republican Party and the Jeffersonian Republican Party at the time, but the term Democratic-Republican

(1732–1799; see entry in volume 1), who was then commanding the Continental Army, Madison consistently argued for a stronger central government than that established by the Articles of Confederation (the equivalent of a constitution from 1781 to 1788).

Madison returned to Montpelier in 1783. He was feeling sad after his engagement to a young woman was broken off. He emerged again in 1784, however, when he was elected to the Virginia legislature. During his tenure (time in office), he pushed through Jefferson's Act for Establishing Religious Freedom in 1786. When commerce issues arose between the

helps distinguish that early political group from the Democratic and Republican parties that were formed later. The Democratic-Republican Party dissolved in the 1820s. Many former members began supporting the formation of the Democratic party led by Andrew Jackson, who was elected president in 1828 and 1832. The modern-day Republican Party was formed in 1854.

Federalist: A proponent for a strong national (federal) government.

Impression: The seizure by a government of individuals or goods for military service. Beginning in 1790, thousands of British sailors joined the U.S. Merchant Marine (the U.S. ships involved in commerce). Many became American citizens. The United States was the only country at the time to recognize change of citizenship as a legal right. Britain certainly did not. British ships frequently stopped American ships and took crew members.

Louisiana Purchase: A vast region in North America purchased by the United States from France in 1803 for $15 million.

Nullification: Negation. The Theory of Nullification was proposed by John C. Calhoun, a South Carolina congressman who later served as vice president to Andrew Jackson. In Calhoun's theory, a state has the right to nullify federal laws that it deems harmful to the state's interests.

Republican: A form of government in which supreme power resides with citizens who elect their leaders and have the power to change their leaders.

Tariff: A tax a nation places on imported goods to increase their price.

War hawks: Those who support the use of military force to carry out foreign policy.

states of Virginia and Maryland, Madison helped arrange a meeting and invited representatives from all the states. Only five states sent delegates to that convention held in Annapolis, Maryland, in September 1786, but they discovered many areas of mutual concern and cooperation. Alexander Hamilton (1755–1804; see box in **George Washington** entry in volume 1) of New York was there. He and Madison became powerful allies for a time before they parted as leaders of opposing political parties. A second convention was scheduled for the following May in Philadelphia. Madison's long-held desire to strengthen the central government in the Articles of Confederation was on the agenda.

Father of the Constitution

Madison arrived early for the convention and was well prepared. He had researched and written a paper on ancient and modern confederacies (groups of people, states, or nations that form an alliance). He had prepared another paper detailing his observations on the strengths and weaknesses of the Articles of Confederation. He immediately introduced resolutions calling for a new central American government that would have stronger powers. His plans included an elected executive (chief administrative official) who had veto power over legislation, a federal judiciary branch (system of courts and justice), and a bicameral (two-chamber) legislature (the body of persons elected to decide on the laws of the nation). The various branches of government would have specific responsibilities, but they would also have the ability to take part in checks and balances with each other (that is, approve or disapprove actions taken by another branch). All these ideas, which had been proposed and favored by several Americans for some time, were adopted into the Constitution, which replaced the Articles of Confederation.

Madison's Virginia Plan for a bicameral legislature called for a House of Representatives and a Senate. In the House, the number of representatives from each state was determined by a state's population. The Senate would be elected by the House of Representatives. Smaller states supported yet another approach, the New Jersey Plan. This plan proposed that each state would have equal representation in a unicameral (single) legislature. After much debate, a compromise—called the Connecticut Plan—was reached. The House of Representatives was established under the Virginia Plan model. The U.S. Senate would have equal representation for all states.

Madison attended every session of the convention and was present at every major debate, speech, and vote. While fighting for his views, he was tactful and reasonable. Madison's notes on the gathering were collected and published in 1840 as *Journal of the Federal Convention*.

The United States begins

In order for the Constitution to have legal authority, at least nine of the thirteen states had to ratify it. Madison

George Mason

Born in Fairfax County, Virginia, in 1725, George Mason was the son of a wealthy planter who died when Mason was nine years old. Mason was privately educated. Inheriting several large estates along the Potomac River, he became a friend and neighbor of George Washington. Mason married Ann Eilbeck in 1750. He became a county justice and was elected to the Virginia House of Burgesses in 1759. In 1773, his wife died, leaving him with nine children. He never aspired for high public office, but he proved influential in pursuing ideals that form the basis of American government.

Mason served at the Virginia Convention (July 1775), where the colony prepared for armed struggle with Great Britain. At Virginia's constitutional convention in 1776, he introduced the Virginia Declaration of Rights, which protects individual liberties and was a forerunner to the Bill of Rights in the Constitution. Mason's drafts of the Declaration of Rights and the constitution emerged as models for other colonies. Mason was a force for religious tolerance, helping make Virginia an attractive destination for immigrants of various faiths. An expert in land laws, he outlined a plan in 1780 that was later used to form the Northwest Territory as settlers moved into present-day Ohio, Indiana, and Michigan.

George Mason.
Reproduced by permission of Archive Photos.

Mason was a delegate to the 1787 Constitutional Convention in Philadelphia, Pennsylvania. He was unhappy with the extent of federal power outlined by the Constitution, its failure to limit slavery, and the lack of a bill of rights. On those grounds, he opposed its ratification. After the Bill of Rights was adopted in 1791, Mason conceded that with a few more alterations "I could chearfully put my hand and heart to the new government." He died at his Virginia plantation home, Gunston Hall, on October 7, 1792.

worked tirelessly for passage. With Hamilton and U.S. secretary of foreign affairs John Jay (1745–1829; see box in **George Washington** entry in volume 1), Madison published a series of essays called *The Federalist Papers*. In this work, issues concerning the Constitution were carefully explained and criticisms were countered. In all, eighty-five *Federalist* papers were issued under the pseudonyms "A Citizen of New York" or "Publius." Madison is generally credited with having written twenty-six of them. He consistently argued for the federal government plan and stated that government in a democratic society can allow for conflicting views.

Meanwhile, Virginia's convention to ratify the Constitution proved challenging. Madison found himself debating against Patrick Henry, **James Monroe** (1758–1831; see entry in volume 1), and George Mason (1725–1792; see box). All felt that individual states would be dominated by the new national government and that individual rights were not guaranteed in the document. Madison convinced enough delegates otherwise. The Constitution was ratified (formally approved) in Virginia by a slim margin—89 votes to 79. Addressing concerns about federal power, Madison pointed out that a national government would be a more forceful power for negotiating treaties than would individual states.

Elected to the U.S. House of Representatives in 1788, Madison became one of the first great legislators of that body. He was instrumental in passage of the Bill of Rights—the first ten amendments to the Constitution. (See **James Madison** primary source entry in volume 1.) While serving in Congress, Madison worked closely with the nation's first president, George Washington, to help establish Cabinet posts.

But Madison was soon at odds with the Washington administration, particularly with Alexander Hamilton, Washington's secretary of the treasury. In 1790, Hamilton proposed financial plans for the federal government that favored commercial development and a national banking system, policies generally more favorable to northern states. Madison, like Jefferson, wanted a government that supported self-reliant farmers and artisans—people who produced products over those engaged in banking and selling. Additionally, Hamilton's plan called for the federal government to assume all state debts, which would require

taxes to collect the revenue needed to pay that debt. Madison represented Virginia, a large and prosperous state that had no debts.

Montpelier, the five-thousand-acre estate of James Madison.
Reproduced by permission of Kathleen Marcaccio.

With Washington's backing, Hamilton's Federalist plan (called that because it emphasized a strong federal government) passed through Congress. By election time in 1792, Madison had aligned with Thomas Jefferson against the administration. The Madison-Jefferson faction became known as Anti-Federalists. The split widened when Great Britain and France went to war in 1793. Federalists favored keeping ties with Great Britain to maintain high trade revenue (income from taxes). Anti-Federalists favored France. The United States had an alliance with that nation dating back to the Revolutionary War (1775–83). France had also adopted a more republican form of government. Again, the Federalists—in the form of **John Adams** (1735–1826; see entry in volume 1)— won the presidential election of 1796. Dismayed at the emphasis on commercial development, Madison continued to fight, but he retired from Congress in 1797.

Resurgence

Madison was not despairing during those disappointing times. His personal life had changed significantly. In 1794, at age forty-three, he married Dolley Payne Todd (1768–1849; see entry on **Dolley Madison** in volume 1), a vivacious (lively) twenty-six-year-old widow. They had had a passing acquaintance through social circles in Philadelphia, then the seat of the U.S. government. After becoming favorites of the Philadelphia social circle, the Madisons moved to Montpelier in 1797 and enjoyed an extremely happy domestic life.

Madison farmed and kept politically active. He jumped back into an important political role following the 1798 passage of the Alien and Sedition Acts (see box in **John Adams** entry in volume 1). Among other things, the acts limited freedom of the press. Working through the Virginia legislature, Madison sponsored the Virginia Resolution. A similar resolution was passed by the Kentucky legislature through the efforts of Vice President Jefferson. The resolutions, which insisted that states have the right to protest unconstitutional federal laws, were more significant as ideals than as results. Still, they helped to solidify anti-Federalist support that turned the Democratic-Republican party led by Jefferson into the nation's most powerful political group. When Jefferson was elected president over Adams in 1800, he appointed his longtime friend and ally Madison to the post of secretary of state.

The Virginia dynasty

As Jefferson's closest advisor, Madison supported and shared in the president's first-term successes—the Louisiana Purchase, a huge area of land purchased from France for $15 million (see **Thomas Jefferson** entry in volume 1 for more information), and victory at sea over Barbary pirates (see box in **George Washington** entry in volume 1), who controlled trade routes in parts of the Mediterranean Sea and who demanded payments from ships using those routes. Jefferson's second term was made difficult by war between England and France. Both nations seized cargoes from American ships and

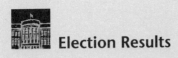 **Election Results**

1808

Presidential / Vice presidential candidates	Popular votes	Presidential electoral votes
James Madison / George Clinton (Democratic-Republican)	—	122
George C. Pinckney / Rufus King (Federalist)	—	47

1812

Presidential / Vice presidential candidates	Popular votes	Presidential electoral votes
James Madison / Elbridge Gerry (Democratic-Republican)	—	128
DeWitt Clinton / Jared Ingersoll (Federalist)	—	89

Popular votes were not yet part of the presidential elections of 1808 and 1812. (The public at large did not vote.) In the 1812 election, New Hampshire governor John Langdon was originally nominated as Democratic-Republican vice president, but he declined.

sealed off areas around the world from American trade. Jefferson instituted the Embargo Act of 1807. The act was intended to teach those nations a lesson about the importance of American trade and to have them respect the nation's neutrality. However, the Embargo Act proved disastrous. England and France both benefited by the lack of American trade competition. The embargo (restriction on foreign trade) also hurt Americans at home—from thriving industries in the North to farmers in the agricultural South.

Even with the vastly unpopular embargo, Democratic-Republicans remained powerful nationally. Jefferson repealed the embargo shortly before leaving office. He was succeeded by Madison, who was elected president in 1808. Madison was still confronted with disrespect toward the United States from England and France—the world's two most powerful nations.

Madison's inauguration (formal ceremony installing him as president) was impressive. The Madison administra-

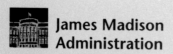

James Madison Administration

Administration Dates
March 4, 1809–March 4, 1813
March 4, 1813–March 4, 1817

Vice President
George Clinton (1809–12)
None (1812–13)
Elbridge Gerry (1813–14)
None (1814–17)

Cabinet
Secretary of State
Robert Smith (1809–11)
James Monroe (1811–17)

Secretary of the Treasury
Albert Gallatin (1809–14)
George W. Campbell (1814)
Alexander J. Dallas (1814–16)
William H. Crawford (1816–17)

Secretary of War
William Eustis (1809–13)
John Armstrong (1813–14)
James Monroe (1814–15)
William H. Crawford (1815–16)

Attorney General
Caesar A. Rodney (1809–11)
William Pinkney (1811–14)
Richard Rush (1814–17)

Secretary of the Navy
Robert Smith (1809)
Paul Hamilton (1809–12)
William Jones (1813–14)
Benjamin W. Crowninshield (1815–17)

Postmaster General
Gideon Granger (1809–14)
R. Jonathan Meigs Jr. (1814–17)

tion began with great fanfare—the first-ever inaugural ball followed Madison's spirited inaugural address. In his speech, he announced that the United States would not tolerate foreign interference. Still, England and France continued to frustrate American shipping. England impressed some American sailors into war service. (Impressment means the seizure by a government of individuals or goods for military service.) England was confident that the United States was weak militarily and growing disunited.

Madison surrounded himself with ineffective Cabinet officials. As attempts at diplomacy with England and France were ignored, New England Federalists were growing rebellious. Southern Congressional war hawks (those who support the use of military force to carry out foreign policy) led by Henry Clay (1777–1852; see box in **John Quincy Adams** entry in volume 1) of Kentucky and John C. Calhoun (1782–1850; see box in **Andrew Jackson** entry in volume 1) of South Carolina clamored (called loudly and publicly) for war. By 1812, Madison had exhausted all diplomatic efforts. War against Great Britain was declared in June of 1812. Reflecting growing divisions nationally, the war declaration barely passed both houses of Congress. Opponents of Madison promptly called the War of 1812 (1812–15) "Mr. Madison's War." In spite of the war, Madison was reelected in a close contest in 1812 over New York lieutenant governor DeWitt Clinton (1769–1828). Massachusetts statesman Elbridge Gerry (1744–1814) was elected vice president; his predecessor, George Clinton (1739–1812), had died during Madison's first term. In 1814, Gerry, too, would die in office.

The rocket's red glare

The weakness of the American military was exposed early on. War hawks had hoped that the United States could expand its territory by winning British Canada and Spanish Florida. Instead, the country was in for a serious struggle. The United States started out the war with a bankrupt national treasury, a poorly equipped and poorly led army, and an increasingly hostile Congress. Some New England congressmen threatened that their states would secede (separate) from the union over the war.

The War of 1812 proved futile. By the end in 1814, little had been accomplished. The United States did not win any new territory, nor was the nation able to persuade Great Britain to respect American rights at sea. Both nations were exhausted by the effort. Washington, D.C., was invaded by a British force in 1814 and burned. But the British failed to advance further, stalling in nearby Chesapeake Bay during battles near Fort McHenry that were watched by poet Francis Scott Key (1779–1843; see box). He was inspired to write "The Star-Spangled Banner," which later became the national anthem.

A naval battle during the War of 1812.

Source unknown.

There were some highlights for the United States in the War of 1812. America secured power on the Great Lakes with victories on Lake Erie by commander Admiral Oliver Hazard Perry (1785–1819). An army commanded by future president **William Henry Harrison** (1773–1841; see entry in volume 2) proceeded to free Fort Detroit from British occupation and pursued a coalition (alliance) of British and Native American forces into Canada, emerging victorious in the Battle of the Thames in the present-day province of Ontario. With those victories, the

Francis Scott Key

Francis Scott Key was born on his family's 2,800-acre estate, Terra Rubra, near Frederick County, Maryland, on August 1, 1779. He was the son of John Ross Key, a soldier who had distinguished himself in battle during the Revolutionary War (1775–83). The Key family was friends with President George Washington. Key became an excellent horseman and attended St. John's College in Annapolis, graduating in 1796, then earning a degree in law. He established a law practice in Frederick, Maryland, in 1801. The following year he married Mary Tayloe Lloyd, who also came from a prominent Maryland family. The couple eventually had eleven children.

In 1803, Key and his family moved to Georgetown, in the District of Columbia. He was an active member of St. John's Episcopal Church and composed a popular hymn, "Lord, with Glowing Heart I'd Praise Thee." His faith led him to maintain a pacifist stance (a belief in non-violence) as relations between England and the United States grew increasingly tense and culminated with the War of 1812 (1812–15).

When England defeated France in 1814 and turned its full attention to fighting the United States, Key reversed his position and enlisted in the District of Columbia militia. American forces clustered around Baltimore, anticipating that it would be the main target of British attacks. Instead, the British landed near Washington, D.C., and in August 1814 they managed to capture the city and burn the Capitol building and the White House.

Key embarked on a mission on September 3, 1814, to help secure the release of an American physician, William Beanes, taken prisoner by the British. At first, the captors refused to release Beanes, but they eventually agreed after reading the testimonials Key had secured. The two men's departure was delayed, however, to prevent them from revealing British plans to launch a full-scale attack on Baltimore. Their boat was put in tow behind the British fleet as it approached Fort McHenry. As sixteen British warships formed a semicircle around the fort, Key noticed a thirty-by-forty-two-foot American flag flying over it. The ships

frontier from the Ohio River north to the Great Lakes was made secure for further American expansion and settlement.

After a peace settlement had been agreed on in December of 1814, General **Andrew Jackson** (1767–1845; see entry in volume 1), another future president, led American forces to an overwhelming victory in the Battle of New Orleans in January 1815. News of the peace agreement had not yet reached that far south. By the time the treaty ending the

Francis Scott Key.
Courtesy of the Library of Congress.

commenced bombing on September 13 and continued for the next twenty-four hours. When the shelling finally stopped, it was still dark, and Key waited impatiently to learn how the fort had fared. At dawn, he saw the American flag still flying defiantly over Fort McHenry. In the early morning hours of September 14, 1814, Key wrote a poem conveying his patriotic feelings about the battle. Key's poem, "The Defense of Fort McHenry," was published in a newspaper. The verse quickly gained popularity as it was reprinted in newspapers across the country and set to the tune of a popular song, "To Anacreon in Heaven." Key's song, renamed "The Star-Spangled Banner" in 1815, was adopted by the Union Army during the Civil War (1861–65) and was declared the anthem of the American military during World War I (1914–18). It was recognized by Congress as the national anthem of the United States in 1931.

After the War of 1812, Key enjoyed a flourishing law practice. He was appointed district attorney for the District of Columbia in 1833 and held the post through 1841. In this position, Key negotiated several important agreements between the government and Native Americans. He also became active in the antislavery movement. Key died of pneumonia at the home of his daughter on January 11, 1843.

War of 1812 was signed in 1815, a stronger sense of national spirit had arisen. Though it had not emerged victorious, the United States had proved that it could defend its rights against international powers.

Madison and the nation showed new confidence and began thinking more in national terms. Madison supported the formation of the Second National Bank to handle federal finances. He backed a moderate tariff (tax on imports) to protect American commerce. He pursued plans for road and canal improvements. All these efforts were similar to Federalist policies Madison had previously opposed, but the times had changed and the imperfections of the American system demanded attention. Involving the federal government in national improvements of finance and transportation, and enhanced by national pride at having stood up against the British Empire, Madison was popular. The president's last two years in office were his most effective, and Madison left office on a positive note in 1817. The nation was enjoying prosperity and expansion.

Farmer again

The Madisons retired to Montpelier. Madison took up the life of a gentleman farmer, employing the latest scientific advances to agriculture. He served as an advisor to James Monroe, his successor as president. He became rector (president) of the University of Virginia following Thomas Jefferson's death in 1826. He wrote and revised papers ranging from his days as a young politician, to his position as a leader of the Constitutional Convention, to his time as president.

Madison attended the 1829 Virginia Convention at which the state's constitution was revised. Madison argued for expanding voting rights and attempted to limit slavery in the state. He spoke against the theory of nullification during President Andrew Jackson's administration (1829–37), when the state of South Carolina attempted to nullify (negate) a federal tariff it opposed. When Madison died on June 27, 1836, he was the last of the Founding Fathers who had steered the nation to independence.

Legacy

James Madison has the distinction of having presided during an unpopular war that accomplished little but from which the nation emerged stronger. The War of 1812 succeeded in giving Americans a sense of national identity. Madison had always recognized the necessity for having a strong federal government. He proceeded to expand upon his own ideas to begin programs that would further strengthen the nation.

A Selection of Madison Landmarks

James Madison Museum. 129 Caroline St., Orange, VA 22960. (540) 672-1776. Exhibits about James and Dolley Madison. See http://www.jamesmadisonmuseum.org/ (accessed on June 9, 2000).

Montpelier. P.O. Box 67, Montpelier Station, VA 22957. (540) 672-2728. Home, gardens, and burial site of the president and first lady. Exhibit and walking tour. See http://www.montpelier.org/ (accessed on June 9, 2000).

Todd House. Fourth and Walnut Sts., Philadelphia, PA (215) 597-8974. Home where Dolley Madison and her first husband, John Todd, lived before he died in 1793. She married James Madison less than a year later. See http://www.ushistory.org/tour/_todd.html (accessed on June 9, 2000).

Appropriately, before beginning federal programs such as improving the nation's roads and canals, he encouraged debate about the constitutionality of such actions. Still, during his last two years he expanded the power of the presidency, putting the nation's concerns above the interests of individual states.

Madison's legacy rests with his tireless actions in forging the Constitution. His approach was exemplary. He was always well-informed, well-reasoned, able to express his convictions without flamboyance (excessive showiness), and willing to compromise for the greater good.

Where to Learn More

James Madison University. *James Madison: His Legacy.* [Online] http://www.jmu.edu/madison/ (accessed on July 31, 2000).

Leavell, J. Perry, Jr. *James Madison.* New York: Chelsea House, 1988.

Madison, James. *Notes of Debates in the Federal Convention of 1787.* Athens: Ohio University Press, 1966. Reprint: New York: W. W. Norton, 1987.

Malone, Mary. *James Madison.* Springfield, NJ: Enslow, 1997.

Polikoff, Barbara G. *James Madison: 4th President of the United States.* Ada, OK: Garrett Educational Corp., 1989.

University of Virginia. *The Papers of James Madison.* [Online] http://www.virginia.edu/pjm/home.html (accessed on July 31, 2000).

Dolley Madison

Born May 20, 1768
Guilford County, North Carolina
Died July 12, 1849
Washington, D.C.

Popular first lady energized the White House and assisted other presidential families

Charming and fashionable, Dolley Madison was an energetic first lady with a flair for entertaining. Her service as first lady expanded beyond the eight years (1809–17) in which her husband, **James Madison** (1751–1836; see entry in volume 1), was president. She also counseled and helped host social functions for three other presidents: **Thomas Jefferson** (1743–1826; see entry in volume 1), **Martin Van Buren** (1782–1862; see entry in volume 1), and **John Tyler** (1790–1862; see entry in volume 2).

"The profusion [great quantity] of my table is the result of the prosperity of my country, and I shall continue to prefer Virginia liberality [casualness] to European elegance."

Dolley Madison

Modest beginnings

Dolley was born in Guilford County, North Carolina, on May 20, 1768, to John and Mary Payne, settlers from Virginia. Raised in a devout (deeply religious) Quaker household, Dolley was taught to dress plainly and behave humbly. Though sometimes referred to in biographies as Dorothy or Dorothea, Dolley was the name she always used. That name was recorded in her birth record by the Quaker community (also called the Society of Friends) in Piedmont, North Caroli-

Dolley Madison.
Portrait by Stuart Gilbert. Courtesy of the National Archives and Records Administration.

na. Quakers believe that each individual can directly feel the presence of God. They value work, community cooperation, and modesty in dress and behavior.

In 1769, the Payne family moved to Virginia; in 1783, when Dolley was fifteen years old, they moved to Philadelphia, Pennsylvania. By that time, Dolley had received private tutoring and had attended Quaker schools. She also learned to cook and sew. Although she continued to dress plainly, Dolley learned more colorful social customs from her maternal grandmother, who introduced her to fine food, clothing, and jewelry. Her grandmother gave her a gold brooch (large pin), which Dolley wore beneath her humble clothing. She would later name her grandmother as her greatest influence.

After her father failed in a laundry business in Philadelphia, the family ran a boardinghouse (a private home that provides meals and lodgings for paying guests), with Dolley serving as the cook. Anxious to begin her own life and to assert her identity as a lively young woman, Dolley married Philadelphia lawyer John Todd in 1790. They had two children. However, a yellow fever epidemic (a rapid spread of an infectious disease caused by a virus) swept through the area in 1792. That same year, her husband and one of her children died. Dolley was left to carry on as a young widow with a young boy.

The "great little Madison"

As a personable and attractive widow, Dolley had several suitors. She moved in a social circle that included national politicians in Philadelphia, the nation's capital from 1790 to 1799. In May of 1794, New York senator Aaron Burr (1756–1836; see box in **Thomas Jefferson** entry in volume 1), who had stayed in the Payne boardinghouse, informed Dolley that Virginia representative James Madison was interested in being introduced to her. Excited at the prospect of meeting him, Dolley sent a note to a friend of hers, stating, "Aaron Burr says that the great little Madison has asked to be brought to see me this evening." Famous as an influential congressman and for his contributions to the U.S. Constitution, Madison was great, indeed, even though he was physically small— five-foot, four-inches tall and weighing about 100 pounds. He was also eighteen years older than she was.

Dolley and "Little Jemmy," as she called Madison, hit it off. Their romance was encouraged by others. At a state dinner, for example, President **George Washington** (1732–1799; see entry in volume 1) and first lady **Martha Washington** (1732–1802; see entry in volume 1) each on separate occasions spoke to Dolley in glowing terms about Madison. Dolley, meanwhile, delighted political social circles with her friendliness, fashionable dress, and love of dancing. Madison, who had always been reserved and somewhat formal, became more sociable, proving to be a lively conversationalist and a graceful dancer. The couple was married on September 15, 1794.

Dolley was soon the toast of Philadelphia. She wore elegant gowns, modeled the newest trends in clothes and shoes, and was a spirited entertainer. After Madison retired from Congress in 1797 and the couple moved to his home, Montpelier, in Virginia, they continued to entertain regularly.

In 1801, the Madisons moved to Washington, D.C., the nation's new capital. Madison served as secretary of state under Thomas Jefferson. Dolley occasionally served as hostess for official functions, since Jefferson's wife, **Martha Jefferson** (1748–1782; see entry in volume 1), had died nineteen years earlier. Dolley helped instill Jefferson's preference for informal and simple social occasions. She collected recipes from throughout the United States in order to establish a distinctly American cuisine (style of preparing food). In addition to dressing in the latest fashions, she often started fashion trends. Her distinctive headdress of scarves wrapped around her head became known as the Dolley turban. She was likely the best known and most popular woman in America by 1808, when her husband ran for president. Madison's opponent, Charles C. Pinckney (1746–1825), thought so. After losing the election to Madison, he remarked, "I might have had a better chance had I faced Mr. Madison alone."

"Lady Presidentess"

As first lady, Dolley introduced a more elegant style to White House occasions. There was a first-ever White House inaugural ball when President Madison took office. Soon after, Dolley successfully lobbied (sought to influence) con-

A view of the White House after the British burned it on August 24, 1814.
Courtesy of the Library of Congress.

gressmen for funds to improve the White House. She hired a chef and expanded guest lists for parties beyond the usual political crowd. She invited writers, artists, and other newsmakers. Her regular Wednesday drawing room parties (parties in a formal reception room) and special events were all spirited occasions and earned her the nickname "Lady Presidentess."

During the War of 1812, Dolley toned down social occasions, except for opportunities to celebrate American successes. When British forces began marching toward Washington, D.C., in 1814, President Madison abandoned the city with retreating soldiers, while Dolley was to move in with friends in Virginia for safety. Instead, she remained at the White House until the last possible moment. She supervised the removal of precious items, including a famous painting of George Washington, for safekeeping. The items were placed in carriages and moved from the White House just ahead of British troops.

The British occupied the capital for a few days, long enough to set fire to government buildings, including the White House. Upon her return to Washington, Dolley was cheered by people in the streets and promised them that the capital would be rebuilt. It was, and the new White House was stocked with items she had helped to save.

Afterglow

When Madison's presidency ended in 1817, the couple returned to Montpelier. Dolley continued her habit of hosting elegant parties. The ex-president and ex–first lady enjoyed festive and quiet times together until Madison's death in 1836. Dolley nursed her husband during the illness from which he eventually died. She took dictation as he expressed his final thoughts on government.

A widow again, Dolley returned to Washington, D.C., in 1837. She was short on finances and had to sell Montpelier because of debts incurred by her son. She was still known and celebrated as the grand dame of Washington social circles. She remained as likable and demonstrative as ever, greeting fellow guests with hugs and always knowing everyone by name.

In 1838, Dolley acted as adviser to White House hostess Angelica Van Buren, the daughter-in-law of President Van Buren and his late wife, **Hannah Van Buren** (1783-1819; see entry in volume 1). In the early 1840s, Dolley assisted first lady **Letitia Tyler** (1790–1842; see entry in volume 2) and her daughters during the early part of John Tyler's presidency. Letitia Tyler died in 1842, three years after a stroke had left her incapacitated. In the mid 1840s, Dolley also counseled first lady **Sarah Polk** (1803–1891; see entry in volume 2)—a highly intelligent woman who was not accustomed to large social functions—to create her own style. Dolley was chosen in 1844 to send the first personal message using the Morse telegraph. Even as she turned eighty, Dolley Madison was still active and vibrant in Washington, D.C. Upon her death in 1849, President **Zachary Taylor** (1784–1850; see entry in volume 2) noted, "She will never be forgotten because she was truly our first lady for half a century."

Where to Learn More

Arnett, Ethel Stephens. *Mrs. James Madison: The Incomparable Dolley.* Greensboro, NC: Piedmont Press, 1972.

Davidson, Mary R. *Dolly Madison: Famous First Lady.* Champaign, IL: Garrard, 1966. Reprint, New York: Chelsea Juniors, 1992.

Flanagan, Alice K. *Dolley Payne Todd Madison, 1768–1849.* Children's Press, 1997.

Moore, Virginia. *The Madisons: A Biography.* McGraw Hill, 1979.

University of Virginia. *The Dolley Madison Project.* [Online] http://moderntimes.vcdh.virginia.edu/madison/index.html (accessed on July 31, 2000).

Madison's
Bill of Rights Proposal

Delivered on June 8, 1789; excerpted from
The Congressional Register, **Vol. I**

*The "Father of the Constitution" proposes
amendments to guarantee the rights of citizens*

Beginning on May 25, 1787, fifty-five delegates representing twelve of the thirteen states united by the Articles of Confederation (1781) met in Philadelphia, Pennsylvania. Many felt that the national government created by the Articles was too weak to be effective. Virginia delegate **George Washington** (1732–1799; see entry in volume 1) was among those calling for a stronger central government. He presided over the convention.

After much debate, the new U.S. Constitution was completed on September 17, 1787. The document was submitted to individual states: nine of them had to ratify the Constitution in order for it to go into effect. Representatives of the state of Delaware voted to ratify the Constitution on December 7, 1787, and, thus, Delaware became the first state in the union. On June 21, 1788, the state of New Hampshire became the ninth state to approve the Constitution, and the U.S. government became official.

There were lively debates in each of the states. Virginia was typical: such leaders as Patrick Henry (1736–1799; see box in **Thomas Jefferson** entry in volume 1), **James**

"The people shall not be deprived or abridged of their right to speak, to write, or to publish their sentiments; and the freedom of the press, as one of the great bulwarks of liberty, shall be inviolable."

James Madison

Monroe (1758–1831; see entry in volume 1), and George Mason (1725–1792; see box in the **James Madison** entry in volume 1) were against the Constitution, fearing that the federal government it outlined was too powerful; they also objected to a lack of guarantees for individual liberty. **James Madison** (1751–1836; see entry in volume 1) was able to argue convincingly enough for Virginia's ratification by a slim margin, 89–79. Madison did not believe that a bill of rights was necessary. He vigorously pursued amendments (additions) that would guarantee liberties, however, to honor those who wanted it and to calm those who were unhappy with the Constitution and were calling for another constitutional convention.

Madison was elected to the House of Representatives, which began convening on March 4, 1789. He soon proposed a series of amendments that would become known as the Bill of Rights—the first ten amendments to the U.S. Constitution.

Things to remember while reading an excerpt from James Madison's proposal for a Bill of Rights:

- The speech proposed amendments to the Constitution that would guarantee individual liberties. Since Madison was introducing discussion on this issue, the rights he proposed were often worded differently than they are in the final amendments that appear in the Constitution. Ten amendments were ratified two-and-a-half years later, on December 5, 1791. An amendment to the Constitution must be approved by at least three-fourths of the states in the union in order to become law.

- The excerpted portions of Madison's speech focused on those areas in which Madison specifically discussed amendments concerning individual liberties.

- Madison proposed that amendments he offered should be worked into the text of the Constitution. For example, most of the individual liberties he proposed were to be inserted in Article I, Section 9. When the amendments were finally approved, they were placed after the original text of the Constitution. All subsequent amendments to the

Constitution are numbered and follow in the order of when they were adopted.

- At the time of Madison's speech, two states—North Carolina and Rhode Island—had still not ratified the Constitution.

James Madison's Bill of Rights proposal

*It appears to me that this house is bound by every motive of **prudence**, not to let the first session pass over without proposing to the state legislatures some things to be incorporated into the constitution, as will render it as acceptable to the whole people of the United States, as it has been found acceptable to a majority of them.*

*I wish, among other reasons why something should be done, that those who have been friendly to the adoption of this constitution, may have the opportunity of proving to those who were opposed to it, that they were as sincerely devoted to liberty and a **republican** government, as those who charged them with wishing the adoption of this constitution in order to lay the foundation of an **aristocracy** or **despotism**. It will be a desirable thing to extinguish from the bosom of every member of the community any apprehensions, that there are those among his countrymen who wish to deprive them of the liberty for which they valiantly fought and honorably bled. And if there are amendments desired, of such a nature as will not injure the constitution, and they can be **engrafted** so as to give satisfaction to the doubting part of our fellow citizens; the friends of the federal government will **evince** that spirit of deference and concession for which they have **hitherto** been distinguished.*

It cannot be a secret to the gentlemen in this house, that, notwithstanding the ratification of this system of government by eleven of the thirteen United States, in some cases unanimously, in others by large majorities; yet still there is a great number of our constituents who are dissatisfied with it; among whom are many respectable for their talents, their patriotism, and respectable for the jealousy they have for their liberty, which, though mistaken in its object, is laudable in its motive. There is a great body of the people

Prudence: Wisdom.

Republican: A form of government in which supreme power resides with citizens who elect their leaders and have the power to change their leaders.

Aristocracy: Government in which power resides with a minority of people considered to be the best qualified.

Despotism: Rule by fear and violence.

Engrafted: Added on.

Evince: Reveal.

Hitherto: Up until now.

*falling under this description, who as present feel much inclined to join their support to the cause of **federalism**, if they were satisfied in this one point: We ought not to disregard their inclination, but, on principles of **amity** and moderation, conform to their wishes, and expressly declare the great rights of mankind secured under this constitution.*

*The **acquiescence** which our fellow citizens show under the government, calls upon us for a like return of moderation. But perhaps there is a stronger motive than this for our going into a consideration of the subject; it is to provide those securities for liberty which are required by a part of the community. I allude in a particular manner to those two states who have not thought fit to throw themselves into the bosom of the confederacy: it is a desirable thing, on our part as well as theirs, that a re-union should take place as soon as possible. I have no doubt, if we proceed to take those steps which would be prudent and **requisite** at this juncture, that in a short time we should see that disposition prevailing in those states that are not come in, that we have seen prevailing [in] those states which are.*

*But I will candidly acknowledge, that, over and above all these considerations, I do conceive that the constitution may be amended; that is to say, if all power is subject to abuse, that then it is possible the abuse of the powers of the general government may be guarded against in a more secure manner than is now done, while no one advantage, arising from the exercise of that power, shall be damaged or endangered by it. We have in this way something to gain, and, if we proceed with caution, nothing to lose; and in this case it is necessary to proceed with caution; for while we feel all these inducements to go into a **revisal** of the constitution, we must feel for the constitution itself, and make that revisal a moderate one. I should be unwilling to see a door opened for a re-consideration of the whole structure of the government, for a re-consideration of the principles and the substance of the powers given; because I doubt, if such a door was opened, if we should be very likely to stop at that point which would be safe to the government itself: But I do wish to see a door opened to consider, so far as to incorporate those provisions for the security of rights, against which I believe no serious objection has been made by any class of our constituents, such as would be likely to meet with the concurrence of two-thirds of both houses, and the **approbation** of three-fourths of the state legislatures. I will not propose a single alteration which I do not wish to see take place, as intrinsically proper in itself, or proper because it is*

Federalism: A form of government in which power is distributed among components of a central authority.

Amity: Friendly relations.

Acquiescence: Acceptance.

Requisite: Necessary.

Revisal: Alteration.

Approbation: Official approval.

wished for by a respectable number of my fellow citizens; and therefore I shall not propose a single alteration but is likely to meet the concurrence required by the constitution.

There have been objections of various kinds made against the constitution: Some were leveled against its structure, because the president was without a **council;** because the senate, which is a legislative body, had judicial powers in trials on impeachments; and because the powers of that body were compounded in other respects, in a manner that did not correspond with a particular theory; because it grants more power than is supposed to be necessary for every good purpose; and controls the ordinary powers of the state governments. I know some respectable characters who opposed this government on these grounds; but I believe that the great mass of the people who opposed it, disliked it because it did not contain effectual provision against encroachments on particular rights, and those safeguards which they have been long accustomed to have interposed between them and the magistrate who exercised the sovereign power: nor ought we to consider them safe, while a great number of our fellow citizens think these securities necessary.

It has been a fortunate thing that the objection to the government has been made on the ground I stated; because it will be practicable on that ground to **obviate** the objection, so far as to satisfy the public mind that their liberties will be perpetual, and this without endangering any part of the constitution, which is considered as essential to the existence of the government by those who promoted its adoption.

The amendments which have occurred to me, proper to be recommended by congress to the state legislatures are these:

First.

That there be prefixed to the constitution a declaration — That all power is originally vested in, and consequently derived from the people. That government is instituted, and ought to be exercised for the benefit of the people; which consists in the enjoyment of life and liberty, with the right of acquiring and using property, and generally of pursuing and obtaining happiness and safety. That the people have an **indubitable,** unalienable, and **indefeasible** right to reform or change their government, whenever it be found adverse or inadequate to the purposes of its institution. . . .

Fourthly. That in article 2nd, section 9, between clauses 3 and 4 [1:9:3], be inserted these clauses, to wit,

Council: Advisers.

Obviate: Anticipate and prevent.

Indubitable: Unquestionable.

Indefeasible: Incapable of being undone.

The civil rights of none shall be abridged on account of religious belief or worship, nor shall any national religion be established, nor shall the full and equal rights of conscience by in any manner, or on any pretext infringed. The people shall not be deprived or abridged of their right to speak, to write, or to publish their sentiments; and the freedom of the press, as one of the great **bulwarks** *of liberty, shall be* **inviolable.**

The people shall not be restrained from peaceably assembling and consulting for their common good, nor from applying to the legislature by petitions, or remonstrances for redress of their grievances.

The right of the people to keep and bear arms shall not be infringed; a well armed, and well regulated militia being the best security of a free country: but no person religiously scrupulous of bearing arms, shall be compelled to render military service in person.

No soldier shall in time of peace be quartered in any house without the consent of the owner; nor at any time, but in a manner warranted by law.

No person shall be subject, except in cases of impeachment, to more than one punishment, or one trial for the same offence; nor shall be compelled to be a witness against himself; nor be deprived of life, liberty, or property without due process of law; nor be obliged to relinquish his property, where it may be necessary for public use, without a just compensation.

Excessive bail shall not be required, nor excessive fines imposed, nor cruel and unusual punishments inflicted.

The rights of the people to be secured in their persons, their houses, their papers, and their other property from all unreasonable searches and seizures, shall not be violated by warrants issued without probable cause, supported by oath or affirmation, or not particularly describing the places to be searched, or the persons or things to be seized.

In all criminal prosecutions, the accused shall enjoy the right to a speedy and public trial, to be informed of the cause and nature of the accusation, to be confronted with his accusers, and the witnesses against him; to have a **compulsory** *process for obtaining witnesses in his favor; and to have the assistance of counsel for his defense.*

The exceptions here or elsewhere in the constitution, made in favor of particular rights, shall not be so construed as to diminish the just importance of other rights retained by the people; or as to en-

Bulwarks: Strong supports.

Inviolable: That which cannot be violated; a law.

Compulsory: Required.

Complete American Presidents Sourcebook

large the powers delegated by the constitution; but either as actual limitations of such powers, or as inserted merely for greater caution.

Fifthly.

That in article 2nd, section 10, between clauses 1 and 2, be inserted this clause, to wit: No state shall violate the equal rights of conscience, or the freedom of the press, or the trial by jury in criminal cases. . . .

It has been said by way of objection to a bill of rights, by many respectable gentlemen out of doors, and I find opposition on the same principles likely to be made by gentlemen on this floor, that they are unnecessary articles of a republican government, upon the presumption that the people have those rights in their own hands, and that is the proper place for them to rest. It would be a sufficient answer to say that this objection lies against such provisions under the state governments as well as under the general government; and there are, I believe, but few gentlemen who are inclined to push their theory so far as to say that a declaration of rights in those cases is either ineffectual or improper.

It has been said that in the federal government they are unnecessary, because the powers are enumerated, and it follows that all that are not granted by the constitution are retained: that the constitution is a bill of powers, the great **residuum** being the rights of the people; and therefore a bill of rights cannot be so necessary as if the residuum was thrown into the hands of the government. I admit that these arguments are not entirely without foundation; but they are not conclusive to the extent which has been supposed. It is true the powers of the general government are circumscribed; they are directed to particular objects; but even if government keeps within those limits, it has certain discretionary powers with respect to the means, which may admit of abuse to a certain extent, in the same manner as the powers of the state governments under their constitutions may to an indefinite extent; because in the constitution of the United States there is a clause granting to Congress the power to make all laws which shall be necessary and proper for carrying into execution all the powers vested in the government of the United States, or in any department or officer thereof; this enables them to fulfil every purpose for which the government was established. Now, may not laws be considered necessary and proper by Congress, for it is them who are to judge of the necessity and propriety to accomplish those special purposes which they may have in contemplation, which laws in themselves are neither necessary or proper; as well as

Residuum: Something that remains after a part has been taken away.

improper laws could be enacted by the state legislatures, for fulfilling the more extended objects of those governments. I will state an instance which I think in point, and proves that this might be the case. The general government has a right to pass all laws which shall be necessary to collect its revenue; the means for enforcing the collection are within the direction of the legislature: may not general warrants be considered necessary for this purpose, as well as for some purposes which it was supposed at the framing of their constitutions the state governments had in view. If there was reason for restraining the state governments from exercising this power, there is like reason for restraining the federal government. . . .

Having done what I conceived was my duty, in bringing before this house the subject of amendments, and also stated such as wish for and approve, and offered the reasons which occurred to me in their support; I shall content myself for the present with moving, that a committee be appointed to consider of and report such amendments as ought to be proposed by congress to the legislatures of the states, to become, if ratified by three-fourths thereof, part of the constitution of the United States. By agreeing to this motion, the subject may be going on in the committee, while other important business is proceeding to a conclusion in the house. I should advocate greater dispatch in the business of amendments, if I was not convinced of the absolute necessity there is of pursuing the organization of the government; because I think we should obtain the confidence of our fellow citizens, in proportion as we fortify the rights of the people against the encroachments of the government. (The Congressional Register, *Vol. I, pp. 423–37*)

What happened next . . .

After debate, the amendments suggested by Madison granting individual liberties were formed into twelve amendments that were sent to states for ratification. Ten amendments—collectively called the Bill of Rights—were added to the Constitution after being ratified by three-fourths of the states in the union. The first nine amendments are similar to Madison's original proposals. The tenth amendment—"The powers not delegated to the United States by the Constitution,

Bill of Rights

The first ten amendments to the Constitution were ratified December 15, 1791. The amendments form what is known as the Bill of Rights. The original constitutions of the states of Virginia (1776) and Massachusetts (1780) had such stipulations protecting the rights of individuals. Those states, Pennsylvania, and New York ratified the Constitution on the expectation that statements safeguarding individual liberties would be added. As a representative from Virginia, James Madison proposed amending the Constitution to include a Bill of Rights.

Amendment 1: Congress shall make no law respecting an establishment of religion, or prohibiting the free exercise thereof; or abridging the freedom of speech, or of the press, or the right of the people peaceably to assemble, and to petition the Government for a redress of grievances.

Amendment 2: A well regulated Militia, being necessary to the security of a free State, the right of the people to keep and bear Arms, shall not be infringed.

Amendment 3: No Soldier shall, in time of peace be quartered in any house, without the consent of the Owner, nor in time of war, but in a manner to be prescribed by law.

Amendment 4: The right of the people to be secure in their persons, houses, papers, and effects, against unreasonable searches and seizures, shall not be violated, and no Warrants shall issue, but upon probable cause, supported by Oath or affirmation, and particularly describing the place to be searched, and the persons or things to be seized.

Amendment 5: No person shall be held to answer for a capital, or otherwise infamous crime, unless on a presentment or indictment of a Grand Jury, except in cases arising in the land or naval forces, or in the Militia, when in actual service in time of War or public danger; nor shall any person be subject for the same offence to be twice put in jeopardy of life or limb; nor shall be compelled in any criminal case to be a witness against himself, nor be deprived of life, liberty, or property, without due process of law; nor shall private property be taken for public use without just compensation.

Amendment 6: In all criminal prosecutions, the accused shall enjoy the right to a speedy and public trial, by an impartial jury of the State and district wherein the crime shall have been committed, which district shall have been previously ascertained by law, and to be informed of the nature and cause of the accusation; to be confronted with the witnesses against him; to have compulsory process for obtaining witnesses in his favor, and to have the Assistance of Counsel for his defence.

Amendment 7: In Suits at common law, where the value in controversy shall exceed twenty dollars, the right of trial by jury shall be preserved, and no fact tried by a jury, shall be otherwise re-examined in any Court of the United States, than according to the rules of the common law.

Amendment 8: Excessive bail shall not be required nor excessive fines imposed, nor cruel and unusual punishments inflicted.

Amendment 9: The enumeration in the Constitution, of certain rights, shall not be construed to deny or disparage others retained by the people.

Amendment 10: The powers not delegated to the United States by the Constitution, nor prohibited by it to the States, are reserved to the States respectively, or to the people.

nor prohibited by it to the States, are reserved to the States respectively, or to the people"—was added by those who insisted that the powers of states needed to be recognized.

Did you know . . .

• North Carolina became the twelfth state to ratify the Constitution, but Rhode Island resisted. Only a threat by Congress to regard Rhode Island as a foreign nation and to impose taxes on its trade with other states convinced Rhode Island's state representatives to ratify the Constitution. It became the thirteenth state on May 29, 1790.

Where to Learn More

Douglas, William O. *A Living Bill of Rights*. Garden City, NY: Doubleday, 1961.

Heymsfeld, Carla, and Joan W. Lewis. *George Mason, Father of the Bill of Rights*. Alexandria, VA.: Patriotic Education Inc., 1991.

Meltzer, Milton. *The Bill of Rights: How We Got It and What It Means*. New York: Thomas Crowell, 1990.

Quiri, Patricia Ryon. *The Bill of Rights*. New York: Children's Press, 1998.

Rutland, Robert Allen. *The Birth of the Bill of Rights, 1776–1791*. Chapel Hill: University of North Carolina Press, 1955. Reprint, Boston: Northeastern University Press, 1991.

James Monroe

Fifth president (1817–1825)

James Monroe

Born April 28, 1758
Westmoreland County, Virginia
Died July 4, 1831
New York, New York

Fifth president of the United States (1817–1825)

Served during "The Era of Good Feelings,"
a period of peace, national expansion,
and the absence of party rivalry

J ames Monroe, elected in 1816, presided during the "Era of Good Feelings." The young United States was establishing its national identity in exciting times. The War of 1812 (1812–15) was over. The nation was expanding beyond the original thirteen colonies, and people were moving west for new opportunities. Political conflicts were few, as a political party called the Democratic-Republicans enjoyed widespread support and influence. Monroe was a popular president. In 1816, he won the electoral votes of all but three states; in 1820, he won the electoral votes of every state. Electoral votes are the votes a presidential candidate receives for winning the majority of the popular vote in a state.

The United States began its development as a major international power with the Monroe Doctrine (see **James Monroe** primary source entry in volume 1), announced in December of 1823. The young nation had been involved in a series of international disputes in the Americas with Great Britain, France, Spain, and Russia. The doctrine declared that the United States would not tolerate any further acts of intervention (interference in the affairs of another nation) or colo-

"National honor is national property of the highest value."

James Monroe

James Monroe.
Courtesy of the Library of Congress.

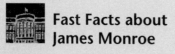

Fast Facts about James Monroe

Full name: James Monroe

Born: April 28, 1758

Died: July 4, 1831

Burial site: Gouverneur Vault, Second Street Cemetery, New York, New York; moved in 1858 to Hollywood Cemetery, Richmond, Virginia

Parents: Spence and Elizabeth Jones Monroe

Spouse: Elizabeth Kortright (1768–1830; m. 1786)

Children: Eliza Kortright (1787–1840); James Spence (1799–1800); Maria Hester (1803–1850)

Religion: Episcopalian

Education: Attended College of William and Mary

Occupations: Farmer; lawyer; military man

Government positions: Virginia state assemblyman; Continental congressman; U.S. senator; minister to France and England; Virginia governor; envoy to Spain; secretary of state and secretary of war under James Madison

Political party: Democratic-Republican

Dates as president: March 4, 1817– March 4, 1821 (first term); March 4, 1821–March 4, 1825 (second term)

Age upon taking office: 58

nization (establishment of new settlements) in the Americas on the part of European nations.

By the time Monroe's second term began, the Era of Good Feelings was gradually fading. An economic downturn occurred in 1819 and the issue of slavery continued to divide the nation. Still, Monroe remained popular. He is considered by historians to have been one of the most effective presidents. He was the last of the "Virginia dynasty" that included his predecessors, **Thomas Jefferson** (1743–1826; see entry in volume 1) and **James Madison** (1751–1836; see entry in volume 1). Combined, the three Virginians held the office of president for twenty-four years.

Modest beginnings

The oldest of five children, James Monroe was born on April 28, 1758, on his family's small farm in Westmoreland County, Virginia. His father, Spence Monroe, was a carpenter. Because he lived in an isolated area, Monroe had to travel several miles to attend school. At times, he studied with John Marshall (1755–1835), who would later become chief justice of the U.S. Supreme Court.

Monroe went on to the College of William and Mary in 1774. When the American Revolution (1775–83) broke out the following year, Monroe began training with student-formed military companies. He was assigned to the Third Virginia Regiment of the American army, called the Continental Army. In August of 1776, the regiment moved north to help support the Continental Army in a battle at Harlem Heights, New York. The regiment arrived during the Army's retreat and moved west with them through New Jersey, crossing the Delaware River into Pennsylvania.

Many militia groups formed during the American Revolution. A militia is not part of a regular army. Instead, citizens organize themselves for military service during an emergency. With a letter of recommendation from General **George Washington** (1732–1799; see entry in volume 1), Monroe was commissioned to command a new Virginia militia regiment. However, the militia group never came together. Monroe instead became an aide to Virginia governor Thomas Jefferson, with whom he quickly became friends. Monroe began studying law with Jefferson and decided to go into politics. Monroe was elected to the Virginia legislature in 1782 at the age of twenty-four.

The Articles of Confederation created a federal government in 1781. The Articles, which were created before the U.S. Constitution, were the first attempt at writing a document to define the powers and the duties of the new government. The Articles also discussed the rights of the people. Monroe was elected to the Congress of the Confederation in 1783. Greatly interested in the potential for American expansion beyond the thirteen colonies, Monroe took a trip to the Northwest. In those days, the Northwest contained the lands west of the Allegheny Mountains to the Mississippi River.

 James Monroe Timeline

1758: Born in Virginia

1775: American Revolution begins; Monroe is assigned to Third Virginia Regiment of the Continental Army in 1776

1783: Is member of Continental Congress

1787: Monroe votes against ratification of the Constitution on grounds that it establishes excessive federal power; supports Constitution after it is ratified

1790–94: Serves as U.S. senator

1794: Resigns from Senate to serve as a diplomat to France

1799–1802: Serves as governor of Virginia

1803–7: Serves as minister to France and England; helps negotiate the Louisiana Purchase

1811–17: Serves as secretary of state

1814–15: Serves as secretary of war

1816: Monroe elected president; "Era of Good Feelings" begins

1819: Florida ceded by Spain to the United States

1820: Missouri Compromise forbids slavery above the southern border of Missouri; Monroe reelected

1823: Monroe Doctrine delivered to Congress

1831: Dies in New York

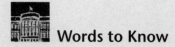

Words to Know

Articles of Confederation: From March 1, 1781, to June 21, 1788, the Articles served as the equivalent of the U.S. Constitution (1787). The Constitution replaced the Articles, which had failed to produce a strong central government.

Censure: Publicly condemn an individual; in Congress, the act of censure expresses Congress's condemnation of an individual's actions and is entered into the *Congressional Record*.

Continental Army: The army representing American interests during the Revolutionary War (1775–83).

Democratic-Republicans: Supporters of a political party in the United States led by Thomas Jefferson and James Madison in the 1790s to oppose the Federalist Party and close ties with Great Britain.

The political group was also called the Republican Party and the Jeffersonian Republican Party at the time, but the term Democratic-Republican helps separate the early political group from the Democratic Party and the Republican Party, which were formed later. The Democratic-Republican party dissolved in the 1820s as many of its members supported the formation of the Democratic Party led by Andrew Jackson, who was elected president in 1828 and 1832. The modern-day Republican Party was formed in 1854.

Electoral votes: The votes a presidential candidate receives for having won a majority of the popular vote in a state. Electoral votes are distributed among states in ratios based on population. A candidate must win a majority of electoral

---

The Ohio River formed the southern boundary, and the Great Lakes region formed the northern edge. Monroe traveled north from New York City up the Hudson River and other waterways to reach the Great Lakes. From there he traveled west and made several stops to tour inland areas (areas not along the rivers and lakes).

The trip made a great impression on Monroe. Upon his return to New York, where the Congress of the Confederation held its sessions, he began contributing to a plan that became the Northwest Ordinance of 1787. The ordinance formed a territorial government of the lands bordered by the Ohio River to the south and the Mississippi River to the west.

votes (over 50 percent) in order to win the presidency.

Louisiana Purchase: A vast region in North America purchased by the United States from France in 1803 for $15 million.

Missouri Compromise: Congressional bill that was intended to maintain a balance of slave and free states in the union. The Compromise set a dividing line at the southern border of Missouri: all states formed south of the dividing line could enter as slave states, depending on the will of the people, while all states formed north of the line would be free states.

Monroe Doctrine: A policy declared in 1823 as part of President Monroe's annual address to Congress. The Doctrine declared that the United States would not tolerate interference from European nations in North and South America.

Ratification: A vote of acceptance. A majority of the representatives from each of the thirteen colonies had to vote for the U.S. Constitution (1787) in order for the document to become legally binding.

Tariff: A tax that a nation places on imported goods to increase their price, making imported goods as expensive or more expensive than similar products produced in the home nation.

War of 1812: A war fought from 1812 to 1815 between the United States and Great Britain. The United States wanted to protect its maritime rights as a neutral nation during a conflict between Great Britain and France.

While he was serving in New York, Monroe met Elizabeth Kortright (1768–1830; see **Elizabeth Monroe** entry). She was the daughter of a wealthy merchant. They married in 1786. The Monroes would have three children—two daughters and a son who died in early childhood.

Monroe had hoped to attend the Constitutional Convention, the formal assembly of statesmen who met in Philadelphia, Pennsylvania, in 1787 to strengthen the Articles of Confederation. However, he was passed over as a representative of Virginia in favor of Madison. The convention's participants replaced the Articles of Confederation with a new document called the Constitution. The Constitution established a stronger federal government.

Major General Lafayette

Marie-Joseph-Paul-Yves-Roch-Gilbert du Motier de Lafayette was born on September 6, 1757, to the Motier family—better known by their noble title of La Fayette ("Lafayette" is an American spelling). After three years of study in the Collège du Plessis, a distinguished secondary school in Paris, France, Lafayette joined the French army in 1771. In 1773, Lafayette married Adrienne de Noailles (1759–1807), daughter of the Duc d'Ayen. After the outbreak of the American Revolution in 1775, Lafayette decided to put his military training to use by assisting America against France's historic enemy, England. Refused the king's permission to go to America, Lafayette sailed anyway, after buying and equipping a ship with his own money.

On June 13, 1777, he landed in North Carolina. The Continental Congress had given the distinguished volunteer an honorary commission as a major general, but his actual duties were as aide-de-camp (a top assistant) to General George Washington. After performing well in battles against the British in Pennsylvania and New Jersey, Lafayette was given command of a division of American troops. He became friends with future president James Monroe during battles in Pennsylvania. The next year, Lafayette was sent back to France with the mission of obtaining greater French support for the Americans. Upon landing in his homeland early in 1779, Lafayette was arrested for having disobeyed the royal command in going to America. But he was soon summoned by the king, who wanted a first-hand report on how things stood in America.

Lafayette returned to America in April 1780 in command of French auxiliary forces. His maneuverings in 1781 in Virginia eventually drew English commander Charles Cornwallis (1738–1805) into the trap at Yorktown, where he was blockaded by the American forces and by French troops brought by a French fleet. Cornwallis's surrender on October 19 brought the American war of independence to its military conclusion and was the culmination of Lafayette's career as a soldier. When Lafayette returned to France in 1782, it was as a hero—Washington's friend—and he was made a brigadier general in the French army.

Lafayette was influential in the first months of the French Revolution, which began in 1789. The Declaration of the Rights of Man and the Citizen was adopted at his initiative, and his military fame and political reputation combined to win for him, on the day after the Bastille fell (July 14), the command of the Parisian national guard, the force of citizen-soldiers created to defend the new regime. Lafayette favored

Major General Lafayette.
Reproduced by permission of the National Portrait Gallery, Smithsonian Institution.

a parliamentary monarchy like England's but one based on a formal written constitution, like that just adopted in America. However, he had to cope with radical mob violence. His efforts to hold the Revolution to a moderate course proved unpopular, and his command to his troops to fire on a mob in July 1791 led to his retirement in September from command of the national guard.

However, the onset of war against Austria and Prussia in 1792 brought Lafayette's return to military life as the commander of the Army of the Ardennes. He invaded the Austrian Netherlands (Bel-

gium) and then withdrew for lack of support. He was treated as a prisoner of war until 1797, when the victorious Napoleon obtained his release from jail. He was not allowed to return to France until 1799, when he was given a military pension as a retired general and allowed to live quietly on his country estate.

Lafayette did not engage in political activity again until 1814, when he was elected to the Legislative Chamber. From 1818 to 1824, he sat in the Chamber of Deputies as a leading member of the second most powerful political group in France. In 1824, Lafayette was invited by the U.S. government during the administration of President Monroe to visit America as its guest, and his triumphant tour of the country lasted fifteen months. Congress gave him a gift of $200,000 and a sizable tract of land, and Lafayette returned to France in 1825 to great acclaim as the "hero of two worlds."

Lafayette did not regain political prominence until the outbreak of revolution in 1830, when he became the symbol of moderate republicanism (a form of government in which citizens elect their leaders). When Lafayette died in Paris on May 20, 1834, he had few followers left.

First, the Constitution had to be approved by representatives from all the states. Monroe represented Virginia as a delegate during the process of acceptance, or ratification, of the Constitution. He opposed the new document, believing that the federal authority it outlined created a national government that was too powerful. He also wanted protection of individual liberties guaranteed. Monroe voted against the Constitution, but he welcomed the new government when the document was ratified.

In 1788, Monroe lost his race for a seat in the House of Representatives to Madison. The relationship between the two Virginia men was strained, but they would eventually patch up their differences. Meanwhile, the Monroes established an estate in Virginia called Ash Lawn, which is near Jefferson's home of Monticello.

Monroe was elected in 1790 to the U.S. Senate. In the early days of the nation, there were no political parties. Politicians generally divided themselves into two smaller groups, or factions. Those favoring a strong national government were called Federalists. Those who favored limited federal power and strong states rights were known as Anti-Federalists. Monroe, Madison, and Jefferson were among the most powerful Anti-Federalists.

Mixed results in Europe

Monroe resigned from his senate seat in 1794 to accept a ministry post in France. (In diplomatic work, a minister ranks below an ambassador.) President George Washington wanted Monroe to maintain friendly relations with France while the United States worked more closely with Great Britain. France and Britain were enemies at the time. Monroe became a great favorite in France. While there, he helped secure the release of writer Thomas Paine (1737–1809; see box), who had been imprisoned for opposing the execution of the king of France, Louis XVI (1754–1793), during the French Revolution (1789–97).

President Washington recalled Monroe in 1796 for fear that relations between America and France might upset Great Britain. This development resulted in the end of friendship between Washington and Monroe. Monroe had served under Washington during the Revolutionary War, and Washington had helped Monroe begin his political career. Monroe joined such politicians as Jefferson and Madison in criticizing Washington for not being more aggressive toward Great Britain.

After returning to Virginia, Monroe was elected governor of that state in 1798. Meanwhile, the divide between Federalists and Anti-Federalists grew larger. Washington, in his farewell address in 1797, urged the nation to avoid splitting into political parties, but that is exactly what happened during the presidential election of 1800. Anti-Federalists transformed into the Democratic-Republican Party. Its leader, Thomas Jefferson, was elected president.

In 1803, President Jefferson appointed Monroe as a special envoy to a delegation that was negotiating with France on the purchase of New Orleans, a port city of the French colony in the Louisiana Territory. Monroe and chief negotiator Robert R. Livingston (1746–1813) quickly showed interest when French emperor Napoleon I (1769–1821) suggested that France might be interested in selling the entire Louisiana colony to the United States. The negotiations concluded with the largest ever real estate acquisition—the Louisiana Purchase (see **Thomas Jefferson** entry in volume 1 for more information).

Monroe stayed on in Europe after the Louisiana Purchase, but he failed in two missions. He was unsuccessful in attempting to convince Great Britain to stop seizing the cargoes of American ships bound for France, with whom Great Britain was at war. As a neutral nation—that is, a nation not taking sides—America claimed the right to trade with all countries. When diplomacy failed, President Jefferson issued the Embargo Act of 1807, which cut off U.S. trade to all nations in an attempt to punish Great Britain. This move did not work, however. Great Britain was able to increase trade in the absence of American competition.

In between diplomatic sessions with Great Britain, Monroe traveled to Spain to try to convince that nation to sell its colony of Florida. Spain refused. Monroe returned to the United States near the end of Jefferson's presidency.

Thomas Paine

Thomas Paine was born in Thetford, Norfolk, England, on January 29, 1737. After seven years of school, he apprenticed to his father, a corsetmaker. Paine ran away to sea at the age of sixteen, but soon returned, finished his apprenticeship, and worked in several towns before starting his own shop. In 1759, he married Mary Lambert. When she died suddenly the following year, Paine abandoned his trade to become an exciseman (collector of taxes on goods produced and sold in a country). He remarried in 1768 and continued his education by reading books, attending lectures, and conducting scientific experiments.

In 1772, Payne wrote a pamphlet calling for pay increases for excisemen. The new salaries were denied and Paine was fired from his job. He went bankrupt and was divorced from his second wife, but his career of fighting for reform had begun. His work caught the attention of Benjamin Franklin (1706–1790), who was in London at the time. Franklin encouraged Paine to sail to America and gave him a letter of recommendation. Paine arrived in Philadelphia in 1774 and found work with the new *Pennsylvania* magazine. Inspired by the revolutionary spirit growing around him, Payne published a pamphlet, *Common Sense,* in which he presented arguments for America's independence from England. Written in clear and common language, the pamphlet proved popular, with twenty-five editions published during 1776.

Paine served as a military aide during the Revolutionary War (1775–83), but he continued to raise support for the American war effort through his writings. In December 1776, he began publishing *The Crisis,* a set of sixteen inspiring essays, the first of which began with the famous line, "These are the times that try men's souls." General George Washington often had the essays read to his soldiers.

A few years after the war ended and America gained independence, Paine sailed back to England to work on the design of an iron bridge. With the outbreak of the French Revolution in 1789, however, he was drawn back into political conflict. Many people criticized the Revolution for trying to overthrow the monarchy. Paine, on the other hand, supported it and responded to this criticism in 1791 by writing a two-part work, *The Rights of Man.*

Paine was influenced by the Enlightenment, a philosophical movement that held that natural laws (civil rights) existed for all people, and governments were only formed to protect them. Paine argued that if people were fighting for a truly rep-

Thomas Paine.
Courtesy of the National Archives and Records Administration.

resentative government, then their fight was just. He further argued that it was the duty of governments to provide universal education, unemployment relief, and assistance for the poor. Because he criticized the English monarchy in this work, Paine was threatened with imprisonment for treason. In 1792, he fled to France where he was welcomed as a hero and was elected to the National Convention, the country's new body of representatives. Paine, however, soon opposed the mob violence of the French Revolution and the execution of French king Louis XVI (1774–1793).

Branded a traitor, Paine was jailed from December of 1793 to November of 1794.

While he was imprisoned, Paine wrote *The Age of Reason,* in which he attempted to define his belief in the religious philosophy called Deism. Deists did not reject God, but thought God set up the universe like an intricate clock and left it running, never to interfere with it. They believed the Bible was only a moral guide, and that the natural laws of the universe (and God's perfection) could be discovered through education and reason. Paine urged people to abandon Christianity, which he called absurd and contradictory, and to follow a natural religion of good deeds and humanitarianism.

Paine's work on Deism proved to be his undoing. Upon his return to America in 1802, he faced great hostility. Many people saw *The Age of Reason* as an attack on society and labeled him an atheist (a person who does not believe in God). Even those people who had supported his earlier writings turned against him. His great accomplishments as a champion of liberty soon faded from their memories. Paine, who had argued on behalf of the poor throughout his life, lived his last seven years in poverty. He died alone in New York on June 8, 1809.

When James Madison won the presidential election of 1808, Monroe expected to receive a Cabinet post. But relations between the two men had not been good since Monroe had lost to Madison in a battle for a seat in the House of Representatives. Their relationship became further strained when Madison did not make a Cabinet offer. While serving again in the Virginia legislature and then again as the state's governor, Monroe had opportunities to settle differences with Madison. In 1811, Madison appointed Monroe as his secretary of state.

Great Britain and France were at war, again. Both nations seized American cargoes bound for the other nation. France relented to American demands to stop the practice, but Great Britain refused to recognize the United States as a neutral nation. Monroe opposed going to war over the matter, but once the War of 1812 began, he supported the conflict against Great Britain.

Emerges as national leader

Monroe's support for the war included an active military role. He helped the Maryland militia in its failed defense of Fort Bradenburg against British assault. When British forces moved in on Washington, D.C., and burned the nation's capital, President Madison fired his secretary of war, John Armstrong (1758–1842). Madison then placed Monroe in the dual role of secretary of state and secretary of war. Monroe faced tremendous challenges—a bankrupt (moneyless) national treasury, a poorly equipped and poorly led army, and an increasingly unfriendly Congress. Congress included some New England officials who threatened that their states would secede (separate) from the union over the war.

Monroe acted quickly and decisively. He secured loans to help finance the war effort. To lift soldiers' spirits and to attract additional soldiers, he increased the size of parcels of land that war veterans could claim after their military service. He combined state armies with the federal army to form a larger, stronger, and united force.

The War of 1812 officially ended early in 1815. Americans could take heart that although the nation did not emerge as a victor, it was not defeated either. When news of

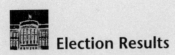

Election Results

1816

Presidential / Vice presidential candidates	Popular votes	Presidential electoral votes
James Monroe / Daniel D. Tompkins (Democratic-Republican)	—	183
Rufus King / John E. Howard (Federalist)	—	34

Popular votes were not yet part of the presidential election. (The public at large did not vote.)

1820

Presidential / Vice presidential candidates	Popular votes	Presidential electoral votes
James Monroe / Daniel D. Tompkins (Democratic-Republican)	—	231
John Quincy Adams / Richard Stockton (Democratic-Republican)	—	1

Popular votes were not yet part of the presidential election. (The public at large did not vote.) Due to the demise of the Federalist Party, candidates in the 1820 election represented different factions of the same party. For all intents and purposes, however, due to Monroe's popularity, he ran unopposed. One elector voted for Adams to ensure that George Washington remained the only president to be elected unanimously.

the Battle of New Orleans (1815) spread, the national mood brightened. A resounding victory for the United States, the Battle of New Orleans was actually fought after the warring sides had agreed on a cease-fire (truce) and a peace treaty. But news traveled slowly in those days. The winning commander, **Andrew Jackson** (1767–1845; see entry in volume 1), became a national hero.

In 1816, Madison decided not to run for a third term. Monroe defeated U.S. senator Rufus King of New York to become the nation's fifth president. At his inauguration, Monroe's old classmate, Chief Justice Marshall, administered the oath of office. As one of the new president's first acts, Monroe toured New England, wanting to smooth over differences that had made some New Englanders call for secession (separation) from the union over the war. Monroe's tour was so successful that a Boston newspaper—the *Columbian Centinel*—exclaimed that the new president had ushered in "an era of good feelings."

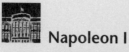

Napoleon I

Napoleon Bonaparte rose from a lieutenant in the army to become emperor of the French. Many of the reforms and institutions he set up still exist in the French government and in French society. The empire he created through war and diplomacy was the largest since Roman times. Born in Ajaccio, Corsica, on August 15, 1769, Napoleon was the son of a lawyer. Most people living on Corsica were of Italian heritage, but the island came under French rule a year before Napoleon's birth. That made him a French citizen. So he entered a French military school when he was ten.

An excellent student, Napoleon attended the famed military academy in Paris in 1784. He graduated a year later, receiving the rank of lieutenant in the French army. In 1789, the French Revolution broke out. Frenchmen were divided over the Revolution, but Napoleon supported it. While mob violence raged in France, Napoleon and the French army fought against Austria, Prussia, and England. In 1795, Napoleon held off an angry mob in Paris that threatened the National Convention, an elected body that was writing a new constitution. The government rewarded Napoleon by appointing him commander of the army of Italy.

Napoleon left for Italy to fight Austria. His army was poorly trained and supplied. But through his military genius—Napoleon never fought two battles using the same method—his army soon became a superior fighting force. By October 1797,

Napoleon had defeated the Austrians and had gained Belgium and the west bank of the Rhine River for France. He returned to France a hero. Soon, Napoleon took troops to Egypt hoping to seize the country and cut off trade routes for England, but the English soon destroyed the French navy. Napoleon was forced to return to France.

Napoleon and a few others seized control of the government in November of 1799. Napoleon presented a new constitution calling for three consuls to rule, each for ten years. Napoleon became the first consul. He restored law and order by establishing a strong police force, and he signed peace treaties with Austria and England. Because of these policies, the French voted Napoleon consul for life in 1802. Two years later, the people made him emperor of France. Napoleon now had unlimited power.

The French Empire prospered under Napoleon's leadership. He stabilized the nation's financial system, built new roads, and introduced new crops. He established the Napoleonic codes, laws that regulated such social rights as individual liberty, religious freedom, and divorce (with some revision, these codes are still in use today).

Despite an existing peace treaty, Napoleon was determined to invade and defeat England. Feared Napoleon's presence on the European continent, England convinced Austria, Russia, and Sweden to ally against him. Napoleon's mighty army, how-

Napoleon I. *Source unknown.*

ever, defeated the Austrians and Russians in 1805. Austria lost possession of its German and Italian states and with them, the crown of the Holy Roman emperor. In 1806, Napoleon gathered these territories together into the Confederation of the Rhine, and the Holy Roman Empire was no more.

Napoleon proceeded to conquer powerful Prussia. He now dominated Europe, but he still wanted to defeat England. Since he could not invade the country, he decided to destroy its economy. In 1806, Napoleon established the Continental System, which forbade European countries from trading with England. However, countries began secretly opening their ports to the English. Napoleon retaliated by warring with Spain in 1807 and Austria in 1809. Although Napoleon quickly defeated them, his troubles were not over.

By the end of 1810, Russia withdrew its support of the Continental System and broke any alliance it had with France. Napoleon responded in 1812 by invading Russia. Greatly outnumbered, the Russians retreated, burning villages and crops along the way. The French found no food or shelter in this barren land and when winter set in, they suffered. The Russians refused to negotiate and, without supplies, the French had to retreat. Napoleon's Russian campaign was a tremendous defeat. European nations banded together and attacked the weakened French army. On March 31, 1814, Paris fell, and Napoleon abdicated (gave up the throne) a few weeks later.

Napoleon was moved to the island of Elba, near Italy, to live as an outcast. In March 1815, however, he escaped, went to the French coast, and gathered support as he marched to Paris. King Louis XVIII (1755–1824) fled and Napoleon reclaimed the crown on March 20, 1815. Napoleon appealed to the other European countries for peace, but they did not trust him and warfare began again. British and Prussian forces combined to overwhelm Napoleon. It was his last battle, and his second period of rule—known as the Hundred Days—ended. He surrendered to the British on June 15, and was banished to the island of Saint Helena, hundreds of miles off the coast of Africa. He died there on May 5, 1821, of stomach cancer.

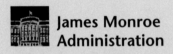

James Monroe Administration

Administration Dates
March 4, 1817–March 4, 1821
March 4, 1821–March 4, 1825

Vice President
Daniel D. Tompkins (1817–25)

Cabinet
Secretary of State
John Quincy Adams (1817–25)

Secretary of the Treasury
William H. Crawford (1817–25)

Secretary of War
John C. Calhoun (1817–25)

Attorney General
Richard Rush (1817)
William Wirt (1817–25)

Secretary of the Navy
Benjamin W. Crowninshield (1817–18)
Smith Thompson (1819–23)
Samuel L. Southard (1823–25)

Postmaster General
R. Jonathan Meigs Jr. (1817–23)
John McLean (1823–25)

The Era of Good Feelings

Along with a sense of increased national pride, the Era of Good Feelings was highlighted by several developments. American territory continued to expand. Settlers were finding new opportunities in former frontier land. Ports along the Atlantic Ocean were fortified—strengthened militarily—to provide the nation with a better defense. There were few signs of political division within the nation.

Still, the United States was not without problems. When a patrol crossed the border from Georgia into Spanish Florida in search of runaway slaves, Seminole Indians of Florida responded by making raids into Georgia. General Andrew Jackson, the hero of the Battle of New Orleans, was summoned to help drive Seminoles from Georgia. He pursued retreating Seminoles into Spanish Florida. Jackson captured two forts and executed two British citizens for inciting (encouraging) the Seminoles to make surprise attacks.

This action became a major international incident and the possibility of war with Great Britain loomed. Spain demanded return of the forts to their possession. Many in Congress wanted to censure (publicly condemn) Jackson. Monroe, who surrounded himself with excellent Cabinet officials and consulted regularly with ex-presidents Jefferson and Madison, was urged to apologize to Great Britain and Spain. Instead, he followed the advice of his secretary of state, **John Quincy Adams** (1767–1848; see entry in volume 1). The forts were returned, and a simple explanation of Jackson's actions—but not an apology—was made to Great Britain. The Monroe administration used the incident to display to European nations the difficulty of maintaining order in lands across the ocean. Adams took the opportunity to negotiate with Spain for the purchase of Florida.

The purchase of Florida was made during Monroe's first term. Meanwhile, Adams negotiated with Great Britain over western lands beyond the territory the United States had acquired in the Louisiana Purchase. The two nations agreed to joint control of the Oregon Territory and established a border at the 49th parallel latitude. The border, running from Lake of the Woods in present-day Minnesota to the Pacific Ocean, forms the present-day division between the United States and Canada west of the Great Lakes.

Meanwhile, 1819 was a year of ill feeling. An economic downturn led to financial problems for many citizens and a halt to road and canal projects that were improving the nation's infrastructure (physical resources). Then, when Maine and Missouri petitioned (formally requested) to enter the Union as states, the issue of slavery caused a bitter divide in Congress. Slavery was outlawed in much of the North, and Maine petitioned to enter as a free state. Missouri, however, petitioned to enter as a slave state. Much heated debate on the slavery issue occurred in Congress. The conflicts were eased with the Missouri Compromise of 1820.

The Missouri Compromise was intended to maintain a balance of slave and free states in the Union. To address the fear that slavery might expand to new states formed in the area acquired in the Louisiana Purchase, the Compromise set a dividing line at the southern border of Missouri. All states formed south of the dividing line could enter as slave states, depending on the will of the people; and all states formed north of the line would be free states.

Monroe easily won reelection in 1820. The nation continued to grow and prosper during his second term. Monroe faced three difficult issues during that term. In an effort to assert the international influence of the United States and restrict European nations from controlling parts of North and South America, he issued what came to be known as "the Monroe Doctrine" in 1823. He was against slavery, but signed the Missouri Compromise in 1820 because it offered the best alternative to dividing the nation at that time. Both Monroe and secretary of state Adams (who would follow Monroe as president) believed that great debate and battles over slavery

In the election of 1820, Monroe won the electoral votes of each state in the union. However, in the Electoral College, one elector cast his vote for John Quincy Adams. The action ensured that George Washington would remain the only president to win election unanimously (with all voters agreeing).

The Missouri Compromise

The Missouri territory applied for admission to the union as a slave state early in 1819. The application spurred a full-fledged congressional debate on the nature of slavery and the expansion of the institution into new territories. In February 1819, Representative James Tallmadge (1778– 1853) of New York offered an amendment to the Missouri Enabling Bill to prohibit the further introduction of slavery into the territory and to provide for the gradual emancipation of slaves already in Missouri. The amendment was passed by the House of Representatives (dominated by Northerners) and was sent to the Senate, where the amendment was eliminated from the bill. The House refused to follow the Senate action, but Congress soon adjourned and the slavery issue awaited the organization of the Sixteenth Congress.

That body hammered out the Missouri Compromise.

The Tallmadge Amendment stirred up the South, which was just entering an era of great expansion westward. The plantation system was advancing beyond the Mississippi River. The Tallmadge Amendment challenged the doctrine of states' rights, which had become accepted as a defense of slavery throughout much of the South. The Sixteenth Congress debated all aspects of the question from December 1819 through March 1820.

A compromise was proposed by Senator Jesse B. Thomas (1777–1853) of Illinois. The Thomas Amendment coupled the admission of Missouri as a slave state with that of Maine as a free state and prohibited the introduction of slavery into the remain-

would follow. Like the issue of slavery, Monroe questioned whether Congress had the authority to enact laws for federally-led improvements of roads and canals. He vetoed an improvements bill on that ground. Debate on slavery and the powers of the federal government heated up considerably after Monroe left office.

Monroe called slavery the "most menacing" issue confronting the nation. He supported a law that returned illegally captured African slaves to their home continent. A group called the American Colonization Society had purchased land in Africa; the nation of Liberia was formed shortly thereafter. The group intended it as a colony where returned slaves could live. To honor the president's support for the cause, the Liberian capital was named Monrovia.

ing areas acquired through the Louisiana Purchase. The bill was passed by both Houses with this amendment. But Congress and the nation were not quite finished with Missouri. A second, if less dramatic, debate occurred with the submission of Missouri's proposed constitution to the Congress.

In the proposed constitution, the Missouri Assembly was ordered to pass laws prohibiting free blacks or mulattoes (persons of white and black heritage) from entering the state. This prohibition went against the U.S. Constitution's clause guaranteeing that "the citizens of each State shall be entitled to all of the privileges and immunities of citizens of the several States." The status of free blacks in the North was at stake. For instance, free blacks in Massachusetts were considered citizens. Were their rights to be denied? Under the leadership of Speaker of the House Henry Clay (1777–1852; see box in **John Quincy Adams** entry in volume 1), Congress passed a resolution admitting Missouri on the condition that the legislature of that state refuse to pass any laws that denied privileges of citizenship. Later, Missouri passed acts (in 1825 and 1847) designed to prohibit the immigration of free Negroes and mulattoes into the state.

The Missouri Compromise debate of 1820 was the start of great discussions over the nature of the Union and the expansion of slavery, which dominated the political life of the nation during the 1840s and 1850s. The Compromise of 1850 was another attempt to address the sectional dispute over slavery.)

Monroe also wanted to protect the rights of Native Americans, especially as white settlers moved into the frontier. He supported a policy that set aside certain areas as Native American land for "as long as grass shall grow and rivers run." Despite Monroe's best intentions, however, within a decade the United States would adopt policies that forcefully removed Native Americans from their lands.

End of an era

Monroe's policies toward Native Americans and African Americans did not last beyond his presidency. On the other hand, the most noted historical event of his second term—the introduction of the Monroe Doctrine—

would have much greater impact in later years than it had at the time. A series of revolutions in Latin America and ongoing disputes between the United States and Russia over lands of the far west in North America created international tension. In the early 1820s, an alliance of Russia, Austria, France, and Prussia helped restore the fallen monarchy of Spain. (Prussia was a state in north central Germany [it was dissolved in 1947 and divided among the former East and West Germany; Poland; and the former Soviet Union, now fifteen independent republics, the largest of which is Russia].) With revolutions brewing in Spain's Latin America colonies, the United States and Great Britain both feared that the alliance would help Spain maintain its colonies in the Americas.

Great Britain and the United States agreed to withstand any such interference. The two nations were planning to issue a joint policy, a statement of cooperation. Monroe, as usual, took his time to carefully examine the issue from several angles. He consulted his Cabinet, congressmen, and ex-presidents Jefferson and Madison. Most were in favor of the joint policy, but Secretary of State Adams favored the United States making its own individual statement on the matter. Monroe agreed with Adams. In his annual address to Congress in December of 1823, Monroe announced the policy that would become the Monroe Doctrine (see **James Monroe** primary source entry in volume 1).

The Monroe Doctrine was applauded at home as another sign of the emergence of the United States as a major nation. Internationally, it was largely unnoticed. Great Britain had planned to fight any attempt by other European nations to protect or expand influence in the Americas. European nations could no longer afford to maintain their vast colonial empires. Still, the Monroe Doctrine was a major statement. The doctrine would be used and expanded by U.S. presidents several times through the years to challenge European intervention in the affairs of the Americas.

Meanwhile, the political unity that Monroe had enjoyed gradually began to dissolve. The Federalist Party had disappeared. The Democratic-Republican Party was splitting into factions around potential candidates for the 1824 presidential election. Slavery continued to divide the nation. Re-

gional difficulties grew larger over the introduction of a new tariff—a tax on imports—in 1824 that was more favorable to northern states.

Following the precedent set by George Washington and Monroe's Virginia Dynasty predecessors, Monroe limited his presidential tenure to two terms. When Monroe left office in 1825, he found himself deeply in debt. All his years of public service had brought him only a small part of the financial stability he could have attained as a private citizen. After Elizabeth Monroe died in 1830, he sold his estate, Ash Lawn, and moved to New York City to live in the home of his youngest daughter, Maria. Only several years after he left office did Monroe receive some form of reimbursement and a pension from the government he had served so well.

Monroe died on July 4, 1831, five years to the day after the deaths of two previous presidents, **John Adams** (1735–1826; see entry in volume 1) and Thomas Jefferson.

An editorial cartoon shows European rulers observing the newfound foreign policy strength of the United States, following the creation of the Monroe Doctrine.
Reproduced by permission of the Corbis Corporation.

A Selection of Monroe Landmarks

Ash Lawn–Highland. 1000 James Monroe Pkwy., Charlottesville, VA 22902-8722. (804) 293-9539. Home of Monroe from 1799 to 1826. Site—on the grounds of the College of William and Mary—includes Monroe memorabilia and a plantation. See http://monticello.avenue.gen.va.us/Tourism/AshLawn/home.html (accessed on June 13, 2000).

Hollywood Cemetery. 412 South Cherry St., Richmond, VA 23220. (804) 648-8501. Burial site of James and Elizabeth Monroe. See http://www.hollywoodcemetery.org/ (accessed on June 13, 2000).

James Monroe Museum and Memorial Library. 908 Charles St., Fredericksburg, VA 22401. (703) 899-4559. Monroe exhibits and artifacts on property once owned by Monroe. See http://www.artcom.com/museums/vs/gl/22401-58.htm (accessed on June 13, 2000).

Monroe was buried in New York, but in 1858 his remains were moved to Richmond, the capital of Virginia.

Legacy

James Monroe was the last president to govern with nearly full political support. The election of 1824 bitterly divided Democratic-Republicans, and the political landscape in America was forever altered soon after by the establishment of modern-day political parties. Like Washington, Monroe had warned against such a development, in which the interests of a party could be put above those of the nation.

The Monroe Doctrine became perhaps the most significant foreign policy statement in American history. Several U.S. presidents invoked the doctrine through the years to challenge European intervention in the affairs of the Americas, and later to protect island nations of the Pacific Ocean.

The Missouri Compromise of 1820 offered a temporary calming of divisiveness (disagreements) on the issue of slavery and served as a guide into the 1850s. Monroe, following his principles that Congress should act independent of the president, did not engage in the debate. The issue of slavery continued to be a threat to the nation. Meanwhile, harsher government policies toward Native Americans followed soon after Monroe's presidency.

Monroe's personal legacy rests with his ability to unite the nation and to help instill a sense of national identity. The young nation matured during his presidency. John Quincy Adams, who had served with distinction as an American diplomat and as secretary of state, followed Monroe as president. He was rendered ineffective because of political differences with Congress. Adams, who later would redistinguish himself as a congressman, wrote that the Monroe years would be looked back to as "the Golden Age of this Republic."

Where to Learn More

Ammon, Harry. *James Monroe: The Quest for National Identity.* New York: McGraw-Hill, 1971. Reprint, Newtown, CT: American Political Biography Press, 1997.

Bains, Rae. *James Monroe, Young Patriot.* Mahwah, NJ: Troll Associates, 1986.

Gerson, Noel Bertram. *James Monroe: Hero of American Diplomacy.* Englewood Cliffs, NJ: Prentice-Hall, 1969.

The James Monroe Memorial Foundation. [Online] http://www.monroe foundation.org/ (accessed on July 31, 2000).

Kallen, Stuart. *James Monroe.* Edina, MN: ABDO Publishing Company, 1999.

Kelley, Brent P. *James Monroe.* Philadelphia: Chelsea House Publishers, 2000.

Elizabeth Monroe

Born June 30, 1768
New York, New York
Died September 23, 1830
Loudoun County, Virginia

Quiet future first lady helped spare the life of Madame Lafayette in 1795

E lizabeth Monroe was a woman of calm dignity who disliked fanfare and social activity. However, her quiet personality did not stop her from helping to free Madame Adrienne de Noailles Lafayette, Marquise de Lafayette (1759–1807), from execution in 1795.

Elizabeth Kortright Monroe was born on June 30, 1768. She came from a wealthy family that moved within a small social circle in New York City. Her father, Lawrence, supported the Tory party of Great Britain and wanted the American colonies to remain under British rule. By the time of the American Revolution (1775–83), he was established as a wealthy merchant. Earlier, he had been a privateer. A privateer was a private trader and merchant who was also licensed to carry arms and provide military support for a nation. Kortright traded with American, Indian, British, and French settlers in North America. If needed, he could serve as a civilian for British military interests. When the American Revolution started, however, Kortright was not involved in fighting for the British cause.

Meanwhile, **James Monroe** (1758–1831; see entry in volume 1) had served valiantly on the American side in the

Elizabeth Monroe had "a complete absorption in the affairs of her family and household and a total detachment from the world of politics and business."

Historian Harry Ammon

Elizabeth Monroe.
Courtesy of the Library of Congress.

Revolution. He met Elizabeth while he was serving in the Congress of the Confederation, which met in New York. Despite their different family backgrounds—he came from a modest family and fought for American independence—they began a romance. They married in 1786.

The Monroes had a daughter in 1787, Eliza Kortright Monroe, and moved to Fredericksburg, in Monroe's native state of Virginia. The couple had two other children: James Spence, who was born in 1799 but died a year later, and daughter Maria Hester Monroe, who was born in 1803.

Madame Lafayette's life is spared

From 1794 to 1796, James Monroe served as a diplomat in France. It was during that period that Elizabeth Monroe helped secure the release of Madame Lafayette. Monroe had been a friend of Major General Lafayette (1757–1834; see box in **James Monroe** entry in volume 1) since helping tend to Lafayette's wounds during the American Revolution. Lafayette was a French citizen who fought for the American cause and was made a major general in the Continental Army. After the American Revolution ended, Lafayette returned to France. There he played an important role in the French Revolution (1789–97) and served in the new French government that emerged. He was commanding the French army in a war against Austria when the French political power shifted to his political opponents. Lafayette was branded a traitor (a person who has betrayed his country). He was captured and held in prison in Prussia and Austria from 1792 to 1798. His wife, meanwhile, was imprisoned in Paris.

Elizabeth Monroe paid a visit to her friend Madame Lafayette and her two children where they were being held in jail. At that time in Paris, carriages were banned from the streets because they represented a status symbol of wealth. Nevertheless, Elizabeth Monroe hired a carriage to take her to the prison. Her ride to the jail and her arrival there drew a crowd of onlookers. The prison gatekeeper was surprised by her arrival, but he allowed her to enter and led her to a waiting room. Madame Lafayette was brought in, saw her friend, and burst into tears. She had been waiting in her cell for a summons: She was supposed to be executed that very afternoon.

Elizabeth Monroe spoke briefly with Madame Lafayette. As she rose to leave, she announced loudly that she would return to visit Madame Lafayette the next morning. Meanwhile, French officials received word of her visit to the prison. Anxious to promote goodwill between France and America, French officials freed Madame Lafayette.

As Monroe's political career blossomed—he was elected governor of Virginia in 1798—Elizabeth Monroe concentrated on raising her daughters. In 1803, President **Thomas Jefferson** (1743–1826; see entry in volume 1) appointed Monroe as a special envoy (a diplomatic position just below the rank of ambassador) to France. He was included in a delegation that was sent to France to negotiate the land sale that eventually became the Louisiana Purchase. Eliza, as she was called, accompanied her husband. She was well liked in Paris society, where she was affectionately called *la belle americaine* ("the beautiful American"). The Monroes enjoyed attending theaters in Paris. Whenever they entered a theater, the orchestra would play the American favorite "Yankee Doodle" in their honor.

The Monroes remained in Europe until 1807, often traveling between Great Britain, France, and Spain while Monroe represented various foreign policy interests of President Jefferson. After returning home, Monroe served in the Virginia legislature and then, again, briefly, as the state's governor. During this period, Elizabeth and her daughters resided at Ash Lawn, the Monroe estate in Charlottesville, Virginia. President **James Madison** (1751–1836; see entry in volume 1) appointed Monroe as secretary of state in 1811.

The Era of Good Feelings

After serving Madison as secretary of state and secretary of war, James Monroe was elected president in 1816. He served two terms during which the young United States became a stronger and more prosperous nation. The period has been called "The Era of Good Feelings."

Those good feelings did not always extend to Elizabeth Monroe. She did not compare well to her more outgoing predecessor, **Dolley Madison** (1768–1849; see entry in volume 1). Dolley Madison often visited the wives of political officials and dignitaries, and she entertained frequently. However, Elizabeth soon developed her own style. She preferred a much less active social role. Social events during the Monroe administration were fewer and more formal. Elizabeth often did not attend dinner parties at the White House. Instead of making the rounds in Washington, D.C., Elizabeth expected the wives of political officials and dignitaries to make appointments to visit her. She and her two daughters, however, served as hostesses for weekly receptions that were open to the public.

The Monroes retired to Ash Lawn following the completion of President Monroe's second term in 1825. However, Monroe had fallen into debt. He had not received sufficient compensation for all his years of public service. The couple eventually benefited from a pension and lived reasonably well. Elizabeth Monroe died in September of 1830. Her husband died less than a year later.

Where to Learn More

Anthony, Carl Sferrazza. *First Ladies: The Saga of the Presidents' Wives and Their Power, 1789–1961*. New York: William Morrow, 1990.

Minnigerode, Meade. *Some American Ladies: Seven Informal Biographies*. New York: Putnam's Sons, 1926. Reprint, Freeport, NY: Books for Libraries Press, 1969.

The Monroe Doctrine

**Delivered as part of Monroe's Seventh Annual Address
to Congress, December 2, 1823; excerpted from
A Hypertext on American History (Web site)**

*The President introduces the Monroe Doctrine, the most
influential foreign policy statement in American history*

During the presidency of **James Monroe** (1758–1831; see
entry in volume 1), there were ongoing disputes between
the United States and Russia over lands in the far west of
North America. In addition, a series of revolutions occurred
against Spanish and Portuguese authorities in their colonies
in Latin America. When an alliance of Russia, Austria, France,
and Prussia (a state in north central Germany that was dissolved in 1947 and divided among the former East and West
Germany; Poland; and the former Soviet Union, now fifteen
independent republics, the largest of which is Russia) helped
restore the fallen monarchy of Spain in the early 1820s, the
United States and Great Britain grew concerned that the alliance would provide assistance to Spain to help it maintain
its colonies in the Americas.

Great Britain and the United States agreed to withstand any such interference. The two nations were planning
to issue a joint policy, but Secretary of State **John Quincy
Adams** (1767–1848; see entry in volume 1) convinced Monroe that the United States should make its own statement on
the matter. In his annual address to Congress in December of

"We should consider any
attempt [by Russia,
Austria, Prussia, Spain, or
France] to extend their
system to any portion of
this hemisphere as
dangerous to our peace
and safety."

*James Monroe, in an address to
Congress*

1823, Monroe announced the policy that would become known as the Monroe Doctrine.

Things to remember while reading an excerpt from the Monroe Doctrine:

- During Monroe's presidency, there were only two states west of the Mississippi River—Missouri and Louisiana. The area from present-day Texas to California was controlled by Spain; the present-day states of Oregon, Washington, and Idaho were occupied under a joint agreement between the United States and Great Britain; and present-day Alaska was owned by Russia, which also claimed fishing rights along the coast of present-day California.

- The best definition of the Monroe Doctrine can be found in the last sentence of the second paragraph and the first sentence of the sixth paragraph in the following excerpt. Monroe affirmed that North and South America could no longer be colonized (controlled) by European powers, and any attempt to do so would be viewed as an act of aggression against the United States.

- In the concluding two paragraphs of the excerpt, Monroe noted that the United States had not interfered in conflicts and governments in Europe. He concluded by demanding the same of European nations toward the Americas. Likewise, Monroe stated, the United States would not interfere with new governments emerging in South America.

Excerpt from the Monroe Doctrine

A precise knowledge of our relations with foreign powers as respects our negotiations and transactions with each is thought to be particularly necessary. Equally necessary is it that we should for a just estimate of our resources, revenue, and progress in every kind of improvement connected with the national prosperity and public defense. It is by rendering justice to other nations that we may expect

it from them. It is by our ability to resent injuries and redress wrongs that we may avoid them. . . .

*At the proposal of the Russian Imperial Government, made through the minister of the Emperor residing here, a full power and instructions have been transmitted to the minister of the United States at **St. Petersburg** to arrange by amicable negotiation the respective rights and interests of the two nations on the North West coast of this continent. A similar proposal had been made by His Imperial Majesty to the Government of Great Britain, which has likewise been acceded to. The Government of the United States has been desirous by this friendly proceeding of manifesting the great value which they have invariably attached to the friendship of the Emperor and their solicitude to cultivate the best understanding with his Government. In the discussions to which this interest has given rise and in the arrangements by which they may terminate the occasion has been judged proper for asserting, as a principle in which the rights and interests of the United States are involved,*

President James Monroe (standing) discusses the Monroe Doctrine with members of his administration: (left to right) John Quincy Adams, William H. Crawford, William Wirt, John C. Calhoun, Daniel D. Tompkins, and John McLean.
Reproduced by permission of the Corbis Corporation.

St. Petersburg: The capital city of Russia at that time.

that the American continents, by the free and independent condition which they have assumed and maintain, are henceforth not to be considered as subjects for future colonization by any European powers. . . .

*The citizens of the United States cherish sentiments the most friendly in favor of the liberty and happiness of their fellow men on **that side of the Atlantic**. In the wars of the European powers in matters relating to themselves we have never taken any part, nor does it **comport** with our policy so to do.*

It is only when our rights are invaded or seriously menaced that we resent injuries or make preparation for our defense. With the movements in this hemisphere we are of necessity more immediately connected, and by causes which must be obvious to all enlightened and impartial observers.

*The political system of the **allied powers** is essentially different in this respect from that of America. This difference proceeds from that which exists in their respective Governments; and to the defense of our own, which has been achieved by the loss of so much blood and treasure, and matured by the wisdom of their most enlightened citizens, and under which we have enjoyed **unexampled felicity**, this whole nation is devoted.*

*We owe it, therefore, to **candor** and to the **amicable** relations existing between the United States and those powers to declare that we should consider any attempt on their part to extend their system to any portion of this hemisphere as dangerous to our peace and safety. With the existing colonies or dependencies of any European power we have not interfered and shall not interfere, but with the Governments who have declared their independence and maintained it, and whose independence we have, on great consideration and on just principles, acknowledged, we could not view any **interposition** for the purpose of oppressing them, or controlling in any other manner their destiny, by any European power in any other light than as the manifestation of an unfriendly disposition toward the United States.*

In the war between those new Governments and Spain we declared our neutrality at the time of their recognition, and to this we have adhered, and shall continue to adhere, provided no change shall occur which, in the judgment of the competent authorities of this Government, shall make a corresponding change on the part of the United States indispensable to their security.

That side of the Atlantic: A reference to Europe.

Comport: Fit.

Allied powers: Nations that unite against a common enemy. In his speech, Monroe is referring to Russia, Austria, Prussia, Spain, and France.

Unexampled felicity: Unprecedented happiness.

Candor: Honesty.

Amicable: Friendly.

Interposition: Intrusion.

*The **late events** in Spain and Portugal **shew** that Europe is still unsettled. Of this important fact no stronger proof can be **adduced** than that the allied powers should have thought it proper, on any principle satisfactory to themselves, to have interposed by force in the internal concerns of Spain. To what extent such interposition may be carried, on the same principle, is a question in which all independent powers whose governments differ from theirs are interested, even those most remote, and surely none more so than the United States.*

*Our policy in regard to Europe, which was adopted at an early stage of the wars which have so long agitated that quarter of the globe, nevertheless remains the same, which is, not to interfere in the internal concerns of any of its powers; to consider the government **de facto** as the legitimate government for us; to cultivate friendly relations with it, and to preserve those relations by a frank, firm, and manly policy, meeting in all instances the just claims of every power, submitting to injuries from none.*

*But in regard to those continents circumstances are eminently and conspicuously different. It is impossible that the allied powers should extend their political system to any portion of either continent without endangering our peace and happiness; nor can anyone believe that our **southern brethren**, if left to themselves, would adopt it of their own accord. It is equally impossible, therefore, that we should behold such interposition in any form with indifference. If we look to the comparative strength and resources of Spain and those new Governments, and their distance from each other, it must be obvious that she can never subdue them. It is still the true policy of the United States to leave the parties to themselves, in the hope that other powers will pursue the same course.* (A Hypertext on American History [Web site])

Late events: Recent social unrest in Spain and Portugal against the ruling monarchies of those nations.

Shew: Show.

Adduced: Shown.

De facto: In reality; actually.

Southern brethren: The people of Americas south of the United States.

What happened next . . .

The Monroe Doctrine was a sign of the emergence of the United States as a major international power. Internationally, it was largely unnoticed. European nations could no longer afford to maintain their vast colonial empires, and

Great Britain was prepared to fight any attempt by other European nations to protect or expand influence in the Americas.

The Monroe Doctrine proved to be one of the most important policies in American history. Several presidents, including **James K. Polk** (1795–1849; see entry in volume 2), **William McKinley** (1843–1901; see entry in volume 3), and **Theodore Roosevelt** (1858–1919; see entry in volume 3), invoked the doctrine to protect U.S. interests. The doctrine would be expanded into the Pacific to include the Hawaiian Islands. President **John F. Kennedy** (1917–1963; see entry in volume 5) referred to the doctrine in 1961 during the Cuban missile crisis between the United States and the Soviet Union.

Did you know . . .

•James Monroe and his wife **Elizabeth Monroe** (1768–1830; see entry in volume 1) first settled on a farm that is now the site of the University of Virginia. In 1793, they purchased land next to Monticello, the estate of **Thomas Jefferson** (1743–1826; see entry in volume 1), so that Monroe could be closer to Jefferson, his mentor. The Monroes were not able to spend much time at their new estate because Monroe was appointed minister to France in 1794. While the Monroes were away, Jefferson supervised construction of their new home and the planting of orchards. The Monroes finally moved into their estate (called Highland, and later, Ash Lawn) in November of 1799. Within four years, they were back in France, as Monroe served as a foreign relations official for the Jefferson administration. From 1811 to 1817, the Monroes lived in Washington, D.C., as Monroe served as secretary of state to **James Madison** (1751–1836; see entry in volume 1), and then from 1817 through early 1825 as president. The Monroes retired to their estate in 1825, but all of those years of public service left them with little money. They had to sell Ash Lawn in 1826.

Where to Learn More

Dangerfield, George. *Defiance to the Old World: The Story Behind the Monroe Doctrine.* New York: Putnam, 1970.

May, Ernest R. *The Making of the Monroe Doctrine.* Cambridge: Belknap Press of Harvard University Press, 1975.

Rink, Paul. *In Defense of Freedom: The Story of the Monroe Doctrine.* New York: J. Messner, 1968.

University of Groningen, Department of Alta-Informatica. "James Monroe: Seventh State of Nation, Washington, DC, 1823-12-02." *A Hypertext on American History.* [Online] http://odur.let.rug.nl/~usa/P/jm5/speeches/jmoson7.htm (accessed on June 30, 2000).

Vaughan, Harold Cecil. *The Monroe Doctrine, 1823: A Landmark in American Foreign Policy.* New York: Watts, 1973.

John Quincy Adams
Sixth president (1825–1829)

John Quincy Adams

Born July 11, 1767
Braintree, Massachusetts
Died February 23, 1848
Washington, D.C.

Sixth president of the United States (1825–1829)

Son of a president and a child of the American Revolution, Adams also served as a diplomat, secretary of state, and U.S. representative

A member of the influential Adams family, a family that contributed greatly to the early years of the United States, John Quincy Adams was the first son of a former chief executive to also be elected president. Like his father, **John Adams** (1735–1826; see entry in volume 1), the second U.S. president, John Quincy Adams served only one term and was not a popular or an effective president. He won a disputed election. No candidate in the 1824 presidential election received enough electoral votes, so the election was decided by the House of Representatives, as required by the U.S. Constitution. Because of the election controversy, nearly every piece of legislation Adams or his allies in the Democratic-Republican Party attempted to pass was blocked by political rivals.

Indeed, shortly after Adams's election, military war hero **Andrew Jackson** (1767–1845; see entry in volume 1) resigned his seat in Congress to begin campaigning for the 1828 presidential election. Jackson had received more popular votes than Adams in the election of 1824. He was able to drum up tremendous opposition, both on Capitol Hill and with the general public, against Adams. The power struggle

"No one knows . . . the agony of mind that I have suffered from the time that I was made by circumstances . . . a candidate for the presidency till I was dismissed from that station by failure of my re-election."

John Quincy Adams

John Quincy Adams.
Courtesy of the Library of Congress.

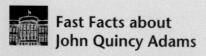

Fast Facts about John Quincy Adams

Full name: John Quincy Adams

Born: July 11, 1767

Died: February 23, 1848

Burial site: First Unitarian Church, Quincy, Massachusetts

Parents: John and Abigail Smith Adams

Spouse: Louisa Catherine Johnson (1775–1852; m. 1797)

Children: George Washington (1801–1829); John II (1803–1834); Charles Francis (1807–1886); Louisa Catherine (1811–1812)

Religion: Unitarian

Education: Harvard College (B.A., 1787)

Occupations: Lawyer

Government positions: Minister to the Netherlands, Prussia, and Russia; U.S. senator and representative (MA); peace commissioner at the Treaty of Ghent; secretary of state under James Monroe

Political party: Democratic-Republican

Dates as president: March 4, 1825–March 4, 1829

Age upon taking office: 57

between Adams and Jackson represented a contest between the entrenched (firmly established) New England political and economic order, as represented by Adams, and the independent-minded new southern and western states that had more recently entered the Union.

Prior to being president, Adams enjoyed a prominent career as a diplomat. He was instrumental in the drafting or signing of several important pacts that helped establish American foreign policy in the early decades of the new nation's history. As secretary of state under **James Monroe** (1758–1831; see entry in volume 1), for example, Adams penned the speech that became known as the Monroe Doctrine (see **James Monroe** primary source entry in volume 1). The doctrine firmly stated American intentions to oppose further European colonization in the Americas.

After failing to be reelected as president in 1828, Adams became the only ex-president to be elected to the House of Representatives. His career in Congress was marked by far greater effectiveness than that of his presidency. A vocal opponent of slavery, Adams spent seventeen years battling—and at times belittling—colleagues who fought to maintain the institution. Adams was nicknamed "Old Man Eloquent" for his impassioned speeches.

Though he was a talented and highly regarded foreign diplomat, Adams probably would have been much happier had he never entered American politics. A skilled speaker and linguist, Adams wrote poetry, kept a journal from the age of eleven, and translated a famous German work, *Oberon,* by

Christoph Martin Wieland (1733–1813), into English. Adams was also an avid collector of books and worked hard to secure a place in American libraries for his many foreign editions. As a legislator, later in his career, Adams helped direct a large bequest (a gift of money specified in a person's will) from an English donor, chemist James Smithson (1765–1829), to form the Smithsonian Institution, which runs a number of important museums and other historical institutions in Washington, D.C.

An auspicious beginning

John Quincy Adams was born at home in Braintree, Massachusetts, on July 11, 1767. His family ancestry stretched back several generations in New England. An Adams forebear (ancestor) arrived from England in 1632. A subsequent Adams descendant had wed the granddaughter of *Mayflower* pilgrim John Alden (1599–1687) and his wife, Priscilla Mullins Alden (1604–1680). The couple's romance had become a legendary tale in Plymouth Colony history. The Smith and Quincy lineage (family line) of Adams's mother, **Abigail Adams** (see entry in volume 1), was equally deep-rooted. The Smiths had long been involved in the shipping business. The first Quincy ancestor had arrived in America in 1633, starting a long line of prominent Quincy figures in early New England history.

Adams was the second child born to John Adams, a prominent Boston lawyer, and Abigail Smith

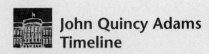

John Quincy Adams Timeline

1767: Born in Massachusetts

1775: American Revolutionary War begins

1787: Earns degree from Harvard College

1790–94: Works as attorney in private practice in Boston

1794–97: Serves as minister to Holland

1796: Father John Adams elected president

1797–1801: Serves as minister to the Court of Prussia

1803–8: Serves in the U.S. Senate as a Federalist from Massachusetts; recalled by special election in 1808

1809–15: Serves as minister to Russia during presidency of James Madison

1812: War of 1812 begins

1815–17: Serves as minister to Great Britain; negotiator of Treaty of Ghent, which ended the War of 1812

1817–24: Serves as U.S. secretary of state; writes the Monroe Doctrine

1825–29: Serves as sixth U.S. president

1831–49: Serves in the U.S. House of Representatives from Plymouth District, Massachusetts

1841: Serves as co-counsel on the *Amistad* case argued before the U.S. Supreme Court, delivering the closing argument

1844: Successful in rescinding a Congressional gag rule on slavery

1846: Opposes U.S. conflict with Mexico

1848: Dies in Washington, D.C.

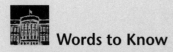

Words to Know

Annual Message to Congress: A speech the president delivers before Congress each year. Originally called the Annual Message to Congress and delivered each November, the speech became known as the State of the Union Address and is delivered each January.

Bar: A term that encompasses all certified lawyers—those who have passed all official requirements (the bar exam) to be certified as lawyers.

Capitol Hill: A nickname for Congress, since the Capitol building where Congress holds sessions is located on a small hill.

Consul: A diplomat stationed in a foreign country who advises people from his or her own country on legal matters.

Continental Congress: The group of representatives who met to establish the United States.

Electoral votes: The votes a presidential candidate receives for having won a majority of the popular vote in a state.

Federalist Party: An American political party of the late eighteenth century that began losing influence around 1820. Federalists supported a strong national government. Growing sentiments for states' rights and rural regions led to the demise of the party. Many Federalists became Democratic-Republicans until that party was split into factions in the mid-1820s. Those favoring states' rights became Jackson Democrats and formed the Democratic Party in 1832.

Infrastructure: The system of public works—the physical resources constructed for public use, such as bridges and roads—of a state or country.

Lineage: Ancestry; family line.

Monroe Doctrine: A policy statement issued during the presidency of James Monroe. The Monroe Doctrine explained the position of the United States on the activities of European powers in the Western Hemisphere. Of major significance was the United States' stand against European intervention in the affairs of the Americas.

Partisan politics: Placing the concerns of one's group or political party above all other considerations.

Tariff: A tax imposed on imported goods that raises their price.

Adams, the daughter of a parson. They had married in 1764. Abigail Adams was a learned, progressive woman. She had had no formal schooling but was an avid reader, writer, and debater. The two thousand letters she left behind reveal a woman of intelligence, with a passion for English literature and a dedication to democratic ideals and the American cause. Her son was named John Quincy after Abigail's great-grandfather, who died two days after John Quincy was born. Adams's siblings included older sister Abigail, whom the family called "Nabby," younger brothers Charles and Thomas Boylston, and younger sister Susanna, who died as a toddler.

Adams's early childhood was spent between homes in Boston and Braintree, where the Quincy clan owned a large seaside estate called Mount Wollaston. In the family since 1633, the parcel had originally been known as Merry Mount and was later immortalized in the tale "The Maypole of Merry Mount," by Nathaniel Hawthorne (1804–1864). Adams inherited this property later in life. The colonial city of Boston, where his father practiced law, was a thriving and increasingly rebellious port town at the onset of the American Revolution in 1775, when Adams was seven.

War brought abrupt changes to Adams's early life. His village school in Braintree closed when its headmaster (principal) departed to serve in the Continental Army. Adams's father left for Philadelphia, Pennsylvania, to take part in the Continental Congress, where he served as a delegate for three years. The elder Adams was a member of a committee that helped **Thomas Jefferson** (1743–1826; see entry in volume 1) write the Declaration of Independence (see **Thomas Jefferson** primary source entry in volume 1). And closer to home, the war's violence came very near the Adams residence when, in 1775, young John Quincy Adams watched the Battle of Bunker Hill with his mother from a neighboring hilltop.

First of many European sojourns

In 1778, when Adams was eleven years old, his father was named the U.S. minister to France, and he took his son along. On a return trip to Europe, the elder Adams again served as a diplomat and again took his son. During this time, John Quincy studied at Holland's University of Leyden, though he was not yet fourteen. Later that year, Francis Dana (1743–1811), the first American envoy (a diplomatic position just below the rank of ambassador) to Russia, requested that the teen serve as his secretary. Adams spent the next fourteen months in St. Petersburg, Russia.

When Adams returned to the United States in 1785, he was a young celebrity for his impressive work as a junior diplomat. He suffered an embarrassing setback, however, when he failed his first oral (spoken) entrance examination to Harvard College. But when he graduated in 1787, second in his class, Adams was the class orator—the most skilled public speaker in his class.

Adams seemed destined to enter a career in law. After being admitted to the Massachusetts bar (the legal profession), he began practicing in Boston. Adams soon began to dislike the daily grind of a lawyer. He preferred writing on political matters for New England newspapers. From 1790 to 1794, he was a leading political commentator. Adams inherited his love of literature and learning from his mother. He spent much of his time in intellectual pursuits. He was also a devoted book collector.

In 1794, President **George Washington** (1732–1799; see entry in volume 1) named young Adams the U.S. minister to the Netherlands. He accepted the job with some hesitation, fearing he was not quite qualified. In 1795, Adams was sent to London for the ratification of Jay's Treaty, which helped soothe increasing tensions between Great Britain and the United States. While in London, England, he met Louisa Johnson (1775–1852; see entry on **Louisa Adams** in volume 1). She was the daughter of Joshua Johnson, who was serving as the American consul (a diplomat stationed in a foreign country who advises people from his or her own country on legal matters) in London. After a long engagement, John Quincy Adams and Louisa were married in London in July of 1797. The event was a major story for the London newspapers, because John Adams had been elected the second U.S. president. John Quincy Adams was called "the American Prince of Wales." Meanwhile, Louisa Adams, half-British by birth, was a topic of some nasty remarks back in America because of her British heritage.

Elected to the U.S. Senate

Soon after his marriage, John Quincy Adams was named envoy to the Court of Prussia by his father, President Adams. (Prussia was a state in north central Germany; it was dissolved in 1947 and divided among the former East and West Germany; Poland; and the former Soviet Union, now fifteen independent republics, the largest of which is Russia). The younger Adams and Louisa enjoyed their time in Berlin, where their first child, George, was born, but they returned to the United States in 1801 when Thomas Jefferson succeeded the elder Adams to the presidency. Back in Boston with Louisa and George, Adams resumed his law practice, but he quickly abandoned it in 1803 when the Massachusetts legislature elected him to a vacant seat in the United States Senate as a member of the Federalist Party.

A young John Quincy Adams.
Courtesy of the Library of Congress.

While serving in the Senate, however, Adams had a falling-out with his party. He supported the rival Democratic-Republican president, Thomas Jefferson, on two major issues—the Louisiana Purchase and the Embargo Act of 1807. Because he sided with a Democratic-Republican, Adams was recalled from his seat by the Massachusetts legislature, which, at that time, elected the state's U.S. senators. The legislators instead chose a Federalist—James Lloyd (1769–1831)—who would routinely support the party's interests. Partisan politics (putting the concerns of one's political party above all other considerations) taught Adams an especially bitter lesson in this case. Nevertheless, he remained true to his own beliefs rather than to those of his political party.

Beginning in 1806, Adams taught at Harvard and soon became an active member of the Democratic-Republican party organization, the rival of the Federalist Party of his father and George Washington. (He resigned from office in 1808.) When fellow Democratic-Republican **James Madison** (1751–1836; see entry in volume 1) was elected president, Adams was named U.S. minister to Russia. He and Louisa departed in 1809, leaving two older sons behind with relatives

Like father, like son, like son: John Adams served as minister to England during George Washington's administration; his son, John Quincy Adams, served in the post during Thomas Jefferson's administration; and John Quincy Adams's son, Charles Francis Adams, was appointed to the position by Abraham Lincoln.

but bringing two-year-old Charles with them for the six-thousand-mile voyage.

By this time, the forty-two-year-old Adams was a respected senior member of the American diplomatic corps. He was part of the team that negotiated the Treaty of Ghent in 1814, which ended the War of 1812 between the United States and Great Britain. He was then given the very desirable assignment of minister to Great Britain in 1815. Adams was later appointed to the U.S. Supreme Court by President Madison, but he turned down the offer.

Another Democratic-Republican president, James Monroe, chose Adams to be his secretary of state when he named his Cabinet in early 1817. Now fifty years of age, Adams had attained a post that was viewed as the stepping-stone to the presidency (Jefferson, Madison, and Monroe had previously held the position before they were elected president). Adams's term as secretary of state was marked by several notable achievements that shaped American history and geography in the century, among them the Monroe Doctrine of 1823. Adams wrote the speech that Monroe delivered in December of that year.

A contested election

Adams ran for president in 1824 against three other men. General Andrew Jackson, a popular hero from the War of 1812 who had support from the new "western" states of Kentucky and Tennessee, received the majority of the popular vote. However, none of the four contenders—all Democratic-Republicans—won the necessary number—a majority—of electoral votes. Thus, the contest went to the House of Representatives, as dictated by the Constitution. The House elected Adams by a narrow margin on February 9, 1825. He became the first president to take office without a majority of Electoral College votes. (For more information on the Electoral College, see boxes in **George W. Bush** entry in volume 5.)

The narrow margin would bring political doom for Adams, however. Among his three rivals for the top office had been Henry Clay (1777–1852; see box), Speaker of the House of Representatives. When neither Adams nor Clay received a

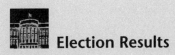

Election Results

1824

Presidential / Vice presidential candidates	Popular votes	Electoral votes
John Quincy Adams (Democratic-Republican)	108,740	84
Andrew Jackson (Democratic-Republican)	153,544	99
William H. Crawford (Democratic-Republican)	47,136	41
Henry Clay (Democratic-Republican)	46,618	37

Only the Democratic-Republican Party was represented in this election; different factions of that party nominated different candidates. When no candidate received a majority of electoral votes, it became the responsibility of the House of Representatives to elect a president. Clay's supporters largely threw their support to Adams, which helped elect Adams president. John C. Calhoun received the most votes as a vice presidential nominee. This was also the first election where popular votes were counted.

majority of electoral votes in the election, Clay allied with Adams and instructed his legislative colleagues to throw their votes to Adams. Adams later named Clay to the post of secretary of state. Jackson's supporters—especially southern politicians—complained that the appointment was unfair.

Clay's acceptance of the secretary of state post was a disastrous move. Jackson and his supporters accused Adams of engaging in a "corrupt bargain" when he named Clay to the Cabinet position. Although Adams and Clay were not friends or political allies, the appointment caused such an uproar that Clay later said it permanently stained his political career. Adams wanted to name Jackson as his secretary of war, but Jackson declined.

An ineffective administration

The four years between 1825 and 1829 were, as revealed by Adams's journals, the most difficult, painful years of his otherwise distinguished career. The press criticized him harshly. He was accused of having European intellectual tendencies and was called a Yankee elitist (someone who thinks himself superior). Although Adams was president during a period of American prosperity, there were no major achievements during his administration.

 **Henry Clay**

Known as "The Great Compromiser" for his ability to convince diverse factions in Congress to agree on legislation that would preserve the union, Clay helped avert—or delay—a national crisis over slavery. He was a forceful proponent of a strong federal government building interstate roads and canals and making other national improvements during a period when the constitutionality of such actions was debated.

Clay was born on April 12, 1777, in Hanover County, Virginia. His father died in 1781, his mother remarried in 1791, and the family moved to Richmond, Virginia, where Clay began working as a store clerk. From 1793 to 1797, Clay served as secretary to George Wythe, a court administrator. Clay had little education, but he read widely in Wythe 's library.

Clay moved to Lexington, Kentucky, in November 1797 and worked as a lawyer. In 1803, Clay was elected to the Kentucky legislature. In 1806 and again in 1810, he finished the terms of U.S. senators who left office. In 1811, he was elected to the House of Representatives. He was immediately chosen Speaker and was re-elected five times to that position. Clay was a "war hawk"—one who favored armed conflict against Great Britain, with whom the United States had been feuding for several years. The ensuing War of 1812 (1812–15) accomplished little, but the nation emerged stronger.

Beginning in 1815, Clay pushed for his "American System," a program intended to protect American industries against foreign competition, provide federal financing for improvements of highways and canals, and bolster the United States Bank to provide centralized financial control. Clay succeeded for a time: the Federal Bank was strong from 1815 to 1832 and tariffs (taxes on imported goods) were enacted, but the internal improvements, opposed by those who believed they infringed on the powers of individual states, were not carried out.

Missouri's application for statehood in 1819 shocked the North. If accepted, Missouri would be the first new state to permit slavery. Clay had advocated gradual emancipation of slaves in Kentucky in 1798, but by 1819 he was a slaveowner. In the Missouri debate, he did not devise the basic compromise that allowed Missouri to enter the Union as a slave state. Instead, he resolved a crisis caused by the Missouri constitutional provision that free blacks could not enter the state. The Missouri legislature assured Clay that it would pass no law abridging the privileges and immunities of U.S. citizens of whatever race.

Clay was a candidate for the presidency in 1824, but three others received more votes, so he was not a candidate when the election was decided in the House of Representatives. He defied Kentucky's instruction to cast the state's votes

Henry Clay, secretary of state under President John Quincy Adams.
Courtesy of the Library of Congress.

for Jackson, saying he could not support a "military chieftain"; instead, he supported eventual victor John Quincy Adams. When Adams named Clay secretary of state, opponents accused the pair of devising a "corrupt bargain." Clay had merely supported the man whose views were closest to his own, but the charge lingered for the rest of his life.

When Adams lost in his reelection bid in 1828, he offered to appoint Clay to the Supreme Court, but he declined and returned to Kentucky. In 1831, he was elected to the Senate and served until 1842. In the mid-1830s, anti-Jacksonians formed the Whig Party. Clay expected the Whig nomination for president in 1840 but aging military hero William Henry Harrison won it instead. When Harrison, who lacked political savvy, won the election, Clay anticipated that he would be the actual leader of the administration. But Harrison died after only a month in office, and his successor, John Tyler, a states' rights advocate, opposed the principles of Clay's program. Clay resigned from the Senate in disgust.

Clay was the Whig presidential candidate in 1844, but his unwillingness to take a firm stand on the annexation of Texas cost him the election. He made another effort for the 1848 nomination, but that went to General Zachary Taylor, a Mexican War (1846–48) hero. American victory in the war brought on another sectional crisis, with threats to dissolve the Union over the expansion of slavery into new territories. Clay returned to the Senate in poor health and led in working out the Compromise of 1850. This series of measures admitted California as a free state, organized new territories, and enacted a fugitive slave law that denied protection of the laws to African Americans who escaped from slavery and fled to the North. The Compromise helped preserve the Union, but merely delayed the inevitable conflict that erupted into the Civil War in 1861. Clay died in Washington on June 29, 1852, confident that armed conflict had been averted.

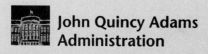

John Quincy Adams Administration

Administration Dates
March 4, 1825–March 4, 1829

Vice President
John C. Calhoun (1825–29)

Cabinet
Secretary of State
Henry Clay (1825–29)

Secretary of the Treasury
Richard Rush (1825–29)

Secretary of War
James Barbour (1825–28)
Peter B. Porter (1828–29)

Attorney General
William Wirt (1825–29)

Secretary of the Navy
Samuel L. Southard (1825–29)

Postmaster General
John McLean (1825–29)

In his first Annual Message to Congress (now called the State of the Union Address), Adams called for such public improvement projects as a national university and an astronomical observatory. He noted that Europe already had 130 such scientific stations, whereas America had none. The anti-Adams press made great fun of his proposal, explaining to a skeptical American public that Adams wanted to spend federal money on scientific explorations of the heavens. (Nearly two decades later, however, Adams attended the opening of the first American observatory in 1843. The observatory was built on a hill named Mount Adams near Cincinnati, Ohio.)

Adams tried to push forward bills or acts that would expand the American road and canal system, believing that westward expansion would secure the nation's power and economic strength. However, his enemies in Congress blocked every piece of legislation he introduced. After the midterm Congressional elections of 1826, which brought a new group of anti-Adams opposition to Congress, Adams wrote in his journal that "days of trial are coming again." He observed that Washington seemed populated by "thousands of persons occupied with little else than to work up the passions of the people." Even his vice president, John C. Calhoun (1782–1850; see box in **Andrew Jackson** entry in volume 1), had become a supporter of Jackson by 1826.

Ironically, Adams's belief that the federal government should play an active role in creating an infrastructure (for example, bridges and roads) that would benefit and strengthen all regions became another of his political liabilities. Clay had earlier proposed what he termed the "American system," a strategic plan that would impose tariffs (taxes) on imported goods and create an infrastructure that would encourage

greater trade between the factories of the North and the farm-based economies of the South and the West. Opponents in Congress believed that such a plan would benefit the North at the expense of the South. Debate continued about the power of the federal government to implement such programs against the wishes of individual states. Adams's administration managed to pass an act that allowed the Cumberland Road—the first federal road in the United States—to expand into Ohio. Adams also succeeded in pushing through legislation that funded a canal linking the Chesapeake Bay with the Ohio River.

Land-rights issues for Native Americans also caused much disagreement during this era. Adams sought fairness in dealings with Native Americans; in the 1828 presidential campaign, his opponents called him "pro-Indian." However, Adams was not successful with his Indian policy. Georgia landowners submitted an agreement, said to be signed by

John Quincy Adams worked hard to improve roads and canals. The Erie Canal in New York (above) was built during his administration. *Reproduced by permission of Archive Photos.*

Cherokee chiefs, that forced several thousand Creek and Cherokee Indians from richly fertile land. Adams signed the treaty against advice. When the treaty was revealed to be a fake, a more moderate treaty replaced it. The fairer treaty was opposed by the Georgia legislature. Adams contemplated sending in federal troops to Georgia to enforce the treaty, but he decided against using force. Then two other southern states, Mississippi and Alabama, followed Georgia in taking a strong position against federal intervention (interference) in matters regarding Native Americans.

Though he was often overworked and depressed, Adams still rose at five o'clock every morning for a long, vigorous walk or a swim in the Potomac River. In this era, there was little security in the White House, and a constant stream of visitors and tourists frequently interrupted him. For instance, one day, Adams was greatly entertained by his conversations with a man who sat down and claimed to be the Messiah.

The Tariff of Abominations

One of the more infamous (widely and unfavorably known) acts passed by Congress during Adams's tenure was the so-called Tariff of Abominations, formally known as the Tariff of 1828. Adams had been a strong advocate for a higher tariff. Andrew Jackson's supporters in Congress amended Adams's original tariff bill to include much higher taxes on imported raw materials as well. They believed that northern legislators and Adams supporters would never vote for such legislation, since it would mean that New England manufacturers would pay much higher prices for their raw materials. However, the bill passed, and consumer prices for a selection of goods jumped considerably. Needless to say, it was an extremely unpopular piece of legislation with the general public.

Despite his disappointment and growing distaste for the job, Adams ran for reelection in 1828. Adams took part only halfheartedly in a campaign that was one of the ugliest in American history—with both sides continually on the attack. Andrew Jackson won fifty-six percent of the popular vote, and Adams lost the election by a wide margin in the Electoral College. He became the second president in American history to serve only one term; his father had been the first.

Andrew Jackson (left) defeated John Quincy Adams in the heated election of 1828.
Courtesy of the Library of Congress.

Old Man Eloquent

After leaving office, Adams's health and outlook brightened considerably. He regained much of the energy and spirit that the job had drained from him. Nevertheless, a series of personal setbacks struck the family after Adams's defeat, including the death of the two elder sons, George and John, while still relatively young men. Both sons had been heavy drinkers and gamblers.

In 1830, Adams—over the objections of his wife—ran for and won a seat from Massachusetts in the U.S. House of Representatives, making him the only former president to serve in the House, also called the lower chamber. He was re-elected eight more times and enjoyed a legislative career marked both by great acrimony (bitterness) but also by much respect as an elder statesperson. He became a member of the newly formed Whig Party that opposed the policies of President Jackson and his newly formed Democratic Party. He relished the opportunity to tangle with his political enemies from the South in floor debates. Opposed to slavery, he became known as "Old Man Eloquent." (An eloquent debater speaks smoothly, expressively, and convincingly.) As leader of the House's antislavery faction, he coined the term "slavocracy" to describe the powerful faction that represented southern landowners and supporters of slavery, whom he believed ran counter to the nation's sacred democratic principles.

Adams's abolitionist (antislavery) politics were part of the reason that he was asked to serve as co-counsel on the 1841 *Amistad* case when it was argued before the U.S. Supreme Court. Roger S. Baldwin, a prominent lawyer, requested Adams's help in defending Africans who had mutinied on a Spanish slave ship. The Africans had been tricked into sailing to Long Island, New York, instead of back to Africa and were captured by the American navy. Adams delivered an eloquent closing argument against returning the Africans to Spanish jurisdiction (territory under Spanish law). The High Court declared the men set free.

One of Adams's greatest achievements in the House was his success in repealing a Congressional gag rule on slavery. A gag rule puts a limit on debate of a particular issue. The gag rule on slavery, in place from 1836 to 1844, had been pushed through by southern politicians to bar discussion of the slavery issue in both the Senate and the House. Adams had hectored (verbally annoyed) his colleagues during those years by reading aloud numerous petitions from his constituents (voters) that called for a repeal of the rule under the First Amendment guarantee of free speech. When he read one petition that called for the dissolution (breakup) of the Union—on grounds that federal money was being used to support the enslavement of human beings—there was an outcry in the House. Southern legislators voted to eject him from his seat on grounds of high treason. Appearing before a House judicial committee, Adams argued successfully for the repeal of the gag rule. His acquittal in the matter was seen as a significant early victory in the battle to end slavery.

As a congressman, Adams was vehemently (passionately) opposed to the U.S. conflict with Mexico in 1846. He called it an unfair war. In February of 1848—well into his eighties—Adams rose to voice his opposition to a proposal to award swords of honor to some of the American generals of the war. During the speech, he collapsed from what was probably a stroke (a sudden loss of consciousness and motion caused by an interruption of blood flow to the brain). He died two days later. Adams's body was laid out in the Capitol Building, where thousands came to pay their respects. Thirty members of Congress accompanied his funeral procession to Boston. He was buried in the Adams family vault in Quincy, Massachusetts. The vault is now part of the Adams National Historical Site.

Legacy

John Quincy Adams's term as president was the most difficult period of his long career. He achieved little as president, but the foresight behind many of his ideas to invest in the national infrastructure would be borne out later by successors. Ironically, Adams was portrayed as an elitist, whereas his opponent Andrew Jackson was considered more representative of the common man. Adams, however, wanted the federal government to take an active part in improving roads and education, which would have benefited poorer areas of the nation.

The detested Tariff of Abominations would grow into an even larger political problem during his successor's administration. Jackson's vice president, John Calhoun (who also served under Adams), firmly believed that it violated states' rights as set forth by Thomas Jefferson. He argued that states could choose to nullify, or willfully disobey, such federal laws. This idea is called the Theory of Nullification. Congress passed a law in 1832 that reduced some of the tariff rates, but South Carolina still objected. The possibility of using federal troops to enforce federal acts loomed as a harbinger (something that indicates what is to come) of the American Civil War.

A Selection of Adams Landmarks

Adams National Historic Site Visitors Center. 1250 Hancock St., Quincy, MA. 02169.
   (617) 773-1177. Videos, slide shows, and exhibits about the Adams family. The historic site includes three Adams houses: the birth site of President John Adams at 133
   Franklin Street, the birth site of President John Quincy Adams at 141 Franklin Street,
   and "Peacefield," a home owned by John Adams at 135 Adams Street. See
   http://www.nps.gov/adam/ (accessed on June 5, 2000).

United First Parish Church. 1306 Hancock St. (Quincy Center), Quincy, MA 02169. (617)
   773-1290. John Quincy and Louisa Adams, as well as John and Abigail Adams, are entombed in the family crypt in the church's basement. See http://www.ufpc.org/ (accessed on June 5, 2000).

During his nine terms as a U.S. representative, Adams was vocally opposed to the South's threat of nullification. The debate over state-versus-federal power would eventually ignite in full over the issue of slavery and spark the Civil War.

Adams's entire presidential administration was a battleground between political forces. On his side were the "federalist" lawmakers who believed that a strong federal government would lead America to economic prosperity and international power. On the other side stood forceful newcomers from the South and West, encouraged by regional economic success.

Adams's rival, Andrew Jackson, united some of the groups opposing Adams. This union would eventually cause the Democratic-Republican Party to dissolve. Jackson's followers would become the Democratic Party in 1832. Jackson's opponents formed the Whig Party in the mid-1830s.

Where to Learn More

Adams, John Quincy. *Memoirs of John Quincy Adams, 1795–1849.* (12
   vols.) Edited by Charles Francis Adams. Philadelphia: J. B. Lippincott, 1874–77. Reprint, Freeport, NY: Books for Libraries Press, 1969.

Miller, William Lee. *Arguing About Slavery: The Great Battle in the United States Congress*. New York: Knopf, 1996.

Nagel, Paul C. *John Quincy Adams: A Public Life, A Private Life*. New York: Alfred A. Knopf, 1997.

Shepherd, Jack. *The Adams Chronicles: Four Generations of Greatness*. Boston: Little, Brown, 1975.

Louisa Adams

Born February 12, 1775
London, England
Died May 15, 1852
Washington, D.C.

Half-British first lady suffered through political criticism

Louisa Adams was much beloved by her husband, **John Quincy Adams** (1767–1848; see entry in volume 1) for her intelligence, temperament, and sense of daring, but she was often the target of political gibes (sarcastic remarks) from his opponents because of her heritage: Her mother was British. As the daughter of a British mother, Louisa Adams remains the only first lady to have been born outside the United States.

Louisa Adams also had an uneasy relationship with **Abigail Adams** (1744–1818; see entry in volume 1), her famous mother-in-law. Abigail Adams thought Louisa represented extravagant "foreign" tendencies. Indeed, John Quincy Adams feared that his mother might try to arrange a marriage for him with an American woman if she learned that he was courting Louisa. He romanced Louisa for some time in England, where he was a diplomat, before revealing by letter to his family his intention to marry her.

> "Try as she might, the Madam could never be Bostonian, and it was her cross in life."
>
> *Henry Adams, in reference to his grandmother, Louisa Adams*

Louisa Adams.
Courtesy of the Library of Congress.

London years

Born Louisa Catherine Johnson on February 12, 1775, she spent her earliest years in Nantes, France. The outbreak of war between the New England colonies and Britain had forced American sympathizer Joshua Johnson to relocate his family from Great Britain. The Maryland-born Johnson was the American consul in London. His English wife, Catherine Nuth, was known for maintaining a lavish (luxurious) household. No expense was spared for food or entertainment. Louisa and her two sisters—all close in age, attractive, and musically gifted—were popular debutantes in London at the time. (A debutante is a young woman who has been formally presented to society.)

In 1795, John Quincy Adams arrived in London for the formal ratification of Jay's Treaty. The treaty settled commerce issues between the newly created United States and the powerful British Empire from which the United States had won independence. Adams, the son of America's first vice president, **John Adams** (1735–1826; see entry in volume 1) was already a well-known diplomat with several notable career achievements to his name. The twenty-eight-year-old Adams first met Louisa when he came to their home one evening to drop off some official papers and was invited to stay for dinner.

Adams and Louisa began to date. One of the qualities that attracted the diplomat to Louisa was her love of literature. She penned essays, poems, and plays, though they were never published, in addition to maintaining a journal for many years. Louisa also spoke French fluently, as did Adams.

The courtship between the two independent-minded spirits was somewhat stormy. Adams was apparently hesitant to set a wedding date until he was almost forced into it by Joshua Johnson. Initially, Adams had been led to believe the Johnsons possessed a vast Georgia plantation. As the couple's relationship developed, it became clear to Adams that Joshua Johnson had deep financial troubles.

The couple was wed on July 26, 1797, at All Hallows Barking, a church inside the Tower of London with origins dating back to the year 675. Adams's father had recently been elected the second American president. The couple departed not long afterward for the new diplomatic post to which his father had assigned him: minister to the Court of Prussia. (Prussia was a state in north central Germany; it was dissolved in 1947 and divided among the former East and West Germany; Poland; and the former Soviet Union, now fifteen independent republics, the largest of which is Russia.)

A traveling life

The Adamses spent the first years of their marriage in Berlin, Germany. Louisa suffered four miscarriages before giving birth to a son, George Washington Adams, in 1801. The Prussian king, Frederick William III, was fond of the Adamses. In a gesture that demonstrated how well liked the American minister and his wife were, the king issued an order that prohibited traffic on the street where the Adamses lived. This was so that Adams's infant could sleep undisturbed.

During the first few years of marriage, Adams's diaries reveal a deep appreciation of his choice of mate. Among other qualities, he noted that Louisa was a skilled conversationalist, which made her a valuable companion during the numerous official functions that the couple were required to attend. Privately, Louisa suffered the trials of travel and the miscarriages with a fortitude that surprised her husband. Abigail Adams, however, had called the young bride a "halfbreed" and proclaimed her to be a European beauty accustomed to a lavish lifestyle who would likely bankrupt her son.

After the elder Adams's presidency ended in 1801, John Quincy, Louisa, and their son returned to the United States. They settled in Boston's Hanover Square area. During this period, Louisa continued to have an uncomfortable relationship with Abigail Adams. Her father-in-law, the former president, however, greatly admired Louisa and recognized that the marriage was solid. During brief separations, Louisa received passionate poems from her husband.

The Adams family expanded with the arrival of two more sons, John II in 1803 and Charles Francis in 1807. Both were born in the United States while Adams was a Boston lawyer and then a member of Congress. In 1809, when Adams was named U.S. minister to Russia, he and Louisa left the two elder boys behind with relatives and set out with the two-year-old Charles on the six-thousand-mile voyage to St. Petersburg.

The capital of Imperial Russia was a rough place at the time, with dreadful winters and a poor water supply. Finding a warm apartment also proved difficult. In 1811, a daughter, Louisa Catherine, was born, but she died a year later, a terrible tragedy for her parents. When Louisa Adams departed the city in early 1815 to join her husband in London, the child was left buried in St. Petersburg's Anglican cemetery.

Adams had been named minister to Great Britain. There, he and Louisa were reunited with sons George and John, whom they had not seen in six years. During this period in Adams's career, from 1815 to 1817, the family lived in a suburb of London. The couple grew increasingly worried over the undisciplined habits of the two older boys.

The family returned to the United States when Adams was named secretary of state in the administration of newly elected president **James Monroe** (1758–1831; see entry in volume 1). After spending so many years abroad, the Adamses found adjusting to life in the United States difficult. Living in the District of Columbia, a national capital with a distinct absence of grandeur at that time, proved one of their most challenging assignments. Washington was a muddy and isolated town. John Quincy Adams was elected sixth president of the United States in 1824. The White House was not yet the grand presidential home that it eventually became. Cows, horses, and sheep grazed nearby. There was no indoor plumbing. Security was so lax (relaxed) that anyone could simply walk in unannounced.

Louisa worried greatly about her husband during his term as president, for he was under tremendous strain. He was severely criticized in the press—which usually described him as a Yankee aristocrat with a foreign wife—and subject to harsh attacks by the opposition party. For the duration of his term, Adams was hindered by supporters of political rival **Andrew Jackson** (1767–1845; see entry in volume 1), who thwarted nearly every piece of legislation he introduced. As a result, Adams lost a great deal of weight and suffered from periods of depression. Louisa made the best of her stay in the White House, participating in elegant receptions and showing hospitality to her guests.

Even after Adams lost the 1828 election to Jackson and his health rapidly returned, the Adamses were beset by worse trials. Their eldest son, George, a heavy drinker and gambler, disappeared from a vessel in the Atlantic in April of 1829. His hat and overcoat were found, and his body washed up on Long Island Sound a month later. John II, also a drinker, went into a coma at the age of thirty-one in 1834. He died debt-ridden, leaving his wife and two children to the care of Adams and Louisa.

Louisa was initially depressed about the prospect of returning to Washington when her husband was elected to Congress in 1830. She enjoyed summers at the family estate in Quincy, Massachusetts. After she settled down in Washington, she eventually came to be known as one of the capital's most eminent partygivers alongside another former first lady, **Dolley Madison** (1768–1849; see entry in volume 1).

John Quincy Adams suffered a stroke and died in 1848. Louisa also died as a result of a stroke four years later. She left behind a large collection of writings, including a diary, a great deal of correspondence, poems, and plays. The whole collection became part of the vast Adams Papers archive of the Massachusetts Historical Society. Louisa was laid to rest next to her husband inside the United First Parish Church—also known as the Adams Temple—in Quincy.

Where to Learn More

Bobbé, Dorothie De Bear. *Mr. & Mrs. John Quincy Adams: An Adventure in Patriotism*. New York: Minton, Balch & Company, 1930.

Heinrichs, Ann. *Louisa Catherine Johnson Adams, 1775–1852*. New York: Children's Press, 1998.

Nagel, Paul C. *The Adams Women: Abigail and Louisa Adams, Their Sisters and Daughters*. New York: Oxford University Press, 1987.

Adams's Closing Argument in the *Amistad* Case

**Delivered on February 24 and March 1, 1841;
excerpted from *The Amistad* . . . (Web site)**

*The former president, known as "Old Man Eloquent" for his
impassioned speeches in Congress against slavery, argues a case
on behalf of slaves before the Supreme Court*

In 1839, fifty-three Africans sold into slavery were to be taken
to Cuba, then a colony of Spain, aboard the *Amistad,* a Spanish vessel. The men seized control of the ship off the coast of
Cuba; they killed two crew members and directed the remaining crew to sail the ship back to Africa. Instead, the crew pilot-
ed the ship off the American coast, where it was seized by a U.S.
warship. The Africans were jailed in the United States. President
Martin Van Buren (1782–1862; see entry in volume 1) intended to surrender the men to Spanish authorities in Cuba.

Citing an international law that prohibited the slave
trade, the Africans were defended in American courts. Murder
charges were dropped, but the Africans remained in confine-
ment while claims on them were made by planters who
bought them as slaves and by the government of Spain. A
lower court ruled that claims to the Africans as property were
unwarranted because they were held illegally as slaves.

The case was eventually heard by the U.S. Supreme
Court. Former president **John Quincy Adams** (1767–1848;
see entry in volume 1) was enlisted to present closing arguments before the court in defense of thirty-six of the Africans.

"The Court, therefore, I
trust, in deciding this
case, will form no
lumping judgment on
these thirty-six
individuals, but will act
on the consideration that
the life and the liberty of
every one of them must
be determined by its
decision for himself
alone."

*John Quincy Adams, in his
closing defense in the* Amistad
trial

Adams, a staunch abolitionist (person in favor of eliminating slavery), had become known as "Old Man Eloquent" for his impassioned speeches in Congress during the 1830s against slavery. Adams served in Congress from 1831 to 1848 after having served as president from 1825 to 1829.

Things to remember while reading an excerpt from Adams's closing argument in the *Amistad* case:

- Van Buren intended to surrender the Africans to Spanish authorities. Adams and Van Buren were political enemies; Van Buren had been a key political adviser and second-term vice president of **Andrew Jackson** (1767–1845; see entry in volume 1), who defeated incumbent president Adams in the 1828 presidential election. During his closing arguments in the *Amistad* case, Adams made sure to announce that his presence was as a representative for justice for the Africans, and not as a means for revenge against his political enemy. He used the word "justice" on several occasions, attempting to impress upon the Supreme Court judges that the human rights of the defendants outweighed any political differences he had with Van Buren.

- Only a portion of Adams's long closing argument follows. In parts not included, he presented a great volume of evidence that indicated President Van Buren and his secretary of state, John Forsyth (1780–1841), among others, were motivated to surrender the defendants to Spanish authorities by political reasons, rather than by justice or international law. An example of Adams's use of such evidence occurs in the excerpt when he quotes from letters written by Forsyth on the *Amistad* matter.

- In his closing, Adams referred to the *Antelope* case of 1825, when a U.S. ship, the *Arraganta,* seized control of the *Antelope,* a slave ship sailing under a Venezuelan flag with a cargo of 281 Africans. The dispute over the ship and the Africans was settled when the U.S. Supreme Court ruled unanimously that the slave trade was a violation of natural law, which means that an actual law has to be enacted by a nation to make slavery legal. The ruling set free only some of the Africans, as the court noted that the slave trade was legal in Spain, Portugal, and Venezuela. Thirty-nine Africans were designated by the court as Spanish property and were returned to that nation.

- The case for the *Amistad* defendants hinged on whether or not they could be considered free when their ship anchored in American waters.

Excerpt from Adams's closing argument in the Amistad case

May it please your honors—

(This) Court is a Court of JUSTICE. And in saying so very trivial a thing, I should not on any other occasion, perhaps, be warranted in asking the Court to consider what justice is. Justice, as defined in the **Institutes of Justinian,** *nearly 2000 years ago, and as it is felt and understood by all who understand human relations and human rights, is—*

> Constans et perpetua voluntas, jus SUUM cuigue tribuendi *("The constant and perpetual will to secure to every one HIS OWN right.")*

And in a Court of Justice, where there are two parties present, justice demands that the rights of each party should be allowed to himself, as well as that each party has a right, to be secured and protected by the Court. This observation is important, because I appear here on the behalf of thirty-six individuals, the life and liberty of every one of whom depend on the decision of this Court. The Court, therefore, I trust, in deciding this case, will form no lumping judgment on these thirty-six individuals, but will act on the consideration that the life and the liberty of every one of them must be determined by its decision for himself alone.

They are here, individually, under very different circumstances, and in very different characters. Some are in one predicament, some in another. In some of the proceedings by which they have been brought into the custody and under the protection of this Court, thirty-two or three of them have been charged with the crime of murder. Three or four of them are female children, incapable, in the

Institutes of Justinian: The legal system established by Justinian I (483–565), ruler of the Roman empire from Constantinople (present-day Istanbul, Turkey) from 527 to 565. His system still remains the basis for the law of most European countries.

judgment of our laws, of the crime of murder or piracy, or, perhaps, of any other crime. Yet, from the day when the vessel was taken possession of by one of our naval officers, they have all been held as close prisoners, now for the period of eighteen long months, under custody and by authority of the Courts of the United States. I trust, therefore, that before the ultimate decision of this Court is established, its honorable members will pay due attention to the circumstances and condition of every individual concerned.

*When I say I derive consolation from the consideration that I stand before a Court of Justice, I am obliged to take this ground, because, as I shall show, **another Department of the Government** of the United States has taken, with reference to this case, the ground of utter injustice, and these individuals for whom I appear, stand before this Court, awaiting their fate from its decision, under the array of the whole Executive power of this nation against them, in addition to that of a **foreign nation**. And here arises a consideration, the most painful of all others, in considering the duty I have to discharge, in which, in supporting the motion to dismiss the appeal, I shall be obliged not only to investigate and submit to the **censure** of this Court, the form and manner of the proceedings of the Executive in this case, but the validity, and the motive of the reasons assigned for its interference in this unusual manner in a suit between parties for their individual rights. . . .*

*It is . . . peculiarly painful to me, under present circumstances, to be under the necessity of **arraigning** before this Court and before the civilized world, the course of the existing Administration in this case. But I must do it. That Government is **still in power**, and thus, subject to the control of the Court, the lives and liberties of all my clients are in its hands. And if I should pass over the course it has pursued, those who have not had an opportunity to examine the case and perhaps the Court itself, might decide that nothing improper had been done, and that the parties I represent had not been wronged by the course pursued by the Executive. In making this charge, or arraignment, as defensive of the rights of my clients, I now proceed to an examination of the correspondence of the Secretary of State with the ambassador of **her Catholic Majesty**, as officially communicated to Congress, and published among the national documents.*

The charge I make against the present Executive administration is that in all their proceedings relating to these unfortunate men, instead of that Justice, which they were bound not less than this hon-

Another Department of the Government: A reference to the executive branch led by President Martin Van Buren.

Foreign nation: A reference to Spain.

Censure: Punishment or scolding.

Arraigning: Officially charging someone of a crime.

Still in power: A reference to the fact that Martin Van Buren had lost the presidential election of 1840 but still held the office until March 4, 1841, when his successor, William Henry Harrison, would take over.

Her Catholic Majesty: The king of Spain.

orable Court itself to observe, they have substituted Sympathy!—sympathy with one of the parties in this conflict of justice, and **Antipathy** to the other. Sympathy with the white, antipathy to the black—and in proof of this charge I **adduce** the admission and **avowal** of the Secretary of State himself. In the letter of **Mr. Forsyth** to the Spanish Minister [Chevalier] d'Argaiz, of 13th of December, 1839, [Document H. R. N. S. 185,] defending the course of the administration against the reproaches utterly groundless, but not the less bitter of the Spanish Envoy, he says:

> The undersigned cannot conclude this communication without calling the attention of the Chevalier d'Argaiz to the fact, that with the single exception of the **vexatious detention** to which **Messrs. Montes and Ruiz** have been subjected in consequence of the civil suit instituted against them, all the proceedings in the matter, on the part both the Executive and Judicial branches of the government have had their foundation in the ASSUMPTION that these persons ALONE were the parties aggrieved; and that their claims to the surrender of the property was founded in fact and in justice.

At the date of this letter, this statement of Mr. Forsyth was strictly true. All the proceedings of the government, Executive and Judicial, in this case had been founded on the assumption that the two Spanish slave-dealers were the only parties aggrieved—that all the right was on their side, and all the wrong on the side of their surviving self-emancipated victims. I ask your honors, was this JUSTICE? No. It was not so considered by Mr. Forsyth himself. It was sympathy, and he so calls it, for in the preceding page of the same letter referring to the proceedings of this Government from the very first intervention of **Lieut. Gedney**, he says:

> Messrs. Ruiz and Montes were first found near the coast of the United States, deprived of their property and of their freedom, suffering from lawless violence in their persons, and in imminent and constant danger of being deprived of their lives also.
>
> They were found in this distressing and perilous situation by officers of the United States, who, moved towards them by sympathetic feeling which subsequently became, as it were national, immediately rescued them from personal danger, restored them to freedom, secured their oppressors that they might abide the consequences of the

Antipathy: Without sympathy.

Adduce: Offer as example.

Avowal: Acknowledgment.

Mr. Forsyth: Secretary of State John Forsyth.

Vexatious: Distressing.

Detention: Act of being held in custody.

Messrs. Montes and Ruiz: The planters who purchased the Africans as slaves.

Lieut. Gedney: The American commander whose ship seized the *Amistad.*

acts of violence perpetrated upon them, and placed under the safeguard of the laws all the property which they claimed as their own, to remain in safety until the competent authority could examine their title to it, and pronounce upon the question of ownership agreeably to the provisions of the 9th article of the treaty of 1795.

This sympathy with Spanish slave-traders is declared by the Secretary to have been first felt by Lieutenant Gedney. I hope this is not correctly represented. **It is imputed** *to him and declared to have become in a manner national. The national sympathy with the slave-traders of the* **barracoons** *is officially declared to have been the prime motive of action of the government: And this fact is given as an answer to all the claims, demands and reproaches of the Spanish minister! I cannot urge the same objection to this that was brought against the assertion in the libel—that it said the thing which is not—too unfortunately it was so, as he said. The sympathy of the Executive government, and as it were of the nation, in favor of the slave-traders, and against these poor, unfortunate, helpless, tongueless, defenseless Africans, was the cause and foundation and motive of all these proceedings, and has brought this case up for trial before your honors.*

After seven years of litigation (in the case of a similar revolt aboard the ship, the Antelope*) in the Courts of the United States, and, of course, of captivity to nearly all of these Africans who survived the operation; after decrees of the District Court, reversed by the Circuit Court, and three successive annual reversals by the Supreme Court of the decrees of the Circuit Court; what was the result of this most troublesome charge? The vessel was restored to certain Spanish slave-traders in the island of Cuba. Of the Africans, about fifty had perished by the* **benignity** *of their treatment in this land of liberty, during its suspended animation as to them; sixteen, drawn by lot from the whole number, (by the merciful dispensation of the Circuit Court, under the arbitrary enlargement of the tender mercies of the District Judge, which had limited the number to seven,)—sixteen had drawn the prize of liberty, to which the whole number were entitled by the letter of the law; and, of the remainder, THIRTY-NINE, upon evidence inadmissible upon the most trifling question of property in any court of justice, were, under the very peculiar circumstances of the case, surrendered! delivered up to the Spanish vice-consul—AS SLAVES! To the rest was at last extended the benefit of the laws which had* **foreordained their emancipation.**

It is imputed: The blame is placed.

Barracoons: Barracks used for confining slaves.

Benignity: Gentleness.

Foreordained their emancipation: Predetermined their freedom.

| Complete American Presidents Sourcebook

They were delivered over to safe keeping, support, and transporta-
tion, as freemen, beyond the limits of the United States, by the Chief
Magistrate of the Union.

And now, by what possible process of reasoning can any deci-
sion of the Supreme Court of the United States in the case of the An-
telope, be adduced as authorizing the President of the United States
to seize and deliver up to the order of the Spanish minister the cap-
tives of the Amistad? Even the judge of the District Court in Georgia,
who would have enslaved all the unfortunate of the Antelope but
seven, distinctly admitted, that, if they had been bought in Africa
after the prohibition of the trade by Spain he would have liberated
them all. In delivering the opinion of the Supreme Court, on their
first decree in the case of the Antelope, Chief Justice [John] Marshall,
after reviewing the decisions in the British Courts of Admiralty, says,
"The principle common to these cases is, that the legality of the cap-
ture of a vessel engaged in the slave-trade depends on the law of the
country to which the vessel belongs. If that law gives its sanction to
the trade, restitution will be decreed: if that law prohibits it, the ves-
sel and cargo will be condemned as good prize." It was by the ap-
plication of this principle, to the fact, that, at the time when the An-
telope was taken by the Arraganta, the slave-trade, in which the
Antelope was engaged, had not yet been made unlawful by Spain,
that the Supreme Court affirmed so much of the decree of the Circuit
Court as directed restitution to the Spanish claimant of the Africans
found on board the Antelope when captured by the Arraganta. But
by the same identical principle, applied to the case of the Amistad,
if, when captured by Lieutenant Gedney, she and her cargo had
been in possession of the Spaniards, and the Africans in the condi-
tion of slaves, the vessel would have been condemned, and the
slaves liberated, by the laws of the United States; because she was
engaged in the slave-trade in violation of the laws of Spain. She was
in possession of the Africans, self-emancipated, and not in the con-
dition of slaves. That, surely, could not legalize the trade in which
she had been engaged. By the principle asserted in the opinion of
the Supreme Court, declared by Chief Justice Marshall, it would have
saved the vessel, at once, from condemnation and from restitution,
and would have relieved the Court from the necessity of restoring to
the Africans their freedom. Thus the opinion of the Supreme Court,
as declared by the Chief Justice, in the case of the Antelope, was in
fact, an authority in point, against the surrender of the Amistad,
and in favor of the liberation of the Africans in her, even if they had
been, when taken, in the condition of slaves. How monstrous, then,

Restitution: Payment for damages.

is the claim upon the Courts of the United States to re-inslave them, as **thralls** *to the Spaniards, Ruiz and Montes, or to transport them beyond the seas, at the demand of the Minister of Spain!. . . .*

I said, when I began this plea, that my final reliance for success in this case was on this Court as a court of JUSTICE; and in the confidence this fact inspired that, in the administration of justice, in a case of no less importance than the liberty and the life of a large number of persons, this Court would not decide but on a due consideration of all the rights, both natural and social, of every one of these individuals. I have endeavored to show that they are entitled to their liberty from this Court. I have avoided, purposely avoided, and this Court will do justice to the motive for which I have avoided, a recurrence to those first principles of liberty which might well have been invoked in the argument of this cause. I have shown that Ruiz and Montes, the only parties in interest here, for whose sole benefit this suit is carried on by the Government, were acting at the time in a way that is forbidden by the laws of Great Britain, of Spain, and of the United States, and that the mere signature of the Governor General of Cuba ought not to prevail over the ample evidence in the case that these negroes were free and had a right to assert their liberty. I have shown that the papers in question are absolutely null and insufficient as passports for persons, and still more invalid to convey or prove a title to property. (The Amistad . . . [Web site])

Thralls: Servants.

What happened next . . .

The Supreme Court ruled in favor of the *Amistad* defendants in March of 1841. They were set free and allowed to return to Africa. It took several months for enough money to be raised for the voyage. The Africans arrived in Freetown, Sierra Leone, in January of 1842.

Adams continued to serve in the House of Representatives and agitate for an end of slavery until his death in 1848. His performance during the *Amistad* trial dazzled spectators and the Supreme Court judges. Adams was able to draw on fifty years of experience in negotiating treaties and fighting for human rights.

Did you know . . .

The leader of the Africans was named Cinque (c. 1810–c. 1880). A charismatic and forceful leader, he helped rally support in the United States for the cause of the Africans, though he spoke very little English at the time. Cinque disappeared shortly after his group returned to Africa.

Where to Learn More

Freedman, Suzanne. *United States v. Amistad: Rebellion on a Slave Ship.* Berkeley Heights, NJ: Enslow, 2000.

Jurmain, Suzanne. *Freedom's Sons: The True Story of the Amistad Mutiny.* New York: Lothrop, Lee & Shepard Books, 1998.

Kromer, Helen. *Amistad: The Slave Uprising aboard the Spanish Schooner.* Cleveland: Pilgrim Press, 1997.

MultiEducator Incorporated. "Argument of John Quincy Adams Before the Supreme Court of the United States. . . ." *The Amistad . . . A Hypertext on American History.* [Online] http://www.multied.com/amistad/amistad.html (accessed on June 30, 2000).

Myers, Walter Dean. *Amistad: A Long Road to Freedom.* New York: Dutton Children's Books, 1998.

National Archives and Records Administration. "The *Amistad* Case." [Online] http://www.nara.gov/education/teaching/amistad/home.html (accessed on July 31, 2000).

Zeinert, Karen. *The Amistad Slave Revolt and American Abolition.* North Haven, CT: Linnet Books, 1997.

Andrew Jackson
Seventh president (1829–1837)

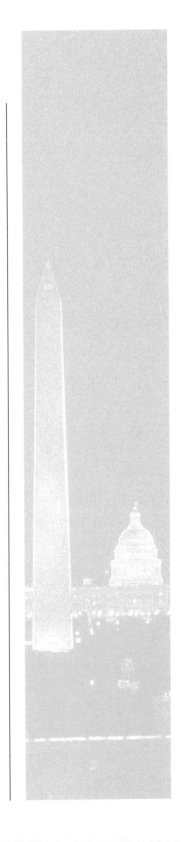

Andrew Jackson

Born March 15, 1767
Waxhaw, South Carolina
Died June 8, 1845
Nashville, Tennessee

Seventh president of the United States
(1829–1837)

The first "log cabin" president rose from back country origins to become a renowned military leader and commander-in-chief

A ndrew Jackson was nicknamed "Old Hickory" after the tough hardwood tree. He had a fiery temper and an iron will, but like the hickory tree, which produces flavorful nuts that can be used as a sweetener, Jackson had a soft side. He was devoted to his wife, **Rachel Jackson** (1767–1828; see entry in volume 1), his friends, his troops, and his extended family.

Jackson's long and colorful life included living a wild boyhood on the frontier, becoming a self-made man (one who succeeds through hard work and without the financial help of others), and serving as one of the original political leaders of the state of Tennessee. In his forties he won fame as a controversial military commander. While in his sixties he led a national political dynasty. (A political dynasty is a succession of government leaders from the same political party.) The dynasty lasted twenty years, from 1828 to 1848. This period in American history is often called "The Age of Jackson" to describe how Jackson and his followers dominated (controlled) the American political scene. Two of his key supporters—**Martin Van Buren** (1782–1862; see entry in volume 1)

"The brave man inattentive to his duty is worth little more to his country than the coward who deserts her in the hour of danger."

Andrew Jackson

Andrew Jackson.
Courtesy of the Library of Congress.

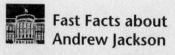

Fast Facts about Andrew Jackson

Full name: Andrew Jackson

Born: March 15, 1767

Died: June 8, 1845

Burial site: The Hermitage Estate, near Nashville, Tennessee

Parents: Andrew and Elizabeth Hutchinson Jackson

Spouse: Rachel Donelson Robards (1767–1828; m. 1791 and in a second ceremony in 1794)

Children: Andrew Jr. (adopted; 1808–1865)

Religion: Presbyterian

Education: No formal education

Occupations: Attorney; soldier

Government positions: U.S. representative and senator from Tennessee; Tennessee state supreme court justice and senator; Florida territory governor

Political party: Democratic

Dates as president: March 4, 1829–March 4, 1833 (first term); March 4, 1833–March 4, 1837 (second term)

Age upon taking office: 61

and **James K. Polk** (1795–1849; see entry in volume 2)—followed him as president.

Like the tough but flavorful hickory tree, Jackson had his contradictory sides: Sometimes he seemed to hold two opposing views at the same time. For example, he and his wife Rachel raised an orphaned Native American boy. But Jackson was a fierce fighter of Native Americans and played a significant role in the removal of Native Americans from the Southeast to "Indian Lands," an area in and around what is now Oklahoma. As a politician, Jackson opposed federal influence on state governments, but he came close to using national force when the state of South Carolina threatened to nullify federal tariffs and secede from the Union (that is, the state threatened to willfully disobey rules about taxes on imported goods and separate from the Union).

The nation was changing at the time Jackson took office. The generations born after the ratification (acceptance by state representatives) of the U.S. Constitution were coming of age. People were settling in former frontier lands. Industrialization and modern urban centers were taking hold. People were looking beyond aristocrats (upper class people) from New England and Virginia for leaders to represent them. Jackson was their man. He was the first president who came from west of the Appalachian Mountains. He appealed to small farmers, laborers, and the common folk. Viewing himself as the highest-elected representative of the people, Jackson became one of the most powerful presidents in the nation's history.

Andrew Jackson Timeline

1767: Born in South Carolina a few days after his father dies

1780: American Revolution spreads to the Carolinas; Jackson's oldest brother is killed; Jackson and his surviving brother Robert are imprisoned by British soldiers; Robert and mother die of smallpox

1787: Certified to practice law

1792: Marries Rachel Donelson, whose husband, Lewis Robards, had petitioned for divorce in 1791

1793: Robards, who never completed the original divorce proceedings, sues to divorce Rachel Jackson as an adulterer; Andrew and Rachel marry again in 1794

1796: Jackson attends convention where the state of Tennessee is established

1796–97: Serves as Tennessee's first member in the U.S. House of Representatives

1797–98: Serves Tennessee as U.S. senator

1798–1804: Serves as justice on Tennessee Supreme Court

1803: Commissioned as major general of Tennessee militia

1815: Soundly defeats British forces in the Battle of New Orleans

1818: Controversy over his killing two British citizens for inciting Seminole Indians to raid nearly leads to his censure by Congress

1821: Serves as governor of the Florida Territory

1823–25 Serves as U.S. senator from Tennessee

1829–37: Serves as seventh U.S. president

1833: Removes funds from the Second National Bank of the United States and disperses them in state banks; censured by Congress and vilified by opponents as "King Andrew"; censure is later erased (1836) from the Congressional Record

1837: Retires to his home, the Hermitage

1845: Dies in Tennessee

Wild youth

Andrew Jackson was born in frontier country—the backwoods of the Waxhaw River community in South Carolina. His parents had emigrated there from Ireland with his two older brothers in 1765. His father, also named Andrew Jackson, died just a few days before young Andrew was born on March 15, 1767.

Jackson learned to read and write in makeshift (quickly assembled) frontier schools. Class was held in buildings not

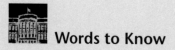

Words to Know

Annexation: Incorporation of a state into the Union.

Armistice: An agreement to cease fire while warring parties negotiate a peace settlement.

Censure: To publicly condemn an individual; in Congress, the act of censure expresses Congress's condemnation of an individual's actions and is entered into the *Congressional Record.*

Charter: An agreement made by a governing party that allows an institution to function for a specified period.

Deregulation: Removal of guidelines and laws governing a business or financial institution.

Electoral votes: The votes a presidential candidate receives for having won a majority of the popular vote in a state.

Land speculation: The purchase of land with the hope that its value will rise significantly in the near future.

Militia: A small military group.

Panic of 1837: A sudden downturn in the economy in 1837 that led to a rush of financial activity that further worsened the economy.

Political dynasty: A succession of government leaders from the same political party.

Secede: To officially withdraw.

Second National Bank: The federal bank, empowered to regulate the flow of currency and to perform functions for the Department of Treasury.

Tariffs: Taxes placed on imported goods to raise their price and make them less attractive than goods produced by the nation importing them.

War of 1812: A war fought from 1812 to 1815 between the United States and Great Britain. The United States wanted to protect its maritime rights as a neutral nation in a conflict between Great Britain and France.

originally constructed to be schools or wherever it was convenient. After the American Revolution broke out in 1775, Jackson often read newspaper articles and messages from Philadelphia, Pennsylvania, and other northern towns to residents in the Waxhaw River community.

The Revolution spread to the Carolinas by 1780, when Jackson was thirteen. He served as an orderly and a messenger for Colonel William Richardson Davie (1756–1820) and his troops. Jackson's oldest brother died during this time. Andrew and his other brother, Robert, were captured and imprisoned by British troops for having aided the American rebellion. Andrew was beaten by a British soldier for refusing to shine the soldier's boots. He suffered wounds that left permanent scars on his face and body.

A smallpox epidemic spread through the area where the Jackson brothers were imprisoned. Their mother, Elizabeth Hutchinson Jackson, arrived to secure their release, but Robert Jackson had fallen ill and died from smallpox. Elizabeth remained to help nurse some of the other victims of the disease. She also became infected and died.

Left an orphan, Jackson learned the art of saddle making and also taught school to earn money. He began studying law with an attorney in Salisbury, North Carolina, and was certified (given approval in written form) to practice in 1787. At age twenty, he set up an office in McLeanville, North Carolina. Meanwhile, Jackson indulged in horse racing, cardplaying, and other gambling pursuits. He eventually gambled away a small inheritance.

With his friend John McNairy (1762–1837), Jackson traveled to Nashville, a frontier village in what was then called the Western District of North Carolina. McNairy became a judge and named Jackson to the post of solicitor general. Jackson was responsible for preparing cases on behalf of the state and for prosecuting (conducting legal action against) debtors. Often accepting small parcels of land instead of money for his services, Jackson formed an estate that would become known as the Hermitage in 1804. In the meantime, however, Jackson himself fell into debt when he was unable to make payments for loans he had received.

In 1790, Jackson rented a room from John Donelson, a former surveyor (someone who measures land), Virginia legislator, and settler in Tennessee. Jackson met Donelson's daughter, Rachel, who traveled to the area to escape her jealous and violent husband, Lewis Robards. Rachel planned to join her sister in Natchez, Mississippi, a rough journey of over three hundred miles. Jackson was asked to escort her. He did, and he fell in love with Rachel along the way.

Rachel Donelson Robards and her husband had agreed to divorce. Divorce was rare in those days and involved petitioning the state legislature for permission. When learning that Lewis Robards had been granted legal permission to seek the divorce, which left only minor paperwork to fill out, Jackson returned to Natchez to find Rachel. They were married there in 1791.

A couple of years later it was discovered that Rachel's first husband had not completed the divorce proceedings. Upon learning that Rachel had married in the meantime, the mean-spirited Robards completed new divorce proceedings based on the grounds of adultery (relations with someone other than a spouse) against Rachel.

Jackson and Rachel were married again in 1794. Although the awkwardness of the incident was the fault of Rachel's ex-husband, that Jackson had wooed and wed a married woman became an issue for slander (harmful talk meant to damage a person's reputation) by his opponents through the years. Jackson fiercely protected the honor of his wife—often with his fists, and sometimes in duels.

In 1806, he dueled, either over slander or a gambling argument, with an excellent gunfighter named Charles Dickinson. Dickinson shot first and hit Jackson in the chest, leaving a wound that never completely healed during Jackson's life. Jackson maintained his position and shot back at Dickinson, killing him.

Jackson built a strong reputation in the Nashville area. He was invited to attend the state constitutional convention through which Tennessee became a state in 1796. He was the first person to represent Tennessee in Congress, where he expressed his view that President **George Washington** (1732–1799; see entry in volume 1) was not being tough enough in dealings with Great Britain. The following year, Jackson was elected to the Senate by the Tennessee state legislature. He resigned after one year. He disliked the responsibilities of senator and also wanted to attend to his own personal debts and responsibilities.

Jackson was appointed to be a judge of the Tennessee State Superior Court and gradually improved his plantation, the Hermitage, where he bred racehorses. Jackson was named major general of the Tennessee militia (a civilian military group on call for emergency duty) in 1803. The first decade of the nineteenth century was the happiest period in the lives of Andrew and Rachel Jackson.

War hero

Jackson spent most of the first decade of the 1800s tending to the Hermitage, training troops in the state militia, and serving as a judge. He was a strong supporter of war against Great Britain as hostilities between the nations increased toward what became the War of 1812 (1812–15). Jackson offered to lead a raid into British-controlled Canada. Instead, he was dispatched by the governor of Tennessee to lead a group of men to help protect the vital port city of New Orleans.

Jackson and his group of twenty-five hundred men were ill equipped for the journey. They made it as far as Natchez, Mississippi, still over a hundred miles from New Orleans, when they received orders to disband. Jackson's orders were to leave the men and return to Tennessee. Instead, he led the exhausted and hungry men back with him. During that difficult march home, the men gave him the nickname "Old Hickory."

In 1813, Jackson received orders to lead two thousand men to fight the Upper Creek Indian nation. That tribe had allied with the British and killed 250 settlers at Fort Mims in what is now Alabama. Despite poor equipment and supplies, Jackson's forces won a series of skirmishes (minor battles), culminating with the March 1814 battle at Horseshoe Bend on the Tallapoosa River. Jackson allowed Indian women and children to cross the river. Then his forces systematically wiped out the Upper Creek warriors. He wrote a treaty that forced the Creek nation to cede (hand over) nine million acres of land. That land forms about twenty percent of present-day Georgia and over sixty percent of present-day Alabama.

Jackson's victory led to his promotion to major general in the federal army, with orders to defend New Orleans against British attack. Leading troops south from Tennessee, Jackson made a slight detour to attack and capture a British base in what is now Pensacola, Florida. Then he led his men to New Orleans, where he found the town virtually defenseless. In addition to his group of Tennessee and Kentucky militiamen, Jackson pressed into service local Creoles (American descendants of French settlers), blacks, and Frenchmen to form a force of five thousand men to fight British troops estimated at nine thousand men.

Jackson set up three lines of defense beyond a dry canal. British forces began a massive attack but they were exposed as easy targets to the well-concealed and surprisingly large defense Jackson established. Over two thousand British soldiers were killed in the assault on January 8, 1815, that would become known as the Battle of New Orleans. Americans suffered fewer than one hundred casualties: thirteen dead, thirty-nine wounded, and nineteen missing.

The Battle of New Orleans was actually fought after British and U.S. officials had called an armistice (an agreement to cease fire while a peace treaty is being worked out). The Treaty of Ghent was agreed to on December 24, 1814, but news traveled slowly in those days and had not yet reached New Orleans. The Treaty of Ghent, officially ending the war, was signed soon after the battle, in February of 1815. In a war in which U.S. forces were vulnerable and the nation's military leadership proved weak, Jackson had enjoyed a huge victory and became a national hero.

More exploits, more controversy

Jackson's military exploits continued over the next few years, often with controversy. Named commander of the Southern District of the U.S. Army in 1815, he led a punitive (designed to punish) expedition against Seminole Indians. The tribal warriors had engaged in raids in southern Georgia and then returned to Florida, which was under command of Spain. Jackson led his forces into Spanish Florida, against orders. Jackson himself killed two British citizens whom he accused of having incited the Seminoles against the United States.

Jackson was rebuked (sharply criticized) by the governments of Great Britain and Spain for the action. Many in Congress called for his censure (public condemnation). President **James Monroe** (1758–1831; see entry in volume 1), however, was persuaded by his secretary of state, **John Quincy Adams** (1767–1848; see entry in volume 1), not to formal-

General Andrew Jackson at the Battle of New Orleans.
Photograph by Charles Severin. Courtesy of the Library of Congress.

ly punish Jackson. Ironically, Adams and Jackson would later become bitter political rivals.

Adams soon negotiated the sale of Florida from Spain to the United States. Jackson was appointed governor of the Florida territory. He took the position to vindicate (prove that earlier criticism was wrong) his earlier actions in Florida. However, Jackson returned home after one month to begin pursuing other goals. In 1822, he became a candidate for the presidential election of 1824. In 1823, he was elected by the Tennessee legislature to the U.S. Senate, giving him more national exposure to build on his large base of popular support.

Jackson was indeed popular. In the election of 1824, he bested three other candidates—John Quincy Adams; William H. Crawford (1772–1834), a Georgian who had been secretary of the treasury; and Henry Clay (1777–1852; see box in **John Quincy Adams** entry in volume 1), Speaker of the House from Kentucky—in popular and electoral votes. However, none of the candidates had won a majority of electoral votes. As mandated (commanded) by the Constitution in such an event, the election was to be decided in the House of Representatives. Each state was to have one vote to cast for one of the top three finishers in the election.

When Clay, who was out of the running, threw his support to Adams, Adams ended up winning the House vote and was elected president. Adams later named Clay as his secretary of state. Jackson followers responded angrily, accusing the two men of having made "a corrupt bargain." Jackson immediately began campaigning for the 1828 presidential election. The accusation of corruption (in politics, bribery or illegal political favors) would prove to be a key issue in his campaign for democratic reform.

Adams's presidency was largely ineffective. Jackson had many political allies in Congress, including future presidents Martin Van Buren and James K. Polk. Both men were making rapid progress in their young national political careers. New Yorker Van Buren helped Jackson carry that state in Jackson's sweeping victory in the 1828 election, in which there would be no electoral dispute: Jackson won 178 electoral votes to 83 for Adams.

The campaign of 1828 was among the ugliest in American history. Slanders against Jackson and his wife were common. The factions (groups) represented by Adams and Jackson were willing to use any means to defame their opponents.

The age of Jackson

Jackson's triumph was a difficult period for him. Rachel died of a heart attack shortly after the election. Jack-

Election Results

1828

Presidential / Vice presidential candidates	Popular votes	Electoral votes
Andrew Jackson / John C. Calhoun (Democratic)	647,231	178
John Quincy Adams / Richard Rush (National Republican)	509,097	83

1832

Presidential / Vice presidential candidates	Popular votes	Electoral votes
Andrew Jackson / Martin Van Buren (Democratic)	687,507	219
Henry Clay / John Sergeant (National Republican)	530,189	49
Others	unknown	18

son blamed her death on the insults his enemies routinely made about her, especially as they pertained to Rachel's first marriage. Jackson was sixty years old when he took office and afflicted with pain from old war wounds and other ailments. He was tall and extremely thin, with a scar on his face and two bullets from old wounds still in his body. He had trouble breathing and had frequent headaches.

Still, his triumph at the polls and his inauguration (a formal ceremony that begins a person's term of office) gave him strength. After his inauguration, wild festivities attended by huge crowds spilled onto the White House grounds. Showing the same iron will and fighting spirit he displayed in military battle, Jackson proved to be among the most powerful presidents. Reflecting his view that the president is the nation's highest elected leader, he set out a course to promote the interests of the common man and to protect the rights of states from undue federal influence.

Several issues challenged Jackson's views. Before he took office, Congress had passed a tariff that Southern states felt was unfair to their region. John C. Calhoun (1782–1850; see box), who was elected vice president under Jackson after having served a term as Adams's vice president as well, announced his Theory of Nullification. He believed that a state had the right to disobey federal laws that it deemed harmful

Andrew Jackson Administration

Administration Dates
March 4, 1829–March 4, 1833
March 4, 1833–March 4, 1837

Vice President
John Caldwell Calhoun (1829–32)
None (1832–33)
Martin Van Buren (1833–37)

Cabinet
Secretary of State
Martin Van Buren (1829–31)
Edward Livingston (1831–33)
Louis McLane (1833–34)
John Forsyth (1834–37)

Secretary of the Treasury
Samuel D. Ingham (1829–31)
Louis McLane (1831–33)
William J. Duane (1833)

Roger B. Taney (1833–34)
Levi Woodbury (1834–37)

Secretary of War
John H. Eaton (1829–31)
Lewis Cass (1831–36)

Attorney General
John M. Berrien (1829–31)
Roger B. Taney (1831–33)
Benjamin F. Butler (1833–37)

Secretary of the Navy
John Branch (1829–31)
Levi Woodbury (1831–34)
Mahlon Dickerson (1834–37)

Postmaster General
John McLean (1823–29)
William T. Barry (1829–35)
Amos Kendall (1835–37)

to the state's interests. Jackson was a champion of states' rights, but not in matters that undermine the supreme power of the federal government.

Southerners expected Jackson to support their cause, which was led by South Carolinian Calhoun, but the president sided with federal powers. His stand and Calhoun's dissenting views were made clear at a ceremonial dinner on the occasion of the birthday of **Thomas Jefferson** (1743–1826; see entry in volume 1). President Jackson rose to make a toast. Looking directly at Calhoun, Jackson said, "Our federal union! It must be preserved." Calhoun replied: "The Union, next to our liberty, most dear."

Around election time in 1832, the nullification issue heated up again. South Carolina not only planned to nullify a new tariff passed in 1832, it threatened to secede from the

Union over the matter. Jackson responded quickly. He rallied the support of the people and threatened to send federal troops to South Carolina to enforce federal law. Meanwhile, a compromise was worked out and a lower tariff passed Congress in 1833.

Another major issue revolved around the charter (government authorization) for the Second National Bank, the federal bank. The bank was empowered (given the authority) to regulate (monitor and adjust as needed) the flow of currency and to perform functions for the Department of Treasury. Jackson felt the bank was dominated by wealthy, private interests and did not represent the people. When he vetoed (turned down) a bill rechartering the bank, many in Congress were outraged and planned to make the veto a major campaign issue for the election of 1832.

Meanwhile, Jackson and Vice President Calhoun were at odds. In addition to clashing (arguing) over the nullifica-

Crowds gather in front of the White House during President Andrew Jackson's first inaugural reception in 1828.
Courtesy of the Library of Congress.

John C. Calhoun

John Caldwell Calhoun was born on March 18, 1782, in rural South Carolina. He was the fourth child of Patrick and Martha Calhoun. Descendants had arrived in Pennsylvania from Ireland in 1733 and eventually settled in an isolated area bordering on Cherokee country near present-day Abbeville, South Carolina. Patrick Calhoun quickly became the military and political leader of this rural community by leading friends and neighbors against Tories (Americans who supported the British during the American Revolution, 1775–83).

While in school, Calhoun read volumes on philosophy and history. Upon his father's death, Calhoun returned home to manage the farm. With financial support from friends and family, Calhoun enrolled at Yale College (now Yale University) as a junior in 1802. After graduating in the fall of 1804, he studied law in a Charleston, South Carolina, office and moved on to the Litchfield Law School in Connecticut. After completing his studies, he returned to Abbeville to establish his practice. His business did well, but he was not happy as a country lawyer.

In the summer of 1807, Calhoun led the small community in protest against the British attack on the American frigate *Chesapeake,* and drafted a set of resolutions denouncing the outrage. The resolutions brought him to public attention as a champion of national honor. He was elected to the state legislature in 1808. He won election to the U.S. Congress in 1810 as part of the "War Hawks," a group of youthful southerners and westerners who demanded territorial expansion and war against Britain. Right after the election, Calhoun purchased a plantation above the Savannah River and married a distant cousin, Floride Bonneau Calhoun.

Calhoun quickly established himself as a strong supporter of the War of 1812 (1812–15) between the United States and Great Britain. By war's end, Calhoun dominated Congressional debate in favor of a national bank and a protective tariff (tax on imports). He also championed an ambitious scheme of federally-sponsored improvements to roads and canals. In December 1817, Calhoun accepted the post of secretary of war under James Monroe. Calhoun ran for president in 1824, but settled for the vice presidency under John Quincy Adams when it became apparent that he could not win. With his eyes still on the presidency, Calhoun supported Andrew Jackson against Adams in 1828 and was elected for a second term to the vice presidency. The next four years brought events and issues that had a profound impact upon Calhoun's future.

Declining cotton prices and a steady departure of people from his native state had led South Carolinians to denounce protective tariffs as instruments of Northern domination. Calhoun sought to balance his position at home and his presidential ambitions in the nation by writing a doctrine on nullification. In essence, he believed that a state could not be bound by a law the state considered unconstitutional.

John C. Calhoun.
Courtesy of the Library of Congress.

In such a case, a state could nullify (negate) the law, declaring it void in that state. When an even higher protective tariff was passed into law in 1832, Calhoun quickly returned to South Carolina, where the state legislature initiated the nullification procedure. A subsequent state convention voted to nullify the tariffs of 1828 and 1832. Calhoun resigned his post as vice president in December 1832 after being elected as a U.S. senator from South Carolina.

Attention focused on Calhoun—now called the Great Nullifier—when he took his Senate seat and defended a policy he believed was constitutional. In 1833, Calhoun worked with U.S. senator Henry Clay of Kentucky to produce a compromise tariff. Some in South Carolina called for the state to secede from the Union; President Jackson, in turn, threatened to use force to keep the Union together.

In February 1844, President John Tyler appointed Calhoun secretary of state after Daniel Webster resigned from the position. In his brief tenure (1844–45), Calhoun completed negotiations for a treaty that eventually admitted the Republic of Texas into the Union as a slave state in 1845. Calhoun returned to manage his plantation after James K. Polk replaced Tyler as president in 1845, but he returned to the Senate later that year to oppose war with Mexico over the boundary of Texas. Calhoun was against the Polk administration's conduct in the Mexican War (1846–48) to such an extent that Polk declared him the most mischievous man in the Senate. Calhoun believed the war was a pretense for invading and taking over Mexican territory stretching west from Texas to the Pacific ocean.

When the war ended, Calhoun focused his attention against the growing Northern demand to exclude slavery in the territories (much of present-day New Mexico, Arizona, and California) acquired in the war. When California sought admission to the Union as a free state, a gravely ill Calhoun entered the Senate chamber on March 4, 1850, to vehemently oppose it. Too weak to speak, Calhoun listened as Senator James Mason read Calhoun's warning that the balance between North and South would forever be destroyed if California entered the Union. It would be Calhoun's last major speech. He died on March 31, 1850.

Hickory canes were popular souvenirs during the 1832 presidential campaign; they reminded voters to support "Old Hickory," as Jackson was called.

tion issue, they differed in their approach to a scandal involving Secretary of War John Eaton (1790–1856), an ally to Jackson. Eaton married a recently widowed woman, Margaret (Peggy) Eaton (1799–1879), in 1828. Rumors persisted that he romanced the woman before her husband's death. Jackson, who had been the victim of gossip, supported his friend Eaton. All other administration officials and their wives, except for Secretary of State Martin Van Buren, snubbed Eaton. Van Buren soon became the head power broker in Jackson's administration. Calhoun's fall from power was sealed when Jackson learned that Calhoun was among those congressmen back in 1818 who had wanted Jackson censured after he killed two British citizens in Florida.

Near the end of his first term, Jackson wanted to change members of his Cabinet, but a clash with Calhoun could pose problems in the upcoming election. Van Buren helped solve the issue by resigning from his position as secretary of state. Jackson then asked all Cabinet members to resign so that he could reshuffle his Cabinet if he should win a second term. Calhoun wound up resigning anyway, on December 28, 1832, after being elected to the U.S. Senate.

The election in 1832 was a landmark in American political history. Following the contentious (quarrelsome) election of 1824, the Democratic-Republican Party became split among supporters of Adams, who were called the National Republican Party, and supporters for Jackson, who were called Jacksonian Democrats. Van Buren helped solidify the Jackson group of Northern and Southern supporters who were for states' rights and the common people. In 1832, they held their own convention and emerged as the Democratic Party, with Jackson as their nominee (candidate).

Jackson was opposed in the national election by Henry Clay, leader of the short-lived National Republican Party. Clay and his party were strongly in support of a national bank. Jackson easily won reelection.

"King Andrew"

Jackson viewed his second victory as a mandate to dismantle (take apart) the federal banking system. He with-

drew funds from the national bank and dispersed them to various state banks. This act, following not long after he had threatened to use federal force in South Carolina, drew the ire of Congress. Through a joint resolution of both the Senate and the House of Representatives, Jackson was censured—the only time in history that Congress has voted to go on record as rebuking a president. He was ridiculed by political and journalistic opponents as "King Andrew."

Jackson, however, continued to be so popular that his political allies were successful in having the censure erased from the Congressional Record. Jackson's victory was complete when the charter for the Second National Bank expired in 1836.

Meanwhile, Jackson had promised to pay off the national debt. In keeping with this aim and maintaining his states' rights principles, he vetoed the Maysville Road bill. This legislation provided federal funds to build a road in Ken-

A cartoon mocks Andrew Jackson's attempt to destroy the federal banking system. The president (left) and his vice president, Martin Van Buren (center), are shown struggling with the multiheaded snake, which represents individual states. *Courtesy of the Library of Congress.*

tucky between the towns of Maysville and Lexington. The veto was sustained and established a trend that made states responsible for the building and improving of roads and canals that exist completely within its borders.

Jackson successfully paid off the national debt. There were other triumphs for the president. A trade agreement with Great Britain opened up the West Indies as a market. His administration convinced France to make reparations (payments for damage or problems caused during war) dating back to the Napoleonic wars (a series of wars fought between France and other European countries). American merchant ships and trade had been disrupted during the war. Finally, Jackson had the opportunity during his two terms to nominate five Supreme Court justices to fill vacancies. He stacked the court with supporters, ensuring that Jacksonian politics would be carried on through the judicial branch of government.

In several other areas, Jacksonian policies caused lasting problems. Jackson's decision to place federal funds in state banks led to a deregulation of (removal of laws about) the currency supply as well as an overextension (an expansion beyond what could be paid back) of credit. The dollar lost value. Previously, the value of currency matched the nation's gold supply (one dollar for each dollar's worth of gold), but the increased amount of currency inflated the ratio of currency to gold—$12 for each dollar's worth of gold. Money lost value and individuals became indebted for not being able to pay off their credit. Much of the credit had been extended for land speculation (the purchase of land with the hope that its value will rise significantly in the near future). Jackson helped ease the problem by declaring that land could be bought only with gold or silver, but the economy had already taken a downturn near the end of Jackson's second term.

Jackson's Native American policy was harsh. When the state of Georgia began confiscating Indian lands, Jackson viewed the matter as a states' rights issue. Even after the Supreme Court ruled that the dispute was a federal matter, Jackson did not enforce treaties honoring Cherokee claims to the land.

In 1834, a large area of the frontier (mostly in present-day Oklahoma) was set aside as "Indian territory," and Native Americans of the Southeast were forcibly moved there.

Last stands among Native American warriors, such as the Black Hawk War of 1832 and the Seminole War of 1835, failed to stem the flow of broken treaties and forced removal.

Settlers in the frontier areas supported Jackson's policies, and he continued to be a popular president through the end of his tenure. He hand-picked his replacement, Martin Van Buren, who went on to win the election of 1836.

White House celebrations during the Jackson administration often overflowed with people and got out of hand. The party after Jackson's first inauguration spilled into the White House, where furniture was broken and walls were scarred. At his farewell bash, crowds could freely help themselves to hunks of cheese—while it lasted: a wheel of cheese weighing fourteen hundred pounds was eaten in two hours.

After a raucous farewell party in Washington, D.C., attended by thousands of well-wishers, Jackson retired to the Hermitage, his plantation in Tennessee. He remained politically active, vigorously supporting the annexation (incorporation of a state into the Union) of Texas, states' rights, and, above all, preservation of the Union. Jackson died at the Hermitage in 1844 shortly after the election of one of his longtime allies, James K. Polk, to the presidency. Polk defeated Jackson's longtime adversary, Henry Clay.

Legacy

Andrew Jackson was among the most powerful officeholders of the presidency. Previous presidents often allowed Congress to guide national policies and pledged to remain above party concerns. Jackson was unabashedly (without shame or embarrassment) the head of his political party and intended to lead the course of the nation. The six presidents preceding Jackson had vetoed Congressional legislation a combined total of nine times. Jackson used the presidential veto twelve times to enforce his views.

Jacksonian politicians continued to dominate the American political scene for the next dozen years after Jackson's presidency. Martin Van Buren and James K. Polk each won an election. In between their respective administrations, Whig party president **John Tyler** (1790–1862; see entry in volume 2), who succeeded **William Henry Harrison** (1773–1841; see entry in volume 2) upon his death, was largely ineffective. Though Tyler had deep anti-Jackson sentiments, he, too, vetoed the rechartering of the Second National Bank and maintained a strongly Jackson-like pro-states policy.

Ironically, the Second National Bank was twice revived—first by Van Buren, then by Polk. The rechartering under Polk was sustained through 1913, when the Federal Reserve system replaced the national bank. Jackson's removal of funds to states had negative repercussions (indirect effects) shortly after he left office. One such result was the Panic of 1837. (In economic terms, a panic is a sudden downturn in the economy that leads to a rush of financial activity that further worsens the economy.) Banks failed, and businesses and individuals went bankrupt. The prosperous times of the Jackson presidency quickly ended.

Jackson's Native American policy left a bitter and tragic mark on American history. He supported the rights of states to decide for themselves on the institution of slavery. This position did nothing to improve national disagreement on the issue. Jackson's threat of using federal force against South Carolina in order to preserve the Union was played out on a much larger scale three decades later, with the Civil War (1861–65).

Jackson's presidency reflected a shift to a new America, led by individuals born after the nation was founded. His successor, Martin Van Buren, was the first president born after the Declaration of Independence. Jackson himself was the first president from west of the Appalachians. His presidency represented a majority—consisting of the common people—who looked to him as their national leader.

Where to Learn More

Collier, Christopher, and James Lincoln Collier. *Andrew Jackson's America, 1824–1850.* New York: Benchmark Books, 1999.

Curtis, James C. *Andrew Jackson and the Search for Vindication.* Boston: Little, Brown, 1976.

Gutman, William. *Andrew Jackson and the New Populism.* New York: Barrons Educational Services, 1987.

Judson, Karen. *Andrew Jackson*. Hillsdale, NJ: Enslow, 1997.

Lindop, Edmund. *George Washington, Thomas Jefferson, Andrew Jackson: Presidents Who Dared*. New York: Twenty First Century Books, 1995.

Meltzer, Milton. *Andrew Jackson: And His America*. New York: Franklin Watts, Incorporated, 1993.

Remini, Robert V. *The Life of Andrew Jackson*. New York: Harper, 1988.

Rachel Jackson

Born June 15, 1767
Halifax County, Virginia
Died December 22, 1828
Nashville, Tennessee

After her character was attacked by her husband's political opponents, Rachel Jackson died only two months before Jackson became president

Rachel Jackson was raised on the frontier. Her early life took place in a backwoods environment, where there were few comforts or opportunities to be educated. Yet this life proved more hospitable and dignified than did her later life as the wife of a military hero and politician. She was often the object of gossip and slander (statements meant to damage a person's reputation).

Rachel and **Andrew Jackson** (1767–1845; see entry in volume 1) were married in Tennessee in 1791 after learning that Rachel's first husband, Lewis Robards, had divorced her. Two years later it was discovered that Robards had filed for divorce in Kentucky but had not followed through on minor legal proceedings. He promptly renewed his divorce claim upon learning that Rachel had remarried, claiming that she had committed adultery (relations with someone other than a spouse). The divorce was granted on those grounds.

The mistake of believing Rachel had been divorced when she and Andrew first married was in all likelihood an honest one. Legal proceedings on the frontier were often complicated, news traveled slowly, and Robards had done lit-

"In the presence of this dear saint, I can and do forgive all my enemies but those vile wretches who have slandered her must look to God for mercy."

Andrew Jackson, about his late wife

Rachel Jackson.
Courtesy of the Library of Congress.

tle to distinguish himself as an honest gentleman. But the legal technicality (a matter of concern in principle only) of being an adulterer allowed Andrew Jackson's enemies to show disrespect and to undermine his political fortunes. Jackson often responded with his fists, and he even dueled over the matter. Rachel bore the insults with quiet dignity, but the strain eventually affected her health.

Girl of the wild frontier

Rachel Donelson Robards Jackson was born in Halifax County, Virginia, on June 15, 1767, the eighth of eleven children of John and Rachel Stockley Donelson. Her father was a surveyor, a member of the Virginia legislature, and a militia leader. As a young girl occasionally accompanying her father on politically related visits, Rachel met fellow Virginians and future U.S. presidents **George Washington** (1732–1799; see entry in volume 1) and **Thomas Jefferson** (1743–1826; see entry in volume 1).

When Rachel was twelve, her family moved as part of an expedition to help settle a remote area of modern-day eastern Tennessee. She had little schooling, but she learned to read and write and played the harpsichord. She spent most of her time helping with the chores necessary to establish a backwoods community.

The family moved to Kentucky when Rachel was seventeen. There she met Lewis Robards, who came from a prominent local family. They were married in 1785 in Harrodsburg, Kentucky. Robards proved to be an abusive and extremely jealous man. The couple separated and reconciled (got back together) on three occasions. In 1790, Rachel fled to what was then the Western District of North Carolina (now Tennessee), fearing for her safety. Robards responded by beginning legal proceedings for divorce on the grounds of desertion.

Andrew Jackson, a young lawyer based in the Nashville area, was a boarder at a home owned by Rachel's father. Jackson was asked to help Rachel relocate to Natchez, Mississippi, where one of her sisters lived. During the long journey of over three hundred miles, Jackson fell in love with her.

After returning to Nashville, Jackson soon learned that Robards had followed the proper legal procedure for a divorce, which was very rare in those days. Jackson assumed that the divorce had been finalized. As a lawyer, he knew that after the party seeking a divorce received permission from the legislature, only minor details were left to complete by the party who had sued for divorce.

Jackson immediately headed to Natchez. He asked Rachel to marry him. They were wed, likely in a civil ceremony (a ceremony authorized by the local government; not a church wedding), in 1791. They began sharing a happy life together, but Robards reentered the picture in 1793, bringing with him what would prove to be a lasting sense of grief to the couple. Robards had not completed the divorce proceedings, even though he simply had to sign papers and return them. He renewed divorce proceedings, able to claim adultery against Rachel in the decree (legal document) that was finalized on September 1793.

Rachel and Andrew Jackson married again in 1794. They were devoted to each other, her extended family, the child they adopted, and other children they helped raise, but people would make judgments about their relationship throughout the rest of their lives.

The Hermitage

Jackson gradually became a major figure of his time. In 1796, he was involved in the actions that led Tennessee to statehood. He became the state's first representative in Congress. In the early 1800s, he was able to transform land he had acquired gradually into an estate called the Hermitage. He served as a judge and was named head of the Tennessee state militia (civilian emergency military force). Those were happy years for the couple.

Still, the Jacksons frequently faced insults over events surrounding their marriage. Jackson had grown up in rough circumstances on the frontier. He knew how to fight, and often he replied to insults with his fists.

Jackson's life became even more adventurous beginning in 1812. He led American forces from Tennessee into

Mississippi, Florida, and Louisiana during the War of 1812. He fought in Florida against Seminole Indians in 1818. He was named governor of the newly acquired Florida territory, which the United States purchased from Spain in 1821. Jackson was a war hero to the nation, but he was accused of overstepping his bounds as a military leader in 1818, when he allegedly killed two British citizens in Florida for encouraging Seminole Indians to raid American settlements.

Throughout Jackson's stormy military life, Rachel and Andrew remained a devoted couple. She maintained the Hermitage during his frequent absences and occasionally joined him at outposts in New Orleans and Florida. Rachel Jackson preferred a quiet, domestic life. She helped raise thirteen children—nieces, nephews, the couple's adopted child, and other children they cared for. She provided guidance and tools for new settlers in the region, and she often put in a full day of domestic and farm work followed by a rest in the evening when she could smoke her pipe.

Andrew Jackson began serving in Congress in 1823 as he prepared for a run for the presidency in 1824. He won a majority of the popular vote in that election, but not enough electoral votes to secure election. Since none of the candidates that year received enough electoral votes, the election was decided by Congress. After **John Quincy Adams** (1767–1848; see entry in volume 1) was chosen, Jackson immediately began campaigning for the 1828 election.

Although Rachel supported her husband, she could not have been delighted by the prospect of becoming first lady. In both the 1824 and 1828 campaigns, opponents used the controversy surrounding the Jacksons's marriage in an attempt to discredit Andrew with voters. In addition, Rachel Jackson was a simple woman not used to the formal parties and conversations of the political social circle of Washington, D.C. The couple had each turned sixty years old and were in frail health when Andrew Jackson was elected in 1828.

Rachel became ill not long after the election. Perhaps seeing her death near, she made arrangements with her niece, Emily Donelson, to learn the techniques of hosting large gatherings. Rachel did not look forward to returning to Washington, D.C., to be among "cave dwellers" and the persistence of rumor and slander. The Jacksons's friend and political ally

John Eaton (1790–1856), who himself would face gossip and accusations of improper behavior after he married a recently widowed woman, urged her to go to Washington. Otherwise, he told her, her "persecutors" would laugh at her and say that they managed to keep her away.

Rachel Jackson died in 1828 before Andrew was inaugurated. Andrew Jackson remained convinced that the ongoing slander and accusations had been the strain that led to the heart attack from which she died. He buried her at the Hermitage. The inscription on her tombstone reads, "A being so gentle and so virtuous slander might wound, but could not dishonor."

Where to Learn More

Anthony, Carl Sferrazza. *America's Most Influential First Ladies*. Minneapolis: Oliver Press, 1992.

Caldwell, Mary French. *General Jackson's Lady: A Story of the Life and Times of Rachel Donelson Jackson*. Nashville: Kingsport Press, 1936.

Cruse, Katherine W. *An Amiable Woman, Rachel Jackson*. Hermitage, TN: Ladies' Hermitage Association, 1994.

Sandak, Cass R. *The Jacksons*. New York: Crestwood House, 1992.

Jackson's Veto Message Regarding the Bank of the United States

Sent to Congress on July 10, 1832; excerpted from
The Avalon Project **(Web site)**

The states' rights president argues against rechartering the national bank

The creation of the First National Bank in 1791 during the administration of **George Washington** (1732–1799; see entry in volume 1) was one of the most controversial issues facing the young nation. Opponents argued that the bank was an expansion of federal power not authorized by the Constitution and an intrusion on the rights of states. Debate over the bank, which controlled the nation's money supply, continued through the 1840s.

The charter (an official form of recognition and guidelines) for the federal bank was authorized in 1791 and renewed for twenty years in 1816, when the Second National Bank was formed. Congress moved early—in 1832—to renew the charter, four years before it was due to expire. That was an election year, and Henry Clay, who led support for the National Bank, was the leading candidate against incumbent president **Andrew Jackson** (1767–1845; see entry in volume 1). The bill to renew the national bank was approved by the Senate on June 11, 1832, and by the House on July 3, 1832. President Jackson, who was suspicious about the wealthy group of leaders of the bank (none of whom were elected of-

"I sincerely regret that in the act before me I can perceive [no] modifications of the bank charter which are necessary, in my opinion, to make it compatible with justice, with sound policy, or with the Constitution of our country."

Andrew Jackson

ficials), vetoed the bill on July 10. He sent a strongly worded message to the Senate explaining his veto.

Jackson's veto and message sparked a serious "Bank War" in which Massachusetts senator Daniel Webster (1782–1852; see box in **John Tyler** entry in volume 2) accused the president of overstepping his authority. Jackson's veto was one of several incidents that led his detractors to call him "King Andrew."

Things to remember while reading an excerpt of President Jackson's veto message:

- In his support for states' rights and arguments against the national bank, Jackson was following a tradition set by **Thomas Jefferson** (1743–1826; see entry in volume 1). Jefferson and Jackson, both southerners, shared some similar concerns. Most importantly, they believed the national bank would primarily benefit northern businessmen at the expense of laborers and farmers throughout the land.

- In the third paragraph of Jackson's veto message, the president remarks that members of the bank's board of directors have benefited for twenty years from their association with the bank. Jackson was concerned that some people were growing extremely wealthy by such an association without performing productive work. In the remaining portion of the excerpt, he expresses concern about wealthy investors, including many from foreign nations, who earned money by investing in a bank that was supposed to benefit all Americans. Since only a few people— not the average citizen—could make money off the government in that way, Jackson called the bank a monopoly. He likens it to a business that prospers because it has overwhelmed all competition—an illegal business practice.

Excerpt from President Jackson's veto message

To the Senate.

The bill "to modify and continue" the act entitled "An act to incorporate the subscribers to the Bank of the United States" was presented to me on the 4th July **instant**. Having considered it with that solemn regard to the principles of the Constitution which the day was calculated to inspire, and come to the conclusion that it ought not to become a law, I herewith return it to the Senate, in which it originated, with my objections.

A bank of the United States is in many respects convenient for the Government and useful to the people. Entertaining this opinion, and deeply impressed with the belief that some of the powers and privileges possessed by the existing bank are unauthorized by the Constitution, subversive of the rights of the States, and dangerous to the liberties of the people, I felt it my duty at an early period of my Administration to call the attention of Congress to the practicability of organizing an institution combining all its advantages and **obviating** these objections. I sincerely regret that in the act before me I can perceive none of those modifications of the bank charter which are necessary, in my opinion, to make it compatible with justice, with sound policy, or with the Constitution of our country.

The present; corporate body, **denominated** the president, directors, and company of the Bank of the United States, will have existed at the time this act is intended to take effect twenty years. It enjoys an exclusive privilege of banking under the authority of the General Government, a **monopoly** of its favor and support, and, as a necessary consequence, almost a monopoly of the foreign and domestic exchange. The powers, privileges, and favors bestowed upon it in the original charter, by increasing the value of the stock far above its **par value**, operated as a **gratuity** of many millions to the stockholders.

An apology may be found for the failure to guard against this result in the consideration that the effect of the original act of incorporation could not be certainly foreseen at the time of its passage. The act before me proposes another gratuity to the holders of the same stock, and in many cases to the same men, of at least seven millions more. This donation finds no apology in any uncertainty as to the effect of the act. On all hands it is conceded that its passage will increase at least so or 30 per cent more the market price of the stock, subject to the payment of the **annuity** of $200,000 per year secured by the act, thus adding in a moment one-fourth to its par value. It is not our own citizens only who are to receive the bounty of our Government. More than eight millions of the stock of this

Instant: With urgency.

Obviating: Anticipating in order to prevent.

Denominated: Authorized with various levels of power.

Monopoly: A powerful corporation that controls a business sector and overwhelms competition.

Par value: Real value; sometimes items like stock or baseball cards rise in value beyond their real worth, allowing owners of those items to sell them for high profit.

Gratuity: An added financial gain beyond what was expected, as when stock rises above par value.

Annuity: A sum of payment made at regular intervals.

*bank are held by foreigners. By this act the American Republic proposes virtually to make them a present of some millions of dollars. For these gratuities to foreigners and to some of our own **opulent** citizens the act secures no equivalent whatever. They are the certain gains of the present stockholders under the operation of this act, after making full allowance for the payment of the bonus.*

Every monopoly and all exclusive privileges are granted at the expense of the public, which ought to receive a fair equivalent. The many millions which this act proposes to bestow on the stockholders of the existing bank must come directly or indirectly out of the earnings of the American people. It is due to them, therefore, if their Government sell monopolies and exclusive privileges, that they should at least exact for them as much as they are worth in open market. . . .

It is not conceivable how the present stockholders can have any claim to the special favor of the Government. The present corporation has enjoyed its monopoly during the period stipulated in the original contract. If we must have such a corporation, why should not the Government sell out the whole stock and thus secure to the people the full market value of the privileges granted? Why should not Congress create and sell twenty-eight millions of stock, incorporating the purchasers with all the powers and privileges secured in this act and putting the premium upon the sales into the Treasury?

But this act does not permit competition in the purchase of this monopoly. It seems to be predicated on the erroneous idea that the present stockholders have a prescriptive right not only to the favor but to the bounty of Government. It appears that more than a fourth part of the stock is held by foreigners and the residue is held by a few hundred of our own citizens, chiefly of the richest class. For their benefit does this act exclude the whole American people from competition in the purchase of this monopoly and dispose of it for many millions less than it is worth. This seems the less excusable because some of our citizens not now stockholders petitioned that the door of competition might be opened, and offered to take a charter on terms much more favorable to the Government and country. (The Avalon Project [Web site])

Opulent: Prosperous.

What happened next . . .

Jackson's veto of the Second National Bank charter ignited "the Bank War," which he fought against the bank's supporters. Jackson won: his veto was sustained, and he was reelected president in 1832. During his second term, Jackson weakened the national bank. He authorized government funds to be deposited in various state banks, rather than the national treasury. That action outraged many in Congress. However, legislators were are not able to successfully challenge the popular president.

The "pet banks" (as the state banks Jackson used were called) were not as stable as the national bank. A severe financial crisis occurred when many people who were loaned money by the pet banks were unable to pay back the money they owed. Thousands of citizens lost their savings. A financial panic swept the nation in 1836, and by 1837, when Jackson left office, the crisis ruined the U.S. economy for several years. As late as 1841, twenty-eight thousand Americans declared bankruptcy.

Did you know . . .

- The controversy over the national bank in the 1830s had lasting significance. The National Bank charter was renewed in the 1840s with more government supervision over the leaders and policies of the institution. Further reform of federal banking practices occurred in 1913, when the Federal Reserve System was established. That system continued in effect into the twenty-first century.

- The Federal Reserve System provides regulation of banking practices that help avoid economic catastrophes, such as the one that occurred in 1837. In essence, the Federal Reserve System represents an effective compromise—reflecting the kind of supervision that Jackson demanded, while providing the kind of financial stability that supporters of the national bank envisioned.

Where to Learn More

Remini, Robert Vincent. *Andrew Jackson and the Bank War: A Study in the Growth of Presidential Power.* New York: Norton, 1967.

Schlesinger, Arthur M. *The Age of Jackson*. Boston: Little, Brown and Company, 1945.

Sister Mary Grace Madeleine. *Monetary and Banking Theories of Jacksonian Democracy*. Philadelphia: Dolphin Press, 1943. Reprint, Port Washington, NY: Kennikat Press, 1970.

Taylor, George Rogers, ed. *Jackson vs. Biddle's Bank: The Struggle over the Second Bank of the United States*. Lexington, MA: Heath, 1972.

Watson, Harry L. *Liberty and Power: The Politics of Jacksonian America*. New York: Hill and Wang, 1990.

Yale Law School. "President Jackson's Veto Message Regarding the Bank of the United States; July 10, 1832." *The Avalon Project*. [Online] http://www.yale.edu/lawweb/avalon/presiden/veto/ajveto01.htm (accessed on June 30, 2000).

Martin Van Buren

Eighth president (1837–1841)

Martin Van Buren

Born December 5, 1782
Kinderhook, New York
Died July 24, 1862
Kinderhook, New York

Eighth president of the United States (1837–1841)

Faced the Panic of 1837, tense relations with Great Britain, and a worsening sectional crisis

M artin Van Buren was the first president to be born after the signing of the Declaration of Independence. He is thus the first president born as an American citizen. He grew up to be a clever and resourceful politician who could anticipate and handle political trends. For his political savvy (practical knowledge), he was called "the Little Magician" and the "Red Fox of Kinderhook." In addition to reflecting his slyness, the nicknames describe his appearance. Van Buren stood only five-and-a-half feet tall and had red hair and long red sideburns.

Van Buren's presidency was eclipsed and made unpopular by the Panic of 1837—the worst depression (drastic economic slump) to hit the United States up to that time. He faced the challenge by introducing policies that would counteract the cycle of boom and bust (repeating periods of up-and-down economic conditions) that had characterized the American economy since the nation began. Nevertheless, in the eyes of the voters, Van Buren never fully rebounded from association with the Panic of 1837. He served only one term as president and later received only ten percent of the vote as a third-party presidential candidate.

"There is a power in public opinion in this country—and I thank God for it: for it is the most honest and best of all powers."

Martin Van Buren

Martin Van Buren.
Courtesy of the Library of Congress.

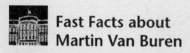

Fast Facts about Martin Van Buren

Full name: Martin Van Buren

Born: December 5, 1782

Died: July 24, 1862

Burial site: Kinderhook Cemetery, Kinderhook, New York

Parents: Abraham and Maria Hoes Van Alen Van Buren

Spouse: Hannah Hoes (1783–1819; m. 1807)

Children: Abraham (1807–1873); John (1810–1866); Martin (1812–1855); Winfield Scott (1814–1814); Smith Thompson (1817–1876)

Religion: Dutch Reformed

Education: No formal education

Occupations: Attorney

Government positions: New York state senator; U.S. senator and governor of New York; secretary of state and vice president under Andrew Jackson

Political party: Democratic

Dates as president: March 4, 1837– March 4, 1841

Age upon taking office: 54

Van Buren's lasting significance in American politics is based more on the periods before and after his administration. He was a prime force in establishing the modern, national political party. Later, he became an uncompromising force against the expansion of slavery and remained so until his death after the Civil War (1861–65) began.

Raised in a political environment

Martin Van Buren was born on December 5, 1782, in Kinderhook, New York, to Abraham and Hannah Van Buren. Abraham was a farmer and innkeeper whose tavern was a popular stopping point for politicians on the road between Albany and New York City. The lively discussions on states' rights and growing anti-Federalist sentiments young Martin overheard at the inn influenced his political views. (Federalists believed in a strong central government; anti-Federalists thought states' rights were more important.) Coming from a more modest background than the aristocrats (upperclass, wealthy landowners) who dominated the American political scene of the time, Van Buren would become a champion of the common man. It was a personal cause and a shrewd political stand. His successful work in New York to expand the base of eligible voters increased the number of people who would likely vote for him.

Van Buren attended local schools and then began clerking in the offices of local attorney Francis Sylvester. Van Buren ran errands, swept floors, studied law, and attended trials. When he was fifteen, according to some accounts, a judge

Martin Van Buren Timeline

1782: Born in New York

1796: Graduates from Kinderhook Academy; serves as clerk for lawyer and begins studying law

1803: Passes New York bar; sets up law practice in Kinderhook

1813–20: Serves in New York senate

1815–19: Serves as New York attorney general

1821–28: Serves as U.S. senator from New York

1828: Elected governor of New York; resigns in March 1829 to join President Andrew Jackson's Cabinet as secretary of state

1831: Resigns as secretary of state and is nominated by Jackson as minister to England, but the nomination is rejected by Congress

1832: Helps establish the Democratic Party, which nominates Jackson for second term; Jackson wins election with Van Buren as vice president

1837–41: Serves as eighth U.S. president

1837: Banks close in Philadelphia and New York City on May 10, beginning the Panic of 1837 and a depression that lasts throughout Van Buren's term

1838: Van Buren continues Jackson's Indian policy, culminating with the Trail of Tears, when thousands of Native Americans are forced westward from the Southeast to present-day Oklahoma

1840: Loses presidential election to William Henry Harrison

1844: Despite being the favorite, Van Buren loses the Democratic Party presidential nomination to dark-horse candidate James K. Polk

1848: Runs for president as a member of the Free Soil Party but receives only ten percent of the vote

1862: Dies in New York

was impressed with his attention and note-taking during a trial and asked him to sum up the case to the jury. Whether the story is true or not, Van Buren did indeed excel in his law preparation and completed his studies in New York City at the firm of William P. Van Ness.

Van Buren was admitted to the bar (the legal profession) in 1803 and returned to Kinderhook to open up a law practice. He soon earned a local reputation as a skillful lawyer and successfully branched statewide into cases against Federalist attorneys who represented more wealthy clients. He be-

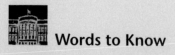

Words to Know

Agrarian: One who believes in and supports issues beneficial to agriculture.

Anti-Federalists: A group who wanted a limited federal government and more power for individual states.

Appropriation: Legislation that sets aside money for a project.

Aristocrats: Wealthy landowners.

Bar: A term that encompasses all certified lawyers; all those who have passed the official requirements to be certified as lawyers.

Boom and bust: An economy characterized by frequent upturns ("boom" periods) and downturns ("busts").

Censure: An official reprimand against a public official.

Coalitions: Groups of people supporting a political issue or cause.

Credit: A loan in which one party (a creditor), usually a bank, extends money to another party (a debtor).

Depression: A period of time when unemployment is very high and business activity slows considerably.

Electoral votes: The votes a presidential candidate receives for having won a majority of the popular vote in a state.

Fiscal: Relating to financial matters.

Nullification theory: The theory that a state can negate a federal law within its borders.

Panic of 1837: An economic slump that hit the United States in 1837.

Platform: A declaration of policies that a candidate or political party intends to follow if the party's candidate is elected.

Recharter: To renew a law or an act.

Reparations: Payments for damage caused by acts of hostility.

Tariff of 1828: Also called the Tariff of Abominations; legislation that placed an extremely high tax on imported goods.

came a rising star among Democratic-Republicans. He gradually assumed a leading role in New York within that political group. The Democratic-Republicans represented agrarian-based (agriculturally based) ideals and appealed to the common man in opposition to the more aristocratic Federalists.

In February of 1807, Van Buren married Hannah Hoes (1783–1819; see entry on **Hannah Van Buren** in volume 1), a childhood friend and distant cousin. They had five children—Abraham, Martin, John, Winfield Scott (who died as an infant), and Smith Thompson. Hannah Van Buren died in 1819, and Van Buren never remarried.

In 1812, Van Buren was elected to the New York state senate. He received some national recognition by proposing conscription (mandatory military service for young men) to beef up the army. His arguments won some approval as American forces struggled during the War of 1812 (1812–15). In 1815, he became New York's attorney general. Almost immediately, he took on a high-profile national case, prosecuting Brigadier General William Hull (1753–1825). (In a case like this, the prosecutor argues the case on behalf of the government.) General Hull was accused of treason (betrayal of one's country) for having surrendered Fort Detroit to the British in the War of 1812. Hull was convicted and sentenced to be shot, but his sentence was commuted (made less severe) by President **James Madison** (1751–1836; see entry in volume 1).

Meanwhile, Van Buren was busy organizing Democratic-Republicans. Political parties, in those days, were regional coalitions (alliances) of like-minded individuals. By organizing Democratic-Republicans on key issues, including expanding the pool of eligible voters, Van Buren was able to forge a powerful political group called the Albany Regency. This group began to challenge the dominant Clintonians, named after New York's governor DeWitt Clinton (1769–1828). Van Buren was able to shift power to his group and ride the new wave of influence to win election to the U.S. Senate in 1820.

Ally to Jackson

As an even-tempered but resourceful and eloquent politician, Van Buren quickly rose to chair the Senate Judiciary Committee. He became a fierce opponent of President **John Quincy Adams** (1767–1848; see entry in volume 1) and was vital in frustrating the Adams administration's plans for providing federal money for improvements for roads. Van Buren viewed the plan as a national intrusion (an unwelcome interference) on states' rights.

Van Buren threw his support to **Andrew Jackson** (1767–1845; see entry in volume 1). Jackson had received more electoral votes than Adams in the first balloting of the election of 1824, but had not received a majority to win the presidency. (Electoral votes are the votes a presidential candidate receives for winning a majority of the popular vote in a state.) When supporters for other candidates switched their votes to Adams, he won. While Jackson immediately began campaigning for the 1828 election, Van Buren skillfully created a coalition of supporters from both the North and the South to promote Jackson's candidacy. Adams and Jackson had both been Democratic-Republicans, but Jackson's faction within the party became known as Jacksonian Democrats. Van Buren helped transform a coalition of antiaristocratic northern politicians and southern planters into the Democratic Party by the 1832 election.

Previously, presidents had viewed themselves as being independent of Congress and tried to avoid influencing the decisions of that branch of government. By 1832, however, incumbent (currently in office) president Andrew Jackson ran for reelection as the head of the Democratic Party, with party congressmen firmly following his leadership. He embraced the Democratic Party's platform (the beliefs and ideals that will form policy if the party is elected).

In a shrewd political move to help secure the 1828 election for Jackson, Van Buren gave up his Senate seat before his term was complete and ran for governor of New York. As expected, Van Buren won the election. His increased recognition within the state helped Jackson to win New York's electoral votes, a surprising result for a southern politician. Van Buren had squeaked by in the gubernatorial election (election for governor). He then promptly resigned after three months when Jackson called him to Washington, D.C., as a reward for his support. Jackson named Van Buren secretary of state. Not coincidentally, the position of secretary of state was as sure a stepping-stone to the presidency as any other office. Four of the first six presidents had held that position.

As secretary of state, Van Buren was effective in opening up the West Indies for trade through a treaty with Great Britain. He was successful in winning reparations (payments for damage caused by acts of war) from France. During the Napoleonic wars (1799–1814), France was at war with other European countries. (Napoleon Bonaparte [1769–1821] was then the leader of France.) American merchants had suffered commercial losses when France seized ships and detoured trade. Van Buren led Jackson's philosophy on states' rights, preparing the speech in which Jackson vetoed (rejected) a federal appropriation bill (legislation that sets money aside for a project) to build a road in Kentucky that would link the towns of Maysville and Lexington. Insisting the road was not a federal matter but of concern only to the state, Jackson vetoed the Maysville Road bill and established a trend that made states responsible for the building and improving of roads and canals.

Van Buren's work drew increasing respect from Jackson, leading to some Cabinet power struggles, particularly between Van Buren and Vice President John C. Calhoun (1782–1850; see box in **Andrew Jackson** entry in volume 1), who aspired to follow Jackson as president. Relations among all Cabinet officials became more strained over a scandal. Secretary of War John H. Eaton (1790–1856) married a woman he was rumored to have romanced while she was still married. Jackson and Van Buren supported Eaton; other Cabinet members and their wives did not.

Another difference developed over the issue of nullification, the theory that a state can nullify a federal law within its borders. Jackson and Van Buren strongly supported states' rights in most matters. But South Carolina threatened to nullify the Tariff of 1828, legislation that placed an extremely high tax on imported goods. This was a tax that Jackson and Van Buren had pushed for to help Western states compete in the American economy. Jackson threatened to send federal troops to South Carolina if the state carried through with its nullification threat. Calhoun, a native of South Carolina, sided for the rights of nullification, further distancing him from Jackson. Calhoun's doom was sealed when Jackson learned that his vice president had supported the censure (public reprimand) of Jackson in 1818, when Jackson was an army general. Jackson had led a raid into Seminole lands in Florida, an area outside of U.S. jurisdiction (authority), to avenge an earlier Seminole attack. It was rumored at the time that Jackson had killed two British citizens in Spanish Florida.

As the end of his first term approached, Jackson wanted to make several Cabinet changes but wanted to avoid public and political criticism. Van Buren helped Jackson tactfully handle the changes. He resigned from his Cabinet position in 1831 and was nominated by Jackson for the post of minister to Great Britain. Van Buren began serving in this position before being confirmed by Congress. (All such appointments require confirmation by Congress.) However, the resulting vote on the nomination in the Senate ended in a tie. Under such conditions, as set forth by the U.S. Constitution, the vice president, who is also president of the Senate, can cast a deciding vote. Calhoun took the opportunity to vote against Van Buren. The move infuriated Jackson and hastened Calhoun's departure from the administration. (Jackson ran with Van Buren in the 1832 election; Calhoun resigned shortly after the election and before Jackson's first term ended.)

Following Van Buren's resignation as secretary of state, Jackson asked all Cabinet members to resign as his first term ended, allowing him to start fresh following the elections of 1832. This election was the first of the modern party system. In this system—still in place in the twenty-first century—party delegates nominate their presidential candidate at a national convention. Van Buren was a leading force in helping to establish the practice. He transformed the Jackson Democrats of the Democratic-Republican Party into the Democratic Party. Jackson won the party nomination easily and triumphed in the national election over candidates of two short-lived parties, the National Republicans and the Anti-Masonics. Van Buren was elected Jackson's new vice president.

Vice president and heir apparent

As vice president, Van Buren spent time defending Jackson's first-term veto of the Maysville, Kentucky, road bill. He also defended Jackson's continued opposition to rechartering (legally renewing) the Second Bank of the United States. The bank, a federal bank, controlled the currency (money in circulation) of the United States. Jackson argued that this bank was not responsive to the will of the people. Van Buren supported Jackson, although he was not wholly convinced the bank should be dismantled. Jackson boldly moved funds from the federal bank to various state banks. This action created political commotion. Congress censured Jackson—the only time

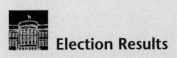

Election Results

1836

Presidential / Vice presidential candidates	Popular votes	Presidential electoral votes
Martin Van Buren / Richard M. Johnson (Democratic)	762,678	170
William Henry Harrison / Francis Granger (Whig)	550,816	73
Hugh Lawson White (Whig)	146,107	26
Daniel Webster (Whig)	41,201	14
Willie Person Mangum (Whig)	unknown	11

The Whig Party presented four regional candidates for president. John Tyler and William Smith were also Whig vice presidential candidates. Democratic vice presidential nominee Johnson did not receive a majority of electoral votes, so his election came as a result of a vote in the U.S. Senate, the only vice president in history to be elected that way.

in the nation's history that Congress has censured a president. Van Buren continued to support President Jackson.

Despite the censure, Jackson remained a very popular president and was the firm leader of the Democratic Party. As such, he ensured that Van Buren would be his heir apparent. Van Buren was unanimously nominated (nominated by all in agreement) as the Democratic Party candidate at its national convention in Baltimore, Maryland, in 1836.

Meanwhile, the National Republican party of 1832 had transformed into the new Whig Party. The Whigs were united in their anti-Jacksonian sentiments, particularly for what they saw as excessive use of presidential power. The Whigs did not hold a convention. Instead, they nominated four regional candidates—General **William Henry Harrison** (1773–1841; see entry in volume 2) of Ohio; U.S. representative Willie Person Mangum (1792–1861) of North Carolina; U.S. senator Daniel Webster (1782–1852; see box in **John Tyler** entry in volume 2) of Massachusetts; and U.S. senator Hugh Lawson White (1773–1840) of Tennessee. Whigs hoped that no candidate would receive the required number of electoral votes, thus throwing the election to the House of Representatives, where they held an edge. The strategy failed, as Van Buren won 170 electoral votes to 125 votes for the Whig candidates.

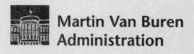

Martin Van Buren Administration

Administration Dates
March 4, 1837–March 4, 1841

Vice President
Richard Mentor Johnson (1837–41)

Cabinet
Secretary of State
John Forsyth (1837–41)

Secretary of the Treasury
Levi Woodbury (1837–41)

Secretary of War
Joel R. Poinsett (1837–41)

Attorney General
Benjamin F. Butler (1837–38)
Felix Grundy (1838–39)
Henry D. Gilpin (1840–41)

Secretary of the Navy
Mahlon Dickerson (1837–38)
James K. Paulding (1838–41)

Postmaster General
Amos Kendall (1837–40)
John M. Niles (1840–41)

A president in the Jacksonian mold

In his inaugural address, Van Buren announced his intention to continue Jackson's policies. He also retained most of his predecessor's Cabinet officials. But soon into his presidency, a worldwide depression struck. The United States, which had enjoyed tremendous economic growth during the Jackson years, was severely affected. The political repercussions (aftereffects) for Van Buren from the Panic of 1837 were major. His popularity nosedived with the economy, as jobs were lost, many businesses went bankrupt, and banks failed.

Van Buren did have financial skills. During his short term as governor of New York, for example, Van Buren was able to establish a then-innovative "safety fund system," which insured individual bank savings. As vice president, he had been supportive against his better judgment of Jackson's opposition to the federal banking system and to his transfer of federal funds to state banks. He recognized, now, that states had used the funds to issue unlimited credit (loans) to customers. The economic downturn was fueled into a depression by this cheap credit that ruined both the banks and their customers.

Van Buren proposed reestablishing an independent banking system that would control federal funds. The Independent Treasury System was approved in 1840. Although it was disbanded by the next administration, the system was revived again during the 1840s. The system served as the federal banking system through 1913, when the Federal Reserve was established during the administration of President **Woodrow Wilson** (1856–1924; see entry in volume 4).

Van Buren lost further popularity over his handling of a crisis with Great Britain. He managed to avoid war and helped settle the conflict; however, his use of diplomacy when American passions were aroused for war lowered his political popularity. The incident grew in significance as Americans began aiding Canadians rebelling for independence from Great Britain. An American steamer, *The Caroline*, stocked with supplies for Canadian rebels, was seized by

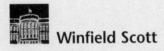

Winfield Scott

From the War of 1812 (1812–15) to the Civil War (1861–65) and many battles in between, Winfield Scott was one of America's leading military commanders. He was so popularly known that he ran for president in 1852. His father, William Scott, had been a captain during the American Revolution (1775–83).

Scott was born on June 13, 1786, on his parents' large farm near Petersburg, Virginia. His father died when Scott was six years old, leaving his mother, Ann, to raise him alone. She died when he was seventeen. After one year each of high school and college, he began to study law. He soon started his own practice, traveling around Virginia to provide legal aid where needed. In 1807, Scott watched the treason trial of former vice president Aaron Burr (1756–1836). Scott declared publicly that he believed Burr and his cohort, General James Wilkinson (1757–1825), were guilty. Scott's statement angered Wilkinson, who, along with Burr, were found not-guilty.

Meanwhile, hostilities between Great Britain and the United States were growing dangerous. President Thomas Jefferson closed American harbors to international trade, beginning the Embargo of 1807. Jefferson had deliberately reduced the size of the army as part of his plan to have a weak central government. Needing troops to keep the British out, Jefferson called for a militia. Scott applied to Jefferson for a permanent position in the army. Impressed with the eager young man, Jefferson gave him the rank of captain. In 1808, Scott and his company proceeded to New Orleans.

Meanwhile, Wilkinson was now in charge of the army in the South. He and Scott disliked each other, but they held an uneasy truce for two years. In 1810, their conflict came to a head when Scott was reprimanded for remarks against his commanding officer. Scott left the army to resume his law practice.

Scott soon returned to service and was promoted to the rank of lieutenant colonel. During the War of 1812 (1812–15), he was given a unit positioned on a high post overlooking British forces in Queenston, Ontario, Canada. Greatly outnumbered, Scott retreated and then surrendered. In spite of the defeat, he showed courage and was promoted to the rank of colonel and, later, brevet major general.

In 1815, Scott turned down President James Madison's offer to become secretary of war. Instead, he withdrew from public life, and traveled to Europe. Upon his return, Scott vied for several years with Edmund Gaines (1777–1849) for the highest rank in the army. In 1821, Scott was named head of the army of the East and Gaines headed the army of the West; both were given the rank of brigadier general. When the position of general of the entire army opened up in 1825, Gaines and Scott were each passed over in favor of Alexander Macomb (1782–1841), a major general during the War of 1812. Scott wrote to the secre-

Winfield Scott.
Courtesy of the Library of Congress.

tary of war stating that he would not take orders from Macomb; Scott was immediately relieved of his command. With no one to command and no official army duties, Scott again headed for Europe.

Scott returned in 1830 and was given command of forces in Atlanta, Georgia. Citizens there refused to accept federal decisions to respect the land of the Cherokee Indians. Scott's balance of military strength and patient explanations of the government's position eased tensions and made him popular with the military and the public once again. When the Black Hawk War erupted in 1832, President Andrew Jackson turned to Scott, whom he respected. Arriving in the Illinois area as the war ended, Scott supervised the treaty at which the Sauk tribe signed away its long-standing rights to land along the eastern border of the Mississippi River.

Meanwhile, Jackson had convinced the head chief of the Seminole to leave the tribe's area and move west. After two years passed and only a few of the Seminole had left, the United States fought against the forces of the great Seminole chief Osceola (c. 1804–1838). His people were eventually defeated, and nearly four thousand of them were forced to move to Oklahoma in 1843. By then, Scott had left to command the removal of the much larger group of the Cherokee. Under Scott's orders, the troops were disposed at various points throughout Cherokee country, where forts were erected for holding the Native Americans before their removal. Scott ordered his soldiers to treat the Native Americans with respect. More than thirteen thousand Cherokee made the move to Oklahoma along what became known as the Trail of Tears.

In 1841, Scott became major general and commander in chief of the army. When war erupted with Mexico in 1845, he took a force of twelve thousand men and seized the national palace. Scott returned home a hero. The Whig Party sought to capitalize on Scott's popularity by nominating him as its presidential candidate in 1852. However, Democrat **Franklin Pierce** (1804–1869; see entry in volume 2) won the election. Scott was still in charge of the army when the Civil War erupted in 1861. But the seventy-five-year-old soon retired. He died on May 29, 1866.

Great Britain and burned. An American named Amos Dufree was killed during the incident. Several American reprisal raids followed. The United States demanded reparations for *The Caroline*, which Britain refused to give. Meanwhile, Van Buren called for order on the American side and sent Major General Winfield Scott (1786–1866; see box) to ensure that raids were stopped.

Trouble brewed again when a Canadian was arrested on charges of having killed Dufree. He had bragged of the deed in a New York City tavern. This development and a renewal of skirmishes (minor conflicts) along the long-disputed border between Maine and Canada renewed passion for war. Major General Scott was again dispatched to the area to maintain peace while diplomatic solutions were ironed out. Van Buren succeeded in eventually winning "peace with honor," even at great political cost for the Little Magician.

Along with conflicts on the northern border, the United States continued to have struggles in the South. The policy of removing Native Americans from the Southeast to the Southwest had met strong resistance from Seminoles in Florida. Efforts were renewed in carrying out the American policy begun by Jackson. In addition to approving raids on Seminoles, Van Buren supported the forcible relocation of the Cherokee nation to "Indian Territory" (mostly present-day Oklahoma). About a quarter of the Cherokee population died during the relocation, which is memorialized as "The Trail of Tears."

Losses and changes

Van Buren was unanimously nominated by the Democratic Party to run for a second term. He was so unpopular by this point, however, that the Whig Party was able to run a spirited public campaign without having to engage deeply in issues of the day. William Henry Harrison, then sixty-seven years old, was the party's candidate. The Whigs presented no platform, concentrating instead on building a sense of good feeling through songs and slogans, such as "Tippecanoe and Tyler Too!" Harrison was still well known for having won a decisive victory against Native American forces some three decades earlier at the Battle of Tippecanoe. **John Tyler** (1790–1862; see

entry in volume 2)—the "Tyler too" half of the slogan—was a handsome statesman. He had the double distinction of promoting states' rights while also being anti-Jacksonian. He had sharply criticized Jackson for transferring funds from the federal bank during his presidency. Van Buren won forty-four percent of the popular vote but was trounced in the Electoral College, 234 to 60. (For more information on the Electoral College, see boxes in **George W. Bush** entry in volume 5.)

Following his defeat, the model politician Van Buren gradually transformed into a statesman while renewing his common-man image. One of his final acts as president was an executive order that limited federal workers to a ten-hour day, a victory for labor reform. He traveled around the United States, became involved in the Texas annexation issue, and twice more ran for president during the 1840s. In the 1850s, he became the first ex-president to tour Europe. European dignitaries were unsure of how to welcome a figure who neither held elective office nor was a member or an associate of

Thousands of members of the Cherokee tribe were forced to march from Georgia to current-day Oklahoma in a massive relocation that became known as the Trail of Tears.
Reproduced by permission of Woolaroc Museum.

A sign in an editorial cartoon points outgoing president Martin Van Buren away from the White House and towards his home in Kinderhook, New York.
Reproduced by permission of the Corbis Corporation.

royalty. Van Buren gladly responded by requesting to be treated as a common person.

On the annexation issue, Van Buren was against admitting Texas into the Union. If Texas were admitted, it would be a slave state and would upset the balance of fifteen slave states and fifteen nonslave states. Van Buren gradually moved from recognizing states' rights on the slavery issue to being against the expansion of slavery to new states. He was the leading contender for the Democratic nomination in 1844, but he could not win the necessary number of delegates at the Democratic convention. The nomination went to **James K. Polk** (1795–1849; see entry in volume 2), who came out clearly for annexing Texas.

Van Buren ran again in 1848, this time as the nominee of the Free Soil Party. The Free Soil Party was led by his son, John, and maintained Jacksonian ideals while being against the expansion of slavery. Van Buren won only ten percent of the national vote, but his presence on the New York ballot stole votes from Democratic nominee Lewis Cass (1782–1866) and tipped the state's electoral votes, and the election, to Whig candidate **Zachary Taylor** (1784–1850; see entry in volume 2).

Van Buren then retired to his farm and Lindenwald estate in Kinderhook, writing his memoirs and occasionally becoming active in national affairs. He opposed the repeal of the Missouri Compromise, which limited the expansion of slavery. The Democratic Van Buren supported the election of the Republican **Abraham Lincoln** (1809–1865; see entry in volume 2) in 1860. Van Buren died at Kinderhook in 1862.

Legacy

Martin Van Buren's role in helping form the Democratic Party in 1832 from a splintered (divided) group of Democratic-Republicans remains his most lasting achievement. His effect on the nation's political affairs was more powerful as a political power broker (one who has a powerful influence over people and votes) during the 1820s and as secretary of state and, later, vice president to Andrew Jackson, then it was as president.

Nevertheless, Van Buren's presidential act of reinstituting the federal bank and his avoidance of war with Great Britain proved to be sound decisions. His fiscal (financial) policies helped address the problem of boom-and-bust cycles. Nevertheless, the cyclical nature of the economy would continue to plague the nation through the nineteenth century.

Van Buren carried on the policies of Andrew Jackson, except for disagreeing on the national bank issue. These practices were also followed by James K. Polk during his term as president in the mid-1840s. Van Buren supported states' rights. His even-tempered approach saw the tradition of Jacksonian politics through a severe economic crisis. His legacy remains as a key political figure of the Jackson era. The era ran from the mid-1820s through the late 1840s, interrupted only from 1841 to 1845 by the largely ineffective Harrison and Tyler administrations.

A Selection of Martin Van Buren Landmarks

Kinderhook Cemetery. U.S. 9, Kinderhook, NY. Final resting place of Martin and Hannah Van Buren.

Martin Van Buren National Historic Site. 1013 Old Post Rd., Kinderhook NY 12106. (518) 758-9689. Site of Martin Van Buren's Lindenwald estate. See http://www.nps.gov/mava/home.htm (accessed on June 20, 2000).

Where to Learn More

Curtis, James C. *The Fox at Bay: Martin Van Buren and the Presidency, 1837–1841.* Lexington: University Press of Kentucky, 1970.

Hargrove, Jim. *Martin Van Buren: Eighth President of the United States.* Chicago: Children's Press, 1987.

Harris, Glenn. *Martin Van Buren Home Page.* [Online] http://www.mindspring.com/~braniff/ (accessed on July 31, 2000).

Niven, John. *Martin Van Buren: The Romantic Age of American Politics.* New York: Oxford University Press, 1983.

Wilson, Major L. *The Presidency of Martin Van Buren.* Lawrence: University Press of Kansas, 1984.

Hannah Van Buren

**Born March 8, 1783
Kinderhook, New York
Died February 5, 1819
Albany, New York**

Early supporter of her husband's political career, she died eighteen years before he became president

When **Martin Van Buren** (1782–1862; see entry in volume 1) became president in 1837, he had been a widower for eighteen years and had four bachelor sons. No one was available to serve in the official capacities of first lady. The situation changed when eldest son Abraham Van Buren married Angelica Singleton. At the end of 1838, Angelica Singleton Van Buren took on the responsibilities of first lady for the Van Buren administration. She had just returned from honeymooning in Europe with her new husband, who served as his father's secretary.

With former first lady **Dolley Madison** (1768–1849; see entry in volume 1) as an advisor, Angelica became the hostess at White House gatherings and brought a feminine sensibility to the Van Buren White House. Angelica was the daughter of a Madison in-law and had journeyed to Washington, D.C., to visit her famous relative. Dolley Madison took Angelica to a White House function soon after the Van Buren administration began. It was there that she and Abraham first met.

"She was a sincere Christian, a dutiful child, tender mother, affectionate wife."

Inscription on Hannah Van Buren's tombstone

Hannah Van Buren.
Courtesy of the Library of Congress.

Hannah died in 1818, shortly after giving birth to the couple's fifth son, Smith Thompson (one other son had died as an infant). Hannah and Martin Van Buren had grown up together in the small Dutch-immigrant community of Kinderhook, New York. They were distant cousins and their families were close friends. Van Buren's parents had been sponsors at Hannah's baptism.

Van Buren began a law career while in his teens and traveled to New York City to finish his preparation to become a lawyer. He returned to Kinderhook and established a successful practice. He and Hannah were married in 1807, when they were both twenty-four years old. Hannah was a modest and unassuming woman, content to remain at home and raise a family. The couple's first son, Abraham, was born in Kinderhook.

In 1812, Van Buren was elected to the New York state senate, and in 1815 he became the state's attorney general. The Van Burens and their three sons moved to Albany, where their home became a whirl of activity. Apprentice lawyers and clerks often worked in the house, as Van Buren took on several high-profile cases.

Hannah Hoes Van Buren fell ill during her fifth pregnancy. After giving birth, she never recovered, dying in 1818 at the age of thirty-five. Her ailment was believed to have been tuberculosis. Though grief-stricken, Van Buren was consoled by the many friends he had made while organizing a strong political party in New York that was dubbed the Albany Regency. He was elected to the U.S. Senate in 1820. Thus began a long and remarkable political career on the federal level that included positions as secretary of state and vice president. In 1836, he was elected president of the United States.

Van Buren had become accustomed to living in a style that combined luxury and a work environment. He and his sons began restoring a sense of elegance to the White House that his more earthy predecessor, **Andrew Jackson** (1767–1845; see entry in volume 1) would have found showy. Angelica Singleton's arrival in late 1838 as daughter-in-law helped complete the transformation. With the help of Dolley Madison, for the next several years White House occasions were lively and festive.

Where to Learn More

Anthony, Carl Sferrazza. *America's Most Influential First Ladies.* Minneapolis: Oliver Press, 1992.

Hargrove, Jim. *Martin Van Buren, Eighth President of the United States.* Chicago: Childrens Press, 1987.

Mayo, Edith P., ed. *The Smithsonian Book of the First Ladies: Their Lives, Times, and Issues.* New York: H. Holt, 1996.

Van Buren's Inaugural Address

Delivered on March 4, 1837; excerpted from
The Republican: A Nation of Laws & Not of Men **(Web site)**

*"Old Kinderhook" announces that he will continue
the policies of the Jackson administration*

Martin Van Buren (1782–1862; see entry in volume 1) was the closest advisor to President **Andrew Jackson** (1767–1845; see entry in volume 1), for whom he served as secretary of state and vice president. As Jackson's hand-picked successor, Van Buren won election to president in 1836. Jackson had been a strong president: his administration was enormously popular and controversial. His support for states' rights against the powers of the federal government (except in cases where national unity is threatened) made him especially popular among southerners and among working people of the North and West.

Southerners were concerned about how fully Van Buren, a New Yorker, would follow the policies of Jackson, a Tennessean. Van Buren answered them in his inaugural address. After expressing optimism for the nation, which had prospered during Jackson's administration, Van Buren announced policies similar to those of Jackson. These policies included support for states' rights in such issues as deciding whether or not to permit slavery.

"Our system, purified and enhanced in value by all it has encountered, still preserves its spirit of free and fearless discussion, blended with unimpaired fraternal feeling."

Martin Van Buren, from his inaugural address

Things to remember while reading an excerpt from President Van Buren's inaugural address:

- The excerpt presents the middle portion of Van Buren's address, which celebrated the success of the United States and indicated a continuation of the policies of the Jackson administration. Van Buren praised the ways in which the American system had adapted to new challenges arising from the expansion of population and territory. He began by saluting the nation's first president, **George Washington** (1732–1799; see entry in volume 1), who helped keep the nation united almost solely by the force of his will. Since then, Van Buren continued, the nation had experienced many challenges but had grown stronger through such tests.

- As a champion of states' rights, Van Buren announced that he was a Constitutional constructionist (one whose political positions are determined by strict adherence to the Constitution). Van Buren's constructionist approach was reflected in his defense of slavery as an issue to be decided by each individual state. In a nod to supporters of slavery, Van Buren insisted that he would not approve any attempt to remove the institution from within the borders of Washington, D.C.

- Van Buren viewed slavery as one of the challenges the government had already undertaken. He wanted to remain on the course of maintaining a balance of free and slave states.

Excerpt from
President Van Buren's inaugural address

*In the early stages of the new Government, when all felt the imposing influence as they recognized the unequaled services of the first President, it was a common sentiment that the great weight of his character could alone bind the **discordant** materials of our Government together and save us from the violence of contending **factions**. Since his death nearly forty years are gone. Party*

Discordant: Uncooperative.

Factions: Political groups.

Complete American Presidents Sourcebook

*exasperation has been often carried to its highest point; the virtue and **fortitude** of the people have sometimes been greatly tried; yet our system, purified and enhanced in value by all it has encountered, still preserves its spirit of free and fearless discussion, blended with unimpaired **fraternal feeling.***

*The capacity of the people for self-government, and their willingness, from a high sense of duty and without those exhibitions of coercive power so generally employed in other countries, to submit to all needful restraints and **exactions** of municipal law, have also been favorably exemplified in the history of the American States. Occasionally, it is true, the **ardor** of public sentiment, outrunning the regular progress of the judicial tribunals or seeking to reach cases not denounced as criminal by the existing law, has displayed itself in a manner calculated to give pain to the friends of free government and to encourage the hopes of those who wish for its overthrow. These occurrences, however, have been far less frequent in our country than in any other of equal population on the globe, and with the diffusion of intelligence it may well be hoped that they will constantly diminish in frequency and violence. The generous patriotism and sound common sense of the great mass of our fellow-citizens will assuredly in time produce this result; for as every assumption of illegal power not only wounds the majesty of the law, but furnishes a pretext for abridging the liberties of the people, the latter have the most direct and permanent interest in preserving the landmarks of social order and maintaining on all occasions the **inviolability** of those constitutional and legal provisions which they themselves have made. . . .*

Certain danger was foretold from the extension of our territory, the multiplication of States, and the increase of population. Our system was supposed to be adapted only to boundaries comparatively narrow. These have been widened beyond conjecture; the members of our Confederacy are already doubled, and the numbers of our people are incredibly augmented. The alleged causes of danger have long surpassed anticipation, but none of the consequences have followed. The power and influence of the Republic have arisen to a height obvious to all mankind; respect for its authority was not more apparent at its ancient than it is at its present limits; new and inexhaustible sources of general prosperity have been opened; the effects of distance have been averted by the inventive genius of our people, developed and fostered by the spirit of our institutions; and the enlarged variety and amount of interests, productions, and pursuits

Fortitude: Determination.

Fraternal feeling: Brotherhood.

Exactions: Strict, particular, and complete accordance.

Ardor: Eagerness.

Inviolability: That which cannot be broken.

have strengthened the chain of mutual dependence and formed a circle of mutual benefits too apparent ever to be overlooked.

In justly balancing the powers of the Federal and State authorities difficulties nearly insurmountable arose at the outset and subsequent collisions were deemed inevitable. Amid these it was scarcely believed possible that a scheme of government so complex in construction could remain uninjured. From time to time embarrassments have certainly occurred; but how just is the confidence of future safety imparted by the knowledge that each in succession has been happily removed! Overlooking partial and temporary evils as inseparable from the practical operation of all human institutions, and looking only to the general result, every patriot has reason to be satisfied. While the Federal Government has successfully performed its appropriate functions in relation to foreign affairs and concerns evidently national, that of every State has remarkably improved in protecting and developing local interests and individual welfare; and if the vibrations of authority have occasionally tended too much toward one or the other, it is unquestionably certain that the ultimate operation of the entire system has been to strengthen all the existing institutions and to elevate our whole country in prosperity and renown.

The last, perhaps the greatest, of the prominent sources of discord and disaster supposed to lurk in our political condition was the institution of domestic slavery. Our forefathers were deeply impressed with the delicacy of this subject, and they treated it with a forbearance so evidently wise that in spite of every sinister foreboding it never until the present period disturbed the tranquillity of our common country. Such a result is sufficient evidence of the justice and the patriotism of their course; it is evidence not to be mistaken that an adherence to it can prevent all embarrassment from this as well as from every other anticipated cause of difficulty or danger. Have not recent events made it obvious to the slightest reflection that the least deviation from this spirit of forbearance is injurious to every interest, that of humanity included? Amidst the violence of excited passions this generous and fraternal feeling has been sometimes disregarded; and standing as I now do before my countrymen, in this high place of honor and of trust, I can not refrain from anxiously invoking my fellow-citizens never to be deaf to its dictates. Perceiving before my election the deep interest this subject was beginning to excite, I believed it a solemn duty fully to make known my sentiments in regard to it, and now, when every motive for misrepresentation has passed away, I trust that they will be candidly *weighed and understood. At least they will be my standard of conduct in the path before me. I then declared that if the desire of those of my countrymen who were favorable to my election was gratified "I must go into the Presidential chair the inflexible and uncompromising opponent of every attempt on the part of Congress to abolish slavery in the District of Columbia against the wishes of the slaveholding States, and also with a determination equally decided to resist the slightest interference with it in the States where it exists." I submitted also to my fellow-citizens, with fullness and frankness, the reasons which led me to this determination. The result authorizes me to believe that they have been approved and are confided in by a majority of the people of the United States, including those whom they most immediately affect. It now only remains to add that no bill conflicting with these views can ever receive my constitutional sanction. These opinions have been adopted in the firm belief that they are in accordance with the spirit that **actuated** the **venerated fathers of the Republic,** and that succeeding experience has proved them to be humane, patriotic, expedient, honorable, and just. If the agitation of this subject was intended to reach the stability of our institutions, enough has occurred to show that it has signally failed, and that in this as in every other instance the apprehensions of the timid and the hopes of the wicked for the destruction of our Government are again destined to be disappointed. Here and there, indeed, scenes of dangerous excitement have occurred, terrifying instances of local violence have been witnessed, and a reckless disregard of the consequences of their conduct has exposed individuals to popular **indignation;** but neither masses of the people nor sections of the country have been swerved from their devotion to the bond of union and the principles it has made sacred. It will be ever thus. Such attempts at dangerous agitation may periodically return, but with each the object will be better understood. That predominating affection for our political system which prevails throughout our territorial limits, that calm and enlightened judgment which ultimately governs our people as one vast body, will always be at hand to resist and control every effort, foreign or domestic, which aims or would lead to overthrow our institutions.*

What can be more gratifying than such a retrospect as this? We look back on obstacles avoided and dangers overcome, on expectations more than realized and prosperity perfectly secured. To the hopes of the hostile, the fears of the timid, and the doubts of the anxious actual experience has given the conclusive reply. We have seen time gradually dispel every unfavorable foreboding and our

Actuated: Energized.

Venerated fathers of the Republic: Founding Fathers.

Indignation: Outrage.

Constitution surmount every adverse circumstance dreaded at the outset as beyond control. Present excitement will at all times magnify present dangers, but true philosophy must teach us that none more threatening than the past can remain to be overcome; and we ought (for we have just reason) to entertain an abiding confidence in the stability of our institutions and an entire conviction that if administered in the true form, character, and spirit in which they were established they are abundantly adequate to preserve to us and our children the rich blessings already derived from them, to make our beloved land for a thousand generations that chosen spot where happiness springs from a perfect equality of political rights.

For myself, therefore, I desire to declare that the principle that will govern me in the high duty to which my country calls me is a strict adherence to the letter and spirit of the Constitution as it was designed by those who framed it. Looking back to it as a sacred instrument carefully and not easily framed; remembering that it was throughout a work of concession and compromise; viewing it as limited to national **objects;** *regarding it as leaving to the people and the States all power not explicitly parted with, I shall endeavor to preserve, protect, and defend it by anxiously referring to its provision for direction in every action. To matters of domestic* **concernment** *which it has entrusted to the Federal Government and to such as relate to our intercourse with foreign nations I shall zealously devote myself; beyond those limits I shall never pass.* (The Republican: A Nation of Laws & Not of Men [Web site])

Objects: Objectives; goals.

Concernment: Something that matters, or is of concern.

What happened next . . .

The great optimism that Van Buren wanted to promote upon taking office was soon overwhelmed when a financial crisis struck the United States in 1837. Van Buren struggled against the effects of a poor economy and waning popular support for much of his term. Meanwhile, his belief that the issue of slavery was, according to the Constitution, to be determined by individual states was severely tested by growing sentiment for abolition of the institution. A great divide between North and South was occurring over the issue of slavery.

Van Buren had helped establish the Democratic Party. The party was formed by members of the Democratic-Republican Party who favored Andrew Jackson against fellow Democratic-Republican **John Quincy Adams** (1767–1848; see entry in volume 1) in the presidential elections of 1824 and 1828. When controversy over Jackson's use of presidential authority erupted in the early 1830s, opponents gradually formed the rival Whig Party. Whigs gained power during the administration of Van Buren as the economy worsened and the issue of slavery became more divisive. Van Buren lost re-election in 1840 to Whig candidate **William Henry Harrison** (1773–1841; see entry in volume 2).

Did you know . . .

- Van Buren failed in a bid to be the Democratic nominee for president in 1844. **James K. Polk** (1795–1849; see entry in volume 2) got the nod instead. In 1848, Van Buren ran for president as a member of the Free Soil Party. By then, he had become a vocal opponent against the expansion of slavery. He never recovered politically, however, from being associated with the hard economic times of the late 1830s. He received only ten percent of the vote in the 1848 presidential election, but he won enough votes in his home state of New York to influence the election: many voters in the state who would have otherwise supported Democratic nominee Lewis Cass (1782–1866) chose Van Buren, instead. Whig candidate **Zachary Taylor** (1784–1850; see entry in volume 2) won the presidency when he ended up winning New York state's crucial electoral votes.

Where to Learn More

Curtis, James C. *The Fox at Bay: Martin Van Buren and the Presidency, 1837–1841*. Lexington: University Press of Kentucky, 1970.

"Martin Van Buren: Inaugural Address." *The Republican: A Nation of Laws & Not of Men*. [Online] http://www.ideasign.com/chiliast/pdocs/inaugural/vanburen.htm (accessed on June 30, 2000).

Niven, John. *Martin Van Buren: The Romantic Age of American Politics*. New York : Oxford University Press, 1983.

Wilson, Major L. *The Presidency of Martin Van Buren*. Lawrence: University Press of Kansas, 1984.

Where to Learn More

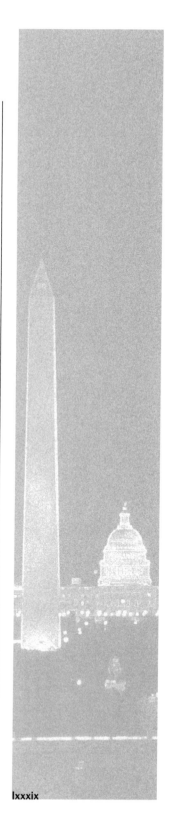

The following list of resources focuses on material appropriate for middle school or high school students. Please note that the web site addresses were verified prior to publication, but are subject to change.

Books

Bailey, Thomas A. *The Pugnacious Presidents: White House Warriors on Parade.* New York: Free Press, 1980.

Barber, James David. *The Presidential Character: Predicting Performance in the White House.* 4th ed. Englewood Cliffs, NJ: Prentice-Hall, 1992.

Barzman, Sol. *Madmen and Geniuses: The Vice-Presidents of the United States.* Chicago: Follett, 1974.

Berube, Maurice. *American Presidents and Education.* Westport, CT: Greenwood Press, 1991.

Boller, Paul F., Jr. *Presidential Anecdotes.* Rev. ed. New York: Oxford, 1996.

Boller, Paul F., Jr. *Presidential Campaigns.* Rev. ed. New York: Oxford, 1996.

Boller, Paul F. Jr. *Presidential Wives: An Anecdotal History.* Rev. ed. New York: Oxford, 1998.

Brace, Paul, Christine B. Harrington, and Gary King, eds. *The Presidency in American Politics.* New York: New York University Press, 1989.

Brallier, Jess, and Sally Chabert. *Presidential Wit and Wisdom.* New York: Penguin, 1996.

Brinkley, Alan, and Davis Dyer, eds. *The Reader's Companion to the American Presidency*. New York: Houghton Mifflin, 2000.

Brogan, Hugh, and Charles Mosley. *American Presidential Families*. New York: Macmillan Publishing Co., 1993.

Bumann, Joan. *Our American Presidents: From Washington through Clinton*. St. Petersburg, FL: Willowisp Press, 1993.

Campbell, Colin. *The U.S. Presidency in Crisis: A Comparative Perspective*. New York: Oxford University Press, 1998.

Clotworthy, William G. *Presidential Sites*. Blacksburg, VA: McDonald & Woodward, 1998.

Cook, Carolyn. *Imagine You Are the . . . President*. Edina, MN: Imaginarium, 1999.

Cooke, Donald Ewin. *Atlas of the Presidents*. Maplewood, NJ: Hammond, 1985.

Cronin, Thomas, ed. *Inventing the American Presidency*. Lawrence: University of Kansas Press, 1989.

Cunliffe, Marcus. *American Presidents and the Presidency*. New York: Houghton Mifflin, 1986.

Dallek, Robert. *Hail to the Chief: The Making and Unmaking of American Presidents*. New York: Hyperion, 1996.

Davis, James W. *The American Presidency*. 2nd ed. Westport, CT: Praeger, 1995.

DeGregorio, William. *The Complete Book of U.S. Presidents*. 4th ed. New York: Barricade Books, 1993.

Fields, Wayne. *Union of Words: A History of Presidential Eloquence*. New York: The Free Press, 1996.

Fisher, Louis. *Presidential War Power*. Lawrence: University of Kansas Press, 1995.

Frank, Sid, and Arden Davis Melick. *Presidents: Tidbits and Trivia*. Maplewood, NJ: Hammond, 1986.

Frost, Elizabeth, ed. *The Bully Pulpit: Quotations from America's Presidents*. New York: Facts On File, 1988.

Genovese, Michael. *The Power of the American Presidency, 1789–2000*. New York: Oxford, 2001.

Gerhardt, Michael J. *The Federal Impeachment Process: A Constitutional and Historical Analysis*. 2nd ed. Chicago: University of Chicago Press, 2000.

Goehlert, Robert U., and Fenton S. Martin. *The Presidency: A Research Guide*. Santa Barbara, CA: ABC-Clio Information Services, 1985.

Havel, James T. *U.S. Presidential Candidates and the Elections: A Biographical and Historical Guide*. New York: Macmillan Library Reference USA, 1996.

Henry, Christopher E. *The Electoral College*. New York: Franklin Watts, 1996.

Henry, Christopher E. *Presidential Elections*. New York: Franklin Watts, 1996.

Hess, Stephen. *Presidents and the Presidency: Essays*. Washington, DC: The Brookings Institution, 1996.

Israel, Fred L., ed. *The Presidents*. Danbury, CT: Grolier Educational, 1996.

Jackson, John S. III, and William Crotty. *The Politics of Presidential Selection*. 2nd ed. New York: Longman, 2001.

Jamieson, Kathleen Hall. *Packaging the Presidency: A History and Criticism of Presidential Campaign Advertising*. 3rd ed. New York: Oxford, 1996.

Kessler, Paula N., and Justin Segal. *The Presidents Almanac*. Rev. ed. Los Angeles: Lowell House Juvenile, 1998.

Kruh, David, and Louis Kruh. *Presidential Landmarks*. New York: Hippocrene Books, 1992.

Kunhardt, Philip B. Jr., Philip B. Kunhardt III, and Peter W. Kunhardt. *The American President*. New York: Penguin, 1999.

Laird, Archibald. *The Near Great—Chronicle of the Vice Presidents*. North Quincy, MA: Christopher Publishing House, 1980.

Mayer, William G., ed. *In Pursuit of the White House: How We Choose Our Presidential Nominees*. Chatham, NJ: Chatham House, 1996.

Murray, Robert K., and Tim H. Blessing. *Greatness in the White House: Rating the Presidents*. 2nd ed. University Park: Pennsylvania State University Press, 1994.

Neustadt, Richard E. *Presidential Power and the Modern Presidents: The Politics of Leadership from Roosevelt to Reagan*. New York: The Free Press, 1990.

Patrick, Diane. *The Executive Branch*. New York: Franklin Watts, 1994.

Presidents of the United States. A World Book Encyclopedia. Chicago: Field Enterprises Educational Corp., 1973.

Riccards, Michael, and James MacGregor Burns. *The Ferocious Engine of Democracy: A History of the American Presidency. Vol I: From the Origins through William McKinley. Vol. II: Theodore Roosevelt through George Bush*. Lanham, MD: Madison Books, 1996.

Robb, Don. *Hail to the Chief: The American Presidency*. Watertown, MA: Charlesbridge, 2000.

Rose, Gary L. *The American Presidency Under Siege*. Albany: State University of New York Press, 1997.

Sanders, Mark C. *The Presidency*. Austin, TX: Steadwell Books, 2000.

Shenkman, Richard. *Presidential Ambition: How the Presidents Gained Power, Kept Power, and Got Things Done*. New York: HarperCollins, 1999.

Shogan, Robert. *The Double-Edged Sword: How Character Makes and Ruins Presidents, from Washington to Clinton*. Boulder, CO: Westview Press, 2000.

Sisung, Kelle S., ed. *Presidential Administration Profiles for Students*. Detroit: Gale Group, 2000.

Smith, Nancy Kegan, and Mary C. Ryan, eds. *Modern First Ladies: Their Documentary Legacy*. Washington, DC: National Archives and Records Administration, 1989.

Stier, Catherine. *If I Were President*. Morton Grove, IL: Albert Whitman, 1999.

Suid, Murray I. *How to Be President of the U.S.A.* Palo Alto, CA: Monday Morning Books, 1992.

Truman, Margaret. *First Ladies: An Intimate Group Portrait of White House Wives*. New York: Ballantine, 1995.

Vidal, Gore. *The American Presidency*. Monroe, ME: Odonian Press, 1998.

Wheeless, Carl. *Landmarks of American Presidents*. Detroit: Gale, 1995.

Video

The American President. Written, produced, and directed by Philip B. Kunhardt Jr., Philip B. Kunhardt III, and Peter W. Kunhardt. Co-production of Kunhardt Productions and Thirteen/WNET in New York. 10 programs.

Web Sites

The American Presidency: Selected Resources, An Informal Reference Guide (Web site). [Online] http://www.interlink-cafe.com/uspresidents/ (accessed on December 11, 2000).

C-Span. *American Presidents: Life Portraits.* [Online] http://www.american presidents.org/ (accessed on December 11, 2000).

Grolier, Inc. *Grolier Presents: The American Presidency.* [Online] http://gi.grolier. com/presidents/ea/prescont.html (accessed on December 11, 2000).

Internet Public Library. *POTUS: Presidents of the United States.* [Online] http:// www.ipl.org/ref/POTUS/index.html (accessed on December 11, 2000).

Public Broadcasting System. "The American President." *The American Experience.* [Online] http://www.pbs.org/wgbh/amex/presidents/nf/intro/intro. html (accessed on December 11, 2000).

University of Oklahoma Law Center. *A Chronology of US Historical Documents.* [Online] http://www.law.ou.edu/hist/ (accessed on December 11, 2000).

White House. *Welcome to the White House.* [Online] http://www.whitehouse. gov/ (accessed on December 11, 2000).

The White House Historical Association. [Online] http://www.whitehousehistory. org/whha/default.asp (accessed on December 11, 2000).

Yale Law School. *The Avalon at the Yale Law School: Documents in Law, History and Diplomacy.* [Online] http://www.yale.edu/lawweb/avalon/avalon. htm (accessed on December 11, 2000).

Index

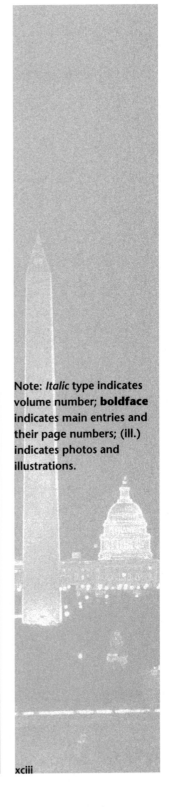

Battle of Vicksburg, *2:* 568; *3:* 640, 644, 650, 667

Battle of Wisconsin Heights, *2:* 435

Seven Days' Battles, *2:* 566; *3:* 649

Baudelaire, Charles-Pierre, *5:* 1301

Bay of Pigs invasion (Cuba), *5:* 1283–84

"Bayonet Constitution," *3:* 831

Beanes, William, *1:* 158

"The Beauty of America" project, *5:* 1344

Bedtime for Bonzo (film), *5:* 1473

Beecher, Catherine, *2:* 470

The Beeches (Coolidge), *4:* 1076

Begin, Menachem, *4:* 1146–47, 1148 (ill.); *5:* 1445

Belgium, World War I, *4:* 973, 1091–92

Belknap, William W., *3:* 658

Bell, Alexander Graham, *3:* 724–25, 725 (ill.)

Bell, John, *2:* 468 (ill.), 562
    election of 1860, *2:* 562

"Belle of Canton." *See* McKinley, Ida

Benton, Thomas Hart, *2:* 408, 468 (ill.)

Bentsen, Lloyd, *5:* 1515
    election of 1988, *5:* 1519

Berlin airlifts, *4:* 1202

Berlin Wall, *4:* 1253; *5:* 1285, 1490 (ill.)

BEST Foundation for a Drug-Free Tomorrow, *5:* 1499

Bethune, Mary McLeod, *4:* 1163 (ill.), 1164

Betty Ford Center, *5:* 1425

Bewick Moreing, *4:* 1089

Bicentennial Celebration, *5:* 1417

Bierce, Ambrose, *3:* 854

"Big Bill" ("Big Lub"). *See* Taft, William Howard

"Big stick" foreign policy, *3:* 891–94, 895–96

Big Three (Paris, 1919), *4:* 975 (ill.)

Big Three (Potsdam, 1945), *4:* 1198 (ill.)

Bill of Rights, *1:* 20, 99, 106, 151, 152, 177

Bill of Rights proposal (Madison), *1:* **169–78**

Bimetallism
    Cleveland, Grover, *3:* 789, 860
    McKinley, William, *3:* 795, 845–46, 848

Birmingham, Alabama, segregation protest, *5:* 1293

Birney, James G., *2:* 404

"Black Codes," *2:* 612, 635

Black Hawk, *2:* 434, 554

Black Hawk War, *1:* 275, 305; *2:* 431; *3:* 770

Black, Jeremiah, *2:* 526 (ill.)

"Black Monday" stock market crash, 1566–67

Blaine, James G., *2:* 442; *3:* 660, 689, 721, 722, 754, 756–57, 757 (ill.), 781 (ill.), 782–83
    "Blaine from Maine," *3:* 756
    election of 1884, *3:* 782, 783
    Garfield's eulogy, *3:* 723

Blair, Francis P., Jr., election of 1868, *3:* 651

Blair House, *4:* 1207

"Bleeding Kansas," *2:* 500 (ill.), 501, 528

Bliss, Alexander, *2:* 590

Bliss, Mary Elizabeth (Betty), *2:* 448, 449

Bloody Angle, Battle of, *3:* 645

Bloomer, Amelia, *3:* 786

Bloomer, Elizabeth Ann. *See* Ford, Betty

Bolívar, Simon, *2:* 335

Bone, Scott C., *4:* 1029 (ill.)

Bones, Helen Woodrow, *4:* 992

Bonus Army March, *4:* 1103–4

Boom and bust cycles, *1:* 293, 309; *3:* 663

Booth, John Wilkes, *2:* 570 (ill.), 571, 578, 596, 610, 635; *3:* 677

Bootleg liquor, *4:* 1059

"Border states," *2:* 563

Borie, Adolph E., *3:* 652

Bork, Robert, *5:* 1379

Bosnia (Bosnia and Herzegovina), *5:* 1563, 1564

"The Boss." *See* Truman, Bess

"The Boss's Boss." *See* Truman, Margaret

Boston, Massachusetts
    Adams, John, *1:* 57–58
    during American Revolution, *1:* 10, 12, 33
    police strike (1919), *4:* 1054

Boston Tea Party, *1:* 9, 76, 77 (ill.)

Boutwell, George S., *3:* 652

Boxer Rebellion (Righteous and Harmonious Fists), *3:* 858; *4:* 1089–91, 1110

Boys' Clubs of America, *4:* 1106

Braddock, Edward, *1:* 8

Brady, James, *5:* 1479 (ill.)

Brady, John R., *3:* 755 (ill.)

Braintree, Massachusetts, *1:* 223

Branch Davidians, *5:* 1570

Brandeis, Louis, *3:* 936 (ill.)

Brandt, Willy, *5:* 1295

Brandywine Creek, Battle of, *1:* 13, 14

Brazil, *3:* 900

"Keep the ball rolling," *2:* 334 (ill.)

"Read my lips: no new taxes," *5:* 1519

"Return to normalcy," *4:* 1016, 1024

"Save the Union," *2:* 523

"Tippecanoe and Tyler Too!," *1:* 306; *2:* 325, 364, 376

Campaign speeches, **"Rugged Individualism"** (Hoover), *4:* **1115–22**

Canada
  in Articles of Confederation, *1:* 43–44
  The Caroline incident, *1:* 303–4
  North American Free Trade Agreement (NAFTA), *5:* 1525, 1560

Canal Ring, *3:* 690

Canals. *See* Infrastructure

Cape Kennedy, *5:* 1305

Capital, location of, *1:* 21

Caribbean, *3:* 891; *5:* 1483

Caricatures, Campaign of 1884, *3:* 781 (ill.)

The Caroline incident, *1:* 303–4

Carow, Edith Kermit. *See* Roosevelt, Edith

Carranza, Venustiamo, *4:* 969, 972

Carter Center, *5:* 1436, 1453, 1467

Carter, Jimmy, *4:* 1207; *5:* 1381 (ill.), **1433–55,** 1435 (ill.), 1439 (ill.), 1441 (ill.), 1448 (ill.), 1449 (ill.), 1453 (ill.), 1562
  administration, *5:* 1443
  Camp David Accords, *5:* 1445
  domestic policy, *5:* 1445–48
  early years, *5:* 1436–39
  election of 1976, *5:* 1418, 1442
  election of 1980, *5:* 1451, 1452, 1477, 1478, 1518
  family peanut business, *5:* 1440
  Ford, Gerald R., *5:* 1419
  foreign policy, *5:* 1436, 1444–45, 1448, 1462, 1466–67
  governor of Georgia, *5:* 1440–41
  "Human Rights and Foreign Policy" Speech, *5:* **1461–68**
  human rights efforts, *5:* 1436, 1452–53
  inaugural speech, *5:* 1419
  inflation problems, *5:* 1445
  Iran hostage crisis, *5:* 1448–52, 1449, 1450–51, 1452 (ill.)
  life after the presidency, *5:* 1436, 1452–54, 1459–60
  marriage and family, *5:* 1439, 1458, 1459
  naval career, *5:* 1439–39

political career, *5:* 1440–42, 1458–59

presidency, *5:* 1442–52, 1459

Soviets invade Afghanistan, *5:* 1467

trouble with Congress, *5:* 1444

Carter, "Miss Lillian," *5:* 1437, 1444

Carter, Rosalynn, *5:* 1381 (ill.), 1457 (ill.), **1457–68**
  human rights efforts, *5:* 1453, 1459–60
  navy wife, *5:* 1458
  peanuts and politics, *5:* 1458–59
  role as first lady, *5:* 1457, 1459

Cartoons, political
  "Bleeding Kansas," *2:* 500 (ill.)
  Campaign of 1884, *3:* 781 (ill.)
  1856 presidential campaign, *2:* 522 (ill.)
  Garfield, James A., *3:* 720 (ill.)
  Johnson, Andrew, *2:* 618 (ill.)
  Kennedy vs. Khrushchev and Castro, *5:* 1285 (ill.)
  Lusitania, *4:* 974 (ill.)
  Nixon tapes, *5:* 1379 (ill.)
  Polk and Webster, *2:* 407 (ill.)
  Roosevelt, Franklin D., *4:* 1144 (ill.)
  Scott and Pierce, *2:* 494 (ill.)
  Stevens and Johnson, *2:* 614 (ill.)
  Taft and Roosevelt, *3:* 932 (ill.)
  Wilson, Woodrow, *4:* 965 (ill.)

Casablanca conference, *4:* 1153

Cass, Lewis, *1:* 309; *2:* 440–41, 441 (ill.), 468 (ill.), 493, 500 (ill.), 526 (ill.)
  election of 1848, *2:* 349, 439

Castro, Fidel, *4:* 1251; *5:* 1283, 1285 (ill.), 1416

Center for National Policy, *5:* 1562

Central America, *2:* 443, 526; *3:* 894, 935–36, 955

Central government. *See* Federal government

Central High School (Little Rock, Arkansas), *4:* 1249

Central Intelligence Agency (CIA), *4:* 1245
  Bay of Pigs invasion (Cuba), *5:* 1283–84
  Bush, George, *5:* 1516
  Ford's overhaul, *5:* 1416

Central Powers (World War I), *4:* 997–99, 1003, 1004, 1005, 1010

Cermak, Anton J., *4:* 1135

Chads, "dimpled," *5:* 1614, 1615

Chamber of Commerce (New York), *4:* 1078

Chamberlain, Neville, *4:* 1148

Chamberlayne, Richard, *1:* 32

L

Meade, George, *2:* 569

Means, Abigail Kent, *2:* 507

Meat-packing industry, *3:* 895

Media coverage, *4:* 968. *See also* Journalism; Radio; Television; Yellow Journalism
Clinton, Hillary Rodham, *5:* 1583–85
Ford, Gerald R., *5:* 1414, 1415
news agencies call election 2000, *5:* 1608, 1609

Medicaid, *5:* 1328

Medicare, *5:* 1328, 1561

Meiji, emperor of Japan, *3:* 660, 668

Mellon, Andrew W., *4:* 1022–23, 1023 (ill.), 1024, 1098

Mellon National Bank, *4:* 1022, 1023

Memoirs, Year of Decisions (Truman), *4:* 1211

Mencken, H. L., on Coolidge, Calvin, *4:* 1068–69

Mercenaries, *1:* 10

Merchant marine, *4:* 1061

Meredith, James, *5:* 1291

Merit system, *3:* 784

Merry Mount (Adams), *1:* 223

Message to Congress Opposing the Annexation of Hawaii (Cleveland), *3:* 803–8

Message to the Senate Supporting the Annexation of Hawaii (Benjamin Harrison), *3:* 831–35

Metal detector, *3:* 722, 725

Methodist Woman's Home Missionary Society, *3:* 703

Mexican Americans, *5:* 1319, 1328

Mexican War, *1:* 229; *2:* 371, 391, 406 (ill.), 406–10, 424, 520, 612
Adams, John Quincy, *1:* 235
Calhoun, John C., *1:* 271
Frémont, John C., *2:* 408, 410
Grant, Ulysses S., *2:* 425; *3:* 640
Kearny, Stephen, *2:* 407, 408
Lee, Robert E., *3:* 648
Lincoln, Abraham, *2:* 425, 556
Perry, Matthew C., *2:* 498
Pierce, Franklin, *2:* 490–93
Polk, James K., *2:* 406, 410
Scott, Winfield, *1:* 305; *2:* 407
Stockton, Robert, *2:* 407
Taylor, Zachary, *2:* 425, 432–36
Van Buren, Martin, *2:* 425

Mexico
Clinton, Bill, *5:* 1565
Grant, Ulysses S., *3:* 660
leased oil lands seized, *4:* 1061
North American Free Trade Agreement (NAFTA), *5:* 1525, 1560

Pershing, John J. "Black Jack," *4:* 971
Polk, James K., *2:* 404
Revolution of 1920, *3:* 937
Rockefeller, Nelson, *5:* 1412
Wilson, Woodrow, *4:* 969–72
Zimmerman note, *4:* 1006

Miami tribe, *2:* 332

Michigan
Ford, Gerald, *5:* 1403–4
Michigan Territory, *2:* 440

Michner, H. T., *3:* 818

Middle class, *4:* 1057

Middle East, *5:* 1370, 1371, 1525

Midnight appointments, *1:* 71, 73

Military, "Don't ask, don't tell" policy, *5:* 1558

Military draft, World War II, *4:* 1152

Military leaders, as presidential candidates, *2:* 468 (ill.)

Military spending. *See* Defense spending

Militia
Massachusetts, *1:* 10
Tennessee, *1:* 262
Virginia (American Revolution), *1:* 6

Militia Act of 1796, *2:* 563

Miller, William E., election of 1964, *5:* 1326

Millie's Book (Barbara Bush), *5:* 1533

Milligan, Lambdin, *3:* 816

Milosevic, Slobodan, *5:* 1564

Milton, John, *1:* 88

Minimum wage, failed New Deal legislation, *4:* 1141

Minnesota, free state, *2:* 547

Minutemen (Massachusetts militia), *1:* 10, 12

"Misdemeanors," *5:* 1572

"Missile gap," *4:* 1248, 1250–51

Missile reduction (Bush-Gorbachev, 1991), *5:* 1522, 1523

Mississippi, *2:* 562
Davis, Jefferson, *2:* 564
Meredith, James, *5:* 1291

Mississippi River, *1:* 113–14
flood of 1927, *4:* 1060, 1093–96

Mississippi River Commission, *3:* 817–18

Missouri
remains in Union, *2:* 563
statehood debate, *1:* 228

Missouri
Japanese surrender, *4:* 1199 (ill.)
Truman, Harry S., *4:* 1191, 1194

Missouri Compromise of 1820, *1:* 197, 198–99, 202–3; *2:* 411, 451, 524, 557

Missouri River, *1:* 112

Mitchell, John, *5:* 1378, 1380

election of 1852, *2:* 483, 494, 495

Screen Actors Guild, *5:* 1474, 1495

SDI (Strategic Defense Initiative) ("Star Wars"), *5:* 1482

Seaton, Josephine, *2:* 417

Secession

formal declaration, *2:* 517

threat by Southern states, *2:* 440–41

Second Continental Congress, *1:* 12. *See also* Continental Congress

Second Inaugural Address (Lincoln), *2:* **593–97**

Second Manassas, Battle of (Second Battle of Bull Run), *2:* 566

Second National Bank, *1:* 141, 159, 269, 276, 285, 300; *2:* 399–401

"Second Reply to Congressman Robert Y. Hayne of South Carolina" (Webster), *2:* 370

The Second World War (Churchill), *4:* 1149

Secretary of State. *See also* administration of specific president

first, *1:* 20

Secretary of the Navy. *See also* administration of specific president

first, *1:* 20

Secretary of the Treasury. *See also* administration of specific president

first, *1:* 20, 24

Secretary of War. *See also* administration of specific president

first, *1:* 20

Securities and Exchange Commission (SEC), *4:* 1140

Sedition Act, *1:* 67, 68, 69, 73, 108

Segregation, *2:* 596; *4:* 1045, 1204, 1249; *5:* 1343

Kennedy, John F., *5:* 1288–89

Kennedy, Robert F., *5:* 1288–89

Marshall, Thurgood, *5:* 1332

Truman, Harry S., *4:* 1229–32

Segregation in the Military: Executive Order Banning (Truman), *4:* **1229–32**

Select Committee to Investigate Presidential Campaign Practices), *5:* 1376–77, 1377 (ill.), 1378

Selective Service Administration, *4:* 1152

Seminole nation, *1:* 196, 264, 305, 306; *2:* 332, 431

Seminole War, *1:* 275

"Semper Fidelis" (Sousa), *3:* 799

Senate. *See also* Congress; House of Representatives

impeachment hearings against Bill Clinton, *5:* 1576, 1577

impeachment hearings against Richard Nixon, *5:* 1377, 1378

impeachment of Andrew Johnson, *2:* 616–17

Johnson, Andrew, *2:* 620

Message Supporting the Annexation of Hawaii (Benjamin Harrison), *3:* **831–35**

treaty ratification, *2:* 369; *4:* 978, 1003

Watergate hearings, *5:* 1376–77, 1377 (ill.), 1378

Sensationalism, *3:* 854, 910, 917, 924

Serbia (Kosovo region), *5:* 1564

Serbians, World War I, *4:* 972–73

Sergeant, John, election of 1832, *1:* 267

Seven Days' Battles, *2:* 566; *3:* 649

"Seventh-inning stretch," *3:* 935

Sewall, Arthur, election of 1896, *3:* 848

Seward, William H., *2:* 464, 559, 571, 612–13, 613 (ill.), 635

Alaska, *2:* 611

radical Republican, *2:* 566

"Seward's Folly," *2:* 611, 613

Sex discrimination. *See* Women's rights

Sexual harassment charges, Clinton, Bill, *5:* 1573, 1574

Sexual orientation, and military service, *5:* 1558

Seymour, Horatio, *2:* 619; *3:* 652

election of 1868, *3:* 651

Shadwell, *1:* 94, 95

Shah of Iran, *5:* 1448–49, 1449 (ill.), 1450, 1467

The Shame of Cities (Steffens), *3:* 924

Shanghai Communique of 1972, *5:* 1371

Shaw, *4:* 1151 (ill.)

Shawnee, *2:* 332

Sheridan, Philip H., *2:* 570

Sherman Antitrust Act, *3:* 819, 915, 933, 935

Sherman, James S.

election of 1908, *3:* 932, 933

election of 1912, *4:* 966

Sherman, John, *3:* 721, 754

Sherman, Roger, *1:* 133 (ill.)

Committee of Five, *1:* 126

Sherman, William Tecumseh, *2:* 570; *3:* 816

Sherwood Forest (Tyler), *2:* 373, 381

Shiloh, Battle of, *2:* 566; *3:* 644, 647, 650

Shriver, R. Sargent, election of 1972, *5:* 1366

W